Writing for an Endangered World

Lawrence Buell

Writing for an Endangered World

LITERATURE, CULTURE, AND ENVIRONMENT IN THE U.S. AND BEYOND

THE BELKNAP PRESS OF

HARVARD UNIVERSITY PRESS

Cambridge, Massachusetts, and London, England · 2001

Library of Congress Cataloging-in-Publication Data

Buell, Lawrence.
    Writing for an endangered world: literature, culture, and environment in the U.S.
and beyond / Lawrence Buell.
        p. cm.
    Includes bibliographical references and index.
    ISBN 0-674-00449-3 (alk. paper)
    1. American literature—History and criticism.   2. Environmental protection in
literature.   3. English literature—History and criticism.   4. Environmental policy
in literature.   5. Nature conservation in literature.   6. Landscape in literature.
    7. Ecology in literature.   8. Nature in literature.   I. Title.

PS169.E25 B84 2001
810.9'355—dc21   00–049796

For Kim

Contents

Introduction   1

"America the Beautiful," Jane Addams, and John Muir   9
Environmental Imagination and Environmental
    Unconscious   18
Outline of This Book   27

1 Toxic Discourse   30

The Toxic Denominator   32
Toxic Discourse Anatomized   35
Toxicity, Risk, and Literary Imagination   45

2 The Place of Place   55

The Elusiveness of Place   59
Five Dimensions of Place-Connectedness   64
The Importance of Place Imagination   74
Retrieval of the Unloved Place: Wideman   78

3 Flâneur's Progress: Reinhabiting the City   84

Romantic Urbanism: Whitman, Olmsted, and Others   90
High Modernism and Modern Urban Theory   103
Whitmanian Modernism: William Carlos Williams
    as Bioregionalist   109
Later Trajectories   120

4 Discourses of Determinism   129

Urban Fiction from Dickens through Wright   131
Rurality as Fate   143
Consolations of Determinism: Dreiser and Jeffers   149
Observing Limits in Literature and Life:
    Berry and Brooks   157
Speaking for the Determined: Addams   167

5 Modernization and the Claims of the Natural World:
Faulkner and Leopold   *170*

    Faulkner as Environmental Historian   *171*
    Go Down, Moses and Environmental Unconscious   *177*
    Faulkner, Leopold, and Ecological Ethics   *183*

6 Global Commons as Resource and as Icon:
Imagining Oceans and Whales   *196*

    Resymbolizing Ocean   *199*
    Moby-Dick and the Hierarchies of Nation, Culture,
      and Species   *205*
    Imagining Interspeciesism: The Lure of the Megafauna   *214*

7 The Misery of Beasts and Humans: Nonanthropo-
centric Ethics versus Environmental Justice   *224*

    Schisms   *225*
    Mediations   *236*

8 Watershed Aesthetics   *243*

    From River to Watershed   *244*
    Modern Watershed Consciousness: Mary Austin
      to the Present   *252*

Notes   *267*

Acknowledgments   *341*

Index   *345*

Writing for an Endangered World

Introduction

> Everyone knows enough to pursue what he does not know, but no one
> knows enough to pursue what he already knows. Everyone knows enough
> to condemn what he takes to be no good, but no one knows enough to
> condemn what he has already taken to be good. This is how the great con-
> fusion comes about, blotting out the brightness of sun and moon above,
> searing the vigor of hills and streams below, overturning the round of the
> four seasons in between. There is no insect that creeps and crawls, no crea-
> ture that flutters and flies that has not lost its inborn nature. So great is the
> confusion of the world that comes from coveting knowledge!
>
> —Chuang Tzu, "Rifling Trunks," trans. Burton Watson

This is my second book about environmental imagination, written in
the conviction that environmental crisis is not merely one of economic
resources, public health, and political gridlock. Not by alleviation of
these alone will the ingredient "missing from American environmental
policy today" be supplied: "a coherent vision of the common environmental good that is sufficiently compelling to generate sustained public
support."[1] As sociologist Ulrich Beck remarks about debates over
species extinction: "only if nature is brought into people's everyday images, into the stories they tell, can its beauty and its suffering be seen
and focused on." The success of all environmentalist efforts finally
hinges not on "some highly developed technology, or some arcane new
science" but on "a state of mind":[2] on attitudes, feelings, images, narratives.

That the advertising budget of U.S. corporations exceeds the combined budgets of all the nation's institutions of higher learning is crude
but telling evidence that trust in the power of imagination is not a literary scholar's idiosyncrasy. It is evidence too, of course, that imagination
is not always a "force for good." Hence in part the recurring desire to
sequester art from the world of affairs. "Poetry makes nothing happen,"

insists W. H. Auden's 1939 elegy to fellow poet W. B. Yeats, reacting against what Auden took to be misuse of imagination in ways that abetted fascism. Shelley's grandiose claim that "Poets are the unacknowledged legislators of the World" made Auden shudder: "Sounds more like the secret police to me."[3] But though his distaste for subjugating art to didacticism was understandable, it remains that acts of environmental imagination, whatever anyone thinks to the contrary, potentially register and energize at least four kinds of engagement with the world. They may connect readers vicariously with others' experience, suffering, pain: that of nonhumans as well as humans. They may reconnect readers with places they have been and send them where they would otherwise never physically go. They may direct thought toward alternative futures. And they may affect one's caring for the physical world: make it feel more or less precious or endangered or disposable. All this may befall a moderately attentive reader reading about a cherished, abused, or endangered place.

This book takes up a wide range of texts in light of these convictions. Its protagonists are largely U.S. writers from the late 1700s to today. I stretch the category of "creative writer," however, to include eloquent observers who did not think of themselves as artists. So my dramatis personae include not only Walt Whitman, Herman Melville, Mary Austin, Theodore Dreiser, Richard Wright, William Faulkner, William Carlos Williams, Gwendolyn Brooks, Wendell Berry, Terry Tempest Williams, John Edgar Wideman, and Linda Hogan but also Benjamin Franklin, Frederick Law Olmsted, Jane Addams, Aldo Leopold, Rachel Carson, and others who have operated across the conventionally drawn border between "literary" and "nonliterary."

Most chapters are organized partly along historical lines, not as continuous narratives but as episodes in the history of environmental writing since the beginnings of industrialization.

Obviously concern for environment did not originate a mere two centuries ago, though the term itself apparently did not enter English usage until the 1830s. Insofar as human beings are biohistorical creatures constructing themselves in interaction with surroundings they cannot not inhabit, all their artifacts may be expected to bear traces of that. It makes sense that the reach of "ecocriticism"—the omnibus term by which the new polyform literature and environment studies movement has come to be labeled, especially in the United States—should extend from the oldest surviving texts to works of the present moment.[4] This is borne out by the sweep of such books as Robert Pogue Harrison's *Forests: The Shadows of Civilization* and Louise Westling's *The Green Breast of the New World*, both of which start with a reading of the Sumerian epic *Gilgamesh* as an allegory of settlement culture's triumph over hunter-gatherer culture, town over forest.[5] Classic texts and genres rightly continue to exert influence. But with accelerated technosocial change has come greatly intensified anxiety about "the environment," and with it a redirection of traditional discourses and a plethora of new ones.

By "environment(al)," I refer both to "natural" and "human-built" dimensions of the palpable world. Though I shall also insist on the distinction, one must also blur it by recourse to the more comprehensive term. Human transformations of physical nature have made the two realms increasingly indistinguishable.[6] Perhaps only the last half-century has witnessed what Bill McKibben apocalyptically calls "the end of nature": a degree of modification so profound that we shall never again encounter a pristine physical environment. But Karl Marx was not far wrong in claiming that by the mid-1800s second nature (nature as reprocessed by human labor) had effectively dominated first nature worldwide.[7] What we loosely call "nature" has often long since become "organic machine," as Richard White calls the painstakingly engineered, computer-monitored Columbia River of today.[8] Indeed, the nature-culture distinction itself is an anthropogenic product, deriving in the first instance from the transition from nomadism to settlement that began millennia ago in southwestern Asia.

Even those who know better can lapse into loose talk about the "natural" look of an exurban landscape.[9] Few poets have been more aware than Robert Frost of countryside as historical artifact; yet one can also catch him at flat-footed moments of mental motoring, musing that "The mineral drops that explode / To drive my ton of car / Are limited to the road," and "have almost nothing to do / With the absolute light and rest / The universal blue / And local green suggest."[10] Frost here seems oblivious to automotive effects, unless one gives a huge benefit of the doubt to that "almost." Not that he should be too chastised for in-souciance. Doubtless this was a country road; and even if it had been the I-89 of today, which winds through miles of lovely Vermont and New Hampshire countryside, civil engineering has done its utmost to preserve the illusion of nature and machines peacefully coexisting in separate spaces. You have to make the effort to notice the bedraggled roadside trees, as well as the ecological studies of how bird and animal species avoid major highways, to gauge the impact.[11] Even warier imag-inings of the early automotive era don't see *that* far, though they resist binary naïveté in some arresting ways.[12]

> He rode over Connecticut
> In a glass coach.
> Once, a fear pierced him,
> In that he mistook
> The shadow of his equipage
> For blackbirds.
>> (Wallace Stevens, "Thirteen Ways of
>> Looking at a Blackbird")

> I ascend
>
> through
> a canopy of leaves
>
> and at the same time
> I descend
>
> for I do nothing
> unusual—
>
> I ride in my car
> I think about
>
> prehistorical caves
> in the Pyrenees—
>> (William Carlos Williams,
>> "The Avenue of Poplars")

Both poems create whimsical-eerie effects by puncturing the illusion of outdoor-indoor, nature-civilization dichotomies coddled by habits of insulated travel.

They do so by making the opposite move from Marx's reduction: dwelling on repressed intimations of first nature's continuing invasion of human-engineered space (Stevens) and the persistence of primordial forms of enclosure like trees and caves into modernity (Williams).[13] This in turn suggests that the history of human modification of environment should not be taken as implying a comprehensive, irreversible transformation of "nature" into artifact. Three-quarters of a century after Stevens and Williams wrote these passages, the United States is far from being paved over. "The production of nature should not be confused with *control* over nature," as geographer Neil Smith warns.[14] Nor is it just during tornadoes and hurricanes that second nature's inability to contain first nature is revealed. Gardeners see the homely truth of this daily.[15]

Then too, the urban-rural distinction cannot be written off as hallucinatory because it is a produced result. It also registers, however sloppily, actual physiographic contrasts: contrasts that in some places local, state, and federal land policies have in modern times accentuated. The acreage of Concord, Massachusetts, is both more densely populated and less cultivated than in Thoreau's day. Some areas of the United States are more sparsely settled than they were a century ago: the western Dakotas and the Green Mountain National Forest, for instance.[16]

So the nature-culture distinction is both a distorting and a necessary lens through which to view both the modernization process and the postmodernist claim that we inhabit a prosthetic environment, our perception of which is more simulacra-mediated than context-responsive. On the one hand, the world's physical environment is being increasingly refashioned by capital, technology, and geopolitics, with so-called nature consumed or reproduced as lawns, gardens, theme parks, habitat zoos, conservancies, and so on. On the other hand, this process has made tracts of (relatively) unfabricated nature in some quarters more salient and, in general, all the more crucial both as concept and as term of value: as a way of designating what has not yet been greatly transformed by pollution, climate change, and the like; as a way of dramatizing the violence and excess of techno-transformation; and as a way of underscoring the importance of the however-modified nonhuman world to the maintenance of life.[17]

That human beings might be ecosystemically constrained as much as vice versa is unfashionable to claim but no less certain on that account. It is doubtful whether earthlings will ever get along wholly without their natural biology and without a high dependence on environmental conditions over which they have limited control. Even if people were to become as "posthuman" as the bionic characters of cyberpunk fiction, they would likely remain physically embodied and permeable to the influences of water cycle, photosynthesis, macroclimate, seismology, bacterial resistance to pharmaceuticals, and the "natural" advantages and disadvantages of regional habitats.[18] Furthermore, environmental psychologists have amassed strong evidence of preference across cultures for environments felt to contain significant "natural" elements: evidence that these seem not only attractive aesthetically but also therapeutic, promoting convalescence from sickness faster than artificial environments do.[19]

A version of the nature-culture distinction, then, will likely remain indispensable as a recognition of empirical fact as well as of human desire. Monist, dualist, and technocultural constructionist theories or myths are likely to prove less convincing than a myth of mutual constructionism: of physical environment (both natural and human-built) shaping in some measure the cultures that in some measure continually refashion it.[20]

My previous book, *The Environmental Imagination,* centered on an attempt to define "ecocentric" forms of literary imagining, as instanced especially by nature writing in the Thoreauvian tradition.[21] I continue to believe that reorientation of human attention and values according to a stronger ethic of care for the nonhuman environment would make the world a better place, for humans as well as for nonhumans.[22] Pressing that argument, however, meant understating the force of such anthropocentric concerns as public health and environmental equity as motivators of environmental imagination and commitment. To those living in endangered communities, the first environmental priorities will understandably be health, safety, and sustenance, and as guarantors of these the civic priorities of political and economic enfranchisement.[23] This is not to countenance the charge of "(eco)fascism" sometimes leveled against ecocentrism's in-principle valuation of ecosystemic concerns relative to human rights and needs, its alleged link to Nazism, and so forth. Such claims oversimplify the diversity of actual ecocentric positions, exaggerate their authoritarianism, and proffer a cartoon version of Nazis as Greens.[24] Nor do ecocentrists warrant deprecation for being "the Puritans of the environmental movement."[25] As with Puritanism, and as with the democratic revolution that Puritan dissent helped bring about, environmentalism of any sort cannot hope to achieve even modest reforms unless *some* take extreme positions advocating genuinely alternative paths: rejection of consumer society, communitarian anti-modernism, animal liberation. As ecocritic Jonathan Bate affirms, "the dream of deep ecology will never be realized upon the earth, but our survival as a species may be dependent on our capacity to dream it in the work of our imagination."[26]

Yet it remains that human beings cannot be expected to live by ecocentricism alone, any more than most "Puritans" were in real life altogether consistent in their Puritanism.[27] A thoroughgoing ecocentrism may strike the world's "ecosystem people"[28] as late eighteenth-century theologian Samuel Hopkins's extreme "New Light" Calvinism struck most fellow New Englanders. Hopkins's test of whether one had received divine grace was willingness to be damned for the glory of God. Judging by what it has taken to rouse sizable numbers of non-white-male, non-highly-educated people to a state of environmental concern, fears for survival of family and self are more powerful motivators than self-sacrificial caring for nature as an intrinsic good. Even Henry Thoreau, now remembered as a green saint, acknowledged this by making a theory of four basic material necessities (food, fuel, clothing, shelter) his starting point in *Walden,* although not his end point.

One of this book's main purposes, accordingly, will be to put "green" and "brown" landscapes, the landscapes of exurbia and industrialization, in conversation with one other. "In order for ecocriticism to earn its claim to relevance," as one ecocritic observes, "its critical practice must be greatly extended . . . the environmental crisis threatens all landscapes—wild, rural, suburban, and urban. South Boston is just as natural (and wild) as Walden Pond. They are equally endangered by the greenhouse effect. And the causes of poverty in one are the causes of development in the other."[29] This is surely just, provided that we understand "just as natural (and wild)" as meaning not "the same ratio of people and buildings to woods and water" but "just as managed (or unmanaged)." Literature and environment studies must reckon more fully with the interdependence between urban and outback landscapes, and the traditions of imaging them, if they are to become something more than a transient fashion. Although their reach in principle extends to any literary transaction between human imagination and material world, in practice they have concentrated (my own work included) on "natural" environment rather than environment more inclusively, and taken as their special province outdoor genres like nature writing, pastoral poetry, and wilderness romance, neglecting (for example) naturalist fiction, muckraking journalism, and the poetics of the urban *flâneur*. No treatment of environmental imagination can claim to be comprehensive without taking account of the full range of historic landscapes, landscape genres, and environmental(ist) discourses.

In U.S. history, indeed, the first expressions of protectionist sentiment about vanishing woods and wilderness on the part of the dominant settler culture, early in the nineteenth century, coincided with the first intensive systematic push toward urban "sanitary" reform. The two initiatives matured about the same time a half-century later as part of the constellation of Progressive-era reforms. They culminated again in the 1960s and 1970s with the concurrent environmentalist initiatives of the Wilderness and Endangered Species acts and the clean air/clean water campaigns catalyzed in part by Rachel Carson's *Silent Spring*. Yet the pre-Carson history of the public health and welfare strand is not—within literary studies anyhow—normally thought of as part of "environmental" history, and in the field of history, where it is, public hygiene and preservationism do not often get dealt with in the same projects or by the same scholars. Yet it has become increasingly clear that these two strands are interwoven,[30] as environmental justice movements challenge traditional preservationism with a more populist message; as bioregionalists call on us to imagine ourselves holding citizenship in environmental units like watersheds that subsume both "urban" and "rural" areas; and as practitioners of nature writing depart from its idyllicizing traditions in order to address issues like toxification that fuse landscapes of wilderness and technology into one like-it-or-not environmental web. It is on the basis of this complex understanding of what counts as environment, environmentalism, and environmental writing that literature and environment studies must make their case for the indispensableness of physical environment as a shaping force in human art and experience, and how such an aesthetic works.

To that end, a U.S.-culture-based study can be of special interest, given the rapidity and vastness of the scale of this country's environmental transformation during the past two centuries, and the history of interwoven controversy and advocacy of civilizationist and naturist persuasions arising from that. But since that history is less unique than symptomatic of the modernization process more generally, any inquiry must also range, as this book does, beyond any one national instance.[31]

"America the Beautiful," Jane Addams, and John Muir

A fine starting point for glimpsing both the trickiness and the necessity of getting beyond the conflation of "environment" with "nature," especially in the United States but in principle elsewhere as well, is the single most iconic work of environmental literature in U.S. settler culture history, the popular hymn "America the Beautiful." Most U.S. citizens know at least the opening stanza:

> O beautiful for spacious skies
> For amber waves of grain,
> For purple mountain majesties
> Above the fruited plain!
> America! America!
> God shed His grace on thee,
> And crown thy good with brotherhood
> From sea to shining sea![32]

I confess that this poem has never been a great favorite of mine. Even as a child, I thought it flatulently grandiose—a prejudice reinforced by my conditioning as an Americanist to read it as a mindless paean to westward expansion. But I was moved to rethink the poem by a happenstance event: the spring 1998 dedication of the Thoreau Institute, a research and teaching facility nestled in the Walden Woods about a quarter mile from the pond.

The climactic portion of the ceremonies started with a rendition of "America the Beautiful" by Tony Bennett, one of many who have argued that it and not the militaristic "Star-Spangled Banner" should be the national anthem. The ritual discipline of the occasion, including crooner Bennett's slow time, made me attend more closely to the lyrics than ever before—and to do some follow-up research.

Those opening lines, declared the author—poet-scholar Katharine Lee Bates, then chair of English at Wellesley College, came to her in an epiphany inspired by the view from the top of Pike's Peak during her first western journey.[33] A deeply self-incriminating anecdote, or so one might at first think. Even as it partially redeems the poem's effusiveness by corroborating the truth of its visual perception (from Pike's Peak one really can see both purple mountain majesties and amber waves of grain in a single sweep), the story seemingly compounds the poem's felony of reducing all America to a beautiful landscape painting—ignoring the legacy of conquest, ignoring the throes of industrial revolution, that new historicist literary studies and revisionist ethnic, immigration, and labor history all lay bare. Surely "America the Beautiful" must be the ne plus ultra of nature escape writing—the cartoon image of ecocriticism in the minds of its detractors.

Yet if instead of focusing only on the nature rhetoric, we recognize the poem's involvement in the double-stranded narrative of U.S. environmentalism just sketched, the picture begins to change. It happens that Bates went to Colorado via the 1893 Columbian Exposition in Chicago, which she also revisited on return: the Exposition at which Frederick Jackson Turner presented his frontier thesis of American democracy and Henry Adams had his vision of the dynamo as the quintessence of twentieth-century civilization. It was from those visits that the image of the "alabaster city" of the last stanza most immediately derived ("Oh beautiful for spacious dream / That lives beyond the years; / Where alabaster cities gleam / Undimmed by human tears"). The lines allude to the "White City" of the Columbian Exposition, as the fairground was called.[34] The human tears obliquely suggest the slums a little beyond the White City's edge, into which Bates forayed when she dined with Jane Addams at Hull-House on her return trip. The poem's first version makes this more explicit than the one we know. The original endings of the final verses underscore that the idealism of "America the Beautiful" is future tense, not present tense: "Till selfish gain no longer stain / The banner of the free!" and "Till nobler men keep once again / Thy whiter jubilee!"[35]

It happens too that Bates concurrently wrote a much gloomier companion piece explicitly about the Exposition, called "The Year of the Vision," which reads in part:

> Beyond the circle of her glistening domes
>   A bitter wind swept by to waste and wither,
> A cry went up from hunger-smitten homes,
>   But came not hither.[36]

If ever there were a stanza fit to express forlorn unfulfillment, this pentameter-cut-to-dimeter quatrain is it. In her collected poems, Bates significantly put "America the Beautiful" and "Year of the Vision" in one-two order at the start.

I do not want to make Bates seem the activist she manifestly was not—although it is notable that one of her more radical colleagues at Wellesley credited her with designing the master plan for the turn-of-the-century women's college urban settlement house movement, even though she did not herself participate.[37] She *did* opt to euphemize in revision. But she grasped the duplicity as well as the utopianism of the alabaster city and with this the interdependence of mountaintop and slum, recognizing that mountaintop exuberance is legitimated not as a thing in itself but only through the ethos of "brotherhood" (as she quaintly calls it).[38] "America the Beautiful" invites one to think the first, then nudges one toward the second, by drawing a line from sublime open space to troubled urban landscape, whose utopian imagery would have been more self-interrogating to an audience of 1890s liberals than it is today, when the last stanza needs a footnote. The poem's cognizance of Chicago's imbrication with the West is more akin than at first seems to Frank Norris's almost contemporaneous novel *The Pit* and William Cronon's history of Chicago's relation to its hinterland in *Nature's Metropolis*,[39] though the poem hardly goes so far as to imagine the amber waves of grain as remote tentacles of the Chicago stockyards. Perhaps it should have. Still, the poem's thrust is not smug affirmation of natural beauty and farm-belt bounty with no strings attached, but affirmation on condition that urban misery be assuaged and social justice achieved. The story that the poem has been made to subserve is not the full story it was written to tell.

In order to tease out further the environmentalist double vision upon which "America the Beautiful" builds, consider the unlikely diptych of Jane Addams and John Muir. Addams, Bates's acquaintance and friend of her Wellesley colleague and Boston-marriage partner Catherine Coman, was the most charismatic figure in the American phase of the turn-of-the-century urban settlement house movement. Muir was the most charismatic celebrator of purple mountain majesty. Though he was a generation older, their apogees as writers and activists coincided: the early 1890s through the early 19-teens. Muir cofounded the Sierra Club within a year or so of Addams cofounding Hull-House.

At first sight Addams's mission of bringing civility to "urban wilderness" (as late Victorian reformers liked to call it) looks irreconcilable with Muir's mission to *preserve* wilderness. The loci are antithetical, the valuations of wilderness are antithetical, and so were their personal environmental preferences (Addams a confirmed urbanite, Muir an agoraphobe). Had Addams lived in northern California, she might well have favored damming Hetch Hetchy to provide water for the urban populace. Addams declared herself a supporter of the conservation movement but her contact among its leaders was Muir's nemesis Gifford Pinchot.[40]

Hence Addams's priorities on open-space policy sharply differed from Muir's priority of sequestering big parcels of land, a value shared by Frederick Law Olmsted, who drew up plans for both Yosemite and Chicago's lakefront park, where the White City was located. For Addams and her colleagues, proximity counted far more than size. They anticipated the modern design principle of "accessible green": they realized that "[p]eople need green open places to go to" but that "distance overwhelms the need," and the need can be met with small patches rather than large tracts.[41] Distressed that the per capita ratio of park acreage to people in Chicago's densest two dozen wards was one-twentieth that of the other dozen, they pushed successfully for "the most ambitious playground system in the world" (as it was then deemed) and for park approval by neighborhood vote. For awhile

Chicago had in place an exemplary large park / small park policy of development. The first of those playgrounds was created near Hull-House as the direct result of Addams's activism.[42]

But here as in other chapters in the history of U.S. environmentalism, the schism between urban and outback reform initiatives is easily overdrawn. Though their priorities clashed, and their paths never crossed, Addams's and Muir's visions of environmental advocacy were complementary. Today it seems increasingly self-evident that a comprehensive public land policy must address both human needs *and* ecosystemic imperilment, and that this requires big and small patches both, with corridors connecting. Even then, it was possible to ally with both Addams and Muir. The same man who turned over to Addams the Chicago lot that became the first playground later moved west to Marin County, California, and in the fullness of time donated to the federal government the tract he named Muir Woods, in order to keep it from being seized by a local water company threatening eminent domain.[43]

I do not know how well this donor understood either figure or if he ever undertook to compare them;[44] but even if not, he would certainly have seen both as self-appointed physicians to a society sickened by industrialization's growing pains. Both Addams and Muir valued open space as therapeutic. Muir commended parks as "fountains of life" to "thousands of tired nerve-shaken, over-civilized people"—referring especially to the neurasthenia of the genteel—though he also called parks "the poor man's refuge," a view Addams would have seconded even while doubting that the urban poor would make the trek to Yosemite. She would have agreed still more heartily with Muir's insistence that "our bodies were made to thrive only in pure air, and the scenes in which pure air is found."[45] Both advocated not spectatorial but physical, "embodied participation," as Shannon Jackson characterizes Addams's rationale for urban playgrounds.[46] Both, furthermore, not only held that optimizing physical environment was crucial to human and social health but also that this took firm and efficient management. Muir supported military protection of national parks against herding, logging, and hunting encroachments no less enthusiastically than Addams supported vigilant municipal law enforcement.[47] Both in short exemplified what Paul Boyer, in his analysis of Progressive-era urban reform, calls "positive environmentalism": that is, belief in proactive shaping of public policy in light of the principle that human welfare is conditioned by physical environment.[48]

Especially striking in this regard is their identification both as persons and as literary personae with specific places: Muir with Yosemite and the Sierras, Addams with the working-class wards of South Side Chicago. This place identification gave Muir his reputation as John of the Mountains, Addams hers as the Mother Teresa of Halsted Street. What they wanted to see done with these places differed hugely: Muir's mountains were to be visited but let be, Addams's slums were to be transformed. But for each a regime of long-term sympathetic immersion and *discipline* in place was key to personal well-being, environmental knowledge, and ethical commitment. Both were self-transplanted outsiders, who then sought to be credible spokespersons and advocates for their chosen places. Both wondered, as Muir said of the wild creatures of the Sierras, "shall I be allowed to enter into their midst and dwell with them?" Both realized that they had to achieve a bona fide existential embeddedness, to "be content [as Addams put it] to live quietly side by side with their neighbors, until they grow into a sense of relationship and mutual interests."[49] For both, this required a considerable measure of voluntary poverty and self-mortifying asceticism. "Just bread and water and delightful toil is all I need," insisted Muir on the subject of backpacking provisions, even as he chafed at feeling weak for lack of bread, "as if one couldn't take a few days' saunter in the God-ful woods without maintaining a base on a wheat-field and gristmill."[50] Addams was no less insistent on the necessity of accepting discomfort with grace and even gusto: the confusions of an overcrowded house, the absence of contemplative time, the chronic anxiety of fighting the intractable hydra-headed problems of inner-city slums.

Their autobiographical writings express an experience of place much more intense and complex than their framing statements can contain. Here is an example from each: first, a passage from *The Mountains of California* (Muir on the experience of entering Bloody Cañon), then one from *Twenty Years at Hull-House* (the start of Addams's recollection of becoming garbage inspector for the nineteenth ward, the one paid public position she ever held).

The effect of [the] expressive outspokenness on the part of the cañon-rocks is greatly enhanced by the quiet aspect of the alpine meadows through which we pass just before entering the narrow gateway. The forests in which they lie, and the mountain-tops rising beyond them, seem quiet and tranquil. We catch their restful spirit, yield to the soothing influences of the sunshine, and saunter dreamily on through flowers and bees, scarce touched by a definite thought; then suddenly we find ourselves in the shadowy cañon, closeted with Nature in one of her wildest strongholds.

After the first bewildering impression begins to wear off, we perceive that it is not altogether terrible; for besides the reassuring birds and flowers we discover a chain of shining lakelets hanging down from the very summit of the pass, and linked together by a silvery stream. The highest are set in bleak, rough, bowls, scantily fringed with brown and yellow sedges. Winter storms blow snow through the cañon in blinding drifts, and avalanches shoot from the heights. Then are these sparkling tarns filled and buried, leaving not a hint of their existence. In June and July they begin to blink and thaw out like sleepy eyes, the carices thrust up their short brown spikes, the daisies bloom in turn, and the most profoundly buried of them all is at length warmed and summered as if winter were only a dream.[51]

One of the striking features of our neighborhood twenty years ago, and one to which we never became reconciled, was the presence of huge wooden garbage boxes fastened to the street pavement in which the undisturbed refuse accumulated day by day. The system of garbage collecting was inadequate throughout the city, but it became the greatest menace in a ward such as ours, where the normal amount of waste was much increased by the decayed fruit and vegetables discarded by the Italian and Greek fruit peddlers, and by the residuum left over from the piles of filthy rags which were fished out of the city dumps and brought to the homes of the rag pickers for further sorting and washing.

The children of our neighborhood twenty years ago played their games in and around these huge garbage boxes. They were the first objects that a toddling child learned to climb; their bulk afforded a barricade and their contents provided missiles in all the battles of the older boys; and finally they became the seats upon which absorbed lovers held enchanted converse. We are obliged to remember that all children eat everything which they find and that odors have a curious and intimate power of entwining themselves into our tenderest memories, before even the residents of Hull-House can understand their own early enthusiasm for the removal of these boxes and the establishment of a better system of refuse collection.[52]

Both passages are about feeling one's way through dangerous territory. Muir has just finished warning that no pack animal emerges from this cañon unscathed, sometimes even falling to its death, and now he wants to soothe the fears he has provoked without denying their basis. Addams wants to stress how noxious and potentially lethal those untended garbage bins can be, without letting her reader disdain the neighborhood. In both passages topophilia and topophobia alternate, clash, and fuse in ways that add up to both an affirmation of bonding to place and a realization that an engagement with place worthy of the name is not just a matter of instinctive rapport but also hard work.

Indeed, these places are singled out for the kind of attention they get because they are so hard to love on first contact. Hence Muir tries to neutralize this landscape of fear[53] by dwelling on the surrounding meadows, peaks, and forest, and then, in the second paragraph, on how the lakelets above and the birds along the way relieve the bleakness, at least in summer. (He has to grant that winter is pretty dreadful.) Addams, for her part, refuses to let one simply think "How deplorable!" by setting forth the residential-insider perspective on the garbage boxes as play places and love seats, doubtless realizing how counterintuitive this will sound; and by following up with a wry self-ironic twist that is one of her stylistic hallmarks: running together the charming Proustian image of olfactory nostalgia and the totally *un*charming image of novice settlement house workers infiltrated subliminally by the nausea of primal stench before they consciously realize its effects.

Once one grasps the elements of similarity within these extremely different landscapes, it becomes easier to see that they also share what I have called a mutual constructionist understanding of placeness. On the one hand, obviously the landscapes both writers portray are culturally constructed. Both avail themselves of conventions of polite literary exchange that reprocess empirical reality so as to subserve their agendas of wilderness bonding or urban concern. In Muir's case, pastoral idealization; in Addams's case, gentle genre-sketch satire of immigrants and do-gooders. In particular, not only Addams but also Muir had a strong post-Victorian drive to domesticize, to reconstitute literal or symbolic wilderness as home.[54] Beyond such common motifs of cultural iconography, furthermore, Muir's Sierra vision and Addams's Chicago vision are products of different kinds of expertise. Muir's arrangement of landscape does not follow the flow of a novice's ground-level experience: the second half, particularly, would not have been so seen or sequenced while negotiating the cañon for the first time. It is a distilled and panoramic image, dependent on knowledge of how the various biotic and geological constituents interlink: the ability to read landscapes from the mountaintop, so to speak, which was a perspective Muir liked to assume both experientially—as mountaineer and field geologist/botanist—and in the mind's eye as a natural historian and theorist of glaciation. Likewise, Addams's descriptivism rests on a thorough grasp of neighborhood sociology and economy (like the rag-picking trade) vis-à-vis the workings (or the nonworkings) of city government.

Yet on the other hand these passages also show that it won't do to reduce platial representation *only* to cultural or disciplinary construct. To do so is to deny their respect for physical environment as destabilizing force; for the experience of resistant first impressions giving way to a more complicated sense of engagement; for the perception that place knowledge may be approximated vicariously but cannot be achieved without long existential immersion; for attachment to place as a creative force. This too is where the *literary* dimension becomes key (Muir's vibration between threatening versus welcoming sensations, Addams's playfulness around the sense of smell), and by the same token this is where the *ecocritical* difference especially enters in. Environmental connectedness requires acts of imagination not at one stage alone but three: in the bonding, in the telling, in the understanding. And though it is true that at each stage imagination can easily interfere, break down, or run amok, imagination remains crucial (whether so recognized or not) as a preservative against "the confusion of the world that comes from coveting knowledge," as Chuang Tzu puts it—meaning, I take it, the fetishization of knowledge, knowledge of an appropriative kind.

In such ways these represented landscapes manifest across the divides of outback-urban, pristine-polluted, an analogous understanding of human experience as formed in transaction with physical environment, and they affirm the centrality of physical environment as a ground of personal and social identity amidst the troubling of pastoral desire (in Muir's case) and even the toxification of neighborhood (in Addams's case).

I deliberately waive for the moment the normative question of what ethical standing or political preference to give to Addams's relatively anthropocentric ethics versus Muir's more ecocentric ethics, and how each might be held up as corrective to the other. To be sure, these are weighty issues in their own right, especially insofar as they necessitate real-life public policy trade-off decisions. But assuming that viable long-run solutions must involve some sort of both-and response rather than an either-or response, then the "Ethics of John versus Ethics of Jane" conundrum must be reckoned a second-order consideration relative to the larger point that the two visions belong in the same history, the same conversation, the same narrative.

Environmental Imagination and Environmental Unconscious

As the case of "America the Beautiful" suggests, a text that evokes a physical environment may not be so exclusively "about" that particular environment as first appears, yet it may also reflect a deeper, more complex engagement with it than one might initially think. On the reader's side also, response even to a simple-seeming rendition of physical environment is likely to be complicated by the tangled set of life experiences and mental training having to do with actual landscapes, landscape simulations, and prior expectations of any sort that a reader brings to an encounter with the work. All this means that acts of writing and reading will likely involve simultaneous processes of environmental awakening—retrievals of physical environment from dormancy to salience—and of distortion, repression, forgetting, inattention.

We do well then to start from the presumption of having to struggle against the limits of habitually foreshortened environmental perception.

"On a day-to-day basis," landscape architect Robert Thayer observes, "we don't comprehend the relationship between nature, technology, and landscape in a deliberate or conscious manner, and what interactions we do experience are merely manifestations of our typical lifestyles, tastes, and desires."[55] Or as social theorist Pierre Bourdieu puts it more fancifully but no less aptly, "when habitus encounters a social world of which it is the product, it is like a 'fish in water': it does not feel the weight of the water, and it takes the world about itself for granted."[56] Much of the time most people, particularly in modernized cultures, may not even want to attune themselves self-consciously to their environments lest this produce sensory overload, confusion, and despondency, as when suburban homeowners, preparing to market their houses, become disconcerted not only by sudden awakening to how differently a home's appearance and site may look through the eyes of others but also to some of its most basic physical conditions: its geology (High radon count likely?), its hydrology (Will the septic system perk?), its chemistry (Is there lead paint? lead in drinking water? asbestos insulation?), not to mention various other local codes that enmesh this and all other "real" estate in layers of invisible barbed wire. The nausea that can overtake one on such occasions is all the more wrenching on account of the prior acculturated practice of repressing such matters or simply not bothering to attend.

Just as one might expect, one of the first American sages of modernity was also one of the first to cope with the modern sense of physical environment as nuisance. Among the most engaging passages in Benjamin Franklin's *Autobiography* are his reminiscences about civic improvements in which he played a role: paving and illuminating the streets of Philadelphia, cleaning and draining the streets of London. "Some may think these trifling Matters not worth minding or relating," Franklin concedes after quoting at length from one of his proposals for urban waste removal, "but when they consider, that tho' Dust blown into the Eyes of a single Person or into a single Shop on a windy Day, is but of small Importance, yet the great Number of the Instances in a populous City, and its frequent Repetitions give it Weight & Consequence; perhaps they will not censure very severely those who bestow some of Attention to Affairs of this seemingly low Nature." On the contrary, "Human Felicity is produc'd not so much by great Pieces of good

Fortune that seldom happen, as by little Advantages that occur every Day. Thus if you teach a poor young Man to shave himself and keep his Razor in order, you may contribute more to the Happiness of his Life than in giving him a 1000 Guineas."[57]

Franklin's problem-solving ingenuity gets activated here by acute sensitivity to small abrasions that most people would either banish from consciousness or never subject to disciplined scrutiny.[58] This prompts him to imagine a new urban ecological order, where the watchmen are armed with brooms and ordered to use them and the "scavengers" or waste removers supplied with new kinds of "carts, not plac'd high upon Wheels, but low upon Sliders; with Lattice Bottoms" that will collect "mud" but drain out the "water," leaving much less to haul away.

Franklin's mental hyperactivity recalls the botanical enthusiasm of his fellow Philadelphian and contemporary William Bartram, whose *Travels in Florida* is the closest rival to Franklin's *Autobiography* as an early republican literary classic. Bartram also loves to transform grains of sand into mental universes, though in an opposite and complementary way. Take his excitement at the philoprogenitiveness of Spanish moss: "Wherever it fixes itself, on a limb, or branch, it spreads into short and intricate divarications; . . . and from this small beginning it increases, by sending downwards and obliquely, on all sides, long pendant branches, which divide and subdivide themselves ad infinitum." Bartram moves from dry taxonomic identification (Tillandsea usneaoides, "growing from N. lat. 35 down as far as 28") through an increasingly lavish description of its proliferation ("it also hangs waving in the wind, like streamers, from the lower limbs, to the length of fifteen or twenty feet, and of bulk and weight, more than several men together could carry") to breathless expatiation on its practical uses:

It seems particularly adapted to the purpose of stuffing mattresses, chairs, saddles, collars, &c. . . . The Spaniards in South America and the West-Indies, work it into cables, that are said to be very strong and durable; but, in order to render it useful, it ought to be thrown into shallow ponds of water, and exposed to the sun, where it soon rots, and the outside furry substance is dissolved. It is then taken out of the water, and spread to dry; when, after a little beating and shaking, it is sufficiently clean, nothing remaining but the interior, hard, black, elastic filament, entangled together, and greatly resembling horse-hair.[59]

Like Franklin, Bartram seeks to activate environmental perception to the end of social improvement; he delights to imagine how the prolific parasite might be put to human use. For him, however, observation is less tied to a utilitarian bottom line; curiosity and wonder are more free-floating: a state of heightened perception to be shared, not a feat of expertise designed to spare others trouble. Unlike Bartram's luminous retrieval of exotic flora, fauna, and landscapes never so evocatively described, Franklin's environmental projects aimed not to stimulate reciprocity with the physical environment but to reduce it, so that pedestrians could go about their business less aware of their surroundings, not more. The Franklin stove was designed, similarly, to reduce bodily discomfort, and with it bodily self-consciousness, as anyone who has lived through a cold winter without central heating knows well.

The absence or repression of a conscious sense of environmental attunement, then, is not necessarily a pejorative. John Muir rightly took pleasure in "having health so good I knew nothing about it."[60] It is the painful consciousness of being deprived of such transparency that drives the speaker in one of the poems of Native American poet Simon Ortiz to remind himself

> that I am only one part
> among many parts,
> not a singular eagle
> or one mountain. I am
> a transparent breathing.[61]

In this way he seeks to compose himself during an airplane ride over Hopi and Navajo country that drives home his separateness. To paraphrase Leslie Silko on the difference between Native and Euro-American landscape representation, particularity of environmental detail may actually betoken lack of connectedness,[62] an observation that can be turned against Bartram's minute and atomized set-piece descriptions of individual species of plant and animals. Hyperfocus is, in part, a recourse for bringing a semblance of order to a series of erratic wanderings through a region whose spatial arrangements, geographical borders, and social organization he can describe only sketchily.

The repressions and exaggerations in Franklin and Bartram are fascinating and instructive, and the same applies to later, more self-consciously literary environmental writers from Thoreau to Rachel Carson, as we shall see below. This mental/textual practice of foreshortening, whether fortuitous or intended, is the negative manifestation of what I shall call, at the risk of sounding overly mystical, "environmental unconscious." By this I mean to refer in part to the limiting condition of predictable, chronic perceptual underactivation in bringing to awareness, and then to articulation, of all that is to be noticed and expressed. As Italian architect Donatella Mazzoleni declares, "the lived experience of non-verbal, pre-logical space is only partly translatable into language or narratable"; the "spatialization of primary pulsations . . . cannot be contained by the web of any structure or story."[63] In my own, more inclusive, conception here, environmental unconscious in its negative aspect refers to the impossibility of individual or collective perception coming to full consciousness at whatever level: observation, thought, articulation, and so forth. I do not pretend to be able to identify all the many causes of foreshortening: scientific ignorance, inattention, specialized intellectual curiosity, ethnocentricity, self-protectiveness, the conventions of language itself—the list is long. Yet environmental unconscious is also to be seen as potential: as a residual capacity (of individual humans, authors, texts, readers, communities) to awake to fuller apprehension of physical environment and one's interdependence with it. Indeed, the various foreshortenings evinced by figures like Franklin and Bartram, serious as they are, are less worth lingering on than the breakthroughs achieved in grasping the significance of the unnoticed detail. Throughout this book I shall especially insist on the power of imagination to achieve such breakthroughs, despite whatever blockages. To my mind, awareness of the chronic presence of these, of the foreshortened or inertial aspect of environmental unconscious, ought not diminish but intensify one's interest in environmental unconscious as an enabling ground condition as it becomes activated in the work of composition and critical reading.

In a moment, I shall offer a more precise definition. But first, by way of further illustration of its sphere and workings, I take it that there is no site that cannot be startlingly and productively reenvisioned in such a way as to evoke a fuller environmental(ist) sense of it than workaday perception permits.[64] Not even the banality of prefabricated tract housing:

> They took the cardboard box and covered
> it with plaster, dry among the evergreens.
> Thinking of the centuries of worship
> that went into those cathedrals built . . .
> . . . like a solid cloud that won't plunge
> into the surging aquamarine, they swept
> the pipes into a large container to be carted
> away by horsepower.
>
>   (Frank O'Hara, "House")

Not even a suburban mall:

> I found myself inside a massive concrete shell
>   lit by glass tubes, with air pumped in, with
>   levels joined by moving stairs.
>
>   (Gary Snyder, "The Trade")

Not even a downtown emporium of luxury goods for the upper crust:

> the savage's romance,
> accreted where we need the space for commerce—
> the centre of the wholesale fur trade,
> starred with tepees of ermine and peopled with foxes,
> the long guard-hairs waving two inches beyond the
>   body of the pelt;
> the ground dotted with deer-skins—white with white spots
>
>   (Marianne Moore, "New York")

Not even a bird's-eye reduction of segregated Manhattan:

> Between two rivers,
> North of the park,

Like darker rivers
The streets are dark.

Black and white,
Gold and brown—
Chocolate-custard
Pie of a town.

(Langston Hughes, "Island [2]")

These passages tersely capture distortions of engineered environments. Not all of them can be said to be primarily "about" the physical sites they portray, but they share the approach of wanting to expose the weirdness of business-as-usual environmental perception.

In doing so these poems activate what Thayer calls "landscape guilt"—a reflex association of "natural" as superior to "built."[65] Yet none of them are simplistically antiurban nor do they line up at the same point on a hypothetical metropolitan-primitivist continuum. Rather, they show that workaday perception can be destabilized from various different directions: for example, by pointing to a more primordial nature existing beneath, outside, or despite restraining civilizational structures, or by exposing the violence of those structures.

These poems seek in various ways to play on and draw out what I have called environmental unconscious in both its occluding and its enabling aspects. Now to specify further what I mean by this neologism. It derives partially, of course, from Freud and thence from literary theorist Fredric Jameson's attempted synthesis of various strains of Freudian and Marxist thought in his theory of a "political unconscious" supposedly operative in narrative texts. Jameson claims that psychological unconscious is mediated by collective social experience and structures according to ideological frameworks, such that a literary text should accordingly "be seen as the rewriting or restructuration of a prior historical or ideological *subtext*."[66] He might wish to claim this of environmental perception too, nor would I wholly disagree. To my mind, however, embeddedness in spatio-physical context is even more intractably constitutive of personal and social identity, and of the way that texts get constructed, than ideology is, and very likely as primordial as unconscious psychic activity itself.[67] As Gadgil and Guha dryly remark apropos the dependence of infrastructure on physical environment in India, "an ecological approach . . . suggests that the mode of production concept [in Marxist thought] is not adequately materialistic in the first place."[68]

In thus privileging environmentality, I do not claim that it is the only dispositional matrix nor that there is any particular *ur*-form of human environmental unconscious,[69] such as preference for a savannah habitat, much less the choice of particular artistic genres or themes.[70] One doubtless can specify certain ways in which environmental unconscious is structured, for example, the sense of a "within" and a "beyond" the perimeter of the body (even when the body is somewhat prosthetic), a domain of the consciously "noticed" and a domain of the "unnoticed." But such contextness admits an immense plasticity according to person, culture, historical moment.

Among those who have recently thought about how imagination of environment finds cultural expression, I am hardly the first to suggest that environmental sensitivity is basic to human psychophysiological makeup or to propose a general term to denote it. The "biophilia" thesis, that humans have an affiliation for other forms of life, is analogous up to a point, but it makes stronger claims than I do for the magnetism of first nature, for the distinguishability of first nature's influence from that of second nature, and (in some versions) for its rootedness in human genetics. Such is even more the case with "the ecological unconscious" advanced by Theodore Roszak as the foundation of ecopsychology, a fusion of gestalt psychology and deep ecology: "the 'savage' remnant within us," the green core of "the collective unconscious [which], at its deepest level, shelters the compacted ecological intelligence of our species, the source from which culture finally unfolds as the self-conscious reflection of nature's own steadily emergent mindlikeness."[71] Somewhat closer to my own idea is Mitchell Thomashow's conception of "ecological identity," a holistic term for "all the different ways people construe themselves in relationship to the earth as manifested in personality, values, actions, and sense of self." Still closer, because more localized in space and more attuned to cultural specificity, is Yi-fu Tuan's "topophilia," the idea that humans have culturally mediated affinities for certain types of landscapes. Even closer is the "homo geographicus" of another humanistic geographer, Robert Sack, who envisions human situatedness as produced by interaction of social construction, territorial physicality, and phenomenology of perception.[72]

Some of the advantages of the idea of "environmental unconscious," as I conceive it, are, first, its ductility in marking situatedness as disposition without specifying particular kinds of environment; second, its value-neutrality, identifying need for some sort of orientation as prior to specific environmental preference;[73] third, its doublesidedness as an orientation that both links individuals to and differentiates them from groups; fourth, its acknowledgment of the impossibility of even trained perception arriving at full understanding of how it is situated; fifth, oppositely, that this disposition nonetheless affords a basis and incentive for efforts to raise unconsciousness to conscious awareness and articulacy; sixth, its implication that disposition and feeling drive theory as much or more than vice versa;[74] and therefore, seventh, its affirmation of the realm of imagination (whether or not articulated) as having a cogency if not also an authority not exhausted by formal reasoning.

The work of environmental unconscious, as I understand its operation in literary and other artistic works, has to do both with the "thereness" of actual physical environments and with processes of emotional/mental orientation and expression that can happen anywhere along a continuum from desultory preconscious intimation to formal imaging. The outer and inner landscapes are never entirely synchronous or continuous,[75] not only because of asymptotic limits of perception and articulacy but also from propensity for reinventing the worlds we see and the linguistic and structural tools we employ. It is never to be taken for granted that a literary image refers unambiguously to a specific place. Snyder's mall and O'Hara's house could be anywhere, and Moore's and Hughes's platial images are also rather generic even though they clearly point to Manhattan. But the generic quality of such images does not mean they lack "thereness," that they fail to suggest particular environments. In each case the poet's approach has been to take a form of readily recognizable spatialized experience, so recognizable as to be taken for granted, and to achieve a certain bringing to awareness by exposure of chronic unawareness. As such, the poems exemplify environmental unconscious as ground condition, seedbed, and creative opportunity.

Again, "a certain bringing to awareness" is not meant to suggest full control over result. Creative writers, like scholars, operate from culturally nuanced repertoires of habits, thoughts, and vocabularies, such that the "finished" work involves not mastery so much as adjudication of discourses over which it maintains an imperfect control. These exercise a force of their own, sometimes even contrary to a writer's intent—one way of reading Katharine Lee Bates's anodyne revisions to "America the Beautiful," further softening its gentle critique of American triumphalism. Or they may conflict, as with sentimental genre sketch versus hygenic parable in the Jane Addams passage. Or they may muffle complications, as with Muir's quickness to supply pastoral reassurance before he has even finished acknowledging his landscape's terrors. But to point out that articulation of environmental unconscious, like its workings at the quotidian level, arises from complex private and collective transactions with environment over which no one ever has full control is hardly to deny the creativity and force of individual acts of imagination.

This idea of an environmental unconscious is not the book's central thesis or subject, however, but rather a preliminary meditation intended to suggest how the acts of imagination that *are* this book's main subject can be oneiric and mimetic, self-referencing and referential, partial, obtuse, and prophetic all at the same time.

Outline of This Book

The eight chapters that follow can be read as separate independent studies but they also form a sequence.

Chapter 1, "Toxic Discourse," deals with a key instance of the rhetoric and ethics of imagined endangerment, which I take to be the most distinctive ground condition of present-day environmental reflection. Here I set discussion of literary discourse(s) in the context of the broadened demographic base of environmentalism during the last quarter-century. The chapter unfolds the premises, antecedents, impact, and cultural significance of toxic discourse by close examination of Rachel Carson's *Silent Spring* in relation to a wide range of other texts from the late eighteenth century to the present.

Following through on this initial emphasis on the felt threat of toxification for specific communities, Chapter 2, "The Place of Place," focuses on place attachment as a resource in the articulation of environmental unconscious. It outlines a theory of place sense and place-connectedness designed to fit a world that is seemingly ever more placeless, trying to give due respect to different facets of placeness sometimes pitted against each other: place as physical environment, as social construct, as phenomenological artifact. The final section, on African-American novelist John Edgar Wideman's retrieval of an abused and neglected place, anticipates Chapter 3, on "Reinhabiting the City." Here I reassess a deceptively familiar staple of urban writing, the *flâneur,* examining its possibilities as a means of "reinhabitory" vision in the work of Walt Whitman, William Carlos Williams, James Joyce, Virginia Woolf, and various other writers, Neoclassical to postmodern. I follow a series of literary experiments in which this figure becomes a means of perceiving the metropolis as ecocultural habitat, and of imagining relational forms of personhood over against the impulse to self-protective autonomy that urban mass society reinforces.

Mindful that Chapters 1–3 convey mixed signals about the degree to which people and communities should be seen as constructed by place, Chapter 4, "Discourses of Determinism," reviews major ways that nineteenth- and twentieth-century writers have imagined lives as place-determined, whether forcibly or voluntarily. The chapter moves from urban realist fiction (Dickens to Richard Wright) through other landscape genres to a paired discussion of the careers and works of Wendell Berry and Gwendolyn Brooks as examples of voluntary submission to the limits and possibilities of place-constrained, community-accountable imagination. Jane Addams gets the last word, however.

Chapter 5, "Modernization and the Claims of the Natural World: Faulkner and Leopold," extends the subject of place-connectedness to the relation between human community and nonhuman. Against the background of a declensionist view of regional environmental history, both Faulkner, particularly in *Go Down, Moses,* and Leopold, particularly in *A Sand County Almanac,* developed parallel ethics of land stewardship and critiques of property, with special emphasis on reimagination of hunting as quest for environmental understanding and connectedness. Their practice of using animals to quintessentialize environmental endangerment is treated more pointedly in Chapter 6, "Imagining Oceans and Whales." This chapter ponders the sudden shift in late-century thinking from ocean as inexhaustible resource and romantically mysterious domain to ocean as endangered global commons, finding in this a striking instance of the beginnings of a global environmentalist culture. I concentrate especially on a specific instance of oceanic reimagination: the revaluation of cetaceans from leviathanic adversaries to lovable kindred in need of protection. A close examination of Melville's *Moby-Dick,* however, also exposes some chronic failures of environmental imagination in contemporary texts even as their whale biology has become more informed and their environmental ethics more humane.

The two final chapters offer complementary reflections on the challenge of getting past the dichotomy of anthropocentric versus nonanthropocentric environmentalist persuasions, without denying its historical, ethical, and aesthetic bases. Chapter 7, "The Misery of Beasts and Humans," historicizes this dichotomy as a legacy of internal contradictions within early moral extensionist thought, crystallized through literary and critical divisions of labor that take unusual resolve and creativity to withstand. It first examines literary instances of this division, then works that mediate it, from British Romanticism to the present, with special emphasis on the fiction of Native American writer Linda Hogan. Chapter 8, "Watershed Aesthetics," gives a critical-historical account of the image that has become contemporary bioregionalism's most important icon, one that may suggest a fruitful way of thinking across the anthropocentric-nonanthropocentric divide. Beginning with early modern works of riverine poetry and prose, the chapter traces the literary invention and reinvention since early modern times of watershed imagination, noting how twentieth-century environmentally conscious writers, beginning with Mary Austin, increasingly deimperialized the watershed topos.

From these chapters I hope the reader will come to share my sense both of the power of environmental influences as a shaping force in works of creative imagination and of the power of those works, contending against the foreshortened vision that afflicts us all, to articulate what "environment" is and might be.

Chapter 1

Toxic Discourse

> There is a real world, that is really dying, and we had better think
> about that.
>
> —Marilynne Robinson, *Mother Country*

> Threats from civilization are bringing about a kind of new "shadow king-
> dom," comparable to the realm of the gods and demons in antiquity, which
> is hidden behind the visible world and threatens human life on this Earth.
> People no longer correspond today with spirits residing in things, but find
> themselves exposed to "radiation," ingest "toxic levels," and are pursued
> into their very dreams by the anxiety of a "nuclear holocaust" . . . Danger-
> ous, hostile substances lie concealed behind the harmless facades. Every-
> thing must be viewed with a double gaze, and can only be correctly
> understood and judged through this doubling. The world of the visible
> must be investigated, relativized and evaluated with respect to a second re-
> ality, only existent in thought and concealed in the world.
>
> —Ulrich Beck, *Risk Society*

> For the first time in history, modern selves are self-consciously aware of the
> need to analyze their actions as transverse interactions within the world
> that is there for *all* humans . . . The accumulation of actions like starting my
> car, spraying my lawn with toxics, leaking chloroflurocarbons . . . from my
> air conditioner, or cutting my trees affects the conditions for human sur-
> vival around the earth.
>
> —Andrew J. Weigert, *Self, Interaction, and Natural Environment*

The fear of a poisoned world is increasingly pressed, debated, de-
bunked, and reiterated. Medicine, political science, history, sociology,
economics, and ethics have been major contributors. Seldom, however,
is toxicity discussed as discourse: as an interlocked set of topoi whose
force derives partly from the anxieties of late industrial culture, partly
from deeper-rooted habits of thought and expression.

The subtler complications of "toxic discourse" will take this whole
chapter to explain. For the moment, however, it can be sweepingly de-

fined as expressed anxiety arising from perceived threat of environmental hazard due to chemical modification by human agency. As such, it is by no means unique to the present day, but never before the late twentieth century has it been so vocal, so intense, so pandemic, and so evidentially grounded.

There seem to be at least two reasons why the discourse of toxicity has not been treated with the same attention as its chemical, medical, social, and legal aspects. One, certainly, is the pragmatism that plays a major part in shaping agendas of public discussion. "Discourse" may seem a low priority when health or property is at risk. Not even intellectuals can be counted on to agree with Emerson's dictum that "to a sound judgment, the most abstract truth is the most practical"[1]—even though basic structures of thought, values, feeling, expression, and persuasion may indeed be more influential in the remediation of environmental problems than the instruments of technology or politics.

A second reason for relative neglect is the more "tribal" factor of the manner in which environmental issues have been framed by the potential contributors to the inquiry. Within literary and rhetorical studies, the impetus to engage environmental issues has mainly come from the ecocritical movement,[2] which has concerned itself especially with creative and critical recuperation of the natural world, although lately it has begun to engage a wider range of texts and positions.[3] The other venue from which environmental issues have chiefly been treated as discourse, cultural studies, has tended to epiphenomenalize physical environment by conceiving it as a production of geopolitics, capitalism, technology, or other human institution,[4] although some recent works of literary-cultural theory have placed environmental concerns more at the center of their analytical maps.[5] Perhaps a better cross-fertilization of approaches can be attained on the basis of such a conception as "mutual construction" of discourse and material world as I sketched in the Introduction or the "constrained constructivism" proposed by N. Katherine Hayles.[6] Toxic discourse makes an excellent test case, since, as we shall see, it arises both from individual or social panic and from an evidential base in environmental phenomena. Both this chapter and the next accordingly attempt to define more precisely the work of discourse as a cultural construction regulated by engagement, whether experiential or vicarious, with actual environments.

The Toxic Denominator

Although toxic concern dates from late antiquity,[7] in recent years it has greatly intensified and spread. Love Canal, Three Mile Island, Bhopal, Chernobyl, the *Exxon Valdez:* this modern mantra refers both to actual incidents and to events in the history of postindustrial imagination that ensured that the environmental apocalypticism activated by Hiroshima and Nagasaki would outlast the Cold War. Even the world's privileged enclaves betray symptoms of what social theorist Ulrich Beck has called "the risk society"—an increasingly global state of "immiseration" characterized by a "solidarity from anxiety" due to inability, even with science's assistance, to calculate the consequences of possibly harmful exposure to environmental hazards in one's everyday life.[8] Concurrently, such anxiety has also increased dramatically among the nonprivileged, seldom previously engaged in green activism. In the United States the antitoxics campaign has changed the face of environmental advocacy since its inception as a large-scale movement in the wake of the Love Canal controversy in the late 1970s,[9] broadening from a relatively few local disturbances to a national network of thousands of community groups.

Whereas preservationist agendas advocated by mainstream environmental groups have been financially supported, and their organizations staffed, by well-educated middle-class whites (typically male), what today is increasingly called the environmental justice movement (of which campaigns against toxic dumping have been the catalyst and remain the centerpiece) has increasingly been led by nonelites, more often than not women, including a strong minority presence[10]—and understandably so, given that "all Americans [are] not . . . being poisoned equally."[11] Nor have these nontraditional activists wanted to identify closely with mainstream preservationists, but like as not to disparage them as "bird kissers and tree huggers."[12] "In their previous lives," notes one account of the early leaders, "each of these folks had led overwhelmingly private lives filled with private, immediate concerns. They did not bother themselves with 'political' matters . . . None of them was eager to get involved. At most, one hears them speak of doing it reluctantly, out of a sense of duty, because someone had to. Then, disillusioned and angered by their experiences, each moved toward a radical critique of society, business, and government."[13]

The 1990s may conceivably be remembered as a time when ecojustice activism built bridges with traditional environmentalism. The first two of the seventeen points in the 1991 manifesto emanating from the First National People of Color Environmental Leadership Summit in Washington, D.C., were (1) "Environmental justice affirms the sacredness of Mother Earth, ecological unity and the interdependence of all species, and the right to be free from ecological destruction" and (2) "Environmental justice demands that public policy be based on mutual respect and justice for all peoples, free from any form of discrimination or bias."[14] These declarations seem to strive for an eclectic blend of old-time American democratic civil religion, '60s-era civil rights guarantees, Native American spirituality, and preservationist ethics. But what seems most distinctive about contemporary ecopopulism is the activism of nonelites, the emphasis on community, and an "anthropocentric" emphasis on environmentalism as instrument of social justice as against an "ecocentric" emphasis on caring for nature as a good in itself.[15]

Even if the theory of environmental justice proves too partisan for most legislators to endorse, the fear of environmental poisoning that energizes it may have at least as good a chance of remaining a compelling public issue as nuclear fear once did, especially given the certainty of future highly publicized emergencies with potentially serious consequences for public health. In the United States the iconographic power of toxic discourse as refracted through the media has been crucial to the quickening of the "scissor effect" of tightened legal regulations on dumping plus local blocking of new waste sites producing "voluntary" moves on industry's part to reduce waste production.[16] Of course, one of those voluntary moves has been to move industry offshore—*maquiladores* along the U.S.-Mexican border, sweatshops in Latin America and southeast Asia, garbage flotillas to Africa[17]—aggravating global ecoinequality, seeming to thrust the world ever closer to the end time of modernization prophesied by Henri Lefebvre: the whole earth subjugated by "the capitalist 'trinity'" (land-capital-labor) into a space of sovereignty at once fragmented and hierarchical.[18] But that metastasis only confirms the potency of toxic discourse itself (which Lefebvre's mordant analysis of runaway modernization antici-pates), a potency confirmed by its very extravagance, which has taken on a life of its own in excess of the "facts."[19] Toxic discourse is both al-ways immoderate and yet always being reinforced by unsettling events. Hence its permeation of the talk, if not the daily behavior, of national leaders and citizenry alike: for example, President Clinton's August 1996 nomination acceptance speech proclaiming as a self-evidently shameful truth that ten million U.S. children under twelve live three miles from a toxic waste dump. At the popular level recent public opinion surveys, like the 1995 Kempton, Bolster, and Hartley survey of a cross-section of five different groups of West-Coasters (Earth First!-ers, Sierra Clubbers, dry cleaners, laid-off sawmill workers, and a random sample of Califor-nians), show a strong consensus for such propositions as "A healthy en-vironment is necessary for a healthy economy."[20] In the developing world to an even greater degree, the sense of looming threat to human life and well-being offers a more cogent basis for global accord on envi-ronment as priority than does traditional preservationism.[21] Though toxic discourse may exacerbate social divisions when it summons up "the environmentalism of the poor" against the rich, and be a bone of contention between the countries of the North and the South and be-tween corporate and individual interests, it also may be a common de-nominator: a shared vocabulary, a shared concern. As literary critic Philip Fisher remarks in another context, fear can be a "route through which reciprocity is broken off," but it can produce a "more profound reciprocity . . . through shared fear, mutual fear."[22]

At the end of the nineteenth century, in a fascinating essay on "The Microbe as a Social Leveller," Cyrus Edson, a physician of socialist sym-pathies, set forth a similar idea: that "disease binds the human race to-gether as with an unbreakable chain"; "the man of wealth" is bound to "the man of poverty" by the unbreakable chain of contagion that quar-antines cannot stop for very long.[23] Edson drew from this a lesson of necessary human cooperation and mutual respect. This made sense be-fore modern medicine, when the bacteriological explanation of the ori-gin of disease was still a new discovery and great importance was attached to environmental causation of illness.[24] But Edson did not reckon seriously enough with the self-insulating propensities of the rich, with racist scapegoating of immigrants and other socially marginal folk as disease-bearers,[25] much less with the pharmaceutical revolution, which has brought a new level of security to those who can buy access. At the turn of the twenty-first century, likewise, perceived environmental crisis will doubtless prompt many affluent individuals, communities, and societies to seek safe havens from which they can blame—or trash—the victims.[26] But the problem may be more inescapable this time around, as the prospect of finding sanctuary anywhere becomes fainter. In any event, if anything like a universal environmental discourse is to come into being, toxic discourse is certain to be one of the key ingredients. But what, more specifically, *is* "toxic discourse" anyhow?

Toxic Discourse Anatomized

Its effective beginning was Rachel Carson's *Silent Spring* (1962). Chapter 1 introduces one of the first of its several defining motifs or topoi: the shock of awakened perception. Carson tells a "Fable for Tomorrow" of a "town in the heart of America" that awakes to a birdless, budless spring. "This town does not actually exist," Carson concludes; "but it might easily have a thousand counterparts in America or elsewhere in the world," for "a grim specter has crept upon us almost unnoticed, and this imagined tragedy may easily become a stark reality we all shall know."[27] She then launches into an indictment of DDT and chemical pesticides in general.

Media coverage of Love Canal, the first widely publicized case in the post-Carson era of a "poisoned community" in the United States, drew on similar images of community disruption, showing "visuals that seemed to signify 'normalcy,' but [revealing] the opposite, through voice-over narration . . . A boy bicycles along a quiet suburban street while the narrator says, 'There have been instances of birth defects and miscarriages among families.' . . . The most frequent, most persistent images throughout these news stories," this same analysis continues, "were of community lands (school yard, suburban field, backyards) that *ought* to be green, vibrant with suburban/domesticated vegetation, but instead show only sparse, half-dead plant cover, punctuated with holes

filled with unnatural-looking chemical soup; house yards and base-
ments invaded by chemical ooze; disrupted neighborhood life."[28]

These images echoed the residents' life narratives. Lois Gibbs, who
became the community's most prominent activist, insisted that when
she arrived in 1972, she "didn't even know Love Canal was there. It was
a lovely neighborhood in a quiet residential area, with lots of trees and
lots of children outside playing. It seemed just the place for our family."
Her awakening was slow and her sense of betrayal commensurate. Returning one night from a Homeowners Association meeting, she was
stunned when a companion remarked "that you could close your eyes
and walk down the street and tell where every single storm sewer opening was just from the smell. It was true; even though I was in the midst
of it, I still couldn't believe the contamination had reached my house."[29]

Studies of other "contaminated communities" report a similar picture: an awakening to the horrified realization that there is no protective environmental blanket, leaving one to feel dreadfully wronged.
Then follows a gamut of possible reactions: outrage, acquiescence, impotence, denial, desperation.[30]

These documents raise insoluble chicken-and-egg questions about
what's constructing what. To what extent did media coverage of Love
Canal shape Gibbs's autobiography? Or did residents' testimony shape
the media coverage? To what extent were both pre-shaped by *Silent
Spring* and its aftermath? Whatever one's answers, the testimony of Carson, Gibbs, and others clearly evince older patterns of thought. In
Nathaniel Hawthorne's mid-nineteenth-century tale "Rappaccini's
Daughter," for instance, the protagonist falls in love with a beautiful
young woman who tends a strange botanical garden that turns out to
be an anti-Eden of poisonous plants created by her mad scientist father.
Indeed, Beatrice herself is toxic, and the price Giovanni must pay to secure her is to accept his own metamorphosis into a creature whose
breath kills ordinary flies and spiders. The setting is medieval, but the
scenario rests on the same techno-dystopian thinking that Hawthorne
displays when rewriting *Pilgrim's Progress* in "The Celestial Railroad."[31] Contemporary Victorian-era "sanitarian" exposés like Catherine
Beecher's "The American People Starved and Poisoned" claim explicitly
what Hawthorne intimates: our snug bastions of bourgeois domesticity
are suffused with noxious lethal vapors.[32]

Both Carson and her populist successors, then, revive a long-standing mythography of betrayed Edens, the American dispensation of which has been much discussed by scholars, most influentially by Leo Marx in his *The Machine in the Garden*.[33] For Marx, traditional mainstream American culture was marked by a naïve doublethink that allayed incipient anxieties about the techno-economic progress to which national policy has always been committed with escapist fantasies of inexhaustible natural beauty. This naïveté was critiqued by a handful of independent-minded creative thinkers like Thoreau and Melville who recognized the inherent contradiction between techno-boosterism and Currier-and-Ives identification of U.S. culture and folkways with pastoral landscapes. The predominant mentality Marx terms "simple pastoral," the contrarian vision of awakened intellectuals "complex pastoral."

It comes as no surprise, therefore, to find contemporary toxic discourse retelling narratives of rude awakening from simple pastoral to complex.[34] As historians of architecture and city planning have shown, the cultural construction of suburbia in the United States and often even of urban neighborhoods has drawn heavily upon pastoral imagery and values: envisioning communities of safe, clean, ample residential and public spaces (including for suburbs green oases of lawn around single-family homes and for cities emerald necklaces, garden parks, and apartment windowboxes).[35] Traumas of pastoral disruption are intensified by the common tendency for people to "have a strong but unjustified sense of subjective immunity" about domains familiar to them: hence failure to read product labels or to take elementary precautions when spraying in home or garden.[36]

It was through the rose-colored lens of pastoral-utopian innocence that Lois Gibbs recalls having seen the extremely modest residential subdivision of Love Canal. Likewise the landfill-plagued north Jersey community of Legler, whose residents had settled there (so affirms the major case study) as "part of an escape from the city to a rural idyll."[37] Likewise Sumter County, Alabama, an impoverished, 70 percent African-American district targeted by the Environmental Protection Agency for one of the nation's largest waste disposal facilities but proclaimed by the head of local activist resistance as "a beautiful agricultural region."[38] The accuracy of these images matters less than their psychological and rhetorical cogency.

In linking ecopopulist protest to pastoral values, one may seem to blur categories, seeing that pastoral sentiment's most obvious environmentalist legacy, preservationism in the Thoreau-Muir tradition, was to become the operating philosophy of the elite environmental organizations against which environmental justice activism has often pitted itself. Not only does the latter have a different demographic mix, it also differs in several core values, being more explicitly anthropocentric,[39] focused more on populated areas than open space and on community betterment rather than alone-with-nature experiences. Yet the two persuasions share the conviction that the biological environment ought to be more pristine than it is, ought to be a healthy, soul-nurturing habitat. So it makes sense for toxic discourse to enlist pastoral support. It refocuses and democratizes the pastoral ideal: a nurturing space of clean air, clean water, and pleasant uncluttered surroundings that ought to be one's by right.

Disenchantment from the illusion of the green oasis is accompanied or precipitated by totalizing images of a world without refuge from toxic penetration. This is a second topos propagated by *Silent Spring*. "For the first time in the history of the world," Carson insists, "every human being is now subjected to contact with dangerous chemicals, from the moment of conception until death."[40] The spectacle of communities, population groups, and finally the whole earth contaminated by occult toxic networks has repeatedly been invoked by environmental justice activists. It has furthered the effort to create a community of the disempowered ("From the time oil is taken out of the ground in Alaska in the land of the Gwichen to the refining process in North Richmond [California] to the final combustion of the oil on the freeways through west Oakland, poor people and people of color pay the cost"). It has helped mobilize groups of previously apolitical women by underscoring "connections between particular health problems in their own lives and the larger world of public policies and power that cause them." It has been invoked by minority neighborhoods threatened by hazardous waste facility sites to persuade white residents in contiguous districts that "no part of a community is an island unto itself; all residents benefit or suffer when any of them do."[41] Not for nothing was the publication of the national organization of antitoxic resistance movements baptized *Everyone's Backyard*.

As with the rhetoric of pastoral betrayal, that of toxic diffusion hardly originates with Carson nor has it been confined to the environmental justice movement. It has pervaded popular culture via, for example, ecocatastrophe novels like Philip Dick's *Do Androids Dream of Electric Sheep?*, John Brunner's *The Sheep Look Up*, Scott Sanders's *Terrarium*, and Paul Theroux's *O-Zone*.[42] Their impetus devolves, just as Carson's diagnostic does, from Cold War-era nuclear fear. Just before *Silent Spring* was published, President John F. Kennedy, who supported Carson's campaign to restrict use of chemical pesticides, warned the United Nations that "every inhabitant of this planet must contemplate the day when this planet may no longer be habitable."[43] Carson explicitly played on such anxieties by branding the pesticides industry "a child of the Second World War" and representing pesticides' consequences with imagery of carnage: weaponry, killing, victimage, extermination, corpses, massacre, conquest.[44]

But theories that locate the origin of global toxification rhetoric in the Cold War or nuclear era cannot account for its long-standingness and complexity. Malthusian anxiety lest the world's resources be ruined by overexploitation is not the "new paradigm" it has been claimed to be[45] but a long tradition in conservationist thought.[46] In the 1930s and 1940s artist-conservationist J. N. ("Ding") Darling popularized the vision of an already depleted world in syndicated cartoons depicting the earth as a globe with a vast crater where the United States once was (to satirize corporate rapacity) or a tiny near-empty kettle tended by a diminutive Mother Nature overshadowed by a hungry giant ("World Population") impatiently holding out a huge begging bowl.[47] Indeed, the ruined world image dates back to the first modern conservationist treatise, George Perkins Marsh's *Man and Nature* (1864), which in turn echoes warnings by European civil servants outposted during the seventeenth and eighteenth centuries on ecologically fragile island enclaves like St. Helena and Mauritius.[48]

When Richard Hatcher, the first African-American mayor of Gary, Indiana, an adroit politician with a keen sense of social justice, managed to rally urban blacks, middle-class suburbanites, and working-class whites behind a campaign for better air quality, they may not have been influenced by Carson, much less by antecedent traditions of toxic discourse. But the success of Gary's environmental coalition—until rustbelt recession hit the city so hard in the 1970s that unemployment over-whelmed other civic concerns—depended on pollution's power as a so-cial unifier: "one of the few issues that could bridge the divide between hostile factions."[49] As Ulrich Beck has written, whereas *poverty is hierar-chic, smog is democratic.*"[50]

No less crucial to the success of Hatcher's coalition building was his strategy of unifying communal hostility by linking environmental re-form with social justice against "a common enemy of corporate greed."[51] This is a third major constituent of toxic discourse: moral pas-sion cast in a David versus Goliath scenario. The motif has a dual prove-nance in U.S. environmentalist thought. The canonical inception point is the struggle between John Muir and Gifford Pinchot for the soul of Theodore Roosevelt over the question of whether to retain the Hetch Hetchy Valley as part of Yosemite National Park or to allow the valley to be dammed in order to bolster the San Francisco area's water supply. Muir accused "mischief-makers and robbers of every degree" of "trying to make everything dollarable," to no avail—although he did manage to unsettle Roosevelt temporarily.[52] Historically simultaneous with Muir's campaign, but rarely mentioned in histories of American environmen-talism,[53] was Upton Sinclair's *The Jungle* (1906), the landmark novel de-nouncing worker victimage by the meatpacking industry. This is the other provenance: not muckraking narrative alone but a congeries of initiatives on behalf of urban and workplace reform that gathered mo-mentum at the end of the nineteenth century, including the Ruskin-inspired settlement house movement, intensified labor agitation, and the birth of industrial toxicology. That the two legacies were not sooner linked bespeaks not simply social compartmentalization by class but compartmentalization of space (workplace versus home and leisure spaces, town versus country). Hatcher interwove these concerns by proclaiming the common victimage of all Gary's neighborhoods.

So too Carson at the global level. In a commemorative essay environ-mental justice activist Victor Lewis praised her exposé of "the de-mented love affair of corporate power with the chemical insect controls" and her protofeminist "denunciation of the outrages of patri-archy."[54] This was said in recognition of Carson's indictment of military and government agencies as well as chemical companies for pursuing eradication programs that don't work and for dispensing poisons without reckoning consequences or warning of known risks. Carson's own ire was less directed against specific organizations and officials, however, than against entrenched recalcitrance: against the "chemical barrage . . . hurled against the fabric of life"—"as crude a weapon as the cave man's club"; against the "tendency to brand as fanatics or cultists all who are so perverse as to demand that their food be free of insect poisons."[55]

The invective gains force by not limiting itself to a single adversary. It carefully preserves an us-versus-them dichotomy without absolving us for our acquiescence and complicity as chemical consumers—even as *Silent Spring* makes clear that ordinary citizens are victims of military, corporate, and government arrogance (with the opposition always masculinized). This universalizing turn within the rhetoric of blame is almost as important as the accusation itself. Even Lewis, who wishes Carson had pressed "the connections between social and environmental justice, between civil and environmental rights," refers to "our rampant misuse of agricultural pesticides."[56] After all, the environmental justice (EJ) activist must guard against insouciance or ignorance, even after having been "awakened," as well as against extrinsic evil. Significantly, Lewis's tribute to Carson is preceded by a hard-hitting how-to article on "The DOs and DONTs of Fighting Pesticides," whose final warning is "DON'T hire a professional and go to sleep."[57] Besides, in many contexts it is not only more accurate but also more effective to name "environmental racism" as the culprit rather than a particular agent.

In either case, the threat of hegemonic oppression is key to toxic discourse. In response, the environmental justice movement has promoted a self-conscious, informed sense of local self-identification, victimage, and grassroots resistance encapsulated by the image of "communities" or "neighborhoods" nationwide combatting "unwanted industrial encroachment and outside penetration."[58] These terms imply population groups with a common sense of place identification and social identity disrupted by toxic menace. The image of the holistic settlement, however, can be quite flexible. It can be extended to comprise not only historically self-identified entities like Alsen, Louisiana ("a rural community of black landowners [that evolved into] its present status as a stable, working-class suburban [98.9 percent black] enclave") but also statistical districts like ZIP code 99058 in South Central Los Angeles

("The *neighborhood* [italics mine] is a haven for nonresidential activities. More than eighteen industrial firms in 1989 discharged more than 33 million pounds of waste chemicals in this ZIP code").[59] This politics of place elasticity, however, is not at all inconsistent with the sociology of place itself. As social geographer John Agnew puts it, "place refers to [a] *process* of social structuration" that "cannot be understood without reference to the 'outside forces' that help define those places."[60] In toxic discourse the forces are, of course, the invader whose unwanted attention has targeted the locale, the EJ activist-facilitator, and the reader whose concern is drawn to this marked territory. Contestation of what counts as "place" is to be expected, then.

As toxic discourse focuses on specific cases, it readily montages into gothic. When Carson goes to the supermarket, her attention is riveted by the spectacle of "substances of far greater death-dealing power than the medicinal drug for which [one] may be required to sign a 'poison book' in the pharmacy next door . . . Within easy reach of a child's exploring hand" are fragile glass containers with convulsion-inducing chemicals. "These hazards of course follow the purchaser right into his home," in the form of such products as kitchen shelf paper "impregnated with insecticide, not merely on one but on both sides."[61] Today's how-to detoxification guides are full of similar cautionary tales like the case of "self-employed suburban engineer" Eugene Beeman, who "tightened his house to make it more energy efficient" and died of carbon monoxide poisoning as a result, or that of Dana Shrier, who traces her recurring "heart palpitations and joint pains" to "pesticide residues" in her mattress.[62]

Gothification becomes most lurid when the victim never had a choice, as Beeman and Shrier did, at least in principle. Consider five-year old Anttwon Suggs, whose story opens a *Los Angeles Times* article on the worldwide increase of asthma among children and especially inner-city African Americans. Overcome by a seizure at school, Anttwon gasped for breath and begged his teacher for help, "but she scolded him for misbehaving." Taken too late to the school nurse's office, "panic began to set in." Anttwon's "eyes bulged with terror as he fought to draw oxygen through his clogged airways." His hastily summoned mother, "fighting back her own hysteria," tried vainly "to calm him as her only son drew his final breath and died,"[63] trapped in the chambers of the school-dungeon. What this report finds especially shocking is that the incident typifies the plight of a whole class of juvenile victims whose life narratives unscroll in an endless series of tragedies in community, neighborhood, and workplace.

As with our previous topoi, here too the precursor forms date back to early industrialization. In U.S. literary history, gothicization of public health issues starts with the first novelist of claim to major importance, Charles Brockden Brown, who luridly portrayed yellow fever epidemics in Philadelphia and New York in *Arthur Mervyn* (1799–1800), *Ormond* (1799), and other works. In early nineteenth-century Euro-America, gothicized environmental squalor intensifies in European and American accounts of rural and especially urban poverty, perhaps the best known being Freidrich Engels's description of Manchester and other British factory towns in *The Condition of the Working Class in England* (1845) and Charles Dickens's novel *Hard Times* (1854), also set in the industrial Midlands.

Surveying mid-nineteenth-century exposés of the lower depths of New York City, Eric Homberger notes their reliance on "the Virgilian mode": "a guided tour of the underworld" slums that allegorizes them in classico-biblical terms as "the home of lost souls" so as to instill shock and compassion in uninitiated readers.[64] Herman Melville carried the Virgilian mode to the milltowns of New England ("you stand as within a Dantean gateway" at the threshold of the ravine leading to the "Tartarus of Maids"); Rebecca Harding Davis carried it to the industrial cities in the hinterland ("take no heed to your clean clothes, and come right down with me,—here, into the thickest of the fog and mud and foul effluvia").[65] It remained a staple of journalistic exposés like Jacob Riis's *How the Other Half Lives* (1890) and Jack London's *The People of the Abyss* (1903),[66] of novelistic equivalents like Sinclair's *The Jungle,* and even the writings of investigative researchers, such as Jane Addams's protégée Alice Hamilton, the American founder of industrial toxicology. In her autobiography Hamilton recalls a bleak January visit to a lead-smelting operation in Joplin, Missouri, "the very dreariest, most hopeless community I had eve[r] seen . . . around the village not a tree, only . . . the refuse from the concentrating mills which formed huge pyramids of ground rock and wide stretches of fine sand as far as the eye could see. As I looked there came to mind that Old Testament verse:

'And the heaven that is over thy head shall be brass, and the earth that is under thee shall be iron.'"[67]

Here we also see the Virgilian mode's potential double bind: advocating social regeneration by reinscribing the polarization of saved versus damned, the guide being so much wiser, so much more like "us," than the hapless hardly human victims. Sometimes the condescension is deliberate. In the macho-adventurer London and in the photographer-voyeur Riis, pity can lapse abruptly into contempt. Dickens's humanitarianism keeps him from this; yet neither Dickens nor Sinclair will abdicate narrative omniscience, any more than Hamilton will question that the best way to diagnose and remediate the environmental problems in the workplace is cooperation between experts and managers. Muriel Rukeyser opens up her long labor-activist poem "The Book of the Dead" to *Spoon River Anthology*-style monologues of Appalachian silicosis victims, but encased within heavy editorial didacticism.[68]

Contemporary toxic discourse inherits this ambiguous legacy. Carson relies at every turn on scientific authority. But in *Silent Spring* the terms of the author-audience relation to the scenes depicted have changed, both parties now being potential if not actual denizens of the toxic Inferno. In contemporary toxic discourse, furthermore, victims are permitted to reverse roles and claim authority. EJ journals contain extensive grassroots affidavits from community representatives along with the corroborating testimony of activist-investigators and scholar-consultants. The insider affidavits make central those moments in Virgilian gothic when—in the spirit of the *Inferno* itself—the sufferer briefly achieves agency by becoming the guide's guide.

Altogether the four interlocking formations, both in their cultural embeddedness and in their contemporary transposition, promote a unifying culture of toxicity notwithstanding recognition of such marks of social difference as race, gender, and class in determining what groups get subjected to what degree of risk. Carson's adoption by the EJ movement as harbinger, prophet, and foremother is exemplary, in that *Silent Spring*'s controlled analytical-satiric tone and documentary circumspection mark it as directed toward a well-educated, middle-class sub/urban citizenry (originally it was serialized in *The New Yorker*) by a person of the same background. Yet it is also a book whose passionate concern about the threat of omnivictimage and whose author's postpublication ordeal as a vindicated and triumphant martyr of industry-led attack (the pathos intensified by Carson's own death from cancer) reidentifies it as a work of "universal" scope speaking from as well as to and for the positions of toxic victims in every place and social niche.[69]

Toxicity, Risk, and Literary Imagination

So much by way of genre analysis. Now let us consider some broader implications of this Virgilian tour for the understanding of the creative and critical work of environmental representation. One implication, clearly, is that toxic discourse calls for a way of imagining physical environments that fuses social constructivist with environmental restorationist perspectives. Against the model often favored by ecocriticism hitherto, of an "ecological holism" to which acts of imagination have the capacity to (re)connect us,[70] toxic discourse holds that belief in the availability of such a holism by such means is chimerical and divisive. Yet it recognizes both the rhetorical appeal and the benefit to human and planetary welfare of the ideal of a purified physical environment as an end in itself, thereby recognizing physical environment's nonreducibility to ideological artifact or socioeconomic counter. Its impetus is both to reinforce the deromanticization and to urge the expansion of "nature" as an operative category.

On the one hand, physical nature's cultural importance, indeed nature's nature itself, ceases to be located in its promise as past, present, or future sanctuary but rather in its standing as humanity's codependent and coconspirator in coping with the fact/awareness that the nature one engages must now inescapably be—if indeed it has not always in some sense been—not pristine but the effect of "second" (i.e., modified) nature or (in Derek Jarman's phrase) "modern nature."[71] However one might wish otherwise, the nature that toxic discourse recognizes as the physical environment humans inhabit is *not* a holistic spiritual or biotic economy but a network or networks within which, on the one hand, humans are biotically imbricated (like it or not), and within which, on the other hand, first nature has been greatly modified (like it or not) by *techne*. This view is neither "preservationist," given its recognition of the impact of human powers and the legitimacy of human needs, nor is it "conservationist," since not resource management so much as viable symbiosis with physical environment is its goal.

On the other hand, the boundaries of "nature" and of "environmental" discourse now become much more elastic than formerly conceived. As Alexander Wilson has observed, the prevalent North American settler culture "ideology of city and country as discrete and exclusive land forms has been destructive" for its impoverishment of the sense of the ecological status and potential of both domains. The stereotypes inhibit recognizing country's status as site of production and city's need for greater ecological self-sufficiency. Though Wilson takes a good argument too far, the basic point is sound;[72] and the same could be said about the traditional linkage in literary studies of "environmental" consciousness to outback genres like wilderness romance and "nature writing" rather than with literatures of the city. Toxic discourse breaks down this binary, opens one to consideration of Richard Wright and Charles Dickens as writers with a sense of the "ecology" of place as keen as that of ruralizing counterparts like Zora Neale Hurston or Thomas Hardy.

Nowhere is this blurring of standard genre distinctions more striking than in contemporary works of nature writing produced under pressure of toxic anxiety, such as Terry Tempest Williams's *Refuge* (1991).[73] *Refuge* unfolds a double plot of a Utah wildlife sanctuary endangered by a rise in the Great Salt Lake and of the women in Williams's family maimed by cancer that might have been caused by downwind fallout from a decade of aboveground nuclear tests at Yucca Flats, Nevada. The book culminates with the narrator's realization that her family might have been put at risk unawares by accidentally being too near a particularly dirty explosion in the early 1950s.[74] After reading this book, it immediately dawns on one how much even the previous generation of green activist writing about this region, like Edward Abbey's *Desert Solitaire* (1968) and *The Monkey Wrench Gang* (1975), has overlooked or suppressed.[75]

The two fields of Williams's vision—wildlife and family illness—pull with and against each other by turns. Wilderness is both antidote to illness and escape from facing it; the deaths of mother and grandmother are both natural processes and profoundly *unnatural*; and the way the narrator splits attention between these foci is both therapeutic and symptomatic of the fitful grasp that she and her culture have of the relation between their mind-bodies and the environmental envelope that contains them. This allows Williams both to acknowledge and to resist the desire to cordon off natural from social—a hazard of traditional preservationist thinking, as we have seen, and the state of innocence from which ecopopulist leaders like Lois Gibbs had to awaken before they could understand what had overtaken their communities. *Refuge* becomes metacommentary on pastoralism's wish-fulfilling turn. Like Carson before her, Williams perceives that human communities and physical environment both stand to gain when the impact on reading audiences of a represented awakening to what is most troubling about that interdependence begins to approximate the startled awakening of victims of actual contaminated communities, for whom "environment becomes much more important to their understanding of life than it was previously likely to be," and this in turn tends to "undermine [their] belief in [human] dominion over earth that characterizes the view of Western civilization."[76]

The emphasis *Refuge* places on the imbrication of outback with metropolis thus not only avoids the circumscription of traditional nature writing but also reconceives that tradition by pointing to an interdependence previously there without having been fully acknowledged. Indeed, the most canonical of such works, Thoreau's *Walden* (1854), acknowledges frankly at start and close that the writer not only once was but now is "a sojourner in civilized life again";[77] and it is from that hybrid perspective that the ecocentric turn in the book is to be read, including Thoreau's political theory (of civil disobedience), which evolved as the book (which mentions his incarceration) was in progress. *Refuge* both levels charges and avoids claiming more than it can prove about the cause(s) of the family's illnesses. This produces a certain tortuousness that points to a second set of critical issues raised by works like Williams's.

Earlier we noted the importance of moral melodrama to toxic discourse, as well as the totalizing rhetoric with which it sets forth claims of environmental poisoning. Reading it, as Martha Nussbaum writes of Dickens's *Hard Times*, one feels "constituted by the novel as judges of a certain sort." Nussbaum readily accepts the propriety of this role, convinced that ability to imagine the lives of socially marginal people empathetically as novelists like Dickens do is an important asset in the crafting of coherent, perceptive legal argument. But what about the question of evidence? Although "the literary judge" may indeed be more apt to wish to read a case "in its full historical and social context,"[78] he or she must also reckon with the phenomenon of narratorial bias in novels like *Hard Times,* not to mention the oxymoronic multigenre of "nonfiction." Toxic discourse raises this question with unusual poignancy.

Although it rests on anxieties about environmental poisoning for which there is often strong evidence, it is a discourse of allegation or insinuation rather than of proof. Its very moralism and intensity reflect awareness that the case has not yet been proven, at least to the satisfaction of the requisite authorities. During two decades of ecopopulism, "almost every claim that a risk is present, almost every attribution of cause, [has been] vigorously contested."[79] It is notoriously hard to demonstrate environmental causation of illness, given the limitation of preexisting research bases, not to mention the multiplicity of possible causal agents. The generation of conclusive data and accompanying regulatory codes is a lengthy and haphazard process;[80] and in any case, as a senior spokesperson for risk assessment theory acknowledges, "*Science cannot prove safety, only the degree of existing harm.* Thus new technologies cannot be proven safe before use."[81] The problem of reaching even approximate certitude is compounded by the predictable reluctance of allegedly responsible parties to concede error and by the cumbersomeness of the process by which error is legally determined. At Love Canal "officials [never] agreed that there was a health problem" other than possible hazard to pregnant women and small children.[82] A suit by families in a leukemia cluster in Woburn, Massachusetts, against W. R. Grace for chemical dumping was settled out of court in 1986 for $8 million after the judge ordered the case retried on the ground that the jury, which had voted to convict, did not understand the hydrogeological evidence.[83]

This climate of scientific and legal complexification calls toxic discourse into question even in advance of its utterance, yet also calls it into being and argues for both its social and ethical import. The deliberate pace and methodological rationalism of scientific and legal procedures run directly counter to the felt urgency of toxic discourse, leaving self-identified victims of environmental illness oscillating between implacable outrage and miserable uncertainty. Williams, for instance, concedes "I cannot prove that my mother . . . or my grandmothers . . . along with my aunts developed cancer from nuclear fallout in Utah. But I can't prove they didn't."[84] This sense of frustrated indeterminacy pushes her toward hesitant but persistent insinuation. The same holds for Todd Haynes's 1995 film *Safe*, about an upscale San Fernando Valley woman with a burgeoning array of what she becomes convinced are environmentally induced allergic symptoms dating back to childhood asthma. Her patriarchal family doctor finds nothing wrong with her and prescribes an equally patriarchal psychiatrist. Does her final retreat to a hermetic igloo-like "safe house" at an exclusive holistic health ranch in the hills above Albuquerque result from undiagnosed physiological vulnerabilities or from psychic dysfunctionality? The film insinuates the former possibility by making it the ostensible catalyst, but equivocates by suggesting the alternative possibility throughout.

The very climate of scientific and legal probabalism that makes Williams cautious and makes *Safe* end ambiguously can also be expected to produce in other quarters a rhetoric of unequivocal assertion as counterweight: a rhetoric with its own ethical force. As Lois Gibbs declared, "I don't see why you need scientific certainty when people's lives and health are at risk."[85] The most thorough study of ecopopulism to date defends the legitimacy of this kind of reaction, the reasonableness of flat refusal to accept indeterminate degrees of environmental risk, at least in such cases as hazardous waste deposits, since "the claim that the risks of *proper* disposal or treatment are known rests on the assumption that permitted facilities operate as advertised, a claim that is not credible in light of the EPA's enforcement record. Given the current state of knowledge and the current state of regulatory enforcement, there is no way to validate claims that the risks are known to be minor or acceptable." On the contrary, "experts have shown that even the best-designed landfills are certain to fail."[86] Add to this decision analyst Paul Slovic's warning that "whoever controls the definition of risk controls the rational solution to the problem at hand," together with the risk assessment community's concession that "public acceptance of any risk is more dependent on public confidence in risk management than on the quantitative estimates of risk consequences, probabilities, and magnitudes,"[87] and alarmism starts to seem not just defensible but indispensable. This is particularly so when the technology in question can be expected to produce what organizational sociologist Charles Perrow calls "normal accidents": that is, when the system's "interactive complexity" and "tight coupling" of sequenced processes are such that accidents must be expected in the nature of the case.[88] The situation is all the more worrisome given that "no system can maintain itself by means of a point-for-point correlation with its environment, i.e., can summon enough 'requisite variety' to match its environment."[89]

From this standpoint, what to some would seem the paranoia of anti-toxic advocacy seems a recourse made needful by the very culture of expertise of which the academy is a part and which intellectuals propagate. The culture that sustains the procedural rigor resulting in repeated findings of indeterminacy stands accused of evading the obligation to *do* something beyond critical interrogation of the problem. An absolutist counterdiscourse seems from this standpoint a necessary outlet for the anxiety formal risk analysis would contain. This is arguably just as true for ambiguated works like *Refuge* and *Safe,* with their self-conflicted wonderment as to whether anxiety might be paranoia. Here indeterminacy at the level of knowledge itself exercises a kind of determination as act of imagination: ensconcing toxic anxiety as a psychological reality and as a cause of immiseration in good part because of the inability to know.[90]

These works thereby also suggest, however, the liability of discourse to become its own sanctuary. Activists have sometimes worried about this. With the hindsight of two decades of committed social work, Jane Addams berated herself "that in my first view of the horror of East London I should have recalled De Quincey's literary description" in "The English Mail Coach" of a case of absorption in literary meditation rendering the persona incapable of preventing an accident in real life. Although the recollection of this literary simulacrum of paralysis seems to have been precisely what jolted Addams from armchair malaise, she took it as a mark of insular decadence that her mind was even fleetingly held captive by intertextuality "at the very moment of looking down from the top of the omnibus" upon real poverty.[91] Though her post-

Puritan scrupulousness may have been overnice, she was not wrong to worry about this form of entrapment. Toxic discourse may repress, fail to fulfill, or swerve away from itself according to the drag of other discourses with which it cross-pollinates.

In the powerful middle section of Don DeLillo's novel *White Noise* (1985), for example, the protagonist Jack Gladney's life becomes transformed when he is exposed to what he fears is a lethal dose during an "airborne toxic event," as local authorities euphemistically call it: a spectacular accident that traumatizes the community. The incident destroys the complacency with which he initially brushes off the explosion, assuring his family that "[t]hese things happen to poor people who live in exposed areas. Society is set up in such a way that it's the poor and the uneducated who suffer the main impact of natural and man-made disasters."[92] For awhile the novel seems to have crystallized around this scene of awakening. But the prospect of ecocatastrophe seems to be invoked mainly to be reduced to the status of catalyst to the unfolding of the culturally symptomatic vacuousness of this professor of "Hitler Studies," as the denouement turns to focus on his and his wife's chronic, narcissistic, long-standing death obsessions, which seem no more than tenuously linked to the precipitating event. Unless one reads the event itself and the characters' subsequent discomfiture as, for example, a deliberate nonevent precipitating a scene of bad risk management whose significance lies in precisely nothing more than "the totality of its simulations,"[93] it is hard not to conclude that a very different sort of "event" might have served equally well: a crime scare, a rumor of kidnapping by aliens, whatever. Otherwise the episode of toxic anxiety and its seeming dissipation seem chiefly a supporting metaphor for the trivialization of Holocaust memory in Gladney's scholarly simulacrum-building (the German expert lacking competence in German) and the book's other (non)event, his high-profile Hitler conference.[94]

White Noise's framing of this toxic event as, chiefly, a postmodern symbol of inauthenticity raises a question raised by Susan Sontag in another context: Is there something inherently problematic about converting affliction into metaphor?[95] My metaphor elides, derealizes, somebody else's pain. For several reasons, I should not want to go so far. First, the novel's insistence on keeping the "event" in quotation marks, and the shallowness of Gladney's response to it, have a pertinence of their own for our inquiry. Bemused detachment, boredom, fecklessness, a sense of unreality about the affair—these are all predictable responses to the passionate, unequivocal engagement of most of the texts we have been considering, howevermuch (for example) an environmental activist might consider them culpably blasé. They make clear what hard work it takes, unless one is preconditioned to think of oneself or one's community as a prime candidate for toxic victimage, for relatively privileged persons to grasp its possibility in a sustained, concentrated way—whether the key issue here be Gladney's attention span or the novel's or both. There is a cultural logic to the "instinctive" reaction that it can't happen here, and to parodistic evasion of toxic discourse as paranoid or banal. Second, relegation to subsidiary metaphor status is something rather than nothing. Once imaged, the "event" cannot be wholly retracted and stands as a "matter" of (literary) record. There is considerable warrant for believing that even "dead" metaphors (e.g., "a black-and-white situation") shape or at least reinforce cultural values.[96] Third, metaphorization in this instance may be better understood as representation of partial emergence from environmental unconscious than as strategy to repress. In the mid-1980s toxicity was only starting to assert itself as a presenting personal reality for the mythical average American. Love Canal and Superfund were only a few years old. A novelist of middle-class manners would have had to contend with the embedded sense of distance between the stuff of headline news about toxic events and the predictable-seeming stability and safety of bourgeois life in middle-class American towns and suburbs.

The metaphorization of waste is an instructive collateral example. For Wallace Stevens, a dump was a purely symbolic place, merely a repository of used-up images. A generation later, Thomas Pynchon made W.A.S.T.E. a symbol of another sort: of the subversiveness of the Tristero.[97] DeLillo, in his massive fictional memoir of the Cold War era, *Underworld,* treats waste more materially as literal garbage and as multinational industry, but oscillating between this literalism and waste as image of modern civilization as detritus.[98] Even for a creative writer of avowedly environmentalist persuasion, the impulse still runs strong to recycle waste as metaphor, as in A. R. Ammons's 1993 National Book Award-winning poem *Garbage.* "Garbage has to be the poem of our time," the speaker insists: but why? Because "garbage is spiritual," a symbol for the age: a multivalent symbol, connoting among other things Stevens's old metaphor of shopworn creativity. The title image remains as much a stimulus to aesthetic play as a socioenvironmental referent.

Yet Ammons remains aware of garbage's materiality, of its sullying of the planet, of the human body in terminal states of materiality: body as imminent garbage. In the process, the poem wryly ironizes its own by-stander status ("I don't know anything much about garbage dumps: / I mean, I've never climbed one"); it "ecologizes" Stevens's trope by insisting on garbage's reuse (poetry "reaches down into the dead pit / and cool oil of stale recognition and words and / brings up hauls of stringy gook which it arrays / with light and strings with shiny syllables"). The seriocomic metamorphism alternates with environmental jeremiad ("poetry to no purpose! all this garbage! all these words: we may replace our mountains with / trash: leachments may be our creeks flowing / from the bottoms of corruption").[99] The poem gathers its energy from angry-bemused nonstop oscillation between the image of garbage as re-cyclable and garbage as shameful refuse, its extravagance of language alternatively fueled and punctured by recognition of humanity's irre-trievably biological condition.[100]

Meanwhile, evidence accumulates of the emergence of toxicity as a widely shared paradigm of cultural self-identification, and of toxic dis-course as an increasingly pervasive irritant: evidence too that the elo-quence of testimony of ordinary citizens' anxiety about environmental degradation can have influence on public policy, especially when the media are watching.[101] Against the economic and procedural conser-vatism of legislative and regulatory bodies, and their susceptibility to lobbying by vested interests, more individuals and communities have developed what some environmental anthropologists call "disaster sub-cultures" (whereby community ethos and social rituals get shaped by the recollection and/or anticipation of environmental disaster).[102] More and more it may become second nature to everyone's environmental imagination to visualize humanity in relation to environment not as solitary escapees or consumers but as collectivities with no alternative but to cooperate in acknowledgment of their like-it-or-not interdependence.

Insofar as a sense of human collectivity can be rendered through a first-person meditative mode, works like *Refuge* and *Garbage* also imagine "disaster subcultures" into being—Williams's feminist-survivalist "Clan of Single-Breasted Women," Ammons's glimpses of cultures united by acknowledgment of garbage crisis:

> toxic waste, poison air, beach goo, eroded
> roads draw nations together, whereas magnanimous
>
> platitude and sweet semblance ease each nation
> back into its comfort or despair: global crises
>
> promote internationalist gettings together,
> problems the best procedure

Not that this prospect inspires much hope and contentment for him, any more than the prospect of a sorority of environmental cancer victims entirely consoles Williams. The poem is, so I take it, provocatively ironic in its formulistic antithesis here, aware as it also is that "our / sins are so many, here heaped, spared given to / false matter."[103] For though toxification may provide a cultural denominator for communities and even for the planet, as Ammons wryly suggests here, the act of imagining it, notwithstanding whatever wishful thinking it inspires about recycling and social mutuality and so forth, will mainly reinforce the desire to do away with it. To the imagination of how that might be done, we now turn.

Chapter 2

The Place of Place

A placeless world is as unthinkable as a bodiless self.
—Edward Casey, *The Fate of Place*

To preserve our places and be at home in them, it is necessary to fill them with imagination.
—Wendell Berry, "Poetry and Place"

There never was an is without a where. Both the bad things and the good that happen to human beings and other life-forms self-evidently occur when their bodies are physically located somewhere, in particular locations. "Environment is not an 'other' to us" but "part of our being."[1] This applies not only to "natural" bodies but also to "cyborgs," the biotechnological hybrids modern humans increasingly have become.[2] Like the reengineerable body, environmental toxification can be conceived abstractly in terms of percentages of chemical compounds diffused throughout earth's atmosphere produced by the macroforces of industrial development, but what gives definition, force, persuasion, *embodiment* to toxic concern are specific events happening at specific times in specific locations to specific beings.

This is the insight behind the double plot of Richard Powers's novel *Gain* (1998). One strand is a pseudohistorical account of a hypothetical soap company, the other the story of a particular woman's losing battle against cancer in a midwestern town whose fortunes have depended on that industry. At the first level, the novel dramatizes the effect of pattern overwhelming presence, to borrow N. Katherine Hayles's characterization of the colonization of consciousness by informatics.[3] In *Gain* the colonizing force is an increasingly decontextualized and transnational capitalism, set forth in a fabulistic chronicle of Yankee enterprise, at once fact-laden and cartoonish: a kind of postmodern update of Dos Passos's *USA* trilogy. The second level, the arena of embodied place specificity, centers on the domestic drama of Laura Bodey, who contracts what she comes to suspect might be cancer environmentally induced by the proximity of the Agricultural Products Division of Clare Soap and Chemical Company. As in other works of sophisticated literary-toxic discourse, the "truth" is left for the reader to infer from a frustrating morass of data bits, disputation, and conjecture. What is most germane for our purposes is that *Gain* deconstructs traditional conceptions of stable body and determinate place as middle-American illusions (from which Laura is awakened with all the trauma of a Rachel Carson or a Lois Gibbs) yet at the same time affirms the necessity of embodiment and place attachment not only as necessary to the operation of pattern but as a means of deconstructing the deconstructor. The novel suggests that corporate dominance, including perhaps (although not conclusively provable) its toxification practices, becomes manifest only through its impact—emotional as well as physical—on particular bodies, families, places, and that it is only by contemplating that impact that pattern hegemony can be questioned, even if not controlled.[4] The forces of embodiment may not win, but they are the only available counterforces.[5]

Place is the specific resource of environmental imagination this chapter will take up. The more a site feels like a place, the more fervently it is so cherished, the greater the potential concern at its violation or even the possibility of violation. That one of literary imagination's traditional specialties has been to evoke and create a sense of place is all the more reason why place should have place in a book such as this. For not only *Gain* but most of the fictive and historical cases we have reviewed so far indicate that an awakened sense of physical location and of belonging to some sort of place-based community have a great deal to do with activating environmental concern. Neither the imagination of environmental endangerment nor, for that matter, of environmental well-being can be properly understood without a closer look at how the imagination of place-connectedness itself works: its multiple dimensions, its cultural significances, its capacity to serve by turns as either an insulating or a galvanizing force.

During the last quarter of the twentieth century "place" has made a comeback in humanistic and social theory, after falling out of favor as a category of analysis.[6] One of the chief reasons for prior skepticism about platiality was the supposition that modernization extinguished it by the triumph of *techne*. "The advent of modernity," as Anthony Giddens puts it, "increasingly tears space away from place by fostering relations between 'absent' others, locationally distant from any given situation of face-to-face interaction," as a consequence of which "place becomes increasingly *phantasmagoric:* that is to say, locales are thoroughly penetrated by and shaped in terms of social influences quite distant from them."[7] Indeed, we still hear such pronouncements daily. On the other hand, place has clearly survived its discreditation as a theoretical category, as the plethora of locally based environmental resistance movements show. As one historian puts it, "regionalism and localism are everywhere in the world today like a grass fire, apparently extinguished but alive at the roots."[8]

This can be a hard doctrine to grasp as one contemplates the action of history in a place undergoing rapid large-scale transformation. From this standpoint all that is solid does indeed seem to be melting into air, place transformed into space. Los Angeles seems particularly to induce such a mentality, whether one is looking askance at its violent, chaotic, self-delusional expansion, like Mike Davis in *City of Quartz* and *Ecology of Fear,* or with postmodernist hauteur at its relentlessly schematic reproduction of space, like Edward Soja in *Postmodern Geographies:*

> Los Angeles has come to resemble more than ever before a gigantic agglomeration of theme parks, a lifespace comprised of Disneyworlds. It is a realm divided into showcases of global village cultures and mimetic American landscapes, all-embracing shopping malls and crafty Main Streets, corporation-sponsored magic kingdoms, high-technology-based experimental prototype communities of tomorrow, attractively packaged places for rest and recreation all cleverly hiding the buzzing workstations and labour processes which help to keep it together. Like the original "Happiest Place on Earth," the enclosed spaces are subtly but tightly controlled by invisible overseers despite the open appearance of fantastic freedoms of choice.[9]

This is immediately recognizable as the city of spatial transformationist theory, of Lefebvre and Baudrillard, and as the nowhere city of Alison Lurie and Thomas Pynchon. But as Dolores Hayden observes in a passage chiding both Soja and Davis for overgeneralization, it simply cannot be the city of lived experience of diverse ethnicities, not the city of history, not a framework for "locating men, women and children in the historic working landscapes of downtown."[10] The passage above has serendipitously conspired with the anonymous corporate purveyors of the "package" to suppress from its image of L.A. the "labour processes which help to keep it together." Doubtless the exaggeration was strategic. In Soja's pronouncements about urban megatrends one detects a ludic version of the grand Nietzschean irony that inflects Foucault's discourse of formations. The passage above suffuses a disdain at totalizing futurism's techno-hallucinations more congruent than it might seem with Hayden's project of strengthening local-particularistic identity through community history work in L.A.'s various ethnic neighborhoods. Davis too would seem to desire reinvigoration of civic consciousness at the neighborhood level, even if the typical form he sees this taking is, ironically, neighborhood crime watch networks.[11]

Place thus potentially becomes part of a "politics of resistance, [seeking] to reinscribe a place-based territorial identity in opposition to the spatial colonizations of capitalist modernity"[12]—or socialist modernity, for that matter: thinking, for example, of post-Soviet disintegration into discrete ethnic-territorial entities. It is hardly strange that this should be so. There is nothing radically new about the desire to affirm place against place-eroding historical forces. In the early industrial era it made sense for romantic idealization of country village life to begin in cities. In the history of U.S. literature probably the four strongest pulsations of regional feeling have been related to consolidations of some sort: during the early nineteenth century, after national unification; at the end of the Civil War, after reunification; following World War I, after industrialization catalyzed the great African-American migration north and began modernizing the rural South, thereby influencing both the so-called Harlem and Southern Renaissances; and in the latter twentieth century, now that large extended suburbanized metropolitan areas, more or less resistant to regional difference, have become the nation's commonest residential choice.

Not all resistances in the name of place speak the same language, however. Some are individualistic and propertarian, some communalistic. Some are intensely local, others self-conscious of belonging in (and/or against) national and even transnational networks. Some seek empowerment within the world economy; some are neotraditonalist, like Chickasaw poet-novelist Linda Hogan's call for "new stories, new terms and conditions that are relevant to the love of land," on the model of first peoples' nondualistic understanding of the oneness of human and nonhuman.[13] These alternatives, moreover, are continuua, not opposites. Indeed, there may be no site in the world commonly thought of as a "place" that is either a hermetic unit or utterly a product of forces outside it.[14]

The Elusiveness of Place

The first task, then, is to specify just what we mean when we say "place." "Place" is if anything more elusive than its sibling "time." "One of the trickiest words in the English language," Hayden calls it: "a suitcase so overfilled one can never shut the lid."[15] Much of this slipperiness derives from "place" having by definition both an objective and a subjective face, pointing outward toward the tangible world and inward to the perceptions one brings to it. "Place" as opposed to "space" implies (among other connotations) "space to which meaning has been ascribed," assigned distinctness and value.[16] "Time," by contrast, seems less malleable, at least since global standard time zones were adopted in the early twentieth century. True, we speak of different persons' "internal time clocks"; African Americans sometimes joke about "c.p. time" (colored people's time); and in Bahasa Indonesian there is a wry formula phrase, *jam caret,* that it is polite to use to apologize when one is late for something, the literal translation of which is "rubber time." But in all these cases there remains the sense of being measured against an objective standard, whereas who would think of measuring the validity of one's sense of place against the grid of latitude and longitude?[17] Even an Indonesian nationalist would recognize the inevitability if not also the desirability of differing regional senses of place: Bali, Java, Aceh.

By the same token, although placeness as such is probably a universal,[18] the range of sites that can count as "places" is infinitely great. A "place" can be as small as a sofa—or even the particular spot on the sofa where your dog lies—or as big as a planet: earth longingly seen by astronauts from the moon, or on the cover of an old *Whole Earth Catalogue,* and felt to be a beautiful blue-green holistic nurturing presence—our home, our habitat, Gaia. Historically, what different groups of humans (and nonhumans) reckon to be a meaningful "place" may diverge and crisscross in innumerable ways. What feels like a place to me may not feel so to you, and likewise with whole cultures. From a Euro-American standpoint, it is self-evident that houses get laid out at right angles, but from another cultural standpoint (Navajo or Mongolian, for instance) round may feel more right. One's sense of place at Thoreau's Walden Pond or in the English Lake Country may differ wildly according to whether he or she is a literary scholar, a restoration ecologist, a small child brought along for a boat ride, a policeman, a tourist from abroad, or a long-term resident whose privacy feels encroached on by the summer influx.

"Place," then, is a configuration of highly flexible subjective, social, and material dimensions, not reducible to any of these. In political geographer John Agnew's definition, "place" can be conceived as a matter of (social) "locale," (geographical) "location," and "sense of place."[19] It "combines elements of nature (elemental forces), social relations (class, gender, and so on), and meaning (the mind, ideas, symbols)."[20] Placeness implies physical site, though site alone does not constitute place. It also implies affect, "a deeply personal phenomenon founded on one's life-world and everyday practices,"[21] though psychological perception of meaningful place is bound to be constructed in part by collective standards as well as by physical terrain and personal proclivity: places are situated within plural "geographies associated with ethnic, political, economic, informational, cultural and religious formations."[22] But those constructs themselves, in turn, are mediated ecologically by the physical environments that they also mediate.[23]

Agnew's triadic postulate is not in itself very controversial, but there have been sharp disagreements over which ingredient(s) of place should be given pride of place. The epicenter is debate between a still-dominant social constructionist view (the only way to make sense of place is to think of it as socially produced) and increasingly assertive rejoinders that argue for the importance of physiography and/or phenomenological experience of place.[24] Perhaps the only points of certainty that emerge from such disputes are that they reveal the interdisciplinarity of geography and place theory more generally; and that in turn suggests that no future theory of place can have much staying power unless it somehow incorporates all three dimensions, recognizing in the process the malleability and contestedness of the concept.

Place is all the harder to conceptualize for being so often taken for granted in lived experience. "Places," Edward Casey observes, "are not so much the direct objects of sight or thought or recollection as what we feel *with* and *around, under* and *above, before* and *behind*" ourselves:[25] a point that social constructionists have made with equal pertinence about the effects of ideological positions into which societies and social groups are acculturated by such conditioners as class, gender, and race. When people try to articulate place sense more fully, they often use a crude vocabulary that hardly begins to grasp the complex network of sensations and value commitments that tie people to the locales they care about. This is one major reason why artists who take it upon themselves to think intently about place can be instructive witnesses to its influence, although of course there is no guarantee that art will itself altogether shake free of the ground condition of place obliviousness that Casey describes, which is after all nothing more than the negative face of environmental unconscious.

Native American novelist Leslie Silko's *Ceremony* (1977) beautifully expresses the delicacy of the problem in an early scene when the tribal medicine man Old Ku'oosh tries to communicate to Tayo, the protagonist, the idea of the "fragility" of the ecocultural world of the Laguna. "The word he chose to express 'fragile,'" says the narrator, "was filled with the intricacies of a continuing process . . . It took a long time to explain the fragility and intricacy because no word exists alone, and the reason for choosing each word had to be explained with a story about why it must be said this certain way. That was the responsibility that went with being human."[26] It is the genius of this passage to be painstakingly clear in stating the general idea of "fragility," yet to refrain from disclosing fully what it means, focusing instead on the tortuous path of the explanation: how every word has to be unpacked by means of some story. Not only are these etymologies not revealed, the native keyword itself is left unspoken: "fragile" is only the English translation of the actual Laguna word the medicine man used. I take it that Silko resorts to this indirection not to be coy but to be faithful to the intricacy of the web of relations and feelings that comprises a deep sense of place. At this juncture Tayo is a long way from his eventual state of understanding about these things, although he has a certain intuitive grasp of them; and as it turns out Ku'oosh himself is too confined within his cultural horizon to heal Tayo's particular pathology. To treat place sense here as an intimation at once proffered and withheld is precisely the right touch.

One's sense of place's elusiveness may actually grow in proportion to one's rapport or expertise. A place may seem quite simple until you start noticing things. Thoreau remarked that the "capabilities of the landscape within a circle of ten miles' radius, or the limits of an afternoon walk" will never "become quite familiar to you" even by the end of "the threescore years and ten of human life."[27] Indeed so. To bring environmental unconscious to anything like full articulation is more than a lifetime's work. I used to take weekend small-group nature walks led by a nonagenarian retired botanist who had tramped around the same fifty-square-mile region (according to the life-log he religiously kept) some 5,000 times, yet he insisted that he had only noticed a fraction of all the observable phenomena. His formidable natural history knowledge made him somewhat impatient and dogmatic with us novices, quick to embarrass us with sudden interrogations; but in the ways that really counted it made him perpetually open. He felt what the poet A. R. Ammons says at the end of his poem "Corson's Inlet," about the place where he takes his daily walk:

> I see narrow orders, limited tightness, but will
> not run to that easy victory:
>> still around the looser, wider forces work:
>> I will try
> to fasten into order enlarging grasps of disorder, widening
> scope, but enjoying the freedom that
> Scope eludes my grasp, that there is no finality of vision,
> that I have perceived nothing completely,
>> that tomorrow a new walk is a new walk.[28]

Especially significant here is Ammons's insistence that "I" can "enjoy the freedom that/Scope [capital S] eludes my grasp": the willing acquiescence in not being able to know no matter how hard one tries. More often than not, that is the like-it-or-not condition to which the serious seeker after place wisdom is reduced, especially if an outsider. Anthropologist Keith Basso's *Wisdom Sits in Places* is particularly shrewd on this point, wryly describing the challenges even a cordially welcomed Anglo faces among the Western Apache as he labors to understand telegraphic place discourses like this one:[29]

LOUISE: My younger brother . . .

LOLA: It happened at Line Of White Rocks Extends Up And Out, at this very place!

EMILY: Yes. It happened at Whiteness Spreads Out Descending To Water, at this very place!

LOLA: It happened at Trail Extends Across A Red Ridge With Alder Trees, at this very place!

LOUISE: [laughs softly]

ROBERT: Pleasantness and goodness will be forthcoming.

LOLA: Pleasantness and goodness will be forthcoming.

LOUISE: My younger brother is foolish, isn't he dog?

Elliptical place allusions (encryptions of events that happened there) are invoked to cheer, to admonish, to instruct. Basso knows he will never learn more than a fraction of them, no matter how skilled he becomes in the language, no matter how long he spends there, no matter how patiently his hosts explain. And his task (of mapping and understanding Western Apache place names) is only one among the whole array of platial tasks he might have undertaken, and a relatively simple one at that compared to, say, the task of discriminating among individual affects or the minuter anthropogenic modifications of physical landscape. As for his informants, although they have a perpetual jump on him and are, as a people, place-connected as he himself will never be, they too know that maintenance of place-connectedness is an ongoing discipline demanding hard work and commitment, in which they must ceaselessly coach and reinforce each other.

Five Dimensions of Place-Connectedness

Even though place cannot be fully perceived or definitively theorized, we may still hope to arrive at a workable conception that will help explain the importance of place sense to literary and cultural imagination, and the cultural work that place-responsive imaginative acts can perform.

Perhaps the most familiar way of imaging place-connectedness is in terms of concentric areas of affiliation decreasing in intimacy as one fans out from a central point. This is the idea behind the whimsical list young Stephen Dedalus scribbles in his geography textbook near the start of James Joyce's novel, *A Portrait of the Artist as a Young Man:* "Stephen Dedalus / Class of Elements / Clongowes Wood College / Sallins / County Kildare / Ireland / Europe / The World / The Universe."[30] Environmental psychologists have found that "children are literally 'attached' to a succession of expanding local places, with their home at the center."[31] Walt Whitman's poem "There Was a Child Went Forth" unfolds more fully this phenomenon of a child's growing awareness as he spontaneously reaches out from parents and home base in farther and farther circles past barnyard, farm pond, orchard, neighborhood, school, and village to seacoast and horizon line—so that by the end of the poem something like a complete Our-Townish kind of farming/maritime region has been portrayed, recalling the Long Island of the poet's early boyhood.

> . . . the fish suspending themselves so curiously below
>   there, and the beautiful curious liquid,
> And the water-plants with their graceful flat heads,
>   all became part of him.

This picture, however, is designedly *not* bent on self-portraiture (although its empathy with beautiful objects predicts a future artist) so much as the creation of a paradigmatic image of the "child who went forth every day, and who now goes, and will always go forth every day."[32] Yi-fu Tuan's *Topophilia* supports the underlying claim. Tuan collects an array of concentric maps embedded in the mentalities of whole civilizations, such as the worldview of traditional China (whose literal meaning is "middle kingdom"), which Tuan diagrams in terms of five zones radiating out from the "imperial center": "royal domains," "tributary lords' domains," "zone of pacification," "zone of allied barbarians," and (finally) the "zone of cultureless savagery."[33]

This model of concentric zones takes us only so far. It makes sense so long as we presume that people operate from home bases and societies from geographically delimited regions. But time once was, and time now is, when such is not so much the case. It would have made less sense, or at least different sense, for ancient nomadic peoples before the dawn of agriculture and cities; and most certainly it suffices less well for postmodern transnationalism, mobility, and diaspora—the age of "DissemiNation" as postcolonial theorist Homi Bhabha punningly calls it[34]—than for the early nineteenth-century lococentric maritime village Whitman describes. Not that the concentric model is wholly obsolete. Much of the world's population still lives a platially-centered existence physically and psychologically even when apparently local worlds revolve economically in somebody else's orbit. Even thoroughly cosmopolitan individuals may operate more than they suppose from modern equivalents of the concentric map, of a Eurocentric world with the "North" as the civilizational center, its area customarily exaggerated on most western maps, and with a limited number of "global" cities like New York and London and Tokyo as financial and/or civilizational epicenters.[35] Hence the postcolonial critique of Eurocentric globalism as de facto provincialism, as in Indian environmentalist Vandana Shiva's charge that "the dominant system" is "merely the globalised version of a very local and parochial tradition" that happens to have colonized the rest of the world.[36] Conversely, even though social theory knows better, a specious concreteness in labeling people as belonging to one geographically finite community or another persists as an ethnological illusion or demographic artifact;[37] and categories like "Texan" or "New Englander" are apt to evoke a much more unitary gestalt than the facts warrant. All the more reason on that account to recognize the insufficiency of concentric models of platiality even while acknowledging their continuing force to arrange lives.

A second model for place-connectedness, accordingly, would be a scattergram or archipelago of locales, some perhaps quite remote from each other. One might begin, like geographer Robert Sack, with the

image of ordinary middle-class life as a patchwork of specific entangle-
ments that make up one's primary life routines: "my home, my work,
my leisure, my relatives, my worshipping"—"all geographically apart,
and often far apart."[38] A rough-and-ready criterion for deciding what to
include might be all the locations so familiar and habitual that even
when you've been away from them six months or more you can remember details well enough to tell a stranger how to navigate them so
he or she will not get lost. Furthermore, in principle each item in this inventory might be unpacked as a platial hybrid: the market where I shop
has links to Venezuela and New Zealand; the building where I work assembles dozens of nationalities from six continents; the loosestrife that
lines the riverbanks where I canoe is an exotic colonizer driving out the
native cardinal flowers; the materials and furnishings that constitute my
house are, as Sack says of his, "a purposely built and maintained part of
a web of interdependencies that can extend over the entire globe."[39]

To understand fully what it means to inhabit place is therefore not
only to bear in mind the (dis)connections between one's primary places
but also the tenticular radiations from each one. And the case I have described is simpler than many in that, for example, it assumes *a* home
rather than the cross-national peregrinations of the Mexican farm
worker who picked some of the vegetables at my market, or of my ex-
patriate colleague who maintains his family home in Paris together with
a long-term residence and tenured appointment stateside.

"Those who know only one country know no country," Seymour
Martin Lipset says in defense of comparative national studies.[40] So with
place. In the literature of place, what often makes the difference between pious obeisance to lococentrism and a more critically aware
place-connectedness is a sense of inhabiting different places simultaneously. The commonest way this is done is via a stylized contrast between attentive witness and bona fide inhabitant, as in Basso's narrative
ethnography, or the travel writing of environmentally attuned writers
like Barry Lopez, William Least Heat Moon, and Bruce Chatwin. But
comparative lococentrists can do the same. Thoreau is simultaneously
the Walden hermit, the sojourner in civilized life, and the vicarious
traveler to foreign lands that he repeatedly compares to Concord. Gary
Snyder's northern California is a palimpsest of contemporary rurality,
Asian classical learning, travel reminiscence, and native mythography

and folklore. In the decisive chapter of Terry Tempest Williams's *Refuge* when her mother's cancer is diagnosed, the text moves in a series of vignettes from wildlife refuge to the narrator's home to department store to hospital to parental home back to refuge again, and so on. These are all familiar, significant places for her, places made more portentous by opening up far beyond themselves (to the thought of North American migratory patterns, of family history, of shopping in other cities, of waiting rooms in hospitals throughout America, etc.). The effect is both to fragment attention and allegiance among places and to accumulate a series of mutually reinforcing instances of place shaping that intensifies and deepens the feel of lived experience. Their disparateness and the fact they create *conflicting* allegiances contribute to the intensification. These places are refuges from each other, enabling compartmentalization of mental and physical existence that gives the narrator the kind of breathing room she needs in order to function in a crisis situation; yet by the same token, the net of personal identity consists of the loose assemblage or mosaic fashioned from them all.

Just as modern place attachment, such as it is, tends to be more or less dispersed, so, conversely, to introduce a third consideration, the places themselves are not stable, free-standing entities but continually shaped and reshaped by forces from both inside and outside. Places have histories; place is not just a noun but also a verb, a verb of action; and this action is always happening around us, because of us, despite us. As Casey puts it, "place is not entiative—as a foundation has to be—but eventmental, something in process, something unconfinable to a thing."[41] In the same spirit, geographer Alan Pred defines place as "what takes place ceaselessly, what contributes to history in a specific context through the creation and utilization of a physical setting."[42]

Consequently, "for those who have developed a sense of place," as ecocritic Kent Ryden observes, "an unseen layer of usage, memory, and significance—an invisible landscape, if you will,—of imaginative landmarks" seems to be "superimposed upon the geographical surface and the two-dimensional map."[43] Sometimes the marks of history and change are in plain view, yet still we ignore them: ignore land forms, settlement markers, even live people—the way romantic landscape painters focused on countryside to the exclusion of the countrymen. A basic, sometimes fatal error made by discoverers and explorers of old as well as by tourists today is to fantasize that a pristine-looking landscape seen for the first time is so in fact—as if it hadn't been changing for eons before they set eyes on it, certainly from natural causes and probably anthropogenic ones as well: from generations of prior inhabitance. Even if I "master" this as a fact of history, as revisionist accounts of the history of colonization are trying increasingly to teach westerners how to do, that is no guarantee I shall be able to look through the New England woods in front of me and "see" the former pasture, or imagine the forest that preceded that, nor the patchwork of one-time villages and towns absorbed into present-day Tokyo or Los Angeles. But "once you know why and what, in terms of time and [specific] landscape history is involved," as ecologist Geoff Park points out in the course of a historically self-conscious circumambulation of a New Zealand lake, "you can never again read this stretch of country the same."[44]

One subgenre of place writing builds on this process by scrolling backward in memory (e.g., Aldo Leopold's "Good Oak," in *A Sand County Almanac* [1949], in which the author chronicles Wisconsin's history in reverse while sawing through a tree that sprouted before the creation of the state) or forward from the dawn of settlement (e.g., Wendell Berry's poem "History," in *Clearing* [1977]) or even from the primordium, as in John Mitchell's *Ceremonial Time* (1984), which unfolds the saga of place history for a particular Yankee community from geologic time to the near present. As Mitchell shows, and as social geographer Doreen Massey has argued in a more scholarly way with reference to the shifting composition of contemporary British towns, today and indeed even yesterday, if not always, places "are not so much bounded areas as open and porous networks of social relations." Whether for better or for worse, "the dominant image of any place will be a matter of contestation and will change over time."[45] The place where you were born is not the same place anymore. Your old home may have been leveled, your neighborhood transformed. In the extreme case, it may be located in a different country, Russia instead of Poland, Tajikistan instead of the Soviet Union, Israel instead of Palestine or Jordan. Or like large hunks of Mauritania and other parts of sub-Saharan Africa, or Cape Cod's southeastern tip, nature may have reclaimed your home place for quite different uses.

It may have been reclaimed for good as well as for bad. So-called urban renewal can produce very bad results, like Stalinesque projects, but good ones also—so that a locale comes to feel more like a "real" place. The environmental and architectural restorations of river districts in Toronto, Cleveland, and Memphis are cases in point. Indeed, it is impossible to set a limit on what restoration ecology can accomplish, although it is seriously underfunded and still in the early stages of unfolding as a discipline.[46] But for the foreseeable future a "timescape" perspective, as social theorist Barbara Adam calls it—a perspective that brings a fourth dimension to the contemplation of landscapes by exposing the history and projected future of "the conflictual interpenetration of industrial and natural temporalities"—seems bound to produce, for the most part, narratives of remembered degradation and anticipated hazard, as with Adam's studies of the BSE ("Mad Cow Disease") anxieties in Britain and the impact of the Chernobyl incident on Europe.[47] "One of the penalties of an ecological education," Leopold remarked, "is that one lives alone in a world of wounds."[48]

Even if places did stay stable, even if a community could be zoned so restrictively that nothing more got built, it might still be impossible to make people stay put or to keep people from moving in as others left. This introduces a fourth dimension of place sense: as an accumulation or composite of all the places that have been significant to a person, or a people, over time: like a coral reef or set of tree rings. "I am a part of all that I have met," asserts Tennyson's Ulysses, adding temporality to Byron's Childe Harold's "I live not in myself, but I become / Portion of that around me."[49] He was not alone. Minimally, one might stipulate that all the places a person has lived that she or he still dreams about sometimes are embedded and responsible for shaping present identity beyond what is consciously realized.

Some believe that, as with much else, childhood is when that place template is formed.[50] Literature supports this, at least somewhat. Thoreau attests that being taken to Walden Pond by his father was one of his earliest memories, and in *Walden* expresses delight that "I have at length helped to clothe that fabulous landscape of my infant dreams."[51] Nor does the infant landscape need to be a happy one for it to have profound long-term impact—quite the contrary. One of Charles Dickens's early memories was the fright and humiliation of his father's incarceration in the Marshalsea debtors' prison in London, which came back to haunt his fiction, as we shall see in Chapter 4. William Wordsworth seems to have been convinced that we derive our greatest emotional energy from place-related moments in the deep past that are connected to remembered experiences of disorientation and fear. "Spots of time," he called them,[52] though "moments of place" would have been as apt.

On the other hand, we can find counterexamples to support the opposite claim that the childhood place template is sufficiently malleable that in time it can be overcome, or nearly so. Robert Frost remade himself as a New Englander, T. S. Eliot and Henry James and Joseph Conrad as Englishmen, Lafcadio Hearn as a Japanese. Their work scripts their life experiments in transplantation: Eliot relocating his *Preludes* (1917) from Boston to London, Conrad creating the self-consciously English persona Marlow, James in *The Europeans* (1878) inventing deracinated Americans who see New England through Europeanized eyes. The richest modern examples are transitional, however, built on the experience of hovering between incompletely integrated platial identities. In Derek Walcott's epic *Omeros* (1990), Major Plunkett's subaltern disaffection with English stuffiness (as well as economic prudence) precipitates his resettlement in St. Lucia, where (as he well knows) he will never be fully accepted within postcolonial society but which he comes to think of as home, albeit not without nostalgic/satiric backglimpses of the old country and his experiences of combat in North Africa. As such, Plunkett is counterpointed with the figure of the poet, his former student, who revisits home occasionally from his venue in the United States, but can never imagine either returning permanently or becoming completely Caribbeanized.

Whether encountered early or later, identity-shaping places are not merely personal but also cultural artifacts. The psalm that sings of the Hebrews who sat down by the waters of Babylon and wept because they remembered Zion was the expression of a people, not just a solitary prophet, and so too with the experience of displacement, diaspora, exile, expatriation today: the single person's experience is mediated by the group's. Such is at least partly the case even for highly idiosyncratic experiences like Thoreau's memory of being taken to Walden Pond. Unique event though it was, he remembers it in terms of a cultural prototype: the *locus amoenus* of traditional pastoral.

By the same token, the past places that stay with a person or a people as an accumulated part of identity get reinvented in the process of absorption. Although the fact that these memories refer to actual places to which we were literally attached is vital, equally so is the transformative process that keeps them with us in a stylized, subjectified way as identity markers.

Such acts of reinvention, again, are always on some sort of continuum between the personal and the collective. At the collective end is the "memorial book" written by Jews to commemorate communities Nazis destroyed (a term since applied to other diasporic communities also);[53] at the individual, Isaac Bashevis Singer's recreation of pre-Holocaust Warsaw in *The Family Moskat* (1950).[54] Perhaps the first great example of this genre in contemporary Anglophone literature is Raja Rao's *Kanthapura* (1938), a novel of Gandhian peasant resistance against the Raj in a south Indian community that Rao tells as a latter-day *sthala-purana* (or legendary village history) in the voice of an elderly woman from the former community, its members now dead or dispersed. This personalized version of a collective narrative corresponds to the autobiographical resonance of this political-historical moment from the standpoint of the recently expatriated author's intense yet attenuated postcolonial commitment. Likewise, with a certain seeming self-reflexive irony as well as gentle satire toward the catalytic character, the novel's imaginary chronicle of public events narrates the intense but transient involvement of the activist Moorthy, who radicalizes the women of the community after he himself becomes radicalized but then leaves them to their own devices to carry on the work of resistance.[55]

The reinventionary aspect of place sense shades into a fifth and final dimension, connectedness with fictive or virtual places. Is it necessary for places actually to have been experienced for them to have influence? Must you have been there before they can be said to matter to you? How much did it matter if some of the Israelites of the psalm were children of captives who themselves had never seen their "native" land? Doubtless it did matter somewhat: "communities are inseparable from particular habitats" in the imagination of the case if not also in the original forming.[56] Whatever the psalm's immediate impact on the Babylonian captives, collective memory of traumatic displacement has had an immense long-range historical impact in perpetuating the dream of a rightful homeland that animated Zionism and ultimately committed the western powers generally to a tortuous and perhaps interminable politics over what places in the Middle East ought to belong to whom. The experience of remote or virtual inhabitation manifestly does not always undermine the force of place as identity shaper and as ideal. Indeed, sometimes quite the contrary: absence may strengthen loyalty to place and sense of entitlement.

The same holds for the region's present-day exiles, the Palestinians. As one child of a refugee camp put it, "Intimate mementoes of a past irrevocably lost circulate among us, like the genealogies and fables severed from their original locale . . . Much reproduced, enlarged, thematized, embroidered and passed around, they are strands in the web of affiliations we Palestinians use to tie ourselves to our identity and to each other."[57] They too kept alive the lost community through memorial books as well as novels of memory and postdisplacement return. In this process of recirculation, as in Jewish discourse of exile and Holocaust, the very impediments to restoration become memory intensifiers: "fragmentary memory means trivial things turn into powerful symbols because, like archaeological artifacts, they are what remain."[58]

In short, whether or not one considers it a good thing, the power of images seems key to making individuals and groups feel place-connected.[59] Sociologist Anthony Smith goes so far as to claim that a "land of dreams is far more significant than any actual terrain,"[60] and he may be right. Especially perhaps at this point in history. Today, if not always, "our experience of the natural world," as Alexander Wilson asserts, "is always mediated. It is always shaped by rhetorical constructs like photography, industry, advertising, and aesthetics, as well as by institutions like religion, tourism, and education."[61] Empirical study bears this out. Take the mundane example of television nature specials. There is good reason to believe that this familiar genre makes certain places seem more luminous and precious and cherished than they might otherwise be, and that this can have consequences for public policy. A recent study of the political fallout from massive oil spills found that a key reason why the wreck of the *Exxon Valdez* off the Alaskan coast moved the U.S. Congress to pass the Oil Pollution Act of 1990 after similar bills had been tied up for two decades was that television literally brought home to millions of Americans how the most deeply held images of Alaska as "a wild, pristine, isolated, scenically beautiful place . . . largely untouched by humans" had been grossly violated and threatened by this catastrophe.[62] In short, visual and other information technologies can enhance place sense in the process of mediating it; and it seems certain that the "complex *co-evolutionary* processes linking new information technologies and space, place and human territoriality" have been underway since industrialization.[63]

Nor is it only modern simulation technology that shapes and reinforces compelling images of unseen places but also media that have been around a very long time: books; storytelling; dreams; religion. As just noted, the Palestinian community in exile has been built in part by story—by oral transmission and printed text. The process of image internalization responsible for causing a plurality of contemporary U.S. citizens to say they want to live in small towns even when in fact they often do not and never have may often have started with bedtime stories read or told to them as toddlers.

Some of the places that move us deeply even though we have seen them only in the mind's eye are actual places, without benefit of which (whatever the inaccuracy of our images) our sense of world citizenship might suffer: the sense of accountability for suffering in Bosnia, Somalia, Rwanda, Kosovo. "Modern media," geographer David Smith argues in a thoughtful revision of the common view of info-technology's simulacra as manipulated hallucinations, "can create a sense of involvement in distant lives" that in turn "can lead to an extension of a sense of responsibility."[64] Certain other imagined places that have moved people no less deeply are more purely visionary, like the traditional Christian image of heaven as a utopian city, or a home, which centuries of writers have tried to describe and believers to visualize: the Celestial City sought by the protagonist Christian in John Bunyan's *Pilgrim's Progress,* the "Jerusalem the Golden" of the folk hymn or William Blake's *Jerusalem.*

In between these two poles of the unseen actual and the imagined utopian are those enticing-but-as-yet-unexperienced small towns of the middle American imagination, of which planned communities like the Disney corporation's Celebration, Florida, are attempted enactments,[65] and, in a more traditional vein, the Hopi *Túwanasavi,* the central place to which the people are called to return from their wanderings: a place whose precise location has been variously identified, but in any event is in principle an actual *there,* the luminous idea of which gives communal

and personal life structure, definition, meaning,[66] even (or especially?)
when the present life-world seems hopelessly degraded. In Hopi poet
Ramson Lomatewama's "Tuuwanasavi," for instance, the title first
seems to point to desolate literality as the speaker notices a derelict ran-
sacking "his dumpster / in his alley / below my easy chair" ("Two purple blades of grass / stood at Tuuwanasavi. / Cracked asphalt / ran
beyond four directions") but this then metamorphoses as the poet's empathy deepens into imagination of the "long lost friends" the man might
be searching for: "At Tuuwanasavi / they stood alone / invisible / like
distant stars / whose radiance / we / do not know."[67]

Personal experiences of arriving at a place that seems a perfect spiritual fit, even if one has never before set eyes on it, have been recorded
by settlers as well as aborigines. Paul Bowles recalls his excitement from
shipboard at the sight of the Algerian mountains as the fulfillment of a
predestined thing, "as if I were drawing close to the solution of an as-
yet-unposed problem." Bowles "had always been vaguely certain that
sometime during my life I should come into a magic place which in disclosing its secrets would give me wisdom and ecstasy—perhaps even
death."[68] Here at last it was. Even more provocative, because (by his
account) it came without any prior wish or expectation, is Alaskan
homesteader-poet John Haines's recollection of stumbling upon the
place where he was, as he puts it, born as a poet. "From the first day I
set foot" on Richardson Hill in Alaska, he writes, "I knew I was home.
Something in me identified with that landscape. I had come, let's say, to
the dream place. Not exactly, of course, for there never was an exact
place [in the dream he had been carrying around with him vaguely for
some years], but here was something so close to it that I could accept it
at once."[69]

The Importance of Place Imagination

A lifeline like Haines's rounds back to where we started, with the lingering question of whether there might in fact be some widespread if not
universal compulsion for humans to seek to connect themselves with
specific places of settlement, failure of which in this era of accelerated
mobility and displacement may be expected to produce in many a

pathological effect equivalent to (say) insomnia or seasonal affective disorder. Call it place deprivation, atopia, topic deficit, displacement anxiety—what you will. Haines by his own say-so was a wanderer who never particularly expected to settle down, starting as the child of a peripatetic military father who took the family all over the map. The sense of a fitness to place so keen that it impelled him to stop there caught him from behind with the force of an unexpected but deep, fundamental, insistent need that would not be denied.

Some would press the point further and contend that there is something deeply wrong with a person who is not able to feel placelessness as loss. As the Kentucky regionalist writer Wendell Berry puts it:

> How you act *should* be determined, and the consequences of your acts *are* determined, by where you are. To know where you are (and whether or not that is where you should be) is at least as important as to know what you are doing, because in the moral (the ecological) sense you cannot know *what* until you have learned *where*. Not knowing where you are, you can lose your soul or your soil, your life or your way home.[70]

For Keith Basso's acquaintances among the Western Apache, likewise, place connection has great moral and therapeutic power. "If we go far away from here to some big city," one informant told him, "places around here keep stalking us. If you live wrong, you will hear the names and see the places in your mind. They keep on stalking you, even if you go across oceans . . . They make you remember how to live right, so you want to replace yourself again."[71] Likewise, Leslie Silko affirmed that she wrote *Ceremony* to recreate her home place in compensation for absence from it; and the novel imagines the psychic reintegration of the protagonist Tayo largely as a matter of reintegration with place.

Indeed, it seems not only a Laguna or Native American but more broadly indigenous or first peoples' way of thinking worldwide for sacrality to be platial and localized. Phenomenologist David Abram, in *The Spell of the Sensuous,* a book full of insights about place sense even though that is not his main subject, remarks that "in the oral, indigenous world, to tell certain stories without saying precisely where those events occurred (or, if one is recounting a vision or a dream, to neglect to say where one was when 'granted' the vision), may alone render the telling powerless or ineffective."[72] Traditional place-based cultures ascribe a kind of wisdom and potency to feeling connected to particular locations that modernized people less likely feel, or at least less often articulate.[73]

As a small-scale experiment in testing the persistence into modernity of what Abram, Silko, Basso, Berry, and Haines have variously reported, in a course in environmental literature I have taught for a number of years at several institutions to groups of reasonable social diversity, I ask each student to locate a particular outdoor place for him or herself during the first two or three days and return to it every week throughout the term both physically, for at least a half-hour, and also creatively: to write a series of ten meditations about the experience of place (e.g., "Write about how the natural and built environments intersect and collide in and around your place," or "Experience your place through one of the nonvisual senses," or "Imagine your place as evolving through time"). For most students, these consciousness-raising exercises turn out to be one of the course's special attractions, despite adding a good deal to its workload. This admittedly directed experiment suggests that the appeal of place-connectedness can continue to thrive in late industrial culture, albeit variously assessed and understood, across lines of region, gender, class, ethnicity, and community of origin.

Clearly it is possible to take a good thing too far. Nothing is easier than to slip into a kind of self-righteous hectoring didacticism when arguing for the importance of place: to make a mantra out of that totem word, like the mantra of "family values" perhaps, as if returning home and committing one's whole life there, or to an adopted place like Richardson, Alaska, would somehow solve all the evils of the world. Your connection to your soil is surely not the sole measure of your health of soul. On the contrary, place attachment can itself become pathological: can abet possessiveness, ethnocentrism, xenophobia. The Palestinian impasse shows this, as does the struggle over Kosovo, sacred to Serbian memory but populated overwhelmingly in recent times by ethnic Albanians agitating for self-determination. Place-centeredness can also produce an opposite extreme of vulnerability: can make one impotent and maladaptive outside one's home range. A certain capacity for self-deterritorialization seems needful for resiliency and even survival. Moreover, as novelist-historian Wallace Stegner cautions, "we may love a place and still be dangerous to it,"[74] through unwise use born of possessiveness or ecological ignorance.

Yet the abuses of place-connectedness hardly invalidate it. At precisely this point our fivefold analysis may help us, precisely because it is so messily complex. To the extent that there is a problem with back-to-the-land, stay-at-home injunctions like Berry's, it is not that they lack value but that they are too narrowly based on the first and third of our vantage points: a strong central home base, fading out to concentric zones, a base valued for strong tribal continuities.[75] The continuing potency of these allegiances makes ethical as well as ethnographic sense: presumably one doesn't want people to become like Mrs. Jellyby in Charles Dickens's *Bleak House* (1853), who spent all her time organizing foreign missionary work to the neglect of family and housekeeping, not to mention the needs of the urban poor in her vicinity. But to take a home-and-community-first paradigm as the litmus test of place-connectedness turns place into something Ptolemaic and retrograde. Do we really want Mrs. Jellyby only to concern herself with home, family, and community and forget about the other side of the world? If, on the other hand, one thinks of place sense as containing within it many different patches besides just home, including what comes to us via the world of images as well as through live transactions, plus the changes in us relative to place and the awareness of landscape as timescape, then we are on the way to arriving at a conception more fit for local, regional, and global citizenship. At the turn of the twenty-first century, "place" becomes truly meaningful only when "place" and "planet" are understood as interdependent.[76]

What transforms this multifold conception of place from analytical model to environmental ethic and aesthetic are such further implications as these, all of which follow from what has been said above. First, that place significantly though differentially affects well-being through physical environment, social context, and phenomenology of perception. What furthers that well-being is therefore, broadly speaking, a good thing provided it does not come at unwarranted expense of others elsewhere. Second, that well-being is maximized by some combination of place-connectedness and a reflexive resiliency that modulates personal and communal sense of place with awareness of others' visions of place, sometimes contending with one's own. Third, that whatever the conventions of ownership, place is more deeply a matter of belonging than of possession. Fourth, "thereness" is indispensable to the vision of place, whether virtually or immediately perceived. Fifth, however, "thereness" is elastic: places evolve, degrade, ameliorate. Sixth, there is no physical space that is not potentially a place. Seventh, therefore it is in the interest of planet, people, and other forms of life, even if not perhaps in the interest of every person or interest group, for "space" to be converted—or reconverted—into "place."

Retrieval of the Unloved Place: Wideman

How and where to put these prescriptions to work? In the western world today, it would not be too offhanded to reply "any place." For "the story a place has to tell," as bioregionalist Freeman House declares with pardonable exaggeration, "is an absence so large in our [i.e., U.S. settlement] culture as to be outside our range of vision. It is invisible like the air is invisible."[77] Almost every community needs to do serious remedial work before it can fully understand its own "invisible landscape," in Kent Ryden's phrase. But among all possible acts of imaginative environmental restoration, few are so potentially important as retrieval of loved places that have been neglected, abused, feared, or despised. That aspiration is basic to toxic discourse: to press the claims of systematically abused places, hitherto without voice or advocate. But toxicity as such need not be the central issue; it could be any number of ecocultural concerns.

These places too can be almost anywhere: at the end of the earth, in the center of the city, in the suburban interstices. In proportion to the unloveliness of the place as conventionally viewed is the gravity of the attempt. Berry's lifetime commitment to eastern Kentucky's Appalachian hills is one such, of which more in Chapter 4. Leslie Silko's Laguna Pueblo-centered oeuvre is another. It is a boldly extravagant effort to make what for most American readers might seem a shabby outback, virtually off the chart as it were, the center of the earth. Still another such project, with which I shall end this chapter, is African-

American writer John Edgar Wideman's return to the gritty Home-wood district of Pittsburgh where he spent his early childhood, and to which his imagination later returned partly because he knew it would seem the antithesis of the usual locus of platial nostalgia.

Wideman's early writing was in a Euromodernist vein: part of a spec-tacular success story of escape from ghetto origins to Ivy League uni-versity and Rhodes scholarship. He began to immerse himself in African-American history (hesitantly, by his account) when teaching at the University of Pennsylvania in the late 1960s, and it took a decade of pondering and family tragedy for him to rediscover Homewood as a place of imagination. But precisely this he did do in the nonfictional nar-rative *Brothers and Keepers* (1984), which focuses on his relation to his younger brother Robby, sentenced to life imprisonment for armed rob-bery and murder, and in a novelistic trilogy of interlinked stories built around this and other episodes in family history (*Damballah* [1981], *Hid-ing Place* [1981], and *Sent for You Yesterday* [1983]). These and such later books as the novel *Reuben* (1987) and the nonfictional *Fatheralong* (1994) mark a return to family, to race, and to place.

Wideman might not be satisfied to have this work categorized as a "return to place,"[78] since he has cautioned that the literary Homewood is not so much a unique "physical location" as "a culture" or "a way of seeing and being seen," the portrayal governed by the wish to generate a counterimage to the reductive stereotype of "black life in America." "Urban ghettoes are dangerous, broken-down, economically marginal pockets of real estate infected with drugs, poverty, violence, crime" and deterioration; the circulation of such images "recycles the classic justifi-cation for slavery," blame the victim. Against that prejudice Wideman wishes to "bear witness to the fact that black life, for all its material im-poverishment, continues to thrive, to generate alternative styles, re-demptive strategies, people who hope and cope."[79] Thus "Homewood is very real," "the family history coincides [although many details are changed] with the history of the actual community"; but Homewood is also paradigm of family and race in place ("My subject is a Black family, a Black family in America, in a particular city"),[80] which means that peo-ple, community, culture, language, voice are all more foregrounded than geography. As these statements suggest, however, central to the fleshing out of Wideman's transposable vision is reminiscence of the specific district, seen through the lenses of family memory and personal recollection.

Wideman does not sentimentalize Homewood. He shows it to be a harsh place, and increasingly so. The years on which the trilogy concentrates, early 1940s through the 1960s, were a time of war-economy-fueled miniboom followed by deteriorating prospects as new arrivals made Homewood markedly poorer and more black (from one-quarter in 1950 to two-thirds in 1960). Other Pittsburgh communities reaped the benefits of the so-called "Pittsburgh Renaissance" while Homewood, like many African-American urban neighborhoods, suffered from botched and halfhearted urban renewal and riots in the wake of Martin Luther King's assassination that devastated the once-"thriving business community" and drove the white merchants out.[81] "Man, they sure did fuck with this place," growls one Wideman character (p. 124). A city guidebook of the mid-1980s acknowledges, "Those residents leave who can."[82] Wideman's nuclear family did. Not so most of the figures in the trilogy, despite their complaints about the neighborhood becoming more impoverished, dingy, unsafe. Homewood is the place where Uncle Carl, a talented art student, dwindles into a barfly after no white firm will hire him; where brother Tommy (the trilogy's Robby-figure) briefly eludes the police after the robbery; where brother-in-law Rashad can't shake his drug dependency; where cousin Hazel lives out a bleak chair-bound life after her brother pushes her downstairs, and the brother comes home to die of an unnamed disease; where Fisk-educated Samantha sees her son burned to death by his siblings and disintegrates into madness; where Carl's friend Albert Wilkes returns to get blown apart by the cops who are waiting for him. Even grandfather John French, a powerful figure in the community, must hang out on the street corner in the freezing early dawn waiting for the slim pickings of white contractors looking for small-job paperhangers.[83]

The materiality of neighborhood decay is insisted on. Homewood Avenue "looks like somebody's bad head with the ringworm," "like somebody's mouth they let some jive dentist fuck with"—the store-fronts "boarded or demolished altogether or transformed to unfamiliar, dirty-looking shops," the unfilled schoolyard pool "a huge garbage can you can smell from blocks away in the summer," the little house in

Westinghouse Park below the train station platform (none stop there anymore) "an empty shell, blind and gutted" (pp. 125, 127, 148, 150). The topographical high point of the neighborhood, Bruston Hill, said to be "the only point in Pittsburgh where it is possible to see a neighborhood in its entirety,"[84] is also the central point in the trilogy's symbolic geography, the point at which—as it connects present events to deeper time—the family narrative metamorphoses from memory into myth. This is the place where family progenitress Sybela Owens (Homewood's first resident according to Wideman family legend) settled after fleeing slavery, the place where a family dwelling and garden still are, where her granddaughter Bess (believed to have magical powers of vision and healing) still lives, where Tommy briefly hides out. But only a fragment of the original house remains after a fire; the rusty tapwater has to be laced with whisky to be drinkable; the vista is foreshortened by smog; and Bess's rumored occult powers are a parody of the legendary Sybela's. She can't heal her dying great-grandniece, she can't shield Tommy.

Altogether, a person bound to Homewood is bound to suffer, like Tommy, who keeps himself emotionally under control during his first prison stint by picturing "the streets gliding past perfect in each detail,"

> even though they were full of broken glass, and cracks, the garbage stacked at the curbs and boards over the empty windows and iron cages over the windows with anything in them, and black stones still smelling of smoke, still smelling of dead winos and dead firemen in the vacant lot after they tried to burn down the streets one hot August night. (p. 286)

This could stand as an authorial statement about the broader impetus behind the literary project. One of its shaping influences is identification with the younger brother. His flight, capture, imprisonment, and the family's anguish and guilt about this (particularly the author's) are central to both *Brothers and Keepers* and the first two books of the trilogy.[85] The preface to *Damballah* (Book I) announces it to be "letters" to Robby "from home," to the brother who wasn't "afraid of becoming instant nigger" by eating watermelon from the middle-class brother who's learning to overcome his fastidiousness. The letter/book is offered up as a symbolic watermelon (p. 3), a belated acknowledgment of desire to go b(l)ack. As in *Brothers and Keepers, Damballah* and the rest of the Homewood trilogy seemingly want to turn the tables: to present the author as in some sense the imprisoned one (by self-division and exile) and Robby/Tommy as the one who has always been more free (by accepting racial/platial identity, notwithstanding rage and pain), and in some sense (so *Brothers and Keepers* has it) all the more so in prison, where his character gets solidified by joining the Nation of Islam and earning a college diploma. To retrace and internalize the ruined streets of Homewood, however painful this may be, is the only way to retrieve the understanding of that life-world with real fullness.

"John," by contrast to Tommy, appears in these books chiefly as a comic, stiffish figure who doesn't know the cues ("tall man . . . looked around real careful like maybe he in the wrong place, like maybe he subject to turn around and split somebody yell *Boo* real loud" [p. 270]), until at the very end he begins to regain the feel of those early days and live up to his "meaningless" childhood nickname "Doot." The people who help him reorient, Carl and his old girlfriend Lucy, are, like Tommy/Robby, sad figures of lost possibility, but also like him able to recuperate Homewood as lived experience. All this is consistent with the judgment of Homewood ethnographer Melvin Williams that "genuine blacks" (those rejecting mainstream values according to criteria that fit the represented Tommy/Robby quite well) are the exemplars of a culturally "successful adaptive strategy" that allows them, despite what look like carceral conditions of life, to "feel a sense of belonging to this neighborhood."[86] Wideman's saltier characters challenge reader-voyeurs the way one of Williams's informants (a "genuine resident") talks back to him:[87]

"This is the ghetto, man, and this is how we have to make it here. Kennedy and Rockefeller want to be president, Howard Hughes wants to be left alone, Mellon wants more money, Nixon wants to be king, and you, you want to be God [understand everything]. I just want to watch the world go by, feeling little pain as possible. But then I can't do no better. I'm on the bottom rung of the ladder and the next step up is outta sight."

By reconnecting with his childhood identity through companionship with Carl and Lucy, "John" tries to take the next step beyond this gritty passage toward retrieving and honoring the "alternative styles, redemptive strategies" invented by people constrained to subsist "on the bottom rung." The trilogy ends, tactfully, without letting the return-of-the-native motif steal the show, and without pushing to closure the question of what "John" will *do* with his long-lost and now seemingly revived Homewood identity. It is enough that Homewood itself has been discovered as a place of value.

It will take more than just Wideman's memory-of-place retrieval to recuperate the literal Homewood. But without such retrievals, no recuperation.

Chapter 3

Flâneur's Progress:
Reinhabiting the City

> To cement and glass I say: you are sand, grains
> banished from the desert, exiled here.
> —Sharon Borg, "In the City We Never See God"

> Harlem and East Saint Louis and Iowa and Kansas and the rest of the world
> where wilderness has been destroyed must come to be loved by enough of
> us, or wilderness is doomed.
> —Wes Jackson, *Becoming Native to This Place*

"Reinhabitation" is a resonant term used since the 1970s by place-committed writers of bioregionalist persuasion[1] to express the goal of mutual renewal implicit in a dedication to ecocultural understanding and restoration. Advocates and practitioners of reinhabitation, whether or not they use the term, start from the premise that not only has the environment been abused, aspiring reinhabitors have themselves been wounded by displacement and ecological illiteracy so that they must (re)learn what it means to be "native" to a place. Moreover, the reorientation process cannot simply be a solitary quest but must also involve participation in community both with fellow inhabitants in the present and with past generations, through absorption of history and legend. In short, reinhabitation presupposes long-term reciprocal engagement with a place's human and nonhuman environments and welcomes the prospect of one's identity being molded by this encounter.[2]

As the "re" prefix and the notion of becoming native imply, the analogue of "inhabitory" or indigenous landwise understanding provides an enabling myth or template for the practice of reinhabitation. By the same token, the usual setting envisaged for enactment is exurban. The reinhabitor is Wendell Berry, returning to Appalachian Kentucky "through my history's despite / and ruin" to make "the beginning / of a farm intended to become / my art of being here." The reinhabitor is John Elder, learning "to pay attention to the stories of the land, and of the previous generations" of Green Mountain village life in Robert Frost country, with Frost's own reinhabitory vision-quest poem "Directive" as one of his main guides. Or he is Gary Snyder rediscovering northern California as Shasta Bioregion, whose tangled cultural history reaches back to the Nisenan.[3] Yet a counterpart of reinhabitation can, must, be attempted in cities also, as Wes Jackson urges. The *Green City Program* designed for "the San Francisco Bay Area and Beyond," for example, ranges from small-scale recommendations like redesigning certain streets with "cul de sacs connected by bike paths" to large-scale ones like "'proximity policies' that encourage people to live near their workplaces."[4] This handbook for urban reform envisages a restoration of a sense of place built around a firmer sense of local and regional ecology, community, and history.

The urban reinhabitation movement might be seen as the latest chapter of a long tradition of urban utopias: the Christian anagogic City of God, Campanella's *City of the Sun*, Benjamin Richardson's *Hygeia: A City of Health*, the socialist paradise of Edward Bellamy's *Looking Backward*, Le Corbusier's *The Radiant City*. The first phase of modern green city thinking was ushered in by the urban landscape and public health reform movements of the mid-nineteenth century, Frederick Law Olmsted being the best-known American examplar. The second came in the early 1900s with visions by designers and cultural critics of how cities, towns, and countryside should be integrated in light of the metropolitan expansion that threatened their integrity but also seemed to establish environmental planning on a more enlightened basis.[5] The contemporary bioregionalist movement has built upon the central insight of the planners and theorists of this second era—Ebenezer Howard, Patrick Geddes, Lewis Mumford, Benton MacKaye—that "every city is part of a region, . . . and depends on the surrounding countryside for many of its resources and much of its market, and every city is built upon a natural foundation."[6] That legacy has influenced a more specifically ecological reconception of urban design arising from interdisciplinary study of a site's particular landscape identity in relation to the history of human settlement.[7]

If in fact it is true that "the city—for better or worse—is our future,"[8] urban reinhabitation becomes all the more important for creative artists and intellectuals at large as well as design and planning professionals, insofar as "the true test in reinhabiting place is our personal and shared abilities to unwrap and tap the inner expressions, experiences and senses that collectively make up our cognitive maps of place."[9] This process must involve simultaneous reimagination of the urban-industrial transformation of natural landscapes and the persistence of physical environment as constitutive influence.

A matched pair of examples of the first sort would include Frank Norris's turn-of-the-century fictional epic of the wheat industry and environmental historian William Cronon's scholarly epic *Nature's Metropolis,* which documents the mind-boggling growth of Chicago in the nineteenth century as a center of transport, trade, and finance by aggressive capitalization on its geographical position as the gateway to a vast hinterland of suppliers and markets. Both works portray Chicago as the center of national and transnational systems of commodity and capital flow, making the city a controlling force throughout the remote corners of the land. When the protagonist of Norris's *The Pit* (1903) risks his fortune buying up wheat futures, "all through the Middle West" go the repercussions: mortgages are "paid off, new and improved farming implements . . . bought, new areas seeded, new live stock acquired," and conversely the corner of wheat collapses under the weight of production that speculative price manipulation has triggered.[10]

An example of the second sort would be Robert Frost's poem "A Brook in the City," a rare sortie into the metropolis to meditate on a former country stream now channeled underground and out of sight. "No one would know except for ancient maps / That such a brook ran water," the poet muses. "But

> I wonder
> If from its being kept forever under
> The thoughts may not have risen that so keep
> This new-built city from both work and sleep."[11]

Frost's supposition that somehow the brook must continue to exert influence if only at a subconscious level is the premise of such green urban design projects as the intensive study and partial restoration of Mill Creek in West Philadelphia, which for many years seemed to exist mainly as an inadequate sewer and intermittent nuisance (causing low places to flood and buildings to settle), but which has become, according to landscape architect Anne Spirn, an exemplary site of "community development, environmental education, and water management."[12] Toronto architect Michael Hough presses the Frostian vision further: "Two landscapes exist side by side in cities. The first is the nurtured 'pedigreed' landscape of mown turf, flowerbeds, trees, fountains and planned places everywhere that have traditionally been the focus of civic design . . . the second is the fortuitous landscape of naturalized urban plants and flooded places left after rain." Yet it is "the formal city landscape imposed over an original natural diversity" that is "the one in need of rehabilitation." Hough goes on to detail various urban systems problems, particularly relating to water supply and waste disposal, caused by planners' neglect of environmental conditions.[13]

As these examples suggest, environmentally conscious urban writing has oscillated between a sense, whether exuberant or appalled, of the self-evident march of urban triumphalism and a sense, also often ambiguated, of the necessary dependence of urban life on physical environment.

Cities being self-evidently built, not "natural," and the modern city being no more than several centuries old, it is understandable that urban literature of the industrial era should look somewhat disillusioned relative to country literature, even in the hands of confirmed urbanites. We still live with the imbalance of sensibility exemplified by the first major English poems of the urban and the rural quotidian, which appeared almost simultaneously: John Gay's *Trivia: or, the Art of Walking the Streets of London* (1716) and James Thomson's *The Seasons* (1726–1740). *The Seasons* is a lavishly attentive pastoral-georgic chronicle of seasonal phenomena, including city glimpses but mostly country-oriented. Gay's is a mock-georgic, also in part seasonally arranged, satirizing the hazards of pedestrian life: mud splatter, pickpockets, chair and carriage mishaps. It is delightfully high-spirited and witty; it does not admonish you to stay indoors, or to flee the plaguy town for salubrious rurality, like that other neglected minor Augustan environmental classic, John Armstrong's "The Art of Preserving Health." *Trivia* is the work of a confirmed urbanite, no doubt about it. But the inhabitance commended is a fastidious, analytic, hold-the-nose disengagement:

> That Walker, who regardless of his Pace,
> Turns oft' to pore upon the Damsel's Face,
> From Side to Side by thrusting Elbows tost,
> Shall strike his aking Breast against the Post;
> Or Water, dash'd from fishy Stalls, shall stain
> His hapless Coat with Spirts of scaly Rain.
> But if unwarily he chance to stray,
> Where twirling Turnstiles intercept the Way,
> The thwarting Passenger shall force them round,
> And beat the Wretch half breathless to the Ground.[14]

Don't let your attention wander! Walk defensively! Watch your step! Although the poem displays, indeed revels in, an insider's sense of what it feels like to haunt the city streets, it cannot bring itself to imagine a walker enjoying himself with impunity. The enjoyments it offers are delight in clever naming, avoidance of hazard, and amusement at the expense of the less agile. Nor does Gay attempt to image "London" as an entity. The city unfolds as "an extended sum of innumerable particulars."[15]

Here we see anticipated the classic formulation of urban experience in early twentieth-century sociological theory: "a series of tenuous segmental relationships superimposed upon a territorial base with a definite center but without a definite periphery and upon a division of labor which far transcends the immediate locality and is world-wide in scope."[16] Already one notes the emphasis on a discontinuous welter of fleeting, incoherent encounters with a barrage of stimuli conceived as a semipathological condition: more as a problem of individual disorientation or civic degradation than as an improvement on rustic stodginess. And already in Gay emerges the canonical form for representing this state of affairs: the impressions of a (usually male) representative observing consciousness as it moves about in the city, among its buildings and crowds, recording scenes and the experience of encounter. Gay's urban traveler is the precursor of the nineteenth-century *flâneur*,[17] and the cross-section of humanity he encounters is the precursor of the crowd of later urban fiction and poetry, from Poe and Baudelaire on down.[18]

These writers, in turn, influenced early twentieth-century urban theory. In particular, Georg Simmel and Walter Benjamin identified the experience of fascinated alienation amidst urban spectacle as the paradigm of metropolitan psychic existence, at least for men of a certain level of class and status.[19] Thus formulated, the *flâneur* figure would seem to reveal more about how to maintain control amid the space, pace, and anonymity of city life than about how or whether cities might be experienced as livable habitats. But within and against the familiar repertoire of *flânerie,* one also finds attempts to deviate or break from the trope of alienated encounter by reimagining the terms of encounter. In this chapter I shall stress in particular several ways in which certain writers endow their *flâneurs* with something like an environmentalist consciousness so as to begin to image the possibilities of urban reinhabitation: imagination of the borders of personal identity such that consciousness extends itself from its perpetually guarded sanctuary into a state of vulnerable, porous transpersonal reciprocity with people and with place; conception of urban environment in ecosystemic terms; and recognition of metropolis, despite alienating abrasions and frustrations, as habitat.

Most of the works treated below feature scenes or plots of urban walking, riding, or roaming about in the mind's eye. One can easily imagine a more comprehensive study than this one, in which *flânerie* from the nature writing tradition or nature poetry traditions— Thoreau's *Journal,* Mary Austin's *Land of Little Rain,* Ammons's "Corson's Inlet"—would be balanced against and fully interwoven with the urban writing on which this chapter concentrates, instead of being confined to short cameo appearances. The device of the roving observer knows no limitation of setting.[20] But given its familiarity as a device of nature writing, I have concentrated here on the more counterintuitive side of the picture: urban ecocriticism.

Romantic Urbanism: Whitman, Olmsted, and Others

Although Neoclassical writers like Gay, Pope, and Swift were much more town-and-city-oriented than the Romanticist generations that followed, Romanticism's commitment to interiority pushed it at times toward a deeper rendering of urban experience, as when Blake stressed the interdependence of the city's extreme juxtapositions (the soldier's moan bleeding down palace walls, the youthful harlot's curse blighting the "Marriage hearse") and when Wordsworth was driven by the crowd "amid those overflowing streets" to ponder the mystery of anonymity such that the biographical placard around the neck of a blind beggar in front of him suddenly seemed to transform into "an apt type / . . . of the utmost we can know, / Both of ourselves and of the universe."[21] Likewise, DeQuincey, remembering his first entry into London at the same period, stresses that "you are no longer noticed: nobody sees you; nobody hears you; nobody regards you; you do not even regard yourself."[22]

Before the mid-nineteenth century, however, perhaps only in Blake's *Jerusalem* does a major work of Anglophone literature attend to the minutiae of city life, and then only at intervals, with anything like an "ecological" sense of interconnectedness between observer and observed, people and landscape. What allowed Blake to achieve such results was a gift more visionary than mimetic. In *Jerusalem* a Christian allegorical diptych of the heavenly city versus the mortal city of destruction montages with a secular allegory of London as national epitome and its historic dispensations from Celtic-primordial to modern-industrial, and this in turn montages with a more personalized Romanticist myth of the artisan Los struggling against his own fallenness to complete the building of the utopian Golgonooza.[23] At first reading *Jerusalem* seems far too abstruse to qualify as a rendering of "modern urban experience." Yet the poem presupposes an insider's sense of how it feels to inhabit a national metropolis of commingled magnificence and desolation, as when Los, in his allegorical search of Albion's bosom culminating in London, finds "every minute particular, the jewels of Albion, running down / The kennels of the streets & lanes as if they were abhorred"; "all the tendernesses of the soul cast forth as filth & mire"; "Dens of despair" built "in the house of bread." Underlying the stylized rhetoric is an identification more intimate than Wordsworth's rendering of the sleeping city in his Westminster Bridge sonnet as a "mighty heart . . . lying still." Los is probing that heart at this very moment: its minute human and environmental particulars, the degradation that is and the beauty that might be, perhaps can be.[24]

The personification of the urban macrocosm by Blake and Wordsworth is both archaic and anticipatory. The modern discourse of urban and regional planning has not been able to do without such holistic metaphorization, whether mechanic ("urban ecosystems") or organic ("urban metabolism").[25] Its disposition is to want to think and express itself in such metaphors even when it realizes they are heuristic at best and misleading at worst.[26] Cybernetics, ecology, and community theory as well as artistic imagination all conspire to corporealize metropolis.

The first major Anglophone creative writers who made the city an object of systematic study and literary portrayal were Charles Dickens (1807–1870) and Walt Whitman (1819–1892). Both reached literature via journalism. Dickens's chief breakthrough of environmental imagination, to be discussed in Chapter 4, was to convert a genius for reportage into unprecedentedly full, varied, chronicles of city dwellers and institutions; Whitman's was to convert the editorial vox populi into an unprecedentedly sensitive barometer of the transformations of selfhood under urban conditions.

One of Whitman's greatest innovations was to destabilize the autonomy of the Romantic persona more radically than any had attempted. The Whitmanian speaker becomes by turns atomized and omniscient, observer and participant, unitary and fragmented into a social collage, interchangeable with others. Animating this strategy were a "democratic" ideal of equality and fraternity and a "Transcendentalist" ideal of the inherent divinity of every person. Neither derives in a simple one-to-one way from metropolitan experience, but it is hard to imagine Whitman making his breakthrough of persona reinvention without benefit of urban context.

Whitman does not always anchor himself there, to be sure. Of the twenty-four prefatory "Inscriptions" that open the final (1891–1892) edition of *Leaves of Grass,* none invoke an unmistakably metropolitan setting. Most roam about ("Dwell awhile and pass on") or inhabit the realm of abstraction. Whitman's most patent borrowing from Dickens, of whom he was an early and ardent admirer, is not from any of the London scenes but from the Brighton seashore. At the climax of "Out of the Cradle Endlessly Rocking," the poet-boy-speaker's exhortation to the fierce "mother" to utter a word that he can "conquer," reprises little Paul Dombey, Jr.'s effort to understand the sea's almost-but-not-quite intelligible language, which he has come to believe is the voice of his mother calling him from beyond the grave. In Dickens by implication, in Whitman explicitly, the word is Death.[27] The village provenance of the archetypal boy in Whitman's "There Was a Child Went Forth," discussed in Chapter 2, suggests that urbanism was for Whitman an acquired taste.

But it was a taste acquired quickly, by young manhood, so that by the first edition of *Leaves of Grass* (1855) Whitman had fashioned a persona "of Manhattan the son." Indeed, that Whitman seized on the *Dombey* passage, and that Dickens created it in the first place, was symptomatic not so much of residual Romantic naturism as of a shared sense of the reciprocity of personhood and environment of whatever sort.[28] Where the two writers achieved their most distinctive effects was in dramatizing the strange but imperative mutual interdependence of people with things and with unknown others in urban contexts. As in this Whitmanian knife-grinder vignette:

> The scene and all its belongings, how they seize and affect me,
> The sad sharp-chinn'd old man with worn clothes and broad
> shoulder-band of leather,
> Myself effusive and fluid, a phantom curiously floating, now here
> absorb'd and arrested,
> The group, (an unminded point set in a vast surrounding,)
> The attentive, quiet children, the proud, restive base of the streets,
> The low hoarse purr of the whirling stone, the light-press'd blade,
> Diffusing, dropping, sideways-darting, in tiny showers of gold,
> Sparkles from the wheel. (p. 390, ll. 8–16)

Such a curbside epiphany would have jolted Wordsworth, but Whitman's comfort with urban inhabitance makes it feel deeply satisfying: to be gripped by the minutest details of a random street scene, such that one feels one's identity come disengaged from one's body—feels it liq-uefy, crystallize in the "unminded point" of "the group," then disperse again into purr, shower, sparkle, as it suffuses through the workman's vernacular magic, itself a fortuitous symbol of what the poem wants to do to the reader.

Whitman's "catalogue" rhetoric of heaped-up parallel images and his fluid "I" presuppose a dense but loose social assemblage, such as only major cities could offer: one so large and diverse that interpersonal communion was imaginable only from the ground condition of juxta-position rather than intimacy, concurrence rather than sequentialism, transience rather than rootedness.

> The butcher-boy puts off his killing-clothes, or sharpens his knife at
> the stall in the market,
> I loiter enjoying his repartee and his shuffle and break-down.
> . . . . .
> I am the mash'd fireman with breast-bone broken,
> Tumbling walls buried me in their debris,
> Heat and smoke I inspired, I heard the yelling shouts of my
> comrades,
> I heard the distant click of their picks and shovels,
> They have clear'd the beams away, they tenderly lift me forth.
> ("Song of Myself," pp. 39, 67, ll. 217–218, 847–851)

At a superficial level Whitman's poetry plays the "identity games" typical of an urban world of strangers: passing, interactive role play, haggling, hustling.[29] At a more transactional level his persona assumes responsibility for the casual surveillance that needs, as Jane Jacobs puts it, to be exercised by *other people without ties of close kinship or close friendship or formal responsibility to you*" in order to create the sense of streets with "eyes" necessary to the preservation of a sense of public ci-vility and community: "the trust of a city street [that] is formed over time from many, many little public sidewalk contacts."[30] At a deeper level yet, his persona models an empathetic civic commitment so fer-vent as to expose himself, ironically, to the charge by more fastidious scholar-voyeurs of not taking the modern city seriously enough: of con-tenting himself with a sanitized, boosteristic version of urban life.

For this charge there is indeed basis. By the 1850s New York had developed into "a city of extraordinary wealth and power but also a city of equally remarkable filth, a sparkling gem set in a pile of garbage."[31] No U.S. metropolis faced worse problems of dirt, pollution, disease, uncontrolled growth, and overcrowding during the years Whitman wrote about New York (1820s through 1860s). Urban poverty as Dickens confronted it in the London of *Oliver Twist* and *Our Mutual Friend,* as Melville in the Manhattan chapters of *Pierre* and in "Bartleby the Scrivener," as Lydia Maria Child in some of her *Letters from New-York,* Whitman's poems treat glancingly. This in spite of the fact that Whitman knew the range and severity of urban problems better than any other American writer of the day now thought "major." For the first two decades of his adult life, as a newspaperman in Brooklyn and Manhattan, he repeatedly called attention to cases of environmental negligence and injustice, sounding like a demotic Franklin. Whitman campaigned for better street repair, better garbage removal, better lighting of streets, better water and sewer systems. He advocated daily swimming exercise (in the East and North Rivers), free public baths, and better habits of personal hygiene. He crusaded against spitting in public places, against unsafe and unhealthy working conditions, and against contaminated "swill" milk sold by dairies that fed their cows on refuse.[32]

When Whitman looked back on his last editorial position in the late 1850s, which was also his most prolific poetic period, he declared that the accomplishment of which he was proudest was his campaign for new water and sewer systems for the city of Brooklyn. Indeed, his newspaper editorials on this subject wax poetic:

> Next to our noble waterworks, and naturally arising out of the existence of them, depending indeed upon them, comes a large and perfect system of Sewerage for Brooklyn. To have interior drains through every street, avenue, and lane, carrying off all impurities— keeping all the houses and yards free from offensive matter—keeping indeed, the whole city sweet and clean—truly there is something cheerful in the vista thus opened to our great city.[33]

Yet when we turn to Whitman's poetry of the city, rarely do we find overt recognition of such mundane infrastructural issues as water supply and waste disposal. This notwithstanding that Whitman's younger brothers George and Tom, in whose careers he took an active interest, both worked in municipal water departments. Thomas Jefferson Whitman, a major news source in the 1850s for his Brooklyn reportage, went on to become chief designer and overseer of the first modern waterworks for the city of St. Louis.[34]

No doubt the discrepancy between Whitman's journalism and his poetry was partly a matter of genre; post-Romantic poetry stylizes social mimesis no less insistently than the gothic conventions favored by William Godwin, Charles Brockden Brown, and Edgar Allan Poe. Victorian poetry did not seriously engage the modern city until the 1860s, a quarter-century after Dickens began publishing novels. A Romantic poet like Whitman, who knew nothing about Blake until Swinburne's comparison of them both caught his attention,[35] would have had every reason to associate "the poetic" mainly with lyric contemplation. A century earlier he might have written differently: as a contemporary of Swift, Johnson, Pope, and Gay. But not in the age of Tennyson, who for Whitman was the high-water mark of Victorian poetry. To this extent, the place in his head where Whitman did poetry was different from the place where he did urban environmental reform.

But a more complicated picture emerges when we look closely at Whitman's greatest poem on a representative urban theme, "Crossing Brooklyn Ferry" (1856). Here Whitman puts a hallmark Romantic genre, hitherto coded rural, to strikingly new uses.[36] "Brooklyn Ferry" may in fact be the first great literary rendering of mass transit experience in all of world literature.[37] Gay, Blake, and Wordsworth present themselves as solitary walkers in the tradition of the limited-scale "walking city" that nineteenth-century metropolises eventually made obsolete. Whitman, however, rides, and he rides en masse. Indeed, more than 25 million passengers annually made the Brooklyn-Manhattan crossing at the time Whitman wrote this poem.[38] The experience is idyllicized. "Brooklyn Ferry" unfolds a lovely description of the speaker's meditations as he relishes landscape, river, and sky during a leisurely seeming homeward commute. ("Sun-down Poem" was the original title.) As he evokes the scene, the speaker imagines himself one with fellow commuters and with readers present and future. The ferry becomes a cosmic symbol, of the transit of individual life, of the body "struck from the float forever held in solution."

The poem culminates in a series of joyous assertions that celebrate the sense of union with all who share this experience either literally or vicariously.

> Consider, you who peruse me, whether I may not in unknown
>   ways be looking upon you;
> Be firm, rail over the river, to support those who lean idly, yet
>   haste with the hasting current;
> Fly on, sea-birds! fly sideways, or wheel in large circles high in the
>   air;
> Receive the summer sky, you water, and faithfully hold it till all
>   downcast eyes have time to take it from you!
> Diverge, fine spokes of light, from the shape of my head, or any
>   one's head, in the sunlit water!
> Come on, ships from the lower bay! pass up or down, white-sail'd
>   schooners, sloops, lighters!
> Flaunt away, flags of all nations! be duly lower'd at sunset!
> Burn high your fires, foundry chimneys! cast black shadows at
>   nightfall! cast red and yellow light over the tops of the houses!
> Appearances, now or henceforth, indicate what you are,
> You necessary film, continue to envelop the soul,
> About my body for me, and your body for you, be hung our
>   divinest aromas,
> Thrive, cities—bring your freight, bring your shows, ample and
>   sufficient rivers,
> Expand, being than which none else is perhaps more spiritual,
> Keep your places, objects than which none else is more lasting.
>   (pp. 164–165, ll. 112–125)

Altogether a ringing tribute to the pleasures of urban experience and the sense of oneness with place, populace, and readership. The passage moves from a sense of particular thisness (the first-person singular observer, the tangible "rail over the river") to mutability of permutation ("fly sideways, or wheel," "pass up or down"), but within a milieu of recurring elements: directing the eye first down to water, then over to ships, then up to flags, and then farther up and out to chimneys in a panorama offered as comprehensive and authoritative yet also with delicate acknowledgment that this apotheosis of I, you, and place is a synergy of subjective impressions ("appearances" and "aromas"): a "necessary film" that envelops the apparatus of perception in a subjunctive "perhaps" that does not so much compromise the sense of wonder as make it the more compelling. The poem thereby opts for an embedded self rather than a transcendent self, and suggests that such transcendence of the specific moment as it has claimed is a shared experience of being situated, bounded, enveloped. The passage astutely perceives how environmental unconscious inevitably brings both recognition and nonrecognition, and seems equally fascinated by both.

Meanwhile, Whitman's ferry journalism was painting a less idealized picture of such experiences. Here too he writes fondly about riding the ferry back and forth from work, and sometimes just for fun; here too his descriptions are sometimes quite lyrical. But he foregrounds more practical concerns as well, respecting the fair, safe, and efficient function of this nineteenth-century equivalent of today's subways and buses. Whitman demanded that ferries run on schedule. He praised fast and efficient vessels over slow ones. He reprimanded inconsiderate and unsanitary behavior by riders like smoking and spitting, and he urged that these be outlawed. He criticized riders who pushed and crowded others in their haste to get off, and he also worried about the safety of such people, who jumped off too soon, fell into the water and drowned, or got crushed between the boat and the dock. He demanded affordable ferry rates. And he complained about the steep, twisting, unsafe paths that led down to the ferry landings.[39] Altogether, Whitman's journalism shows that he could not have failed to realize that "Crossing Brooklyn Ferry" was a selective rendering of an actual mid-nineteenth-century East River crossing, which could be "pleasant enough" in summer but "very dangerous" in winter, and "even in fair weather" made risky by boat traffic so dense that "only by the exercise of the greatest skill on the part of the pilot" could collisions be avoided.[40] Nor does the poem make mention of the nasty spat over ferry rates, including the touchy question of whether reporters like Whitman should be granted free passes.[41]

Yet the poem's silence about transit nuisance and abuse cannot be written off as evasion or amnesia. The reformist emphasis of Whitman's journalism and the idealizing emphasis of Whitman's poetry are symbiotic. Both express commitment to the ideal of a city sweet and clean. "Crossing Brooklyn Ferry" imagines in effect how urban transit ought to be. In its own way, it is just as committed to dramatizing proper ways of thinking and behaving as the newspaper editorials are. The poem too takes fellow citizens by the buttonhole and accosts them directly: "Just as you stand and lean on the rail, yet hurry with the swift current, I stood yet was hurried." Here too the speaker prods readers to reflect more deeply on the implications of their acts, to realize in partic-ular how they are not merely isolated self-interested beings but con-nected with all the other people and things around them.[42] The latitude of poetry permits a more fundamental reorientation of a listener's dis-position (albeit less focused on behavioral specifics) than does topical journalism.

Instead of assuming an insouciantly blissful speaker, then, we should read the poem as a response more oblique but no less sensitive to the all-too-familiar harassments of urban commuting than Gay's prescrip-tion of walking defensively. "Who feels love for his fellow-man at rush hour? Not me," exclaims Jonathan Raban, chafing in the crowd milling through the London tube. "I suspect that the best insurance against urban violence is the fact that most of us shrink from contact with strangers; we don't want to touch one another or feel that close to the stink of someone else's life."[43] Whitman was perfectly aware of this hog-gish side to people (p. 163, l. 75), perfectly aware of the instinct to with-draw into oneself. Indeed, he wants to allow for it, even celebrate it up to a point—but not to leave matters there: to insist also on a reaching out, on restoration of at least a vicarious in-touchness, and preferably a tactile one too. Even if Whitman recognizes, to cite two other "passing stranger" poems, that ordinarily "I am not to speak to you" (p. 127), he wants to raise the question anyhow: "why should I not speak to you?" (p. 14). His "Closer yet I approach you" is an act of deliberate provoca-tion, justified and at the same time rendered more unsettling by the pre-ceding confession that I too "am he who knew what it was to be evil," "Had guile, anger, lust, hot wishes I dared not speak" (p. 163, ll. 86, 70, 73).[44] More like Raban than at first sight, Whitman wants to lay bare the chronic mutual suspicions of strangers in a crowd and make *that* the pathway to common understanding.

To state this aspect of the poem's accomplishment in the strongest possible terms: even at the very start of modern commuting rituals Whitman has perceived the threat they pose to civility and community and sought to counteract that. The experience of commutation quintessentializes the problem of the crowd, as Raban sees, as T. S. Eliot saw in *The Waste Land*, with its phantasmagoria of morning zombies shuffling across London Bridge. Mass transit put large groups of fortuitously converging people in the unprecedented "position of having to stare [defensively] at one another for minutes or even hours on end without exchanging a word." Commutation, in particular, threatened to reduce the space of the urban voyager to "a psychological kind of no man's land," where people treat others as "non-persons," on the shaky presumption that "ultimately, somewhere else—at home? on holiday? in heaven?—both we and they could get back into the business of being real."[45] All this Whitman sees, and against it he imagines how a sense of plenitude, of contact with others and with landscape, might be restored.

Whitman's direction of reformist impulse toward ferry *riders,* rather than ferry *companies,* which his journalism also criticizes, defers to another convention of Romantic lyric: address to the solitary auditor. Yet the tendency to imagine that the key to social reform lay not in institutional change per se but in modification of citizenly behavior through change of attitude was not genre-specific but broadly typical of the urban reform efforts of his day.[46] Whitman is careful, moreover, to set his image of model transit experience within a concentric series of social and environmental controls. "Crossing Brooklyn Ferry" addresses the reader as a specially designated person who at the same time might be anybody and must therefore realize that "any one's head," not just his, is dignified by the nimbus of the sunlit water (p. 165, l. 116).[47] The poem subtly insists on safety and efficiency: that the railings be firm "to support those who lean idly," that the multitude of ships "pass up or down" without colliding, a frequent mishap (p. 165, ll. 113, 117). Even more important, the poem insists on resisting the fragmentation, both spatial and temporal, that Gay and Wordsworth accept as endemic to metropolitan experience. Transit does not occur in an isolated space or as an isolated incident; it should not be thought of merely as a movement from embarkation point X to destination point Y. It should be thought of as a part of the entire commercial and spatial order, and as happening ongoingly and not just in this or that moment. The final "restoration of trust in the sheer physical process of existence" in the poem's final section, which includes the long passage quoted previously, includes affirmation of some highly questionable items, like the belching foundry chimneys.[48] The thrust of the section as a whole, however, is not that this is the best of all possible worlds nor that this particular constellation of phenomena is valid for all time; rather, an urban inhabitance worthy of the name is not to be self-isolating and segmented, but carried on in the awareness of reciprocity with others (recognizing that a "necessary film" will always "continue to envelop the soul" [p. 165, l. 121]), and symbiotically with the built and natural environment.

Whitman's reinhabitory vision of how to counter the influence of industrial speedup and commutational nonbeing surprisingly resembles Thoreau's concurrent prescription, in *Walden,* for living deliberately in a rural context. Reminiscent of Whitman's invitation to "loafe" on the grass at the start of "Song of Myself," Thoreau argued the importance of breaking the hold of the work ethic by cultivating nonlinear attentiveness: to retone psychic existence so as to experience each moment in its fullness, whether one is building a cabin step by step or listening to the sounds of a day hour by hour.[49] Thoreau's antisocialism should not blind one to their common desire to resist routinization through attentive reciprocity with all that surrounds a person, in imagining how a person can live more fully in the moment in a particular place. Whitman's concern for situating the individual among groups of people in place brings him closer, however, to nineteenth-century America's best-known urban environmental reformer, Frederick Law Olmsted, who named the emerging field of landscape architecture and was more responsible than any other person for its professionalization.

The year after "Brooklyn Ferry" was published, Olmsted became superintendent of the new Central Park and soon after its chief architect (in partnership with Calvert Vaux). Though much more the gentleman-authoritarian than Whitman, Olmsted was also at heart a democrat, for whom the justification of public parks was bringing together diverse classes in a countrified space so that poor as well as rich would enjoy the refreshments of nature, and community would be promoted by propinquity and casual observation in a context of collective enjoyment of park pleasures and respect for the grounds.[50] Olmsted both considered the park a feat of interventionary social engineering ("the lives of women and children too poor to be sent to the country, can now be saved in thousands of instances, by making them go to the Park") and believed that salvation, both physical and social, would happen spontaneously, by a kind of natural osmosis, "a distinctly harmonizing and refining influence upon the most unfortunate and most lawless classes of the city."[51] The rhetoric of Whitman's poem contains a similar manipulation of readers to imagine themselves in a particular kind of outdoor scene and trust in the spontaneous efficacy of that vicariousness to produce the "right" psychic reaction.

In their efforts to imagine livable cities, Whitman and Olmsted each resorted to pastoral rhetorics that bore traces of previous life experience. Olmsted was preconditioned to think of himself as a farmer; personal experience as well as ideology made him a believer in rural salubrity. Whitman, we have seen, remained sentimentally attached to the countryside where he spent his early boyhood. Yet both saw urbanization as the way of the future and celebrated cities as offering better possibilities for social life and individual growth.[52]

Both wanted an urbanism that would retain a measure of rural healthfulness. But whereas Olmsted led the nineteenth-century movement to pastoralize cities by dedicating tracts of green space for public use, Whitman was less engaged by the idea of urban parks as such, although he did vigorously support the creation of a park for Brooklyn that would give "lungs" to a congested area of the mushrooming city.[53] On the whole, public works key to the delivery of essential city services like clean drinking water and affordable bathing places mattered more than spending great sums of money on reclaiming sizable tracts for parkland. To Whitman, regular bathing was more important than regular woodsy strolls. From this perspective, the epic achievement of Croton Reservoir was more important than that of the Central Park that surrounded it.[54] His choice and handling of subject in "Brooklyn Ferry" were wholly in keeping with this commitment: to seize hold of a mundane ritual of city life, a familiar and pivotal aspect of metropolitan infrastructure, and to imagine a paradigmatic moment embodying transfiguration of city life within the routine of ordinary experience that Olmsted, more like Thoreau than Whitman in this respect, could envisage happening only in a space apart from mundane activity. Whitman's estimate of the importance of reliable infrastructure like water and sewer systems was less romantic than Olmsted's park project but no less important from a nineteenth-century environmentalist standpoint.[55]

Neither Olmsted nor Whitman was completely right, and neither got his way. Olmsted's grand designs were watered down in the implementation, forever subject to budgetary battles and political infighting, and vulnerable to the criticism that allocation of green space as large parcels tends to benefit those who need it least. Whitman's vision of a city set within nature, Manhattan ringed by glistening water and rural retreats, was sullied by urban sprawl and tenement proliferation. "Brooklyn Ferry" was completely wrong in presuming that ferry transit would remain Gotham's primary mode of commuting "a hundred years hence, or ever so many hundred years hence" (p. 160, l. 18). Yet Whitman did grasp the broader truth that separation of home and workplace, and consequently the experience of daily transit among strangers, would remain down through late industrialism if not forever a typical urban condition; and he was prescient in realizing that this kind of experience called for redefining selfhood so as better to imagine how ever more solitary-feeling individuals could perceive themselves as part of a composite "soul" comprised not only of other people but also of the "dumb beautiful ministers": the entirety of life-forms and inanimate objects in the environmental surround. The poem's hectoring insistence on unity between speaker and reader ("We understand then do we not?" [p. 164, l. 98]) suggests awareness of the audacity and high stakes of the project. If the reader is moved, then maybe he or she will apprehend the sense of emplacement that the poem knows is the actual condition of urban experience, whether or not the reader consciously realizes it.

The poem's impulse to acknowledge that I too "Blabb'd, blush'd, resented, lied, stole, grudg'd" but then turn these "dark patches" into their opposite by using the revelation as a basis for claiming intimacy (pp. 162–163, ll. 72, 65) suggests that Whitman's vision was quickened, as was Olmsted's, by underlying awareness that the opposite was usually the case. Because Whitman knew the city needed to be more sweet and clean and its citizens more mutually trusting, he insisted that it and they inherently were. The closing imperatives rest on an uneasy fusion of moods: satisfaction that things are so, anxiety that they be so.

Whitman's limitations as a literary urbanist are easily glimpsed. He euphemized. His catalogues often too tidily represent disorder. His urbanism was "marred by the panopticism of his age";[56] control anxiety keeps the persona from becoming as malleable and other-directed as Whitman desired to be. Yet such defects are trivial compared with his grasp of early modern city-dwelling as a heteroglot assemblage of discontinuities, as a sensory overload out of which intimations of order fleetingly emerge, as a state of being in which consciousness and identity are continually shaped and reshaped via interaction, in which solitary and collective personhood are fused in unstable synthesis. Though he did not pursue all the implications of this breakthrough, his refashioning of the Romantic persona is one of the richest premodern renderings of the most familiar ordering motif of urban consciousness writing: the lyric or narrative figure who reads the city as he/she goes and builds from this some sense of urban place as habitat—the Baudelairean promenader, Dickens's Boz, Lydia Child's roving epistler in her *Letters from New-York,* the sociological investigator of Friedrich Engels's *Condition of the Working Class in England.* The excursioner can range widely from stereotypical to willfully eccentric, from the document-assembler of muckraking journalism to the interior monologuer of experimental lyric. But only Whitman was capable of imagining a figure that could play all these roles in turn.

High Modernism and Modern Urban Theory

Modernist literary urbanism went beyond the Whitmanian in pushing lyric interiority toward self-dissolution and by extending the reach and inventory of physical environment that could be named and reperceived as psychological space.

> He crossed under Tommy Moore's roguish finger [the finger-pointing statue of the mediocre Anglo-Irish Romantic poet Thomas Moore]. They did right to put him up over a urinal: meeting of the

waters. Ought to be places for women. Running into cakeshops. Settle my hat straight. *There is not in this wide world a vallee.* Great song of
Julia Morkan's. Kept her voice up to the very last.[57]

This is from Leopold Bloom's ramblings around Dublin on June 16,
1904—a short squib, but enough to show *Ulysses'* greater subjective and
material particularity relative to Whitman's "blab of the pave" and so
forth. The passage starts with the monument to a notable Irish lyric
poet and ends with the recollection of a memorable Dublin performer,
but these lyric landmarks are less important than Bloom's fanciful leaps:
from the statue above to the urinal below to the memory of Moore's
poem called "The Meeting of the Waters" to Miss Morkan's singing
of it.

What Joyce does with Bloom predicts how Michel de Certeau will
theorize the practice of ordinary urban walking, with variations that anticipate the theory's limitations. De Certeau's walkers, like Bloom, offer
a model of how to recover the sense of idiosyncrasy and uncanniness in
the interstices of "the clear text of the planned and readable city." In
going about their ambulatory routines in ways that cannot fail to deviate from the strictly canonical, they subtly transform "each spatial signi-
fier into something else."[58] So does Bloom. But whereas de Certeau, for
all his whimsical lists of erratic itineraries, local superstitions, and so
on, doggedly conceives his walkers as unthinking, albeit de facto subversive, figures, Bloom is neither unthinking nor subversive; and
though he isn't "ordinary" either, he is a more plausible approximation
of ordinary personhood than de Certeau's unintentionally disruptive
automatons.[59]

Bloom's thoughtstream shows how idiosyncratic irreverence can
comport with zest for the city as it is. Although there is a sense in which
perhaps Bloom and surely Joyce want to deface that monument to the
overrated sentimentalizer Tom Moore, there is an even stronger sense,
surely for Bloom if not also for Joyce, of wanting to imagine the city as
compatible habitat. Public facilities for women as well as men, so they
can patronize cakeshops without running; icons you can laugh at yet
also mean something for the music to which they gave rise even if the
lyrics themselves are no better than a stream of pee. Bloom's whimsy
promotes a droll but cozy civic solidarity. The song he remembers is re-

called in terms of a public occasion, and though the lyric nominally praises country life it celebrates community, not rurality as such: "the best charms of nature improve, / When we see them reflected from looks that we love."[60]

It is a pleasant coincidence that Joyce has Bloom walking around Dublin almost at the same moment Georg Simmel published his "The Metropolis and Mental Life," the single most seminal classic essay in urban theory. Many touches in Simmel's psychograph of the big-city dweller apply to Bloom, though Simmel would not have deemed turn-of-the-century Dublin (one-twentieth the size of London) a *grosstadt*: "intensification of emotional life" combined with the internalization of the habit of calculating and apportioning time, the maintenance of a spectatorial reserve, and the frequency of peculiar forms of individuation.[61] The estrangement of the city dweller that Simmel also stresses, however, does not typify *Ulysses* nearly so much as *Dubliners* and *A Portrait of the Artist as a Young Man*. "The deepest problems of modern life," Simmel insists, "flow from the attempt of the individual to maintain the independence and individuality of his existence against the sovereign powers of society, against the weight of the historical heritage and the external culture and technique of life."[62] This is accurate enough as a description of a Stephen Dedalus, or of a James Duffy, whose face "was of the brown tint of Dublin streets" but who "lived at a little distance from his body, regarding his own acts with doubtful side-glances."[63]

But in Bloom, Joyce created a sensibility whose desire to connect with its environment was greater than its need to protect itself from it. Bloom was his chief, though certainly not his only, medium for fulfilling the ambition of giving "a picture of Dublin so complete that if the city one day suddenly disappeared from the earth it could be reconstructed out of my book."[64] Joyce's quest for comprehensive reanimation of greater Dublin extends not only to its dramatis personae, peopling *Ulysses* with scores of obscure historical figures, but also to the sensuous feel and physical fact of the material environment: monuments, public buildings, private dwellings (including backyard privy, with an excursus on garden ecology), the city's tramline grid (glimpsed in "Aeolus"), its entire water supply system from reservoir to tap (concisely summarized in one paragraph of "Ithaca"), the grassy earth upturned by the gravediggers' spades, the coarse-grained detritus-strewn sandflats, "the influence of gaslight or electric light on the growth of adjoining paraheliotropic trees."[65]

Simmel's emphasis on the isolation of the individual in a city itself felt to be unreal or hostile has been seized on by some students of city writing as a master key.[66] But against this also needs to be set his important offsetting point: that whereas "the sphere of life of the small town is, in the main, enclosed within itself," the inner life of the metropolis "is extended in a wave-like motion over a broader national or international area," a "functional magnitude beyond its actual physical boundaries" that Simmel sees as a spatial counterpart of personhood itself, rightly understood. "A person does not end with limits of his physical body or with the area to which his physical activity is immediately confined but embraces, rather, the totality of meaningful effects which emanates from him temporally and spatially."[67] The kind of urban consciousness that Joyce has created through Bloom is, likewise, a site at which public and private interpenetrate (statues and urinals linked by subjective associative logic, texts and public figures by personal remembrance) in a loose suspension nominally inside Bloom's head but encompassing the architecture, society, and cultural history of Dublin as well as its people.[68]

Indeed, with regard to the people of the city, as Hana Wirth-Nesher says of *Dubliners*, contra Simmel what is striking in Joyce is "the nearly total *absence* of strangers." Estrangement, she immediately adds, does continue to run strong in Joyce,[69] but it is as if he has made a deliberate decision to extend his imaginative grasp over his city by naming individuals whom Whitman's poetry resolutely kept generic. Whitman's persona understands everybody's inmost nature from a distance; Joyce (and to a lesser extent Bloom) seems to know just about every person in Dublin more circumstantially than Whitman knows anybody. Relatively seldom in *Ulysses* do we see crowds, as against groups of identified individuals.

Polysaturated with Dublin data though *Ulysses* is, it remains more in the abstract space of oscillation between quotidian and mythic landscape[70] than the postwar London of Virginia Woolf's equivalent work, partially provoked by Joyce's: *Mrs. Dalloway*. This novel also builds on a symbolic dyad of socially disparate characters of different generations, but it makes the material cityscape a more dominant shaping force than either the protagonist or her war-traumatized alter ego Septimus Smith. A further extension of urban transpersonality results. Woolf imagines her characters hypersensitively reacting to the minutest stimuli, showing thereby a porousness of ego boundaries bordering on panpsychism. Even if she were to die, Clarissa feels, "somehow in the streets of London, on the ebb and flow of things," she would survive: "she being part ... of the trees at home; of the house there, ugly, rambling all to bits and pieces as it was; part of people she had never met."[71] During the day the novel takes place, all the major characters evince this susceptibility to some degree, and out of that confluence arises the macrocosm of London's West End: a concatenation of human pulsations thrusting in and around each other through a common environment of buildings, streets, walks, parks, traffic, which itself seems to wobble, montage, evanesce, rematerialize, and dissolve again. The novel is exceptionally sensitive to the vibrations of environmental unconscious as it congeals into awareness and subsides back again.

More than with Whitman's Manhattan or Joyce's Dublin, Woolf's London anticipates "the ideal city" of Henri Lefebvre, where inhabitance is to take precedence over habitat. "The ideal city," exclaims Lefebvre, "would be the *ephemeral city,* the perpetual *oeuvre* of the inhabitants, themselves mobile and mobilized for and by this *oeuvre.*"[72] Lefebvre envisions the city ideally, as Woolf envisions it de facto, emanating from a process of collective, interactive celebration.[73] To be sure (and this is a very big "but"), Lefebvre arrives at his vision via the will to unsettle industrial capitalism's totalitarian compartmentalization of space, whereas Woolf arrives at hers via her sense of the plasticity of individual human consciousness in shared space. His is a strategy for enabling citizens to seize control; hers is an acknowledgment, part anxious and part elated, of human uncontrol.[74] Under the circumstances it is bemusing that these opposite trajectories yield analogous images of urban life as aesthetic play. For Lefebvre would have felt nothing but righteous disapproval of the frivolity of capping the novel with Mrs. Dalloway's party after the suicide of her counterpart Septimus, even if Lefebvre had spotted the irony that Woolf directs toward Clarissa, that indeed Clarissa directs toward herself in those moods when she is overcome by a sense of her own triviality. Yet the festive moment, precisely because of its ironies of circumstance, is a logical culminating epitome of the London scene as the novel has defined it, and a fair anticipation of the ludic-ironic dimension of Lefebvre's utopianism too.

Woolf is even more sensitive than Joyce to the interplay between physical stimuli and mental life. Not by coincidence did she title several of her books after natural processes (*Night and Day, The Years,* and *The Waves*) and begin her last (*Between the Acts*) with a shard of conversation about the location of a cesspool.[75] Woolf's *flânerie* is wonderfully sensitive to the interchangeability of nature and *techne* in the lived experience of urban ecology. Take, for example, how the narrative imagines a stimulus form itself in the consciousness of a particular (male) character. First it is a mere "sound," a "frail quivering sound"; then a "voice" but inarticulate, "of no age or sex," as if "an ancient spring spouting from the earth"; then it becomes "a rusty pump," or rather "a wind-beaten tree," until at length it manifests itself as a "battered woman," a street singer, but reevoking as one attends to her words (an immemorial love lyric) the atavistic primordialism of a time "when the pavement was grass, when it was swamp," despite her being "opposite Regent's Park Tube station."[76] This sequence doubles as rendition of urban landscape-constructing consciousness and as ecofeminist critique of Peter Walsh's barely repressed longing for Clarissa, routed through a fantasy of landscape embodying itself as primordial woman singing of love.

The more assertively politicized Lefebvre would have seen at once through the class bias of such foregrounding of vicarious bourgeois pleasures and anxieties, Woolf's no less than Peter's. This is the upside of Lefebvre's reduction of cities to artifacts that ordinary citizens should be able to take back and play with. The downside is a disinterest in what Woolf perceives so well: the feel at ground-level experience of how personhood develops through semifortuitous confluence of people with each other and with physical environment, each shaping the other simultaneously. Woolf's vision of transpersonal inhabitance is by no means naively affirmative either, as the woman-pump-primordium fantasy begins to suggest. The neo-Whitmanian celebratory aspect of individuals montaging with others and with landscape is complicated by anxiety, sometimes bordering on panic, about how to keep ecstasy from producing self-annihilation or madness once the self's borders are felt to be permeable.[77]

Whitmanian Modernism:
William Carlos Williams as Bioregionalist

William Carlos Williams respected Whitman's "raw vigor" but grudgingly, as having made a crude stab at the vernacular poetics Williams aimed to do better.[78] He was also fascinated by Joyce, both by *Ulysses* and by the mythification of Dublin landscape in *Finnegans Wake* as a geomorphic couple of male earth and female river, which influenced Williams's personification of his own city[79] as a primordial couple of (female) landscape and (male) city. In his masterwork, *Paterson* (1946–1951, 1958), this dyad together with a traditional river-equals-flow-of-life symbolism and a Whitmanian fluidity in the persona (who is sometimes personal, sometimes the embodiment of the city) become the major structural constituents.

Very early in his career, Williams dreamed of writing an updated Whitmanian poem of the city. "Crossing the ferry / With the great towers of Manhattan before me," the poet-speaker sighs, "How shall I be a mirror to this modernity?" He felt intuitively that "Moscow's dignity" was no greater "than Passaic's dignity." Yet even after he broke away from conventionalism of voice and language and tempo, Williams remained for a long time—indeed, never ceased to be—an "imagist," an artist of vignettes:

> Leaves are grey green
> the glass broken, bright green
>
> . . . fattened there
> an eel
> in the water pipe—
>
> —a broken fringe of wooden and brick fronts
> above the city, fading out,
> beyond the watertank on stilts,
> an isolated house or two here and there,
> into the bare fields.

the last yarrow
on the gutter
white by the sandy
rainwater
★
Then unexpectedly
a small house with a soaring oak
leafless above it

Immediately after the last passage, he adds: "Someone should summarize these things / in the interest of local / government or how / a spotted dog goes up a gutter."[80] Which is as if to ask: "What purpose do these imagistic bits serve, anyhow, other than to become so many flies in amber?"

That Williams never shook off this quizzicality about whether his poetic would amount to anything more than a series of beginnings continued to be by turns a source of frustration, self-renewal, perspectival suppleness, and predictable mannerism. Meanwhile, his urban ecological imagination was refining itself at the microlevel. He learned how to render the abrupt juxtapositions created by the "second nature" of detritus and remnant growth (passage one), the visual foreshortening of urban niches (passage two), the unexpected excitement of open vistas however banal (passage five). He taught himself how to image the "fortuitous landscape of naturalized urban plants" (passage four) and the "vernacular" landscape of downscale neighborhoods "in the forgotten places of the city" (passage three) whose importance to urban ecology green landscape designers today stress in preference to the "'pedigreed' landscape" of formally dedicated curbsides and manicured parks.[81] He learned to use metaphor to convey symbiosis between human, biological, and artifactual, and also to parody that: learned how to turn people into trees or flowers or beasts and back again, to turn a tumbling sheet of paper into a man and back again. Above all, he adjusted and readjusted in hundreds of experimental short efforts his sense of the proportions, tonality, and directional movement of the relation, in urban settings, among human, built, natural. Let one extended example stand for all, "View of a Lake."[82]

Three scruffily clad children stand by a highway "beside the weed-grown / chassis / of a wrecked car," looking intently down a "waste of cinders" leading to "the railroad and / the lake." What might they be watching, the poem wonders. Its answer is simply to follow the line of their gaze downward past a sign "planted / by a narrow concrete / service hut / (to which runs / a sheaf of wires)":

> in the universal
> cinders beaten
> into crossing paths
>
> to form the front yard
> of a frame house
> at the right
>
> that looks
> to have been flayed
> Opposite
>
> remains a sycamore
> in leaf
> Intently fixed
>
> the three
> with straight backs
> ignore
>
> the stalled traffic
> all eyes
> toward the water

Whatever else this poem is about, it is about coming to terms with the place of nature in cities. The poem does not fully explain itself (we don't know what the kids are thinking, for instance), but it does show that something is there that matters (to them as well as the poet) that tends to get overlooked: you have to look past the traffic, the highway, the "flayed" house, the cinders, the railroad, down to the shore, over the shoulders of the children engaged in their at-first-mystifying vigil; and even at that you feel clued in more by your imagination of their intent than by the landscape itself. But the sense of how "nature" compels and asserts itself even under these bleak conditions, first for the children and then—infected by them—the speaker-*flâneur*, is also stressed. There are the weeds growing up through the car. The sycamore offsets the cindery yard and then montages with the "intently fixed" straight-backed children themselves. It's an antipastoral pastoral. The ruined landscape is the antithesis of anybody's lake country. "View of a lake?"—surely you jest. Whoever created that "view"—maybe the chil-drens' fathers assisted, who knows?—must have anaesthetized them-selves beforehand. But no matter how stomped down, the natural part of the landscape also has the capacity to reconstitute the rest, under cer-tain conditions. And it seems that for the kids at least there really *is* a view. Maybe that just confirms how pathetic they are, these tatter-demalions. But maybe the casual adult observer has missed something. Be that as it may, a poem like this establishes Williams as a poet of what green urbanists have somewhat euphemistically called the "unofficial countryside," the remnant landscapes of "cemeteries, hospital grounds, old churchyards and railway embankments," and abandoned quarries and other industrial sites where nature has reasserted itself.[83] Williams did not quite know what was to be done with these landscapes, but he was intent on reclaiming them for literature in a way that would rise above wishful sentimentality or knee-jerk revulsion.

The visual tableau of "View of a Lake" is only a five-finger exercise compared to *Paterson*, however.[84]

Paterson is nowhere near as controlled by its mythic design as *Ulysses*, much less by a narrative structure such as Woolf's in *Mrs. Dalloway*. In-deed, one of the poem's most distinctive features is repeated break-down: the frequency and insistence with which the speaker interrupts himself ("Give it up. Quit it. Stop writing" [p. 108]), confesses incompe-tence ("There is no direction. Whither? I / cannot say" [p. 17]), derides himself ("How strange you are, you idiot!" [p. 29]), opens himself up to the taunts of others ("Geeze, Doc, I guess it's all right / but what the hell does it mean?"). Such moments positively flaunt the quixoticism of what the poet has bound himself to do: to create a poem faithful to this place, to which he is committed but which he cannot without violently mixed feelings "love." "Say it, no ideas but in things" (p. 6): this, the most famous line Williams ever wrote, states the goal, and also the im-patience and frustration. "Not until I have made of it [the present as it is, in its plenitude] / will my sins be forgiven and my / disease cured,"

Book III extravagantly declares—immediately adding "in wax," one of many anticlimaxes that make light of the replica that the poem can only at best be (p. 145).

In order to achieve the unachievable, "the undisciplined power of the unimaginable poem,"[85] Williams stippled his pages with oddments from the archives of Paterson's history: Native American primordium and decline; grandiose early republican plans for Paterson as model city (by L'Enfant, who designed the national capitol) and as model of American industry (by Alexander Hamilton); sensational newspaper stories about freaks, ghosts, murders, fire, flood; and, amid lyrical and descriptive vignettes, dozens of competing voices of (mostly vernacular) contemporary characters both actual and imaginary, including slightly edited passages from a number of Williams's correspondents, who expose his shortcomings. A woman poet who sought his advice berates him for insensitivity, his friend and rival Ezra Pound patronizes him, his admiring younger townsman-poet Allen Ginsberg intimates he could teach Williams a thing or two about his own city. Amid this collage, Williams's "own" voice emerges as distinctly male (women are consistently associated with sex, earth, and Dr. P's muse), (hetero)sexist (poesis is imaged as wooing, consummation, marriage), and of the privileged classes ("among / the working classes SOME sort / of breakdown / has occurred"). Equally clear, though, is the poet's cognizance of these limitations, and with this his will to displace himself even more than he does from the center of things: "Why even speak of 'I,' he dreams, which / interests me almost not at all?" (p. 18).

Relative to all important predecessors in the epic vein except Pound's *Cantos*, *Paterson* is indeed more multigeneric and multivocal. "Whitman wants to be his world; Williams wants to know his," one critic sums up. "Almost everything that would go toward the building up of a portrait of Williams as a private person has been excluded," another agrees.[86] One sign of this is how *Paterson* undoes the "walker in the city" tradition on which Whitman, Joyce, and Woolf all rely to focus their panoramas at the site of individual consciousness. Only in Part II, where Dr. P takes a stroll around the park, does the poem do this more than fragmentarily. Again and again Williams disperses the *flâneur* into his various inputs. One way is for the poem to let itself get hijacked by all sorts of other voices, living and dead, oral and archival. Some are even seemingly repudiated voices, like the untutored immigrant evangelist orator in the park whose harangue eventually takes over much of Part II, who overrides P's disdain and disgust to transform at least fleetingly both into the voice of the waterfall and into an image of the poet's own ineffective speech.

A particularly striking instance occurs in "The Library" (III.iii). Reading about Paterson's flood of 1902 precipitates an inner flood, "a counterpart, of reading" (p. 130). Up from this roil of environmental unconscious burbles the memory of a face-off between a surly-pathetic baby-carrying man and another figure, likely P himself, over the man's dog, which had been put down after the other reported him for biting.[87] The man insists "He never hurt / anybody" (p. 131). The poem gyrates wildly back to a snippet of pre-Columbian time (the gigantic sachem Pogatticut buried with his favorite dog, ritually sacrificed for the occasion), then to a flood-provoked fantasy of the biting dog's demise, mythically rendered:

> Pursued by the whirlpool-mouths, the dog
> descends toward Acheron . Le Néant
> . the sewer
>   a dead dog
>   turning
> upon the water:
>   Come yeah, Chi Chi!
>   turning
> as he passes .
>
> It is a sort of chant, a sort of praise, a
> peace that comes of destruction:
>   to the teeth,
> to the very eyes
>   (cut lead)
>   I bin nipped
> hundreds of times. He never done anybody any
> harm .
>   helpless .
>
>   You had him killed on me. (pp. 132–133)

Truly this is the Blakean grain of sand that opens up to infinity. At first it seems almost slapstick, comically primitivizing the dogged dog-lover for his obstinate fetish, but on second thought less a cartoon of him than of T. S. Eliot's multimythic allusiveness, and in a way that turns against both Eliot *and* the bitten Dr. P by giving what seemed like an Apeneck Sweeney or Archie Bunker-like fellow the last word, granting him pathos ("helpless"), even granting him a certain antique dignity (cut lead eyes are stone dead eyes, but also resonant artifacts), granting status even to the cur itself as a ritual sacrifice descending not into a mere sewer but "Acheron," "Le Néant." It's impossible to disaggregate the farce, the tour de force, the regretful amends. The one thing that *is* unmistakably clear is the desire to break down fixed boundaries between man, poet, dog; present time, past time, eternal time.

What Williams permits to happen here is the wholesome production of disorder Richard Sennett offers as key to a reinvigorated civic life. Sennett deplores the "reaction of disengagement" to the extreme differences one encounters in cities, claiming that it has "annihilated the human value of complexity, even in a city where differences are an overwhelming sociological fact." Sennett calls for policies of multiple and fluid land use and spatial distribution of city activities that would "increase the complexity of confrontation and conflict in the city, not polarize it." In this way, "the aggression, still there, would channel itself into paths that allow at least mutual survival." Sennett thinks it would be better if (genteel) urbanites felt more uncomfortable than they do "and began to experience a sense of dislocation in their lives."[88] So did Williams. Like Sennett, for the very reason that he recognizes in himself a will to disengagement, Williams lets the hostile confrontation get under his persona's skin and play itself through to the end that citizen and dog (in a rerun of Joyce's "Cyclops" chapter perhaps?) have standing in his panorama, without the cheap grace of reconciliation.

Through such passages, Williams creates an ecopoetics of the city. Even city-averse readers notice this. Wendell Berry, one of literary bioregionalism's leading voices today, praises Williams for "his use of the art of writing as an instrument by which a man may arrive in his place and maintain himself there." His poems, Berry adds, "have helped to satisfy me of the possibility of life wherever I have lived."[89] The passage just quoted shows the precision of the phrase "writing as an instrument by which a man may arrive in his place and maintain himself there." For it seems entirely plausible that precisely the quest and discipline of looking for poetry in the shards of quotidian place-based experience was the means by which that encounter was retrieved from the netherworld of environmental unconscious to serve as an intimation of recognition and connectedness with person, animal, thing, and place across class and time barriers—a connectedness all the more notable for being so chancy.

Williams's perception of the instability of actual places and place sense is itself basic to the contemporary understanding of reinhabitation, which as Gary Snyder puts it, must be built on the awareness that a

> place will have been grasslands, then conifers, then beech and elm . . . And then it will be cultivated, paved, sprayed, dammed, graded, built up. But each is only for a while, and that will be just another set of lines on the palimpsest. The whole earth is a great tablet holding the multiple overlaid new and ancient traces of the swirl of forces . . . A place on earth is a mosaic within larger mosaics—the land is all small places, all precise tiny realms replicating larger and smaller patterns.[90]

Snyder is talking about the backcountry here, but he could have been describing Paterson. "Song of Myself," *Ulysses,* and *Mrs. Dalloway* all tend in their own ways to arrest their outer landscapes at a moment in time. *Paterson* imagines a place where both outer and inner landscapes have been in motion for more than 200 years. Williams has to a remarkable extent anticipated the bioregional premise that however "counter to modern appearances, even urban areas sprang into existence, and most often continue to depend, on environmental circumstances that lie just below the level of our awareness."[91]

At the end of the poem as originally conceived (IV.iii), another man-dog-poet configuration suddenly occurs, this time in the form of a sea-bather and his pet, again with intent to transfigure an ordinary moment in the face of another possible water-death climax toward which the poem seems to have been tending. This time the poem takes a more tranquil turn as the swimmer—a sly collage of Odysseus, Whitman, and

Williams (a.k.a. Noah Faitoute Paterson)—climbs out, suns himself, sleeps, puts on faded overalls, samples a beach plum, and trudges inland, toward Whitman's old-age home of Camden (as Williams later explained), implying continuation of the epic quest from Whitman to Williams, and beyond.[92]

As the self-consciousness of this ending suggests, Williams knew full well that he was not the sole twentieth-century poet of the city to carry on Whitmanian poetics in a more "democratic" idiom than his nemesis Eliot. Before *Paterson,* Hart Crane's *The Bridge* (1930) had in some ways been a more faithfully Whitmanian epic than *Paterson,* more idealizing in spirit, more affirming of technology, grounded in Whitman's own city and in the signature device of the Manhattan-Brooklyn link: Crane's bridge the descendent of Whitman's ferry. Langston Hughes, Louis Zukovsky, Charles Reznikoff, Allen Ginsberg, George Oppen, Charles Olson, LeRoi Jones/Amiri Baraka, and Frank O'Hara are just some of the contemporary and younger poets of urban imagination influenced by Whitman and/or Williams himself. But Williams's experiment in urban ecopoetics stands as a distinctive combination of attainments.

First, for its creation of a post-Whitmanian transpersonal persona alternately coexisting side by side with citizens and physical environment, and montaging into each or being sharply disputed by them so that the executive control of the flow of the poem is interrupted and even usurped.

Second, for its imagination of the mutuality of physical environment and human action—not just as it obtains at a single moment but also historically, from pre-Columbian times, to Dutch colonization, to Paterson's designation as a model industrial village, to its subsequent history as a site of capitalist greed and labor agitation, to its present condition as depressed, polluted outback of greater New York. Paterson is seen continually to have been formed and reformed, with those who lived here constituted by the place as well as vice versa: the topography underlying the human map, the impact of natural disaster, the landmarks of the central waterway and falls (which dominate the last scene of Williams's *Autobiography* too). "When you have read *Paterson* you know for the rest of your life what it is like to be a waterfall," wrote Randall Jarrell. "Williams' knowledge of plants and animals," he adds, "is surprising for its range and intensity; and he sets them down in the midst of the real weather of the world."[93] Like contemporary green design theory, which starts from the ecosystem model, Williams too believes that "'landscape' does not end where cities begin" and imagines "the city as a highly distinctive addition to an expanding catalogue of natural habitats."[94]

Third, *Paterson* shows a bioregionalist grasp of its city in relation to its vicinity. Williams reflects—without, it seems, being directly influenced by—the central insight of new regionalists like Lewis Mumford, whose *The Culture of Cities* (1938) appeared on the eve of *Paterson*'s crystallization: "the *city* as [itself] a component of the ecosystem," not distinct from hinterland as in old-style country-city anthitheses.[95] The geography of Paterson takes in the whole Passaic watershed, from the Ramapo hills to the river's entry into the sea. The story told by the poem's historical geography starts diffusely (marking the presences of Indian, Dutch, and English in the larger region); then focuses on the nodal point of early national Paterson, a vigorous albeit troubled self-contained community into the early twentieth century; then recognizes its decline from "a small metropolis at the center of things" to the grimy periphery of "both Newark and New York, destroying the kind of cultural autonomy which it had."[96]

This is not to say that Williams set out to write a work of "urban ecology" any more than Whitman did. His first priority was to write poetry; and his first priority as a poet was to devise a distinctive American poetic idiom. But in following through on his second priority as poet, which was to write a poem about "my city" that would characterize its distinctive features past and present, Williams displayed a keen sense of certain "ecological" relationships, even where these were not his main subject. Book IV, canto i of *Paterson*, for example, is given over to an "idyl" of a sophisticated New Yorker, Corydon, attempting to seduce her working-class Patersonian masseuse, Phyllis, with P competing unsuccessfully for Phyllis's attention. This sequence has more to do with "abnormal passion" signifying the "poetic" issue of "America" being "unnaturally" tempted (Phyllis) or frustrated (P) by Europeanized high culture than it does with anything else.[97] But what largely drives the choice of configuration is the "regional logic" of New York as magnet for the New Jersey periphery, and the situation in which this places Phyllis, who resents both Corydon's more rarefied indirections and her father's redneck bullying. No less than Faulkner, to be discussed in Chapter 5, Williams made *Paterson* echo the anxiety of the regionalist thinkers of his day at the seduction of "indigenous" community culture by the "modern inorganic siren" of metropolitanism, as Benton MacKaye called it, such that Paterson was threatened with becoming sucked into what Mumford called "the vast amorphous urbanoid wasteland that stretches between Camden and Jersey City."[98]

Williams's fourth contribution to the literature of urban reinhabitation, certainly the point at which he most assertively revises Whitman, is his tough love of Paterson. Williams was both fiercely loyal to and perpetually discontent with his grimy, down-at-the-heel city. He claimed that "the whole theme of *Paterson*" was "the contrast between the mythic beauty of the Falls and Mountain and the industrial hideousness." "But they haven't been able to lick us," he immediately added: "I must be an artist in my own bailiwick—despite the conditions which make it hard."[99] The result was a poem that reads mainly like the "before" part of success stories of contemporary urban restoration.[100] *Paterson*'s most extended affirmative-lyric sequence, which poetizes a sentimental 1901 Currier-and-Ives-style reminiscence of "Old Paterson" as a delightful industrial village (pp. 192–197), occurs only after such nostalgia has been discredited and interrupted by prose passages that stress more sordid realities.

Williams's diagnostic culminates in a complex image of urban pathology in Book IV, canto ii. This canto develops an analogy between medicine and finance: radium cures the disease of cancer as credit cures the disease of capitalism, which is money (more specifically usury). At first sight, this seems one of the poem's more bafflingly repellent sequences—especially the financial themes, which draw on local socialist tracts (p. 180) and Ezra Pound's diatribes (p. 185). The canto makes more sense, however, when one thinks of it as resting on an environmental history-based vision of Paterson as a community despoiled by economic rapacity and industrial blight: this "rusty county of the world," Allen Ginsberg calls it in a letter Williams here inserts, "whose gastanks, junkyards, fens of the alley, millways, funeral parlors, rivervisions" have become "images white-woven in [our] very beards" (pp. 172–173). The city is a uranium atom "always breaking down / to lead" (p. 177): the color of that inferno-bound dog-owner's eyes. Allow it

"LOCAL control of local purchasing / power" and it becomes radiant; deny it and it becomes cancerous, "spreading slums" (p. 185). One of Williams's notes for this canto identifies cancer as "the typical disease" of the local hospital, which was his hospital and the site of the opening scene, a lecture on "atomic fission." "My father / died of it," Williams adds: "I think we'll get it in / the next 25 years."[101] Overall the canto is less about literal disease than social cancer, including that of the hospital policy of charging poor people a surgeon's fee rather than "buffering it into the locality" (p. 181), but it preserves the force of the medical metaphor by making Marie Curie the poem's strongest example of creative genius working in obscurity.

During the last half-century, *Paterson* has "become part of Paterson's history," influencing the partial restoration of the mill area and the museumization of the postindustrial city.[102] Williams might have been pleased to be an agent of reform, appalled by the element of commodification, and unsurprised that the shape of the city has continued to change. As for Blake, so for Williams: the poetic vision of community and community itself are always under threat, always under construction.[103]

Later Trajectories

Whitman, Joyce, and Woolf complicated the figure of the *flâneur/euse* by transpersonalizing it from an isolated self to a more ecological self. Williams further weakens the control of the nominal organizing consciousness by putting other subjectivities in more aggressive competition with it and by stressing the power of platial materiality and history over consciousness as such: the power to interrupt, disarrange, override, fragment, and indeed sometimes positively efface it. Except for *Finnegans Wake*, Williams also disarranges his represented city to a greater degree. It is less clear at any moment where, when, and what the city is. With these complementary destabilizations also comes a greater range of possible moods, from despair to slapstick. Henceforth the urban eco-*flâneur* or *flâneuse* will be even more conscious than otherwise of the wishful and ad hoc nature of literary attempts to formulate holistic urban visions and to negotiate anything like a secure relation between the single individual with urban community or terrain—but no less intent on trying nonetheless, and in fact more variously equipped than before to generate provisional if not definitive visions of urban reinhabitation. A short look at a few examples will give a flavor of the diverse results: from Frank O'Hara (a post-Williams New York poet), Joy Harjo (a poet of Native American displacement), and Gary Snyder (the most self-conscious bioregionalist of the three). The first poem celebrates in playful deadpan the happenstance trivia of a Manhattan walk:

> the strange embrace of the ankle's
> lock
> on the pavement
> squared like mausoleums
> but cheerful

"The country is no good for us," the speaker insists,

> there's nothing
> to bump into
> or fall apart glassily
> there's not enough
> poured concrete
> and brassy
> reflections
> the wind now takes me to
> The Narrows
> and I see it rising there
> New York
> greater than the Rocky Mountains
> (O'Hara, "Walking")[104]

This poem knows it's being silly, as it lets the wind whisk it about from the microannoyance of a cinder in the walker's eye to the macrosublime of the concrete Rocky Mountains. Cheerful mausoleums? The hymn to poured concrete is slightly outrageous. The poem seems to want to be read at least two ways at once, both anticipated by Williams. One, as insouciant false consciousness: it's such a nice day that to this fellow who can't imagine himself anywhere else even the annoyances feel good and the concrete sublime. Two, as a perverse urban pastoral: I know this will drive Wordsworthians up the wall, but skyscrapers are greater than mountains. Either way, however, this is a poem about the constitution of (the experience of) the city as a process of action of wind and light. The "it" that rises at the end of the poem is at once "wind" and "New York," because for all practical purposes "New York"—this version of it—is *produced* by wind. So although the poem, in the tradition of Whitman's "Keep your splendid silent sun" (p. 313, l. 20), makes the gesture of rejecting outback for Manhattan, the comic extravagance with which it embraces the Manhattan of concrete is produced by the "watery and clear and windy" feel of this exuberant day.

Joy Harjo's "Anchorage" is the reciprocal of "Walking" in that it seems to want to efface and dissolve metropolis back into primal matter:[105]

> This city is made of stone, of blood, and fish.
> There are Chugatch Mountains to the east
> and whale and seal to the west.
> It hasn't always been this way, because glaciers
> who are ice ghosts create oceans, carve earth
> and shape this city here, by the sound.
> They swim backwards in time.

Indeed, the great earthquake of 1964, 8.5 on the Richter scale, did just that.[106] From a Native American standpoint, seismic volatility is not aberrant but part of cosmic order, a trickster spirit's joke on settler culture complacency.

> . . . underneath the concrete
> is the cooking earth,
>   and above that, air
> which is another ocean, where spirits we can't see
> are dancing   joking   getting full
> on roasted caribou

First people must reframe the city in this fashion, as the fragile plaything of spirit/nature, in order to survive; otherwise, all that's left is the blankness of "unimagined darkness":

> On a park bench we see someone's Athabascan
> grandmother, folded up, smelling like 200 years
> of blood and piss, her eyes closed against some
> unimagined darkness, where she is buried in an ache
> in which nothing makes
> sense.

As they pass the derelict, the speaker and her companion transform a Whitmanian moment of fleeting empathy ("Miserable! I do not laugh at your oaths nor jeer you" [p. 43, l. 307]) into a more intimate encounter (somebody's grandmother from a particular tribe, her plight the outcome of centuries of exploitation), and this identification helps them breathe and walk, to restore some sense of ecocultural ground: to strengthen their feel for the clouds above and the ocean nearby, to *become* the ocean even:

> . . . to speak of her home and claim her
> as our own history, and know that our dreams
> don't end here, two blocks away from the ocean
> where our hearts still batter away at the muddy shore.

At this point it seems as if the poem might become a "back to the land" narrative, but it doesn't. On the contrary, speaker and companion give no sign of forsaking urban precincts. The poem ends with a jailhouse story told to a group of "mostly Native and Black men" by one who had been shot at and missed eight times outside a liquor store:

> Everybody laughed at the impossibility of it,
> but also the truth. Because who would believe
> the fantastic and terrible story of all our survival
> those who were never meant
> to survive?

The friend's escape is the counterpart of the opening reminiscence of solid-seeming modern Anchorage's devastation. Who would have thought either one was possible, given the relentless efficiency of settlement culture's architectural and enforcement regimes? Although the poem is careful not to draw any grander conclusion from such reversals than a grim laugh at the dominator's expense, obviously it is committed to the thought that for cities to be livable—*and* understandable—built environment must be understood as embedded in natural process.

So too Gary Snyder's repossession of the city in "Night Song of the Los Angeles Basin."[107] Snyder reimagines a city of paths both industrial (freeway traffic laid out in "knot-tying light paths") and nonhuman ("winding pocket-gopher tunnels"). As with "Anchorage," but more peacefully, the cityscape begins to dissolve:

> Houses with green watered gardens
> Slip under the ghost of the dry chaparral,
>
>> Ghost
>> shrine to the L.A. River
>> The *jinja* [shrine] that never was there
>> is there.
>> Where the river debouches
>> the place of the moment
>> of trembling and gathering and giving
>> so that lizards clap hands there
>> —just lizards
>> come pray, saying
>> "please give us health and long life."

Then, after a momentary interruption ("slash of calligraphy of freeways of cars"),

>> Into the pools of the channelized river
>> the Goddess in tall rain dress
>> tosses a handful of meal.

This hybrid, possibly ad hoc ceremony (a Native deity? a Buddhist ritual? a stately Angelina feeding fish?) confirms the potency of the nature
held under restraint as Snyder makes it dream its way to the reader
through the maze of freeways and confirms the obliviousness of the
"godlings" who "ride by in Rolls Royce" on gourmandizing sorties.
Whereas Harjo seizes on first nature as a weapon for combatting metropolitan alienness, Snyder imagines a reinvigoration, responsive to
local plurality of cultures, by recentering the vista from freeway to watershed, and completely away from his or any other single subject position in the process. The perceiver relinquishes selfhood wholly to the
perceived. Snyder's identification of Los Angeles in terms of its river,
not only recalling Williams but also catching hold of a key principle of
green urban design, which advocates rehabilitation of riverways and respect for underground streams.[108] This is Snyder's version of Frost's
"A Brook in the City." Indeed, "watershed" is the bioregional movement's most luminous and fundamental defining image. More on it in
Chapter 8.

Despite their divergences, these poems by O'Hara, Harjo, and Snyder are all reinhabitory efforts: efforts to imagine a city/nature as a
livable, or at least survivable, habitat. But no less a part of the post-
Williams era, and present around the edges of each poem, particularly
"Anchorage," is the anxiety that such visions might be wishful. So it is
with John Edgar Wideman's quasi-autobiographical writer-protagonist
Cudjoe in *Philadelphia Fire* as, roaming the city in desultory pursuit of
his film project, he boozily views the city from the panoptical height of
the art museum steps:

He is sighting down a line of lighted fountains that guide his eye to
City Hall. This is how the city was meant to be viewed. Broad av-
enues bright spokes of wheel radiating from a glowing center. No
buildings higher than Billy Penn's hat atop City Hall. Scale and pattern fixed forever. Clarity, balance, a perfect understanding between
the parts. Night air thick and bad but he's standing where he should
and the city hums this dream of itself into his ear and he doesn't believe it for an instant but wonders how he managed to stay away so
long.

I belong to you, the city says. This is what I was meant to be. You can grasp the pattern. Make sense of me. Connect the dots. I was constructed for you. Like a field of stars I need you to bring me to life. My names, my gods poised on the tip of your tongue. All you have to do is speak and you reveal me, complete me.

. . . From this vantage point in the museum's deep shadow in the greater darkness of night it seems an iron will has imposed itself on the shape of the city . . . Cudjoe fine-tunes for a moment the possibility that someone, somehow, had conceived the city that way. A miraculous design. A prodigy that was comprehensible. He can see a hand drawing the city. An architect's tilted drafting board, instruments for measuring, for inscribing right angles, arcs, circles. The city is a faint tracery of blue, barely visible blood lines in a newborn's skull. No one has used the city yet. No one has pushed a button to start the heart pumping.

He can tell thought had gone into the design. And a person must have stood here, on this hill, imagining this perspective. Dreaming the vast emptiness into the shape of a city. In the beginning it hadn't just happened, pell-mell. People had planned to live and prosper here. Wear the city like robe and crown.

The founders were dead now. Buried in their wigs, waistcoats, swallowtail coats, silk hose clinging to their plump calves. A foolish old man flying a kite in a storm.[109]

This is a tour de force of deconstructive urbanism. Cudjoe is thoroughly seasoned, self-conscious, credentialed in the art of *flânerie*. He knows the city's history—the original geometric design, the defunct ordinance prohibiting buildings higher than Penn's statue—knows too the "right" point from which to view that order. The art museum's steps are Philadelphia's equivalent of John Denham's Cooper's Hill, of Sarah Wentworth Morton's Beacon Hill—just right for the kind of Neoclassical prospect piece whose controlled *concordia discors* would have pleased the kite-flying old man (Ben Franklin). But, warns the passage, the dream of urban order is a trick. This is no simple protest against African-American disenfranchisement, though it is partly that. Cudjoe has the requisite education, sophistication, and conceptual tools to make a place for himself in upper- middle-class America if he should want it. The deeper idea is that the whole idea of a designed city is hubristic. When you try to implement your design, what you get is the MOVE incident, the tragedy that has drawn Cudjoe here: the police eradicating a fractious Afrocentric cult by dropping a bomb that leveled a whole block. Ironically, this retaliation was mandated by the city's first African-American administration, which now considers the city ungovernable. Cudjoe is the black bourgeois torn between the dream of reinhabitation ("I belong to you, the city says") and the sense of its impossibility. The passage's bottom line is not far different from the weary note Barry Cullingworth strikes at the end of his history of U.S. environmental (and other forms of) planning: "There are huge areas where unequivocal solutions of environmental problems simply do not exist."[110] Not that this makes Cullingworth—or Wideman—any less desirous to see alleviated those obstinate problems of squalor, disorganization, bureaucratic gridlock, and waste.

Although this passage focuses on built environment, the decayed legacy of a grand architectural design, the natural ingredients of the cityscape—especially night's magic and the beckoning stars—conspire to produce the seductive hallucination. The climax, significantly, is the vision of the city as the anthropomorphized image of the skull of a not-yet-alive baby, either just born or (still, after centuries) only emerging from the womb. Wideman here recycles that unkillable tradition of naturalizing city-body tropes—Blake's London as Albion's bosom, Wordsworth's London as the mighty heart, the "dumb beautiful ministers" of Whitman's New York cityscape, the "polypus" of Patrick Geddes's London, T. S. Eliot's etherized patient in "The Love Song of J. Alfred Prufrock" (later recalled by Cudjoe).[111] Wideman/Cudjoe deconstructs the whole image-making process, whereby cities are personified in user-friendly ways as people or at least biologized in user-friendly ways as organisms. In this passage, both design-think and nature/body-think seem equally monstrous, delusional, hubristic.

As the grotesque baby image also hints, though, the passage makes a certain appeal to the "natural" over against the imposed or conditioned or constructed. In a 1984 interview, during his Wyoming residence after his Philadelphia years (but before *Philadelphia Fire*), Wideman made this provocative response to an interviewer who asked him about the influence of the West on his conception of space:

In a city, things that you see are man-made things—man-made structures, buildings, lamp posts, street lights—and you're circumscribed
by those. They're on a man scale. Even a skyscraper is just a hundred
floors; the same as one floor, only a hundred stacked on top of each
other. There's also that temporary quality in spite of the density of a
city and the number of people. Sometimes I can look straight
through it—it doesn't exist. I get more of that sense of temporariness
out here . . . you can go five minutes in any direction and [Laramie]
is gone—absolutely gone; it doesn't exist.[112]

Although the passage from *Philadelphia Fire* does not show the overt interest of Harjo, Snyder, and O'Hara in thematizing the symbiotic ten-
sions of city/nature, its skepticism toward utopian urbanism owes
something to the awareness of an excluded elsewhere.

But what if elsewhere is not an option? Such is indeed the case for
many of the novel's characters: for the woman Cudjoe pesters for news
of the MOVE survivors, for the protégée he recalls from his school-
teaching days, for J. B. the Penn-educated, Vietnam-damaged panhan-
dler. As Wideman realized, and our other writers also, environmental
connectedness requires going beyond vicarious sorties to fuller inter-
change with the lives of the entrapped, with environmental determinism in all its forms—and deciding just how far one is willing to go in
sharing that lot. To this we turn next.

Chapter 4

Discourses of Determinism

> Places and landscapes are ideas set in stone that like it or not, we have to act in.
>
> —Tim Cresswell, *In Place*

> We live in an age in which the impact of materialized forces is well-nigh irresistible; the spiritual nature is overwhelmed by the shock. The tremendous and complicated development of our material civilization, the multiplicity and variety of our social forms, the depth, subtlety and sophistication of our mental cogitations, gathered, multiplied and phantasmagorically disseminated as they are by these other agencies—the railroad, the express and post-office, the telegraph, telephone, the newspaper and, in short, the whole art of printing and distributing—have so combined as to produce what may be termed a kaleidoscopic glitter, a dazzling and confusing showpiece which is much more apt to weary and undo than to enlighten and strengthen the observing mind. It produces a sort of intellectual fatigue by which we see the ranks of the victims of insomnia, melancholy, and insanity recruited.
>
> —Theodore Dreiser, *Jennie Gerhardt*

> They do not wish that they were otherwise.
> Perhaps they know that creature feet may press
> only a few earth inches at a time,
> that earth is anywhere earth.
>
> —Gwendolyn Brooks, "Horses Graze"

Reinhabitation presupposes voluntary commitment to place; but not all are free to choose. Indeed, toxic discourse claims the opposite: you are more entrapped than you think in a place more dangerous than you think. It too urges a take-back-the-place ethic, but not on the premise that place-connected peoples are advantaged as such, but that peoples' lives, especially those of nonelites, are inevitably emplaced.

Environmental determinism is apt to seem counterintuitive to those who live above subsistence level. Liberal democracy teaches us to regard people as free agents. Socialist theory, while purporting to demystify free agency, teaches us to believe that human collectives can transform society. Modernization's inexhaustible inventiveness reinforces faith in human power to control environment, notwithstanding technological bungling and "natural" disaster. Yet many who hold these views also place credence in, for example, the power of biogeographical influences to construct human destinies, through regional biotic advantage, through "ecological colonization," or through mass-scale scourges like AIDS—from which standpoint "nature" begins to reassume a kind of fatality—as well as in the power of the "second nature" of a socially "advantaged" or "disadvantaged" environment to shape people more than they shape it.

Although the theory of people and cultures as ecocontextual products may seem, and sometimes be, a pretext for ethnocentricity, imperialism, and racism (with Third Reich doctrines of *Heimat* and *Lebensraum* commonly offered as the example par excellence), it has also, no less strikingly, been invoked as an antidote *to* these, the counterthrust being to exonerate nonwestern cultures from inherent inferiority by ascribing any "backwardness" to climate and geography.[1] Even some who find "environmental determinism" anathema as doctrine may prefer it as an explanation for such conundrums as why standardized test scores of African-American children are lower than those of their white counterparts.

The forms of deterministic imagination treated in this chapter are sharply discrepant: the sense of environment as exercising a tragically blighting force (sections one and two); the neoromantic counterconception of such force as productive energy (section three); and the envisagement of acquiescence to environmental and cultural limits as a necessary ground condition for art and community (section four). The movement, then, will be from determinism as forced constraint to determinism as submission to discipline in identification with the oppressed.

From Herodotus to Montesquieu, character has often been thought to be produced by location. But not until systematic methods of scientific and social observation converged with western journalism and fiction to discover documentary "realism" during the 1800s did it become possible to imagine in detail the construction of character and behavior

by circumstance. In the first half of the nineteenth century, a key catalyst was systematization of public health theory thanks to the emerging
field of statistics and the "sanitarian" theory that epidemic disease was
caused by dirt and bad housing. This made possible a systematic account of social behavior as observance of socioenvironmental norms.[2]
In the later nineteenth century, especially influential was the adoption
of evolutionary theory as a model for human history, such that humanity became conceived as the product of long biogeological processes
and societies as macrocosms comprised of interdependent assemblages
of specialized organisms.[3] The extent to which natural selection was reflection as opposed to perpetrator of the social thought of its day will be
debated until the end of time. That Darwinian science partially res-
onated with prevalent social determinist attitudes is certain,[4] though,
also typically for his day, it was no less rooted in antecedent traditions
of natural theology.[5] The century's creative writers, likewise, probed
and tested with increasing fascination the notion that human communities were determined by inheritance and / or environment.[6]

As we shall see, the literature of industrialization has tended to worry
more about determinism than that which has focused on rural scenes,
owing to the force of traditional liberal beliefs in the corruptibility of
human institutions relative to natural law and in the countryside as a
space of refreshment. But what especially stands out is neither a simple
city-country opposition nor a simple opposition between tragic and ac-
quiescent visions of determinism. The common denominator is not
"Environmental determinism is bad" but "These lives, determined as
they may be, count for more than statistics."

Urban Fiction from Dickens through Wright

Charles Dickens was the first major creative writer in the English language to explore the full repertoire of modern urban "problems."[7] He
anticipated by more than half a century Georg Simmel's insight that
great cities produce higher degrees of idiosyncratic differentiation
than one finds in traditional small communities.[8] Hence Pecksniff,
Micawber, Fagin, Carker, Podsnap, Wegg—that fecund menagerie of
grotesques who bear out Emerson's second law of experience: that persons are prisoners of temperament, "a certain uniform tune which the

revolving barrel of the music-box must play."[9] No novelist of the early industrial era evoked more powerfully the sense of the city impressing itself on its human denizens for better and for worse: its exuberance, its abrupt contrasts, its labyrinthine stultification, its grime.

Particularly in Dickens's later novels houses, neighborhoods, factories, and landscapes of diverse sorts become scenes of confinement. The abandoned mineshaft down which Stephen Blackpool falls and fatally injures himself in *Hard Times* (1854) retroencapsulates the prison of his whole adult life within the Midlands factory town that in a series of cruel, stupid maneuvers has extruded him only to insist that there is no escape. In *Bleak House* (1853) the plot turns on Lady Dedlock's reunion with her long-dead lover at his pauper's grave in a filthy London alley. At the level of individual behavior, this is the opposite of a "determined" action, a willed rebellion against role; but by resolving the mystery of the heroine's identity (she is the child of their union) and embracing what she once disowned, Lady Dedlock's action programmatically demonstrates—almost theorem-like—the interdependence of gentry and lower depths, and of people with physical environment. The fog that pervades the London scenes is not just a symbol of legal obfuscation of social pathology; it is part of "a literal economy of filth and disease." London fogs of the 1850s were aggravated, as here, when the wind blew "the wrong way," westward back through the more affluent districts instead of carrying the noxious vapors through the poorer neighborhoods and out the Thames estuary. The denouement is presaged by smallpox spread from the vicinity of the lover's rotting corpse by a pathetically degraded sweeper-waif who infects the still-disowned daughter, one of the few respectable characters willing to treat him kindly.[10]

Little Dorrit (1857) is the ne plus ultra of the carceral city. After an opening sequence that reduces Marseilles to the synecdoche of its sweltering prison, Dickens turns to London, where the defining institution is the Marshalsea. The protagonist, Arthur Clennam, is greeted upon returning home after a twenty-year absence by the prospect of "fifty thousand lairs surround[ing] him where people lived so unwholesomely, that fair water put into their crowded homes on Saturday night, would be corrupt on Sunday morning . . . Miles of close wells and pits of houses, where the inhabitants gasped for air, stretched far away toward every point of the compass. Through the heart of the town a deadly sewer ebbed and flowed, in the place of a fine fresh river." Clennam fantasizes that even the dead may well "pity themselves for their old places of imprisonment." One of the worst places is his dilapidated family house, "so dingy as to be all but black," down "a narrow alley leading to the river, where a wretched little bill, FOUND DROWNED, was weeping on the wet wall." Housebound in it for decades, bound to a ferociously invariant regime, dwells Clennam's half-paralyzed, totally bigoted pretended mother, who has reduced his will to paste while hers has turned to stone.[11]

The title character, Clennam's eventual bride in one of the most troubled of all Victorian "happy endings,"[12] is equally underactualized: the junior partner in a parent-child relationship hardly less lethal than the Clennams for the fact that it is more loving. Amy Dorrit is psychologically as well as symbolically "the child of the Marshalsea," born there soon after her father was arrested for debt. Prison is the one home she has known; her identity revolves around ministering to her father, who has found his by embracing the role of "father of the Marshalsea," patriarch of a social pyramid that imitates the deference structure of the larger society. Nowhere in Dickens is there a more striking instance than this father-daughter pair of what J. Hillis Miller has called "the process of Mithridatean acclimatization whereby a person can become accustomed to an environment which would be intolerable to anyone else."[13]

Little Amy is redeemed from total self-incarceration by Sunday rambles with a kindly turnkey. As a young woman, she refreshes herself with the view from the Iron (Southwark) Bridge over the Thames, but the very exuberance of this modest self-liberation makes her feel guilty: "to see the river, and so much sky, and so many objects, and such change and motion. Then to go back, you know, and find him in the same cramped place." When Clennam urges her to stay, she insists "My place is there. I am better there" (p. 262).[14] Second nature has so constructed her that though she instinctively hankers after first nature she cannot bear to acknowledge it, especially when it becomes even faintly eroticized. She must flee back to prison to recoup her identity. Arthur knows better, but not much: he fails to perceive Amy's suppressed feelings about him because his own repression of his own favorite scene of pastoral pleasure interposes—the self-denying taboo with which he invested the Meagles' charming abode upstream, when he resolved not to fall in love with their daughter.

In such ways Dickens constructs psychic landscapes to match urban environment, where "nature is buried invisibly behind a thick surface of roads, streets, buildings, signs, values, meanings."[15]

In the long run, *Little Dorrit* refuses to succumb to the determinist vision that haunts it, as Dickens novels always do, though this one is an especially instructive case owing to the exceptional dreariness of its cityscapes, its unrelieved cynicism toward public institutions, and the number of characters whose wills are dominated by forces outside them.[16] For one thing, the characters do not admit to a single principle of classification. A number of them are what they are for whatever reason and remain so in any setting, impervious to context, as essentialized syndromes: Rigaud the shabby Mephistopheles, Doyce the honest inventor-engineer, Mr. F's aunt the bizarrely consistent incarnation of— one can only guess—the suppressed resentment of her nephew's widow, Arthur's twice-spurned fiancée. Amy's timidity is conditioned by prison experience, including separation from virtually all that smacks of first nature,[17] but her older siblings, Fanny and Tip, grow up pretty much according to their characters as small children before their prison years. Arthur's emotional underdevelopment apparently has everything to do with his weak father and the tyrannical woman he thinks is his mother, not with his urban boyhood as such, much less his young manhood in China. Mrs. Clennam was, by her own account anyhow, the artifact of her Calvinist upbringing, more statistically plausible for late seventeeth-century Edinburgh than for late eighteenth-century London.

At a number of points, furthermore, *Little Dorrit* pointedly questions the determinist position. Several of the book's obvious antimodels are determinists: Mrs. Clennam, the providentialist; Mrs. General, the governess whose ruling principle of never forming opinions becomes a weapon for governing the Dorrits; and Mrs. Merdle, who fortuitously parodies the Amy-and-Arthur-on-the-bridge scene with her insistence that she is "a child of nature if I could but show it," but, alas, "society suppresses us and dominates us"—at which her pet parrot laughs (p. 240). These characters form a mocking chorus against which the melodrama of Amy's and Arthur's detoxification gets orchestrated. The novel also features embodiments of persevering integrity (Doyce, Mr. Meagles) and improbable shackle-breaking acts: Ellen Wade confesses, Tattycoram reforms, Pancks resists Casby, Mrs. Clennam amazingly throws off her paralysis.

These transmutations of character happen, however, in defiance of the predominant treatment of place. In particular, *Little Dorrit* employs relentlessly one of literature's most familiar tropes of environmental-deterministic representation: the metonymy of "comparing and conflating buildings with their inhabitants."[18] Arthur Dorrit becomes his prison; Mrs. Clennam mirrors her decaying house; Tite Barnacle nestles in close to a much more fashionable district in "a hideous little street of dead wall, stables, and dung-hills" in "a squeezed house" that smells like "a bottle filled with a strong distillation of mews" that infects its elegant but dirty footman with "a sallow flabbiness" (pp. 109, 110). Dickens was a pioneer in the medium Anthony Vidler calls "the architectural uncanny": the destabilization of a building that "pretends to afford the utmost security," such that it is reimagined as vulnerable "to the secret intrusion of terror," through such means as "partial inva[sion] by its surroundings."[19] Tite Barnacle's residence reveals both social parasitism and literal pollution. The price of cozying up to greatness is that Mews Street residences cannot keep out the excremental stench. In this we see the start of modern toxic gothification.

Such conflations of residence, resident, and context were powerful carriers of middle-class liberal ideals (with their assumption of home as central semiotic unit) and key to the discourse of mid-nineteenth-century public health. The sanitary condition of a dwelling in the context of its neighborhood predicted the inhabitant's state of well-being. The Barnacle vignette is an upscale version of reformist exposés of the dwellings of the "labouring poor," huddled on narrow streets "where, from a proper want of receptacles and sewers, filth is allowed to accumulate, and there necessarily is a constant emanation of fetid effluvia."[20] It was no accident that Chadwick's milestone report, which galvanized sanitarian activism in Britain and the United States, began by documenting the "general condition of the residences," and moved from there outward to neighborhood environment and workplace. The enlightened view on both sides of the Atlantic was that the public needed to be better informed that miasma bred disease and that clean environment helped ensure both bodily and mental health. Where better to start the tour of inspection than with that iconic sanctuary, home? A few years later, Prince Albert's death from typhoid and President James A. Garfield's from infection following what should have been a nonfatal assassination attempt were widely blamed on residential miasma: unsanitary domestic drainage arrangements.[21] At the moment Dickens was composing *Little Dorrit* American reformer Catherine Beecher was warning that "the idea that every pair of lungs needs a hogshead of pure air every hour as much as the stomach needs its daily food, is one that has never been acted on by one man in a thousand in arranging for his house, his place of business, and his family";[22] and Henry Thoreau, perhaps more anxious about the family curse of tuberculosis than he let on, was boasting about the breezy house he had built with his own hands in Walden Woods, "of rough weather-stained boards, with wide chinks, which made it cool at night."[23]

Dickens's and Thoreau's house-person correlations finally remain as much symbolic-oneiric as material-deterministic, however. Thoreau's hut detaches itself from Concord and metamorphoses into an image of "centralized solitude";[24] Dickens's domiciles tend to dissolve from bricks, mortar, and mire into something like the allegorical realm of his "flat" characters' names. Dickens's fondness for transforming his houses into "squeezed" quasi-persons and weird metaphorical bottles furthers this.[25] Barnacle's essence-of-mews townhouse, like Miss Havisham's mansion in *Great Expectations* (1861), is a waystation between the highly subjectified mode of gothic fiction and the materially grounded landscapes of later realist narrative. The end point is the urban ghetto of realist-naturalist tradition. Here too enclosures are symbolic but their function as literal definers of social possibility is paramount.

For example, the property too quickly bought by the Lithuanian immigrant family in Upton Sinclair's *The Jungle* (1906) seems at first sight a dream house but quickly shows itself to be an all-too-literal overpriced jerry-built affair poised atop a never-emptied cesspool in a blighted neighborhood built on a former garbage dump that suffuses "a ghastly odor of all the dead things of the universe." In this place, "one never saw the fields, nor any green thing whatever," for the air is blackened above by factory smoke and blackened below by swarms of flies. There is no question of the house symbolizing aboriginal character, as with those of Barnacle and Clennam. Rather, it forcibly reshapes character against the family's wills.[26]

This company-built enclave, in turn, is defined by the omnipotent workplace, in this *"Uncle Tom's Cabin* of wage slavery," as Jack London called *The Jungle:*

> Hour after hour, day after day, year after year, it was fated that he should stand upon a certain square foot of floor from seven in the morning until noon, and again from half-past twelve till half-past five, making never a motion and thinking never a thought, save for the setting of lard cans. In summer the stench of the warm lard would be nauseating, and in winter the cans would all but freeze to his naked little fingers in the unheated cellar. Half the year it would be dark as night when he went in to work, and dark as night again when he came out, and so he would never know what the sun looked like on weekdays.[27]

This from a glimpse of child labor in the Chicago stockyards. Little Stanislovas, who has just pulled off the coup of landing a five cents an hour job placing empty cans on "a wonderful new lard machine," will now be grotesquely deformed by his place in space. The passage has all the marks of toxic gothification: the relentless literalism of serial detail, solemnized by narrative omniscience; the circles of time like concentric prison walls (hours, days, years); the paralysis of thought and enchainment of body by conformity to routine; the invasion of the most intimate senses (not only sight, but also smell and touch); the denial of the most basic sources of environmental refreshment (sun and seasonality). Sinclair did not invent these motifs: we find them earlier in Engels, in Dickens, in Gaskell, in Ruskin, in Melville's "Tartarus of Maids" and Rebecca Harding Davis's "Life in the Iron Mills," as well as in antebellum slave narrative and fictionalized accounts of slavery like Harriet Beecher Stowe's. But in late nineteenth-century fictions of labor like Emile Zola's *Germinal* and Euro-American slum journalism they take on a new totalizing intensity, in proportion to the fear that urbanism, industrialization, and poverty have reduced people to pawns, workers to tools. Not only by his supervisors but also by his fellows, Zola's Étienne ironically becomes "accepted and looked upon as a real miner, as the crushing mould of habit pressed him a little more each day into the likeness of an automaton."[28] A fully articulated deterministic representation, as in Zola and Sinclair, operates on many planes at once: conceptual (explicitly formulated), tonal (insistent narrative omniscience), spatial (confinement within enclosure), temporal (no relief in sight), sensuous, and psychological (mind colonized to the point that escape becomes unimaginable).

The Sinclair passage is written from the standpoint of the entrapped actor. Its reciprocal is the panoptic view of neighborhood or district or institution as an imprisoning monolith that blights all that lives within. In Jacob Riis's *How the Other Half Lives* (1890), the tenements breed their "Nemesis," the violent proletariat; "the worst houses exercise a levelling influence upon all the rest"; the slums pollute the rest of the city, holding "within their clutch the wealth and business of New York," their children its "growing generation"; the architectural template is stamped on the tenant; the saloon breeds poverty, corrupts children, and thereby "saps the very vitals of society." To the Harlem minister who complains that Riis stresses material conditions to the neglect of the "inner man," he gives the withering reply that "you cannot expect to find an inner man to appeal to in the worst tenement-house surroundings."[29]

Deterministic mimesis need not be so photographic as in Riis or Sinclair. No naturalist novel renders entrapment more starkly than Richard Wright's *Native Son* (1940), but although Wright operated from a gestalt of Chicago determinism analogous to Sinclair's,[30] *Native Son*'s environmental detail is sparse by comparison, apart from the manhunt sequence when Bigger hides out in abandoned buildings and empty rooms. The opening scene establishes privation via symbolic event (Bigger kills the rat that invades his family's run-down apartment, which augurs his own fate as both murderer and victim) rather than by copious documentary, using laconic descriptors like "a black boy standing in a narrow space between two iron beds," "a gaping hole in the molding," and "now and then a street car rattled past over steel tracks." Most of the novel transpires in tautly described enclosed spaces: theater, poolroom, the mansion of the Daltons (who own the Thomases' tenement), Bessie's tiny apartment, Bigger's hideaways within the diminishing "white space" on the map as the police systematically comb the South

Side, and finally Bigger's prison cell and the courtroom where he is tried. The schematic way these enclosures are rendered, and their relative interchangeability as far as Bigger's destiny is concerned, correspond to the "attitude of iron reserve" he tries to maintain toward others, lest he "be swept out of himself with fear and despair." "Iron reserve" is of course euphemistic, referring not so much to Bigger's "self-control"—such as it is—as to the semblance of it created by fear, anger, stubbornness, and ignorance.[31]

Had he so chosen, Wright could have imitated Sinclair's descriptive exhaustiveness. Wright had made himself into an urban sociologist of considerable acumen; he had prepared under WPA auspices a report on "Ethnographical Aspects of Chicago's Black Belt" and a "Bibliography on the Negro in Chicago, 1936";[32] he was personally acquainted with several of the University of Chicago sociology faculty; he drew upon their work for a number of his own fictional and nonfictional publications in the 1930s and 1940s, and was respectfully cited in theirs; and he contributed the introduction to the most authoritative sociological *summa* of his day on Chicago's Black Belt.[33] His documentary "folk history of the Negro in the United States," *12 Million Black Voices,* published the year after *Native Son,* describes (with photographs by Edwin Rosskam) in graphic detail the forced squalor of life in a one-room overpriced "kitchenette" tenement apartment such as the Thomases presumably inhabit ("with its filth and foul air, with its one toilet for thirty or more inhabitants" [a revolting photograph is affixed] which "kills our black babies so far that in many cities twice as many of them die as white babies").

Ghetto fictions of the period often follow the same approach, like Ann Petry's *The Street* (1946), which opens by bombarding the reader with the sensuous as well as emotional wretchedness of Lutie Johnson as she endures the bone-chilling night wind and the claustrophobic filth of the tenement where she is to reside, and the menacing presence of the inmates' bodies as they crowd into her personal space. In *Native Son,* the specifically physical aspect of urban confinement is more played down. Although Bigger sees the apartment as a "rat-infested" "garbage dump," no characters die of disease aggravated by slum living conditions or even get sick; virtually all the *represented* squalor of the Thomases' apartment is concentrated in the rodent, just as the shock-impact of the plot gets concentrated in Bigger's homicides. In fact, the apartment seems orderly and clean relative to the documentary evidence (particularly the photographs) presented in 12 Million Black Voices. The family mops up the dead rat's blood immediately; even Bigger, the troublemaker, after tormenting his sister by dangling it in front of her nose, wraps it in a newspaper and deposits it dutifully in "a garbage can at the corner of an alley."[34] Gwendolyn Brooks's portrait of the same district in A Street in Bronzeville (1945), which Wright admired, puts the same rhetorical question as Native Son, but handles the sensuous feel of urban blight more pointedly:[35]

> could a dream send up through onion fumes
> Its white and violet, fight with fried potatoes
> And yesterday's garbage ripening in the hall,
> Flutter, or sing an aria down these rooms
>
> Even if we were willing to let it in,
> Had time to warm it, keep it very clean,
> Anticipate a message, let it begin?

Scenes of this kind in Native Son feature emotions of fear and hate, not sensations of flavor and texture.

Wright's approach was well adapted to the starkness of ghetto regimentation, where "the imposed conditions under which Negroes live detail the structure of their lives like an engineer outlining the blueprints for the production of machines," the "natural" rhythms of folklife overridden by the clock time whose raspy "brrrrrng" opens Native Son.[36] Regimentation by the dominant culture of time and space is one index, Werner Sollors observes, of Wright's "sociological" analysis of black-white antagonisms as against Zora Neale Hurston's "anthropological" approach to the rhythms and preoccupations of African-American folklife, and may partly explain their mutual antagonism: his dislike of what he took to be her romantic evasion of racism, her dislike of his bitter pugnacity.[37]

A comparison between Wright's and Sinclair's starting points is additionally instructive. Sinclair told the story of how The Jungle came to be in two discrepant ways, revealing it to be a montage of two quite different experiences. One was a six-week on-site investigation that left him awash in indigestible data until he found a particular Lithuanian family whose saga provided the basis of his plot. The other was a personal near disaster: a feckless quasi-Waldenish experiment in frugal country living whereby he had hoped to finance his struggling career. In this account remembered privation had more to do with shaping *The Jungle* than journalistic ethnography did:

> externally, the story had to do with a family of stockyard workers, but internally it was the story of my own family. Did I wish to know how the poor suffered in wintertime in Chicago? I had only to recall the previous winter in the cabin, when we had only cotton blankets, and had put rugs on top of us, and cowered shivering in our separate beds . . . Ona [the heroine of *The Jungle*] was Corydon speaking Lithuanian but otherwise unchanged.[38]

What enabled Sinclair to write so poignantly about his proletarians, it seems, was tapping into the memory of his own petit-bourgeois nightmare.[39]

Wright was far better acquainted with poverty and discrimination than Sinclair, and that he too identified with his protagonist is suggested by his decision to play the role of Bigger in the film version of *Native Son,* despite being twenty years too old for the part.[40] But Wright derived Bigger, so he said, synoptically from representative instances, with some of the details of Bessie's murder taken from a particular 1938 Chicago case, to the end of creating "a symbolic figure of American life" that would embody the misery, alienation, and potentiality for violence of any "native son" living amid "the greatest possible plenty on earth" but denied access to it. "Just as one sees when one walks into a medical research laboratory jars of alcohol containing abnormally large or distorted portions of the human body, just so did I feel that the conditions of life under which Negroes are forced to live in America contain the embryonic emotional prefigurations of how a large part of the body politic would react under stress."[41] *Native Son* was to diagnose a syndrome characteristic of, although not limited to, the plight of black males in northern ghettoes. Sinclair gave an unforgettable description of a child's body becoming mechanized, but it was Wright who attained a better theoretical grasp of what Mark Seltzer terms "the body-machine complex," the realization of which he sees as "a *model* of realism toward which particular realist practices gravitate": namely, "the production of individuals as statistical persons" manifesting syndromes of behavioral norms.[42]

To the extent that Wright conceived Bigger as a syndrome predictable under given conditions, broadly speaking he applied the traditional naturalist theory of fiction as sociological laboratory experiment, set forth most famously in Emile Zola's "The Experimental Novel"; but a more immediate prototype was the "ecological" approach that marked University of Chicago sociology at that time. This involved transposition of the analytic vocabulary of the emerging subdiscipline of biological ecology, intended to give urban sociology a more scientific basis, although in practice it produced a confused blurring of categories and pseudoscientific claims about the "natural" laws of urban structure and growth.

Odd though it may seem according to the canons of late twentieth-century green urban planning, the "ecological organization" of a city in early Chicago School theory referred not so much to its biogeographical setting as to "the spatial distribution of population and institutions and the temporal sequence of structure and function following from the operation of selective, distributive, and competitive forces tending to produce typical results wherever they are at work."[43] This from Wright's first sociological mentor, Louis Wirth. The premises behind this professorial rarefaction that were commonly invoked to justify the "ecological" analogy were, first, the theory of the city as organized spatially in terms of communities defined by/as "natural areas" (referring both to their original physiography and human-constructed gridworks like streets and railways), and, second, the theory of competition as an elemental motivating force.[44] Such thinking implied notional acceptance, though by no means necessarily ethical approval, of residential segregation as a natural law of human distribution, and an environmental-determinist view of urban spatial arrangements. Although Wright did not call himself an "ecologist," nor identify *Native Son* explicitly with Chicago School analysis, his desire to produce a riveting fiction that would stand the test of empirical inquiry would have disposed him to emphasize the sociological-laboratory aspect of *Native Son* to a greater extent than the novelistic precursors he most admired, Dostoyevsky and Dreiser.

Rurality as Fate

During the early industrial era the notion of environmental construction of human identity played through quite differently for writers according to whether the determiner was felt to be nature or culture. That "Nature never did betray/The heart that loved her," as the Wordsworthian speaker affirms in "Tintern Abbey," became a Romanticist axiom. For Emerson, physical nature was "a fixed point" by which humankind might measure "our departure" or slippage from harmonious self-existence.[45] Mary Shelley makes one wonder if Frankenstein's creature would have remained benign, however lonely, had he wandered forever in the Swiss vales without ever meeting a human being.[46] Even urbanites like Dickens and Whitman pitted rural salubrity against urban blight. "Englishness" has traditionally been linked to countryside,[47] just as "Americanness" has traditionally been linked to heartland, nature, and wilderness, both despite and because of national pride in the United States' rapid industrialization—including exploitative treatment of first nature and its native inhabitants.[48] Indeed, it may be the case, as one cultural geographer asserts, that "in most countries the countryside has become the embodiment of the nation,"[49] at least of its traditional essence.

Yet increasingly unfamiliar exurban landscapes could easily transmute themselves from pastoral spaces apart to spaces of entrapment. Wordsworth recognizes this alternative vision in his portrayal of the rural poor, even if at other times he chooses to ignore it in lyric exuberance upon return to cherished rustic places. Though he wished to affirm the spiritualizing effects of the strict discipline and even the privations of rural life (admiring, for example, the leech gatherer's fortitude, in "Resolution and Independence," as a reproach to the poet-speaker's emotional brittleness), Wordsworth was forced in the same breath to admit how rural figures look, indeed often are, battered into misshapenness by place-bound impoverishment. In figures like Simon Lee, Margaret, and even the noble but doomed protagonist of "Michael" we see the beginnings of the persistent malformation of rural character that some of Wordsworth's contemporaries acknowledged more frankly ("own the Village Life a life of pain," George Crabbe insisted),[50] and that marks much later poetry and prose of country and village life both in Britain and in the United States, from Emily Brontë's *Wuthering Heights* to Edith Wharton's *Ethan Frome.*

As these latter works suggest, gothic fiction is another provenance of literary envisionment of the effects of environmental determinism in remote places. The supercharged landscapes of Ann Radcliffe's novels seem to take on a life of their own, projecting but also shaping the mentality of those traveling through them. Passing through a darksome pine forest on her way from Venice to Udolpho under Montoni's grim supervision, Emily St. Aubert "saw only images of gloomy grandeur, or of dreadful sublimity, around her; other images, equally gloomy and equally terrible, gleamed on her imagination." Montoni's castle, the destined scene of physical and psychological entrapment for hundreds of pages to come, "its mouldering walls of grey stone . . . invested with the solemn duskiness of evening," rises out of this landscape as a malevolent quintessentialization: constructed less from the bricks and mortar alone as by the perception of an anxiously disoriented soul daunted by a landscape of fear.[51] So too the first glimpse of the House of Usher by Poe's apprehensive narrator. From passages like these descend not only the prison-estates of Wuthering Heights and Sutpen's Hundred in Faulkner's *Absalom, Absalom* but also, in part, the urban prison-houses of Dombey and Mrs. Clennam.

That early industrial-era writers were nonetheless more likely than otherwise to take nature's part reflected uneasiness about the changing balance of power between humanity and nature. Such was the central concern of the first major conservationist manifesto in the English language, George Perkins Marsh's *Man and Nature* (1864): that human capacity to disrupt nature's course was far greater than anyone had heretofore realized. Marsh's Vermont boyhood during that state's epoch of dramatic deforestation had given him an unforgettable sense of how "the clearing of the woods" could produce "within two or three generations, effects as blasting as those generally ascribed to geological convulsions, and has laid waste the face of the earth more hopelessly than if it had been buried by a current of lava or a shower of volcanic sand." A person so impressed might be expected to be nature's defender, not to conjure up anxieties about environmental determinism. In fact, March was no sentimentalist, and at times had did grimly imagine scenes of "vengeance of nature for the violation of her harmonies."[52]

But his emphasis on environmental fragility and the necessity of proactive remediation presupposed an image of nature as the ward of humankind rather than of humankind as an environmental product.

When the root assumption of natural balance or predictable cycle came under challenge by the image of nature as a scene of biological struggle of no certain teleology, however, natural harmony itself became suspect not only as fact but also as value. For Marsh, who cited *The Origin of Species* (1859) but did not absorb the radical part of its argument, "nature" had a more static look and more normative value than it did for Darwin. Marsh recognized that the operation of natural law might produce inefficient results but he placed credence in and value on the idea of a balance of nature antecedent to human disruption. For Darwin, human intervention of such kinds as plant grafting and stock breeding was both taken for granted as proper management and a stalking horse for a natural selection that undermined in effect if not in intent pious images like Marsh's of man as earth's "noblest inhabitant."[53] Even as first nature seemed unprecedentedly vulnerable, natural selection gave new currency to determinism at the level of biological history. The ironic but predictable result was to make the conception of nature as a human-constructing law seem more ominous.

Nowhere is the depressing effect on older-style Romantic naturism better illustrated than by the career of one of its most earnest and long-lived exemplars, John Burroughs. Burroughs started out as a nature essayist for the *Atlantic* and other magazines, specializing in collage-vignettes of bird-watching that combined the idealizing bent of his literary hero, Emerson, with the fine-grained observations of Thoreau's later *Journal*. The charm of this work lay in Burroughs's ability to suffuse fieldnotes with a mellow satisfaction in the pleasures of country life: to transport to (sub)urban parlors intimate scenes from the northeastern edgelands. In later life, however, he began to forsake his exquisite nature sketches for a more sober and troubled philosophy of nature. The result was an unstable eclectic synthesis, the catalyst for which was Henri Bergson's theory of an *élan vital*, but increasingly the major creative irritant and bugbear for Burroughs was the rigorous "naturalism" that Darwinian evolution seemed to require. Though he found it "impossible" "to think of anything as uncaused," he conceded that modern science had discredited "the transcendental"—a disillusionment he compared to the loss of Santa Claus—and he concluded that "we shall probably be brought, sooner or later, to accept . . . the physical origin of the soul."[54] Burroughs sought to minister to readers who, like himself, had awakened to "the cosmic chill": the Arnoldian sense of feeling "homeless and orphaned in a universe where no suggestion of sympathy and interest akin to our own comes to us from the great void."[55] For the last two decades of his life, he strove to reconcile his will to believe in cosmic purposefulness with an increasing acceptance of human life as defined by organismal and environmental constraints.

The underlying refrain of these later essays is: face it, nature does not meet our spiritual needs, and we had better get used to it. In a sense nature writing had always tended that way, and still does—toward the discomfiture of anthropocentrism—although as an implicit, "embedded" strategy,[56] indeed sometimes without fully realizing it. By focusing on biological or geological realms faraway in space or time, on microscopic worlds too tiny or macroscopic patterns too vast to be assimilated, by eliminating human protagonists and plots, or by relegating them to the periphery, nature writing effectively defines human interests as marginal to nature's motions. "Of no account you who lie out there watching," writes Mary Austin, filled with "the sense of mastery" of the stark, immense astral landscape of the southwestern desert.[57] Jack London's tale "To Build a Fire" dramatizes this point with chilling literalism, recording the hour-by-hour experience of a man freezing in the Arctic at 70 below.

Although Burroughs's dismay at the prospect of human aspiration controlled by natural process did not keep him from relishing the hands-on agricultural work to which he returned in midlife as a gentler reprise of his agrarian boyhood, more alienated writers took a more caustic view of the kind of human life that bound itself closely to nature. Edwin Markham, musing on Millet's painting L'homme à la houe, created a minor sensation with a bleak poem of the same title about the dehumanization of the farmworker:

> Who made him dead to rapture and despair,
> A thing that grieves not and that never hopes,
> Stolid and stunned, a brother to the ox?
> Who loosened and let down this brutal jaw?

> Whose was the hand that slanted back this brow?
> Whose breath blew out the light within this brain?[58]

Markham's laborer is even more determined than Sinclair's immigrants. At least they knew what it was to be alive before Packingtown crushed them. Not so this figure: we are only allowed to see him as always already brutish, though the poem admonishes later on that this is a produced result, the "handiwork" of the "lords and rulers in all lands."

Of course, Markham did not invent this kind of figure, nor did Millet. It stretches back to comic bumpkins in medieval and Shakespearean literature, if not earlier; and it is revived in the eighteenth century by such Neoclassical and Romantic writers as Crabbe and Wordsworth when they turn to the plight of the rural underclass. But the sense of country life as no less grimly determined than city life becomes more pervasive and insistent as the combination of Darwinian thinking, urban migration, and the shrinkage of domestic agriculture as a component of national economies takes hold in the later nineteenth century. The specific portraits vary greatly. The rustic blockhead resurfaces in, for example, the farmer-interlocutor of Robert Frost's "Mending Wall" (1913); the blockheads are made sinister in provincial gothic texts like Eugene O'Neill's *Desire under the Elms* (1924); and the evaluation of a determined existence can vary greatly within the same writer's oeuvre, as, for example, when Mary Wilkins Freeman treats Louisa Ellis's backcountry stolidness with considerable sympathy in "A New England Nun" (1891) because it preserves her from disarrangement, but treats farmer Adoniram's in "The Revolt of Mother" (1891) harshly because it makes him mistreat his wife and family.

Perhaps the greatest genius in this vein was Thomas Hardy, in whose writing the irony and the pathos of post-Romantic disillusionment collide and interpenetrate continually.

> Heart-halt and spirit-lame,
>   City-opprest,
> Unto this wood I came
>   As to a nest;
> Dreaming that sylvan peace
> Offered the harrowed ease—

> Nature a soft release
> —From man's unrest.

Such is the would-be Wordsworthian speaker's first impulse.

> But, having entered in,
> Great growths and small
> Show them to men akin—
> Combatants all!
> Sycamore shoulders oak,
> Vines the slim sapling yoke,
> Ivy-spun halters choke
> Elms stout and tall.

Alarmed by this glimpse of elemental struggle, the speaker quickly retreats, realizing that "no grace" will be "Taught me of trees."[59] The containment of affect by tart, terse line and cramped syntax transfuses the poem with a rhetoric of vexation to match the theme.

A materialistic-reductive view of natural process was but one facet of Hardy's determinism. Even more daunting than a soulless nature seemed the overriding power of class, inchoate passion, and a cosmic fatalism ("the President of the Immortals, in Aeschylean phrase, had ended his sport with Tess") that mockingly echoes Angel Clare's romantic-neopaganist swerve from his preacher-father's Pauline "creed of determinism."[60] But always an important, if not *the* most crucial, aspect of the determinist mix is rootedness in place. That is what lures the novelist to Tess's vale, "an engirdled and secluded region" of Wessex "for the most part untrodden as yet by tourist or landscape-painter," where ancient customs still prevail among the country folk, even the most sensitive of whom will be driven to fatal acts if disrupted by cosmopolitan influences.[61] *Tess of the d'Urbervilles* (1891) undermines any idealization of country as English essence by making Tess's knowledge of her ancestral link to Norman land barons the start of her undoing, and by having her final flight take the form of a symbolic regression back into prehistory to the sanguinary druidical altars of Stonehenge. Not that the novel apparently means to invalidate rural folk culture, although *Tess* renders it much less idyllically than such earlier Hardy novels as *Under the Greenwood Tree* and *The Woodlanders*. The point seems rather that Tess must come to ruin when she tries to move beyond her provincial sphere, just as her Angel stumbles when he tries to step into it. As Gillian Beer observes, "the emphasis on systems more extensive than the life span of the individual and little according to his needs" is central to Hardy's fiction, both affirmatively as a way of magnifying the scale and the stakes of the characters' struggle against the defeat that will overtake them and negatively as a way of underscoring that "even those recuperative energies" that ennoble them "are there primarily to serve the longer needs of the race and are part of a procreative energy designed to combat extinction, not the death of any individual."[62]

Consolations of Determinism: Dreiser and Jeffers

However sobering the prospect of environmental determinism to some writers, as the example of Hardy begins to suggest it was entirely possible to take a kind of relish in the play of cataclysmic natural process; in the drama of social struggle; even in the spectacle of men and beasts reduced to elemental combat where the strong best the weak by realizing their animal natures (the side of Jack London's mind that produced *Sea Wolf* and *The Call of the Wild*) or in the cataclysmic effects of market forces (Frank Norris in *The Octopus* and *The Pit*).

Among major English-speaking novelists, Theodore Dreiser stands out for his efforts to fashion deterministic scenarios that, by their relish for the human scene, would keep closed-allegory programmaticism at arm's length.

For most of his adult life, desultory thinker though he was, Dreiser looked upon "man" as the "sport of nature" and upon "his fellowmen" as an inconsiderable part of "the great economy of nature." He admired *The Riddle of the Universe* by Ernst Haeckel, the man who coined the term "ecology" on the way to becoming a German Herbert Spencer, as a demonstration of "the underlying unity in inorganic and organic Nature" and of the place of humankind within that as an assemblage of biochemical processes. Birth and death Dreiser called "the result of chemic and electrophysical processes of which at bottom we know exactly nothing."[63] Eventually the idea that "the mass is everything, the individual nothing," that individuals live "not wholly and individually" but absorbed within a superorganism "that has constructed me and is using me" led him to a more teleological myth of life's processes, but his predominant view was formed by a youthful encounter with Spencer's *First Principles,* which "blew me, intellectually, to bits" by seeming to reduce human identity to "an infinitesimal speck of energy . . . drawn or blown here and there by larger forces in which he moved quite unconsciously as an atom."[64] Richard Wright, who placed Dreiser "at the pinnacle of American literature" for having "first revealed to me the nature of American life," rightly characterized Dreiser as trying "to rationalize and justify the defeat of the individual in biological terms."[65]

Philosophical pessimism might have driven Dreiser into gloomy preachment; indeed, sometimes it did, as in "it is only the unfit who fail," "the attitude of pity which the world thinks proper to hold toward poverty is misplaced," "it is time that we cleared away the cobwebs of altruism," and so forth.[66] But his first reaction to Spencer's social darwinism was an exuberant sense of liberation from postadolescent religious guilt,[67] and his more considered response was spectatorial fascination: to observe with empathy, gusto, and bemusement how people, including himself, became entangled by the sensuous, material world around them. Having discovered the truth as he saw it, he sought to appreciate human life in light of it, rather than wish it away.

Like Wright, Dreiser remembered Chicago as "the City of Rats," but instead of stressing immiserated entrapment, he turned his memory of slum boyhood into a Tom Sawyerish nostalgia piece about hunting rats for sport. "What a privilege to come as a child and see a modern city in the making!" he exclaims, have-not and loser that he was—hardly less aware than Wright of how trivial and benighted these lads' lives were, hardly less convinced of their profound ignorance of their situation and their powerlessness to affect the way the city makes itself. Whereas Sinclair found conditions in the working-class districts of turn-of-the-century Chicago intolerable, Dreiser, writing of the same place and time, sounds like Courbet on the aesthetic piquancy of smoky railway stations for the impressionistic painter:

> The palls of heavy manufacturing smoke that hung low over the city like impending hurricanes; the storms of wintry snow or sleety rain; the glow of yellow lights in little shops at evening, mile after mile, where people were stirring and bustling over potatoes, flour, cabbages—all these things were the substance of songs, paintings,

poems . . . I liked those sections crowded with great black factories, stockyards, steel works, Pullman yards, where in the midst of Plutonian stress and clang men mixed or forged or joined or prepared those delicacies, pleasures and perfections for which the world buys and sells itself. Life was at its best here, its promise the most glittering. I liked those raw neighborhoods where in small, unpainted tumble-down shanties set in grassless, can-strewn yards drunken and lecherous slatterns and brawlers were to be found mooning about in a hell of their own. And, for contrast, I liked those areas of great mansions set upon the great streets of the city in spacious lawns.

The relish with which this passage recalls a boy's excitement does not mean the mature Dreiser overlooks the cruelties of the system that produces such contrasts. Later, another such scene in Pittsburgh outrages the more seasoned youth ("What were these things called democracy and equality about which men prated?").[68] But one can never predict whether industrial blight will set off a Menckenesque tirade against the stupidity of American city planning or a painterly celebration of it, this landscape "so black and rancidly stale" yet "interesting beyond any intention of those who plan" it. In his sketches of New York before World War I, Dreiser dwells on the abuses of tenement sweatshops but also on the picturesqueness of homeless street people; the tragedy of frequent suicides in the waters of Manhattan but also the pleasures of Christmas in the tenements. In his sketch of a visit to "A Certain Oil Refinery" aesthetic impressionism and outraged dismay clash throughout, at one point prompting the thought that "A Whistler could make wonderful blacks and whites of this," at another the "doubt if one could wish a better hell for one's enemies than some of the wretched chambers here, where men rove about like troubled spirits in a purgatory of man's devising."[69]

It is tempting to berate Dreiser for fatuous self-contradiction or else to grasp after a deeper consistency, for example, in the popular journalist's need to walk a fine line between exposé and entertainment. Either line of speculation, however, must grant his insight into human malleability by the play of environment on impulse and his readiness to expose his narrative persona to that same influence, so that his texts mirror the susceptibility he ascribes to his characters, from the hard-driving Frank Cowperwood to the feckless Clyde Griffith. This is the source of Dreiser's vigor, populism, redundancy, crudity, *and* refinement: the knowledge "that not we, but the things of which we are the evidence, are the realities," and the ability in consequence to invent figures like Lester Kane and Jenny Gerhardt, George Hurstwood and Carrie Meeber, "created with that passivity of soul which is always the mirror of the active world."[70]

Carrie's bedazzlement by the romance of commodity culture has been the *locus classicus* of this sensibility for Dreiser scholars. "No romantic poet," as one Dreiserian remarks, "ever used the pathetic fallacy to unite emotion and natural artifact better than Dreiser uses his social observations and the personifications of material objects to embody and project" her feelings.[71] But because *Sister Carrie* follows its protagonist's consciousness so close to ground level, it comes less close to *formulating* the city in ecosystemic terms than do Dreiser's nonfiction and portions of his later novels.

Among his major characters, the financier Cowperwood grasps this perspective best. In *The Titan* (1914), he nearly achieves a monopoly of the Chicago transit system; for not only does he foresee that Chicago will get very big and very rich very fast, he also perceives the interrelationships among the city's "natural areas" as the Chicago ecologists called them: the distribution of space in relation to infrastructure. Cowperwood has a Whitmanian "natural aptitude and affection for streetrailway work": "the tinkle of car bells and the plop of plodding horses' feet was in his blood." The breakthrough that allows him to get the jump on his competitors happens during and because of frustration at traffic backups approaching the old-fashioned bridges over the Chicago River. Cowperwood notices what his peers had overlooked: two abandoned "soggy and rat-infested tunnels," which he then explores and by various machinations procures and refurbishes in order to establish streetcar service between the North and West Sides, hitherto controlled by different companies.[72]

Although profit and gratification are his ruling passions, Cowperwood could not have managed as he does without grasping urban landscape as system. Environmental imagination assists his push to dominance. Significantly, the account of Cowperwood's discovery of the tunnels is suffused with a kind of tenderness about the river district that would have seemed self-deluded to Sinclair and time-wasting to Wright but is quite in keeping with the relish Dreiser takes elsewhere in such scenes.[73] The "dirty, odorous" river, the chronic congestion, the lackadaisical bridge attendants seem "lovely, human, natural, Dickens-esque—a fit subject for a Daumier, a Turner, or a Whistler."[74]

This gusto for loitering in a moment of perfect rapport with an avowedly shabby landscape, especially when the novel has long since hinted that destiny will take its course and even a controlling figure like Cowperwood will not stay on top of the forces he would control, may strike some readers as self-indulgent bedazzlement by the very material-ism that should, for consistency's sake, have been ironized. I myself read it as *amor fati,* whose expansive geniality prevents it from being recognized as such. On the other hand, few are likely to miss the fatal-ism of Dreiser's younger contemporary, the California poet Robinson Jeffers (1887–1962), for whom it became an increasingly insistent article of faith.

Much nature writing, as noted earlier, follows the convention of ban-ishing humankind to the edges for the sake of concentrating on the non-human landscape. Sometimes this is a deliberately antianthropocentric move, as when the text invites us to see life from the standpoint of an endangered animal or when the earth is held up as a protagonist certain to outlast its human habitants. But such moments usually stop short of implying that human history is nothing more than an epiphenomenal swirl in the cosmic process. Not so Jeffers. Broadly speaking, he belongs in the company of other early American modernist poets who question whether, properly understood, the semiotics of nature yields a reassur-ing or a terrifying result (Frost's "Design"), whether what it seems to yield is merely our own construction (Stevens's "Anecdote of the Jar"), or whether speculating about any such constructedness should be re-pressed in favor of concentrating on the properties of the object (Mari-anne Moore, "The Pangolin"). But Jeffers was driven to make sublime metaphysics out of the sheer materiality of natural process. He truly seems to have meant it when he wrote

> when the whole human race
> Has been like me rubbed out, they will still be here; storms, moon
> and ocean,

> Dawn and the birds. And I say this: their beauty has more meaning
> Than the whole human race and the race of birds.[75]

What is to define "beauty" or "meaning" when humanity is obliterated is evaded here by a grand tautology typical of Jeffers. Because "Things are the God," as he puts it elsewhere, Thingness itself can be thought of both as materiality and as a discursive gravitational field that makes all the honorific abstractions, like "beauty," revolve around itself.[76]

Jeffers took pleasure in imagining himself dead and his ashes diffused through the universe, no longer mere witness but "part of the beauty." In his copious narrative poetry, he favored epiphanic moments when the shell of personality cracks and "white fire flies out of it," when people are commanded by force of primordial imperatives they only half understand—as when Christine in "Roan Stallion" abases herself to the horse she fears, which is to kill her abusive husband and to be killed in turn by her.[77] Indeed, consciousness itself seemed, in principle, "a derogation from the organic unity of being, a malignancy" existing "parasitically on the substance of the world." If we must have such a thing, let it be "Fierce consciousness joined with final / Disinterestedness," such that

> Among stones and quietness
> The mind dissolves without a sound,
> The flesh drops into the ground.[78]

Stones and quietness indeed. The durability of the mutable cosmos was precisely what needed celebration, and the grandest gesture in Jeffers's later work, accordingly, is to reduce all human history, technology, and aspiration to it:

> . . . even the P-38s and the Flying Fortresses are as natural
>   as horse-flies;
> It is only that man, his griefs and rages, are not what they seem
>   to man, not great and shattering, but really
> Too small to produce any disturbance. This is good. This is the
>   sanity, the mercy. It is true that the murdered

Cities leave marks in the earth for a certain time, like fossil
rain-prints in shale, equally beautiful.[79]

To shrink bombers into horseflies, cities into fossil rain-prints, and
World War II (a plague on both their houses) into a dot on the disk of
history was enough to appall even an admirer like the Polish exile-poet
Czeslaw Milosz, for whom, significantly, Jeffers's insouciance was less
culpable than the duplicity of playing God while reducing the rest of humanity to detritus.[80] If there is such a thing as "ecofascist aesthetics,"
this "inhumanism," as Jeffers called his ethic, must surely be it.[81]

Elsewhere Jeffers admits to feeling drawn by humanity's "lesser
beauty, impure and painful; we have to harden our hearts to bear it." "I
have hardened my heart only a little," he confesses.[82] Such grudging admission of vulnerability seems a far cry from that of Dreiser's bemused
acknowledgment of human frailty. Yet there is a quasi-resemblance in
Jeffers's inability to keep his poems from expressing what in more res-
olute moods he knows he should disapprove, as when a painterly-im-
pressionistic glimpse of fishing boats wending their way through
sudden fog overtakes him with this reaction:

> A flight of pelicans
> Is nothing lovelier to look at;
> The flight of the planets is nothing nobler; all the arts lose virtue
> Against the essential reality
> Of creatures going about their business among the equally
> Earnest elements of nature.[83]

In its own way, Jeffers's persona is almost as self-divided as Dreiser's.
The speaker has to keep reminding himself again and again to see
through the enticing world of appearances to bedrock, to see "through
the trick to the beauty," to see lonely starkness as the standard of
beauty. "No imaginable / Human presence here could do anything / But
dilute the lonely self-watchful passion," he wrote of "the coast hills at
Sovranes Creek."[84] Why "self-watchful passion"? Presumably because
inhumanism is such hard work: you have to keep reminding yourself to
grit your teeth and harden yourself.

What brings the two determinists more closely together, however, is that neither really accepts for himself the conditions and limits of a determined *community*. Both identify with strong-minded anticonventional souls, trying to maintain a certain distance in their capacity as determinism's philosophers from the predicament of determinism's ordinary victims.

Indeed, some such gap is doubtless impossible for creative writers of any persuasion completely to erase, even if they want to; nor is that necessarily a bad thing. John Edgar Wideman's Homewood fiction is written in retrospect from a more secure vantage point, but without that aesthetic distance Homewood might have remained virtually unknown beyond the vicinity of Pittsburgh, Pennsylvania. Could the faithful Jane Addams, who voluntarily lived in a Chicago slum the last forty-five years of her life, be called hypocrite for maintaining a vacation home on the Maine seacoast where she could recoup her energies? She may have done well to take issue with Tolstoi's attempt to conform to the rhythms of peasant subsistence culture, despite her embarrassment at his criticism of her fashionable clothing and her income as absentee landlord of inherited property. Can "the wrongs of life," she asks, "be reduced to the terms of unrequited labor and all be made right if each person performed the amount necessary to satisfy his own wants?"[85] Though she shared Tolstoi's conviction that the rich should live alongside the poor, his regime seemed to fetishize personal purity so as to limit the prospects of community betterment.

Yet some writers have gone very far indeed in the direction of embracing determined existences, existentially as well as artistically: accepting the constraints of downscale communities to which they have sworn lifelong vows of solidarity that they knew would pigeonhole them as provincial in the eyes of the world, but that seemed nonetheless to be imperative preconditions of artistic and civic possibility. The most striking case is religious asceticism, the prospect that in fact has attracted a number of environmental writers: Edward Abbey, Annie Dillard, and Kathleen Norris among them. Two less dramatic yet more persevering and self-consistent examples are the careers of Kentucky Appalachian farmer-man of letters Wendell Berry and Chicago poet Gwendolyn Brooks.

Observing Limits in Literature and Life: Berry and Brooks

Berry and Brooks dwell in, contribute to, write about, and defend the claims of the endangered cultures of the places where they were born through visions of community that also situate the local (inter)nationally. Both seek, as Berry puts it, "to substitute for the myths and stereotypes . . . a particular knowledge of the life of the *place* one lives in and intends to *continue* to live in."[86] In some ways they share a remarkably similar understanding of the "beloved community": "common experience and common effort on a common ground to which one willingly belongs."[87] So too their sense of its endangerment: in both Berry's and Brooks's home bases work has been drying up from lack of local or reachable options, threatening family and culture with chronic demoralization.[88]

Berry showed where he stood in the lead poem of his 1980 collection *A Part* by playfully inverting Frost's invitation at the start of his *Collected Poems* ("You come too") to "You stay home too."[89] When an interviewer asked Brooks if she found the South Side of Chicago too confining, she replied, "I intend to live in Chicago for *my* forever"—a response no less passionate than Emily Dickinson's to a similar question about whether she ever hankered to leave Amherst ("I never thought of conceiving that I could ever have the slightest approach to such a want in all future time").[90] Both Berry and Brooks made principled decisions to engage in locally focused civic and political activism, to limit lecture travel and guest-teaching engagements in the interest of community identification (but continuing to remain much in demand), and to shift their work to smaller presses outside the New York publishing establishment. In so doing, both claimed the resources of world literature while declaring allegiance to ethnic-platial community. Both envisage their communities as paradigmatic of embattled communities elsewhere. For Berry, it is a neo-Jeffersonian vision of rural communities of small farmers practicing sustainable agriculture contending against hegemonic agribusiness and metropolitan dominance; for Brooks, a no less nationally distinctive image of the urban ghetto victimized by institutionalized racism and exacerbated by the unfulfilled promise of the civil rights movement.

The two bases of operation could hardly be more different. Each writer would have felt out of place in the other's world: his the ethnically homogeneous white backcountry enclave, hers the urban African-American enclave. Nor is there much resemblance between Berry's masculinist, patriarchal, meditative-orotund persona and Brooks's clipped, intense vignettes, which favor a "concealed narrator" rather than a lyric-essayistic "I" and focus more often on women figures and women's experience than men's.[91] Nor is Brooks the poet of landscapes that Berry tends to be; the poem quoted in this chapter's epigraph is unusual for her. "I start with the people," "I don't start with the landmarks," she replied when asked whether she tries "to evoke place in [her] work."[92] Yet both committed themselves to representing people in place over time, constructing identities in dialogue with place, notwithstanding that for Berry the commonest image is a male farmer working or ruminating in a rural landscape,[93] whereas for Brooks the standard image is a female character or groups of people in enclosed spaces or street scenes.

"The hill pasture, an open place among the trees, tilts into the valley"—such leisurely, ruminative evocation of the physical surround is typical of Berry,[94] whereas Brooks elaborates outdoor settings mostly to express defamiliarization, as when black characters ogle the "Beverly Hills" of Chicago's North Side, or genteel white women do-gooders tremulously venture into the ghetto.[95] She prefers to fit her figures within foreshortened, hyperstimulative landscapes of urban density using elliptical bits of detail, and this rare descriptive set-piece (Satin-Legs Smith taking his Sunday walk) shows why:

> Out. Sounds about him smear,
> Become a unit. He hears and does not hear
> The alarm clock meddling in somebody's sleep;
> Children's governed Sunday happiness;
> The dry tone of a plane; a woman's oath;
> Consumption's spiritless expectoration;
> An indignant robin's resolute donation
> Pinching a track through apathy and din;
> Restaurant vendors weeping; and the L
> That comes on like a slightly horrible thought.[96]

Brooks here converts Eliotic ennui into a more complex image of inner life, starting with the intimation that the rhetorical polish is itself a refraction of Smith's defensive pose. "He hears and does not hear" telegraphs the selective filtration that Bronzeville dwellers must master in order to cope. The alarm, the oath, the spitting, the birdshit, the rackety elevated train are always implicitly there; that they are salient *here* is not an aberrancy of factitious descriptivism but because her subject is the process by which a mind that is sensitive yet self-focused filters out the intimation of "hundreds of hungers mingl[ing] with his own," withdrawing into the self-protective illusion that "he walks most powerfully alone."

The ecopoetics of the portrait poem (the commonest genre in Brooks's earlier canon) is as adaptable to the repressions of small-town life (as in Edwin Arlington Robinson's Tilbury Town poems and Edgar Lee Masters's *Spoon River Anthology*) as to a metropolitan scene. Brooks's work often reads, indeed, like a cross between Langston Hughes's casual impressionism (*The Weary Blues* [1926], Brooks said, first made her realize "that writing about the ordinary aspects of black life was important")[97] and Emily Dickinson's cerebral-intense conciseness. Dickinson does not need to sketch in village greens and church architecture in order to situate her "Soft-Cherubic" gentlewomen as small-town snobs, nor does Hughes need more than an allusion to "frozen rain" to place his "Troubled Woman" as a displaced person in the urban North.[98] Brooks admired how Hughes's impressionistic studies captured a sense of "the street"—"its multiple heart, its tastes, smells, alarms, formulas, flowers, garbage and convulsions"—as she herself did with greater compression.[99]

What especially links Berry and Brooks is the felt need to (re)discover the place one already "knows." For both, this starts with family history, across generations. Their work is full of tributes to parents and grandparents, marriage, ties to children. In this allegiance to family values they are both firmly, almost Norman Rockwellishly, mainstream writers, although Berry's agrarianism is self-evidently more middle American than Brooks's increasingly pan-Africanist aesthetic of black cultural retrieval.[100] Brooks would have agreed that "To be at home on its native ground / the mind must . . . / / receive the lives of the dead,"[101] however she might have felt about Berry's penchant for graveyard elegy. Related to *pietàs* of family is a strong internalized sense of propriety that, for example, leads Berry to reaffirm the holiness of traditional marriage, the great chain of being, the soundness of Alexander Pope relative to Walt Whitman, and the unsoundness of (post)modernism; and led Brooks, in her earlier work, to favor bound forms like sonnet and semiautobiographical portrayals of idealistic young women like Annie Allen and Maud Martha, who grow up yearning to live nice bourgeois lives amid adverse circumstances, and later to embrace an idealistic Afrocentric patriotism. There is a clear resemblance, despite the difference in gender politics, between Berry's anti–Cold-War message of solidarity to "A Siberian Woodman" from one good rustic father to another (your daughter playing the accordion, mine learning "the womanhood / of her mother") and Brooks's call "To Black Women" to "prevail across the editors of the world," as they hold "the civil balance, / The listening secrets" and "create and train your flowers still."[102]

Two long poems by each writer stand out as pivotal rededications to place: Brooks's "In the Mecca" (1968) and Berry's *Clearing* (1977). *Clearing* is a narrative-lyric series about the pivotal act of Berry's life as writer and as person: making a family home that is also to be a working farm out of an abandoned and abused property he and his wife bought in the 1960s and later added to. This was a work of Jeffersonian reenactment and environmental restoration connecting personal history to that of land, region, ultimately even nation. "In the Mecca," built on the grisly murder of little Pepita Smith, one of ten children of a single-mother-domestic struggling to sustain her family in a huge, overcrowded, dilapidated apartment building, is by far the longest poem Brooks ever published; a turning point in her conversion from Negro poet to Black poet;[103] and a long-pondered reprocessing of a disturbing autobiographical episode. The poem is also a conspicuous exception to her practice of starting with people rather than landmarks.

The original Mecca was an elegant apartment building erected at the turn of the century by the firm of Daniel Burnham, the urbanist-visionary most responsible for the White City of the 1893 Columbian Exposition and author of the utopian *Plan for the City of Chicago,* the central text of the so-called City Beautiful movement, satirized obliquely by Katharine Lee Bates in "America the Beautiful" and more openly by Jane Addams when she organized a band of juvenile pseudoparamilitary sanitation workers as Hull-House's part in the Exposition.[104] Originally a showcase, the Mecca deteriorated along with the neighborhood, and by the time of Richard Wright's literary apprenticeship and Brooks's childhood it had become an enormous tenement housing more than 2,000 people (exact number unknown): a half-block disaster area, its courtyard "littered with newspapers and tin cans, milk cartons, and broken glass," as one of the poem's headnotes has it.[105] The building was torn down in 1952, but Brooks remembered it well from the "most haunting and humiliating work experience" of her youth, working after graduation from junior college as assistant to a "spiritual advisor" based there (recycled in the poem as the lecherous charlatan Prophet Williams), who "traded in dreams and frustrations and supplied 'answers' to deeply troubled people" living in the tenement.[106]

Altogether, the Mecca was the very kind of place a respectably brought-up young woman (like Brooks's alter egoes Annie Allen and Maud Martha) would have been reared to eschew—although Brooks's early poems also confess the lure of the forbidden alternative:

> I've stayed in the front yard all my life.
> I want a peek at the back
> Where it's rough and untended and hungry weed grows,
> A girl gets sick of a rose.
> . . . . .
> And I'd like to be a bad woman, too,
> And wear the brave stockings of night-black lace
> And strut down the streets with paint on my face.[107]

In the 1960s Brooks did indeed decide to go "bad." The literary turning point was the collection In the Mecca (1968) and the biographical was her association with such younger generation Black Arts movement poets as Don L. Lee / Haki Madhubuti (who makes a cameo appearance in the poem), and her community work as volunteer writing instructor with members of the South Side Blackstone Rangers gang, begun the same year Mecca appeared, out of which came her anthology, Jump Bad (1971).

In the late 1950s Brooks initially wrote up her Mecca reminiscences in a novel for children about a young woman's coming of age in an alien milieu, then rewrote it during the 1960s into a sardonic social tragedy "thick with story and music and sound-and-fury."[108] She wanted to feature the Mecca's squalor even more pointedly than she did by issuing the 2,000-line poem as a book in itself (but Harper's insisted on a larger collection) and by using for the dust jacket a *Life* magazine photograph of the building's Piranesi-like staircase and a forlorn-looking Pepita-like waif (but *Life* refused permission to reprint).[109] The headnotes and the opening lines nevertheless trigger an unmistakable sense of the architectural uncanny:

> Sit where the light corrupts your face.
> Miës Van der Rohe retires from grace.
> And the fair fables fall.

The first line sets out to destroy composure: this command that we sit where we cannot but be corroded by the sight, this oxymoronic insistence on light as corruption. Warning: *flâneurs* who venture here will be unstrung. No culture here. No looking the opposite way, at the architectural showcase across the street.[110]

The implied voyeurs presumably include her former self. For "Mecca" refuses to maintain the breathing room between observer and observed that Brooks's earlier poems do, poems she once described as coming to her while ensconced, a stationery *flâneuse,* in the panoptical niche of her corner apartment at East 63rd Street and Champlain: "If you wanted a poem, you had only to look out of a window. There was material always, walking or running, fighting or screaming or singing."[111] Be that as it may, what follows is a gallery of grotesques, strung along the wire of Mrs. Sallie's frantic search through the building for Pepita, after an exhausted return to her flat from "the last sourings of the master's Feast" (the leftover anger-envy of a marathon Aunt Jemima act) (p. 407). All her fellow tenants are damaged people, some violent or feeble-minded or insane, some morally repulsive (like the self-righteous dowager whose rancor at her own childlessness makes her pretend-console Sallie with "sinister pianissimos" of a particularly gory juvenile rape-murder [p. 421]). And they are clueless and lackadaisical about the lost Pepita, who in a weirdly abrupt ending is discovered under the cot of her presumed murderer "Jamaican Edward," "in dust with roaches" (p. 433).

In portraying these people, the poem resists the stabler perspective of Brooks's early, concise, tonally modulated portrait poems. As Gayl Jones writes, "In the Mecca" "begins in an 'exclusive' rhetoric—a language that seems to set itself apart from the community's voice," yet "directs itself toward that community." Soon we find that "any kind of language may occupy any space."[112] The pre-kindergartner Pepita is made to speak poetic diction; inarticulacy is rendered as poetic refrain ("Ain seen er I ain seen er I ain seen er"); an old woman's vernacular monologue about roach-killing is orchestrated as blank verse (pp. 416, 417). Most of the weird chorus of tenants are pulled just enough away from frozen-in-place alterity to make even scary figures like gun-collecting Way-out Morgan (who nurses vengeful dreams in memory of lynched buddies and a mob-raped sister) seem, as the narrator says of the artsy-unglued teacher Alfred, "no good" yet "a decent enough no-goodness" (p. 409). So at the end Alfred's loquacity cannot be written off as mere blather for insisting that "something in Mecca," despite its hatefulness,

> continues to call! Substanceless; yet like mountains,
> like rivers and oceans too; and like trees
> with wind whistling through them. And steadily
> an essential sanity, black and electric,
> builds to a reportage and redemption.
> A hot estrangement.
> A material collapse
> that is Construction. (p. 433)

Brooks lets few affirmations stand irony-free. Immediately after this one comes disclosure of the murder, which in turn gives way to tender reminiscence, which in turn gives way to a bizarrely sexualized closing image of Pepita's death struggles ("Odd were the little wrigglings / and the chopped chirpings oddly rising") (p. 433). Yet beneath the ironic patina is diffused the impression that although these characters may be as doomed as the building that entombs them, they can't be dispensed with: there is some "black and electric" "sanity" here, something one wants to dignify by treating it as a natural force, whose action (like natural process? like poetry?) is such that "material collapse" somehow equals "Construction." This scene of human deterioration prior to the building's demolition affirms the worth of these damaged lives as strongly as the 1960s riot scenes of destruction Brooks treats in later poems in the book, like "Boy Breaking Glass," where the "barbarous and metal little man" is made to say/think: "I shall create! If not a note, a hole, / If not an overture, a desecration."[113]

Berry's sense of community victimization can be almost as bitter. Not only his district but "the people of rural America" generally, Berry writes, "are living in a colony," their ecosystems and communities under siege, because the national economy thrives "by the destruction of the principle of local self-sufficiency." Indeed, "if there is any law that has been consistently operative in American history, it is that the members of any *established* people or group or community sooner or later become 'redskins'"—victims of internal colonization.[114] Berry is no less painfully aware than Brooks of inheriting an abused, exploited landscape: "Through my history's despite / and ruin, I have come / to its remainder," he writes at the outset of *Clearing,* about the dilapidated place he hopes to restore.[115] He too is conscious that "Vision must have severity / at its edge" so as to guard against "the wish to make desire / easy" (pp. 21, 22). All his precursors, the exploiters as well as the good stewards, become part of his narrative of the farm's history. By the same token, he is also intent on situating himself not in a lyric or entrepreneurial space apart but as "moving in ancestral motions," in the company of other small farmers "swaying in all weathers in their long rows" (pp. 28, 31).

Brooks might have wished for the assurance of Berry's motto from the *I Ching:* "What has been spoiled through man's fault can be made good again through man's work" (p. 1). Obviously this is easier for Berry to affirm than for Brooks. He battles to redeem a "ruined" landscape (p. 14) from which trees have been stripped and topsoil lost by bad farming and mining practices, but the physical resources at his disposal are greater than for Brooks's South Siders. He and his wife own a sizable tract, which can be made bountiful through the right kind of hard work. Berry's writing also presumes a clan and community network more extensive and intact. Brooks, despite her strong sense of place-based family and community support, stressed to a much greater degree the mutual isolation of her urban figures. Mrs. Smith's frantic search for Pepita and its failure to do more than briefly half-awaken the other residents of the "Mecca" from their self-absorptions show how far these people are from experiencing the kind of "family" and "community" life that Berry feels to be still a lived reality in his home place.[116]

Whatever the difference in degree of embattlement, for each writer the goal of community restoration leads to the extreme of preferring to see one's identity wiped out than not to see this restoration happen. In *Clearing*, Berry wonders whether this passion might lead him away from books and writing:

> What will I say
> to my fellow poets
> whose poems I do not read
> while this passion keeps me
> in the open? What is
> this silence coming over me? (p. 33)

But this mood soon passes. For now, "reverdure / is my calling: / to make these scars grow grass." If this means the end of writing, so be it: "I must turn away / from books, put past and future behind, / to come into the presence of this time." So the poem ends—although not, of course, Berry's career (pp. 33, 50, 52).

For Brooks, that willingness was even greater. She published more sparingly after she became more overtly political; devoted more of her energies to supporting younger talent; deferred to the next generation of more outspoken black poets; accepted her position as "the bridge by which [they] were crossing over into new territory."[117] In such ways she came to accept more limits on expression in proportion to her increased sense of accountability to community. In a 1987 birthday tribute, Brooks's protégé-mentor Haki Madhubuti generously but also somewhat monitorially called Brooks "a woman who cannot live without her art, but who has never put her art above or before the people she writes about."[118] Berry does not seem to have been subjected to such surveillance but to have felt free to play the role of authoritative spokesman for "The New Politics of [Rural] Community," as he has recently called it.[119] Still, one comes away from reading both later Brooks and later Berry convinced that both would cheerfully cease writing and perish if they believed that would ensure the survival of their respective communities. That Brooks published little after 1970 in the fine, pointillist-ironic vein that brought her critical fame followed from a growing sense that that elegantly stylized aesthetic did not mesh with her proper reading community the way Berry had reason to feel his writing always has; or, perhaps more precisely, from a change of view as to how closely the reading community should approximate the life community. Berry, by contrast, never seems to have felt called to target, say, practitioners of sustainable agriculture as his primary reading audience. Yet the claims of that ethos lead Berry repeatedly throughout his work to scroll forward and imagine with profound satisfaction—almost Jeffers-like—his own death, burial, transmogrification into landscape and the *genius loci*. The greatest personal reward he wants to imagine in exchange for whatever form of faithful labor is that

> if we will make our seasons welcome here,
> asking not too much of earth or heaven,
> then a long time after we are dead
> the lives our lives prepare will live
> here, their houses strongly placed
> upon the valley sides, fields and gardens
> rich in the windows. (p. 31)

Brooks would have understood the self-effacing stewardship here, if not the agrarian zeal.

Brooks's vision of community regeneration looks insufficient from Berry's neo-Jeffersonian standpoint, not so much because of the ethnic identitarian turn in later Brooks—for Berry's beloved community is even more homogeneous than hers in every sense: culturally, religiously, economically—as because Brooks's conception of community rarely foregrounds transactions with natural environment as key to the health of persons and communities.[120] One can imagine Berry attentively reading Mumford, MacKaye, and McHarg on green regional planning, even as he fumed at how they contain their fundamental dislike of urban sprawl within an acceptance of the necessity of planned growth. Such work would have interested Brooks little, if it all. But Brooks's representations of the constraints facing urban African Americans clearly presuppose their emplacement within damaged physical environments whose remediation is part and parcel of cultural remediation, even if her emphasis is more on psychograph than on material detail.

Speaking for the Determined: Addams

What to conclude from such polyphony? The voices we have heard define determinism differently according to what they see as the primary determining force—physical nature, human nature, or socioculture; they assess its potency differently; they disagree as to whether it can have constructive as well as blighting effects and, if so, why. One constant, however, is antipathy toward such determinism as ensues from human dictation of the terms of another's existence, even with benign intent. By no coincidence this also happens to be a key ethical-political commitment of toxic discourse.

From this standpoint there can be no more paradigmatic literary reflection on environmental determinism than Jane Addams's magnificent essay, "A Modern Lear," which turns on the irony of railroad entrepreneur George Pullman's obduracy during the strike of 1894 that ignited a union-instigated boycott of Pullman cars.

Pullman was an "unusually generous employer" who had bankrolled the construction of a model town for his workers, with "perfect surroundings," "sanitary houses and beautiful parks," and even a state-of-the-art theater. But his arbitrary reduction of wages and his refusal to negotiate exposed the philanthropist's utopia as a self-serving manipulation. Pullman is Lear, the workers are Cordelia. The angry magnate "who spent a million of dollars on a swamp to make it sanitary for his employes [sic]" and later refuses "to speak to them for ten minutes whether they were in the right or wrong" is a latter-day Lear peremptorily disowning his daughter as "unnatural" for not swearing unconditional fealty.[121] Such being the price of the kingdom, small wonder the workers, like Cordelia, readily left. That no Progressive-era reformer set a higher value than did Addams on a healthy physical environment as precondition for elementary human dignity and accomplishment makes even more striking her denunciation of a case where environmentalism becomes perverted into an instrument of authoritarian control.

Addams does not exonerate the workers; that too is important to her Shakespearean analogy: subaltern overreaction. Up to a point the terms of her indictment of the captain of industry strongly anticipate the ecofeminist critique of the patriarchalist-dominationist tenor of modern science and technology, but her allegory also has a paternalistic cast. Industry in principle is or ought to be like family; reciprocal obligations between employers and employees ought to be like father-child obligations.[122] Yet Addams's image of the worker, especially of Pullman workers,[123] is the child as adult, not the adult infantilized; and the key, as she sees it, to the tragedy of Pullman's ostensibly admirable environmental design was failure to seek the consent of the governed. Even modest reforms that acknowledge "the necessity for consent," Addams concludes, are far more likely to get results than "the most ambitious of social plans and experiments" that disregard this principle.[124]

Addams's antipathy to imposed environmental determination rests on an idiosyncratic and historically specific mix of traditional family and democratic values, together with a vision of social solidarity influenced by socialism and trade unionism that proved, she maintained, the perniciousness of another iconic national value, Pullman's rugged individualism. ("Of the new code of ethics he had caught absolutely nothing.")[125] But her resistance to arrogant imposition is broadly shared by all the writers we have discussed, even Jeffers. One hardly dares claim this to be a universally held conviction, even within the English-speaking world, as can be seen from George Bernard Shaw's *Major Barbara,* which seems to take perverse satisfaction in the reformist daughter's cooptation by her magnate-father's grand schemes, including a model workers' village. But in the main, Anglophone writers have been more drawn to "soft-determinist" visions of consenting acquiescence to communal and/or perceived physical-environmental limits than to "hard-determinist" visions of imposed limits. Calls to reinhabitation will likely always feel more palatable than arguments that people are already place-bound (whether they know it or not), much less that they ought to be made more so. But the cogency of reinhabitory rhetoric, "A Modern Lear" also suggests, is likely to be all the greater when the appeal is not to voluntarism alone but also to identification with the condition of those whose lives—comparatively speaking—are determined: determined, as in the Pullman case, by those who have the power to act as they will. The deepest implication of Addams's essay is the hubris and certain failure of any and all environmental reform initiatives undertaken without regard to what life on the receiving end feels like: how it feels to live, in the first instance and without certain prospect of relief, under another power's control.

Chapter 5

Modernization and the Claims of the Natural World: Faulkner and Leopold

> To him, they were going not to hunt bear and deer but to keep yearly rendezvous with the bear which they did not even intend to kill. Two weeks later they would return, with no trophy, no skin. He had not expected it.
>
> —William Faulkner, "The Bear"

> Some day the hunter will learn that hunting and fishing are not the only wildlife sports; that the new sports of ecological study and observation are as free to all now as hunting was to Daniel Boone. These new sports depend on the retention of a rich flora and fauna . . . There is a growing number of private sanctuaries, private arboreta, and private research stations, all of which are groupings toward non-lethal forms of outdoor recreation.
>
> —Aldo Leopold, "The State of the Profession" [of Wildlife Management]

Both the awakening of obligation to become a reinhabitor and the awakening of a sense of environmental determinism require at some point reconceiving the human relation to the nonhuman, and the ethical borderline between these. A reinhabitory commitment entails extension of moral and sometimes even legal standing to the nonhuman world; a determinist mentality tends to minimize difference between humans and nonhumans, at least so far as exemption from environmental constraints is concerned. The former conditions one to think compassionately of animals and trees as kindred beings; the latter conditions one to think of them all in the same boat. Or perhaps "reconditions" would be more accurate, since the modern vocabulary for expressing these intimations often draws upon images of preindustrial cultures that we take, with a mixture of accuracy and fancifulness, as living in closer symbiosis with the nonhuman world than we.

Nothing conduces to a livelier sense of either mentality than contemplation of scenes of rapid environmental change. Many classics of U.S. environmental writing have been influenced by experience or knowledge of such changes in the author's home districts—James Fenimore Cooper's Cooperstown novel *The Pioneers* and his daughter Susan Fenimore Cooper's literary daybook *Rural Hours* (from wilderness to settlement, from settlement to county seat); Thoreau's *Walden* (from traditional agricultural village to suburban market town); George Perkins Marsh's *Man and Nature* (the deforestation of nineteenth-century Vermont); Willa Cather's *O Pioneers!* and *My Àntonia* (from raw prairie to tidy farms to bustling railroad towns). Another such case is the fiction of William Faulkner. Few writers have reflected on their regions' transits from outback to modernization with more visionary amplitude and deeper historical understanding.

In Faulkner's fiction, particularly *Go Down, Moses,* an incipient environmental ethic begins to take shape in response to regional modernization in many ways compatible with the more fully articulated environmentalism of his near-contemporary, ecologist and nature writer Aldo Leopold. Neither of the two, despite appearances to the contrary, was at bottom an antimodernist, much less a primitivist. Yet each was disconcerted by what he took to be ruthless exploitation of rurality by industry and agribusiness. For each, the history of land transformation from the mid-nineteenth century to the mid-twentieth loomed up as a potentially determinisitic force resistible only through forms of environmental stewardship that took feats of literary imagination to express. Through scenes of imagined leisure, Faulkner and Leopold sought to reconceive the place of nature within the space of culture, and in the process to define an ethics of "ownership" and "possession" for audiences whom they imagined to be, like themselves, both perpetrators and victims.

Faulkner as Environmental Historian

Faulkner is not often considered an "environmental writer," and understandably so. His interest in environmental change was but one dimension of his interest in southern character and history. But the material particularity of regional environment is basic to his representation of place. At the core of Faulkner's first important Yoknapatawpha fiction, *Flags in the Dust* (1927, 1973), is the sense of future shock wrought by technological innovation—cars and airplanes especially—on this backwater. Rarely does Faulkner's mature fiction fail to take shrewd account of southern modernization, especially its casualties and failures, in such a way as to connect people to landscape. *Light in August* (1932) is a good example. The familiar opening phase of this novel seems at first sight to organize itself overwhelmingly around the figure of Lena Grove moving serenely across a more or less undifferentiated landscape: a figure synthesized from several stereotypes (earth mother, Madonna, southern poor white) into a luminous and memorable symbolic image with a soft romantic glow. Yet the reader is also asked to imagine Lena in relation to a more materially specific ground, the world of Doane's Mill, from which she has come, and where she got pregnant by Lucas Burch, the no-good deadbeat she pursues for the rest of the novel. Concerning Doane's Mill, we are told:

> All the men in the village worked in the mill or for it. It was cutting pine. It had been there seven years and in seven years more it would destroy all the timber within its reach. Then some of the machinery and most of the men who ran it and existed because of and for it would be loaded onto freight cars and moved away. But some of the machinery would be left, since new pieces could always be bought on the installment plan—gaunt, staring, motionless wheels rising from mounds of brick rubble and ragged weeds with a quality profoundly astonishing, and gutted boilers lifting their rusting and unsmoking stacks with an air stubborn, baffled and bemused upon a stumppocked scene of profound and peaceful desolation, unplowed, untilled, gutting slowly into red and choked ravines beneath the long quiet rains of autumn and the galloping fury of vernal equinoxes.[1]

In one paragraph the novel provides a concise history of the cut-and-get-out phase of the timber industry in the Deep South: a half-century of intensive exploitation and chronic waste (of forest, soil, people, and equipment), starting in the 1880s, that Faulkner realizes was nearly spent. Southern forest historians identify the early 1930s, the moment of *Light in August*'s publication, as the point when the large tracks of timber in Mississippi's old growth forest finally ran out and lumber production hit a fifty-year low.[2]

The novel's plot intertwines forest history with social history. Initially the rise of the lumber industry (which in the early 1900s rivaled and in some areas exceeded cotton as the Deep South's major cash crop) created, as one historian puts it, an opportunity for employment in mills that acted "as social and economic safety valves by drawing away from cotton tenancy surplus laborers who had no alternative source of employment." Most workers, however, wound up trading "peonage to the sharecropper landlord and the country furnishing store for peonage to the lumber company commissary."[3] "The sawmill worker was underpaid, lived in a nondescript house, and was able to obtain for himself only the plainest of food and clothing. Few were ever able to rise in the social and economic scale. Many were without ambition, easily satisfied with living only in the present, and little concerned about the future of themselves or their children. [Even] had the average worker been dissatisfied with the life he knew, he had little opportunity for improvement."[4]

This supplies the social frame within which a great many things about the characters to whom *Light in August* introduces us can be understood: the anxious stolidity of Lena's unromantic brother and sister-in-law with their too-large family, the rootless dysfunctionality of the seducer Lucas, the reluctant mobility of Lena herself, and the counterpoint between Lucas and his hard-working quasi-namesake Byron Bunch—the superconscientious, repressed, but warm-hearted schlemiel who falls in love with Lena to the point that he quits *his* job at a Jefferson planing mill and forfeits the precarious social standing he has painstakingly built up. All these characters are what they are not just because of who they are but because of where they fit in the history of Mississippi lumbering. Lucas's placelessness, which becomes a stalking horse for his partner Joe Christmas's more extreme placelessness, is as much a product of his culture's shortsightedness about its natural resources as Christmas's is a product of the culture's shortsightedness about race.

That environmental history can illuminate Faulkner's fiction is only to be expected of a person whose enthusiasm for taking his annual hunting trip to the Mississippi Delta almost kept him from traipsing to Stockholm to receive the Nobel Prize. Not only did Faulkner know at least as much about hunting and farming as any American modernist writer, he was also a pretty fair natural historian: "the best scoutmaster [Oxford] ever had," according to the man who was chancellor of the University of Mississippi during the 1920s.[5] He was a close observer in his fiction of regional weather, "its vegetable and animal life, its trees, flowers, insects, birds . . .—as well as of the sounds of nature and the many changes in the play of light."[6] It is symptomatic that the title of *Light in August* refers to a specific seasonal atmospheric effect.[7]

Not that we do full justice to the place of the natural world in Faulkner's work merely by inventorying landscape items and proving their historical or geographical accuracy. For one thing, nature in his writing gets filtered through the lenses of literary convention: stock romantic imagery of pastoral retreat from Andrew Marvell to A. E. Housman, American masculinist wilderness narrative from Cooper to Melville and Twain. In Faulkner's juvenilia especially, the evocation of landscape is passionate but bookish: *The Marble Faun,* his early poetic sequence, looks at landscape and sees rooks and nightingales.[8] Such excrescences get pruned, but it remains a crucial part of Faulkner's mature aesthetics to infuse facticity with myth, legend, and poetic rhetoric. In *Light in August,* a recurring motif of Lucas and especially Lena as vernacularized versions of ancient literary types (the faithless seducer and the Madonna/earth mother) is interwoven with the environmental realism I have stressed. Likewise, the passage quoted earlier starts with an almost photographic approach but then metamorphoses into a highly stylized regional gothic, with the "gaunt, staring" wheels rising up in a way "profoundly astonishing," and the "stubborn, baffled and bemused" look of the "gutted boilers."

Yet when Faulkner stylizes like this he does not "lose touch" with environmental particularity, any more than Henry Thoreau can be said to have lost touch by overstating the seclusion of his retreat at Walden, which was justified in a more historically precise sense by the extreme strangeness of his removal in the eyes of his watchful Concord neighbors. In the Faulkner passage stylized "exaggeration" conveys the ugly wastefulness of industry's leavings and also (no less strikingly) the environment's power to fight back in its own way, as the machinery disintegrates in "the red and choked ravines beneath the long quiet rains of autumn and the galloping fury of vernal equinoxes." Indeed, *Light in August*'s surrealistic image of the blighted landscape is uncannily anticipated by a passage from a 1921 report by Mississippi state geologist E. N. Lowe describing how "cut-over areas" in this part of the country tend to degrade: "Whenever the slightest furrow concentrates the flow of rain a gully begins to form; when this deepens so as to reach the sand beneath, undercutting and slumping begins and progresses with re- markable rapidity, so that a graceful slope in an old field may in an in- credibly short time present a maze of gullies and washes, some of which soon attain enormous proportions. I have seen a pig-trail down a hill slope develope [sic] into a chasm in the hill-side that would engulf a two-story house."⁹

Neither Lowe's nor Faulkner's visions of nature's resurgence are pretty pictures. This is not Gerard Manley Hopkins, in his sonnet on "God's Grandeur," banishing the depressing thought that the world is "bleared" and "smeared" with toil in the assurance that nature will al- ways regenerate. Rather what we have here is an insight into a fre- quently disconcerting kind of environmental effect about which Faulkner's fiction often remarks: the special intensity to subtropical southern nature that gives it power over its human inhabitants as well as vice-versa. In this case, that "nature's revenge" has been set in mo- tion by human wastage intensifies the passage's somber irony. Alto- gether, it makes environmental as well as ideological sense that Faulkner's profuse descriptivism should have influenced the "magical" realism of Gabriel Garcia Marquez and other Latin American novelists. One thinks also of such other Faulknerian signature pieces as the de- scription of the nineteenth-century southern forest as Thomas Sutpen found it in *Absalom, Absalom* (1936) or of Bayard Sartoris's impression in *The Unvanquished* (1938) of the railroad destroyed by Union armies hav- ing quickly become "a few piles of charred ties among which green grass was already growing, a few threads of steel knotted and twisted about the trunks of trees and already annealing into the living bark, be- coming one and indistinguishable with the jungle growth which had now accepted it."¹⁰ Or the hallucinatory experience of the tenderfoot protagonist in the early tale "Nympholepsy," who is used to thinking of trees as timber but now suddenly feels the forest gazing on him threat- eningly, and "above all brood[ing] some god" who regards him "as a trespasser where he had no business being."¹¹

The primordialist vision here, of natural forces bound to assert them- selves, gets worked out most fully in the "Old Man" sequence of *If I Forget Thee, Jerusalem* (1939) and in *Go Down, Moses* (1942). These narra- tives come to opposite conclusions. The first is Faulkner's strongest presentation of nature untrammeled—a gripping narrative of man against flood (probably alluding to the great Mississippi Flood of 1927, which Faulkner believed wiped out the last bear in the Delta).[12] The protagonist in "Old Man"—simply called the "tall convict," as if to refuse him any greater personhood than the river itself, to which the title metaphor refers—despite feats of almost superhuman endurance can do no more than barely cope with the brute force of nature. By contrast, *Go Down, Moses,* published just a few years later, elegaically bears witness to the disappearance of the virgin forest and with it the imminent death of first nature as the protagonist has known it. Had Faulkner realized that the flood was exacerbated by unwise manipulations of the river and its tributaries by a long succession of engineering feats, the emphases of the two works might have converged.[13]

However that may be, Faulkner's straddling between images of nature as independent, irresistible force in "Old Man" versus the "doomed wilderness" (through Ike McCaslin's eyes) in *Go Down, Moses* suggests some reasons Faulkner never developed a coherent environmental ethic, despite his perspicacity as an observer of forest and fauna if not of riverways. First, as with most laypeople, his knowledge of environmental cause and effect was spotty. Second, and more important, the notion of "natural force" as human adversary continued to run strong in his thinking at some level—in which respect he was no different from the overwhelming majority of settlement-culture writers worldwide. Third, he was a professional writer with one eye pragmatically on the marketplace. He was well aware of the almost equally great audience appeal of both man-versus-natural-disaster stories and wilderness initiation stories; and if they cut in opposite directions so far as environmental ethics was concerned, the professional writer in him was not going to strain too much to reconcile the contradiction.

Perhaps the best evidence of this pragmatism on Faulkner's part is his readiness to dumb down episodes in his death of the wilderness saga for mass market consumption: to suspend completion of the *Go Down, Moses* project in order to crank out and sell a compressed version of the early portions of "The Bear" to the *Saturday Evening Post;* to dish up "Race at Morning" for the *Post* in the 1950s; and to collect his more user-friendly hunting stories in *The Big Woods.* This does not mean, however, that he was not even more deeply committed in another part of his being to exfoliating the deeper complexities of the South's historical saga, including serious and sustained works of environmental reflection. A closer look at *Go Down, Moses* shows precisely that.

Go Down, Moses and Environmental Unconscious

Go Down, Moses was one of those books that grows far beyond an author's first conscious intent. Faulkner initially thought of it as a short story collection on the "general theme [of the] relationship between white and negro races here," to be got up like *The Unvanquished* so that it would reap the double harvest of magazine and book publication. His first working table of contents included only five of the eventual seven items: "The Fire and the Hearth," "Pantaloon in Black," "The Old People," "Delta Autumn," and "Go Down, Moses."[14] According to biographer Joseph Blotner, only after revising as far as the middle of "Delta Autumn" (which portrays what may be the last hunt for Ike McCaslin, here figured as a quasi-senile octogenarian) did Faulkner decide to write "The Bear," even though he had previously published a shorter proto-version of the hunting sequence under the title of "Lion" (*Harper's*, 1935).[15] He also added "Was," the farcical tale of the temporary rescue of Ike McCaslin's father-to-be, Uncle Buck, from the clutches of his future mother, Sophonsiba Beauchamp, when Buck's twin brother Uncle Buddy beats Uncle Hubert in a poker game. Therefore the completed novel (as Faulkner came to think of it: not story collection, but novel—he was irked when Random House entitled it *Go Down, Moses, and Other Stories*) came to focus much more on the nineteenth century relative to the twentieth, and—especially pertinent to the point at hand—it also came to foreground environmental reflection to a far greater degree than originally.

In particular, Faulkner invented the figure of the youthful Ike. Until he interrupted his revision of the original story sequence well past the halfway point in order to compose "The Bear," Ike McCaslin seems hardly to have existed for Faulkner except as the crusty old codger of "Delta Autumn" and the farcical 1935 story "The Bear Hunt" (which has virtually no resemblance to the later novella "The Bear"). Both "The Old People" and "Lion" were initially Quentin Compson stories. From *Go Down, Moses* on, however, it is young man Ike who dominates old man Faulkner's imagination. Like his literary forebear, James Fenimore Cooper's Leatherstocking, Ike McCaslin grew younger as his author grew older.[16]

In Faulkner's original group of five stories, the historical center of gravity is the near present, save for a brief retrospect via the middle story ("The Old People") back to the age of the big virgin forests, where the boy novice is vouchsafed a glimpse of an enormous buck by Sam Fathers. The tales that bracket this one, "Pantaloon in Black" and "Delta Autumn," record chapters in the demise of wilderness in black and white. In "Pantaloon," the protagonist, a colossal John Henry-like figure named Rider, who heads a gang of black timber workers at a sawmill, goes haywire when his wife dies, and gets lynched after slashing his white foreman in a game of craps: crunched up like the huge logs he prides himself on being able to sling around from truck to mill down the skidway. What sawmilling does to the woods, what skidway gouges do to the hillsides,[17] is mirrored by what the social system does to uppity black workers—and vice versa. The story seems nightmarish, fantastic; yet it is faithful to history.[18]

Rider's logs come from the same hardwood forests of cypress, gum, and oak whose disappearance old Ike McCaslin laments in "Delta Autumn." Here too the fate of the character is linked to the fate of the woods, in this case by Ike himself—who can take consolation only in the escapist fancy that both his life and that of the wilderness are exactly coeval, "the two spans running out together, not toward oblivion, nothingness, but into a dimension free of time and space where once more the untreed land warped and wrung to mathematical squares of rank cotton for the frantic old-world people to turn into shells to shoot at one another, would find ample room for both—the names, the faces of the old men he had known and loved and for a little while outlived, moving again and again among the shades of tall unaxed trees and sightless brakes where the wild strong immortal game ran forever before the tireless belling [sic] immortal hounds."[19]

Given that the figure of Ike McCaslin has been picked apart by several generations of Faulknerians, I need not belabor the point that Ike's voice is not to be taken as identical with the authorial voice. The evidence does not rest only on Ike's rhetorical senilities, either; "The Bear" has already laid the groundwork by exposing prim young Ike's seduction, the formal parallels between his moral bookkeeping and commissary discourse, his impotence to control the headstrong Boon Hogganbeck, and the sly association of Ike with the forest products industry as the result of his decision to follow a carpenter's trade (which Ike rationalizes as Christ-like).

Indeed, had Faulkner not taken the step of composing "The Bear," thereby shifting the center of gravity in Go Down, Moses from its original base, readers would not even have got the impression in the first place that Ike is the book's central figure, any more than (say) either his cousin Roth Edmonds or Roth's black sharecropper and cousin (via Old Carothers) Lucas Beauchamp. Rather, the main emphasis, at least so far as the environmental history theme is concerned, would have been exposure of the parallel impotence and victimage of both black and white before the juggernaut of Delta enterprise. In the original sequence, not only is the romantic flavor of wilderness initiation narrative in "The Old People" bracketed by "Pantaloon" and "Delta Autumn," it is neutralized in advance by the satirical novella that comes first, "The Fire and the Hearth," whose central section contains a parody of hunting narrative, when Lucas Beauchamp becomes obsessed (as Roth Edmonds puts it) with "poking around in the bottom . . . hunting for" buried treasure with his metal-detecting gadget from Memphis. This seems a wry acknowledgment of the link between hunting rituals and extraction of wealth of all sorts from the woods.[20] The addition of "The Bear" and "Was" to the original sequence places much more emphasis on the romance of preindustrial days versus the shabby present, on wilderness versus settlement culture, and on white innocence versus the hard-bitten wisdom of middle and old age, with the latter no longer represented so centrally by the cranky Lucas but by the more idealized figure of Sam Fathers. In Go Down, Moses as finally published, the significance of ending the book with back-to-back chapters in which uppity third-generation Beauchamps disrupt Jim Crow complacencies threatens to get eclipsed by the much greater emphasis on white angst.

Despite Faulkner's history as a literary entrepreneur, especially after he married and started to try to assume a squirearchical lifestyle in the early 1930s, it is unlikely that the greater romanticization of the revised Go Down, Moses was only a strategy for appealing to readerly nostalgia. There is every reason to believe that with one side of his mind Faulkner

shared a considerable measure of Ike's grief at the demise of the traditional hunting grounds (which were his own hunting grounds as well),
and that this helped prompt him to evoke more fully the memory of a
more pristine past.[21] What's more, Faulkner's nostalgia did not just have
to do with the transformation of nature but with cultural transformation also. In a polite version of the sardonic banter about politics by the
hunters in "Delta Autumn," Faulkner himself later addressed the council of archconservative Delta planters on the evils of government inter-
ference and the virtues of the personal freedom and civic responsibility
exemplified by "the old fathers in the old strong, dangerous times."[22]
Faulkner's affectionate dedication of Go Down, Moses to his family's
Mammy was another obvious mark of reverence for antique social
arrangements.

Faulkner's additions to the book also to some extent qualify and off-
set such idealization of premodernity, however. They make clear that
the space of the hunt, the space of the wilderness, was no safe refuge:
that it was not immune from village and town institutions any more
than Ike could realize his dream of self-extrication from economic en-
tanglements.[23] The long fourth part of "The Bear" was devised not only
as a counter to the hunting sequence (the dialogue between Ike and Mc-
Caslin in the family commissary store when Ike turns twenty-one, in
which the "original sins" of the family patriarch Old Carothers Mc-
Caslin, Ike's grandfather, are revealed—miscegenation and incest with
his female slaves). In addition to injecting these serpents into the hunting narrative, Faulkner revised the denouement of the hunting sequence itself, so as to have Major de Spain sell the timber rights to his
Big Bottom tract to a Memphis logging company—a telling detail not in
the original story, "Lion."

In so doing, Faulkner may or may not have been revisiting a real-life
event: the demise of his own Big Bottom happy hunting ground,
bought and held as an investment property by his friend Phil Stone's father, a successful timberland speculator, until the Depression caught up
with him and he died debt-ridden.[24] This misfortune occurred the year
after "Lion" was published, and after Faulkner and a group of other
local men tried to protect the game on General Stone's holdings (simultaneously reserving the right to hunt it for themselves) by incorporating
the "Okatoba Hunting and Fishing Club."[25] Even if there was no inten-

tional link between the historical Stone's fortunes and the fictional de Spain's decision to turn a buck on his holdings of virgin timber, Faulkner's revisions of Go Down, Moses pretty clearly reflect some of the major cross-currents in 1930s Mississippi so far as treatment and attitude toward forest lands are concerned. During this decade conservationist thinking was gaining ground in the Deep South to a more rapid extent since the advent of large-scale timbering in the 1880s, owing to the depletion of accessible big virgin timber tracts and the advent of such New Deal initiatives as the Soil Conservation Bureau, the Civilian Conservation Corps, and other tree-replacement programs.[26]

In retrospect, at least if one's criterion is the maintenance of a large harvestable acreage, one can read U.S. timber history in the South and indeed the nation generally as melodrama rather than as tragedy: the feared and perhaps threatened extinction of forestlands averted by resourceful implementation, albeit sometimes belated, of prudent conservationist measures.[27] On the other hand, during the 1930s Mississippi lagged behind the rest of the South in this regard. Throughout the decade it "ranked first among southern states in lumber production and last in reforestation": 50 percent more wood was cut than replaced. The Delta region, furthermore, was the most retrograde in the state, the slowest to reverse itself. In the thirties, forties, and fifties, forest acreage in Mississippi as a whole increased, but in the Delta continued to decline.[28]

Altogether we might draw at least four inferences from Faulkner's treatment of the loss of wilderness in "The Bear" in the revised Go Down, Moses. First, the long and irregular saga of bringing to partial articulation the previously much more inchoate ingredients of Faulknerian environmental unconscious makes a haunting case study of the complex mix of those ingredients—biographical event-sequence, sociohistorical assumption structures, literary templates, and phenomenological frames we sometimes grandiosely call "archetypal"—as they work themselves through under the influence of extrinsic distractions like production demands. Second, as an act of historical reflection, to a large degree "The Bear" projects back on the late nineteenth century both a plot of wilderness destruction and an ethos of forest preservation that look somewhat anachronistic when measured against the record of southern environmental history and environmentalism—more like

1930s attitudes than like late nineteenth-century attitudes. Few if any late nineteenth-century southerners were as ecocentric as the young Ike McCaslin, partly no doubt because the really large-scale exploitation of the Deep South's forests ("the years of frantic harvest," southern forest historian Thomas Clark calls them) had only just begun. Part 5 of "The Bear" is set on the eve of this phase of intensive logging, right after the end of Reconstruction.[29]

Yet in the third place, by the same token "The Bear" makes good historical sense as a prophetic intervention reflecting the rise of environmentalist concern in Faulkner's own day. It makes sense that at this moment in local, regional (and indeed national) history the death of wilderness should have loomed up for Faulkner as a pressing concern. It makes sense that he might have felt it more likely there would be an audience for a fiction with a protectionist twist than even just a decade before. But given the still feeble and incipient state of environmentalism in the Deep South, it also made sense that Faulkner would opt for apocalyptic intensification by linking together the advent of late nineteenth-century rapacity in "The Bear" with the more presentist scenes of thoughtless exploitation in "Pantaloon" and environmental deterioration in "Delta Autumn."

Finally, partly for the same reason, it made sense that Faulkner should have turned to hunting narratives as a vehicle for dramatizing environmentalist consciousness. Not only did this vehicle come naturally to Faulkner as an old sportsman, it is historically the case that since the birth of organized environmentalism in the United States in the late nineteenth century, sport hunters have been conservationist advocates rather than the reverse. "Until well into the twentieth century" they were "the largest organized group working to save wildlife."[30] Even though it is going too far to call sportsmen "the real spearhead of conservation," even though their conservationism was self-interested (a way of maintaining game stocks for themselves by legislating against commercial and unlicensed proletarian "pot-shooters"), it is also the case that through their organizations and magazines wilderness-friendly retelling of hunting and fishing stories had become institutionalized as a means of raising public environmental consciousness. "We must preserve our forests and streams to enjoy good mountain hunting and inland fishing" was the enlightened sportsman's typical line.[31] Conversely, before 1930 most of the significant male writers on behalf of conservation and preservation were or had in their early lives been seriously attracted to hunting and fishing.[32] Hunting traditions, hunting narratives, and the intertwinement of hunting and conservation interests have run especially strong in the South, even down to today.[33]

Faulkner, Leopold, and Ecological Ethics

A prime example of a hunter-turned-environmentalist is the man known today as the father of modern environmental ethics, Aldo Leopold, whose period of greatest productivity as a writer coincides closely with Faulkner's. Leopold's most enduring book, *A Sand County Almanac*, adumbrates a "land ethic" based on conscienceful human use of nonhuman nature, in the spirit of awareness that all species have a right to exist "as a matter of biotic right."[34] One of Leopold's prime sources of exempla of how to treat nature properly are narratives about hunting and fishing—narratives in which, like Faulkner, Leopold stresses proper process (mastery of woodcraft knowledge requisite to hunting, for example) as vastly more important than product (bagging the game). Like Faulkner, Leopold had been conditioned from youth by the traditional sportsman's code to see hunting "not as an abomination, nor as an inconsistency, but as active participation in the drama of life, to be conducted in a civil manner." For both, the ideal hunt seemed increasingly to be one in which the act of hunting gave way to nature appreciation.[35] Leopold's "Smoky Gold" is nominally about grouse hunting, but no grouse are shot (despite a misleading illustration in the text of feathers sticking out of the pocket of the hunter's jacket). As his dog flushes a buck, the author placidly eats his lunch and enjoys the needle-fall of the surrounding tamaracks (the source of the title image). The premise behind this whimsical narrative is spelled out in one of the four extended doctrinal pieces in the final section of *Sand County Almanac*, "Conservation Esthetic," in which Leopold urges readers to forsake "trophy"-seeking for the higher, sublimated pleasures of refined perception, cautioning that "it is the expansion of transport [punning here on increased road access and the commensurate increase in mass trophy-fetishism thereby made possible] without a corresponding growth of perception that threatens us with qualitative bankruptcy of the recreational process."[36]

The best-known section of *Sand County Almanac*, "Thinking like a Mountain," is a stylized reminiscence in the form of a kind of deconversion-from-hunting narrative. Looking into the eyes of the dying wolf he has just shot, the author realizes the self-indulgent immaturity of his "trigger-itch," and begins to realize the stupidity of the justification: "that because fewer wolves meant more deer, that no wolves would mean hunter's paradise." Into a few pages is packed the lesson that it took Leopold and other outdoorsmen of his generation many years to learn: from a broader ecological perspective, that of the mountain, wolves are needed to control the deer population that will otherwise deforest the slopes. But Leopold gives no satisfaction to deer hunters either: the best way to control deer, he implies, is to let wolves do it. A more explicit taboo against hunting is created visually by Charles Schwartz's accompanying illustration of a doe guarding her fawn.[37]

From a present-day standpoint, Leopold's didactic stories of how to conduct, or not to conduct, sport hunting in nature-sensitive ways seem somewhat naïvely androcentric and boy-scoutish—as do Faulkner's to some extent. For one thing, readers are apt to be more mindful that these moves had been anticipated long before: as in Thoreau's assessment, during the "Higher Laws" chapter of *Walden*, of literal hunting as a boy's pursuit that mature men should outgrow; and perhaps especially in literary protests against hunting for commercial and/or "scientific" purposes by conservationist-minded women writers later in the nineteenth century such as Sarah Orne Jewett's "A White Heron" (1886), in which a young woman's sense of kindred with wild creatures makes her refuse to tell a specimen collector the location of the bird's nest despite her attraction to him. Then too, from a turn-of-the-twenty-first-century middle-class perspective, the whole notion of hunting seems more atavistic than it did a half-century ago, particularly for city folk and suburbanites. In my teaching experience at various northeastern and midwestern institutions, students from metropolitan areas tend to find themselves at odds over this issue with students from rural areas. To the former (a growing majority) it seems axiomatic that hunting, for sport if not for subsistence, ought to be banned. After one makes the necessary allowances for youthful intolerance and simple naïveté about what rural life is like on a daily basis, it seems clear that second thoughts about metropolitan civilization's increasing dominance (making "wilderness" more remote and more luminously iconic for larger numbers of people) has significantly altered public attitudes concerning the proper treatment of nonhuman creatures and their status as moral agents. Even if it is not true across the board that "hunting has ceased to be a marker of high social status" in the United States today,[38] the heyday of imperial hunting in Victorian Britain and its American macho imitators like Theodore Roosevelt and Ernest Hemingway is long since over.[39] Nature-watching safaris for both sexes, not game-bagging safaris dominated by men, are the Eurocentric norm. From a turn-of-the-twenty-first-century perspective, then, figures like Faulkner and Leopold look distinctly transitional.

"The Bear" represents, as it were, the stage at which the male, classist tradition from which standpoint "wilderness" is a gentlemen's preserve and the underclass subservient to the recreational and aesthetic needs of the ruling classes begins to recoil on itself. Both the rituals of the hunt and the class hierarchy on which their execution rests get held up to question, even though the old traditions retain considerable force even after they have been discredited—as we see from how the geriatric Ike McCaslin, despite having "relinquished" both birthright and conventional hunting protocols, tags along for the now-debased annual event long after his renunciation of settler-culture ways. This transitionalness is another means of connecting the time of the event-sequence (concurrent with the golden age of genteel sport hunting) to a contemporary dispensation when controls on hunting practices had become more institutionalized, as indeed they were at the time of writing.

Leopold, albeit a decade Faulkner's senior, exemplifies that later phase. Trained as an environmental professional (forestry) shortly after the turn of the century, he was among the first wave of Gifford Pinchot's followers, and an increasingly zealous supporter of legalized conservation efforts and scientific principles of nature-friendly environmental management as he moved from the federal bureaucracy into academia. Only in retrospect does *Sand County Almanac* loom up as Leopold's magnum opus. He himself would have thought it to be *Game Management* (1933), the leading textbook in the field. Significantly, if Leopold's editorial team had let the order of chapters in *Sand County* stand when revising the book for its posthumous publication, it would have ended with the assertion that "it is only the scholar who understands why the raw wilderness gives definition and meaning to the human enterprise."[40] Yet as vignettes like "Smoky Gold" and "Thinking like a Mountain" show, and as Leopold's modern readers have perceived, the book's actual trajectory does not reinforce the authority of environmental professionalism, much less that of regulatory institutions, as it does the significance of awakening environmental unconscious to "ecological conscience," as Leopold called it. *Sand County Almanac*—the final result more than the original design—tends to portray the author, as Robert L. Dorman shrewdly remarks, in the guise of a man "*retreating* from politics and policy-making . . . to seek the personal refuge of an authentic ethical life," a self-portrait that may in part signify frustration or uncertainty over how "to translate his new 'ethic' into effective policy or political action."[41]

This diagnosis needs also to reckon with the pragmatics of bookmaking: the pressure on Leopold from editors and associates over a period of years to play up autobiographical narrative and play down prescriptive policy statements in what was, after all, supposed to be a popular book.[42] The privatistic turn was partly market-driven, in other words. Yet it is less important to haggle over the extent to which Leopold's late-life emphasis on personal narrative and the aesthetics of environmental perception was truly voluntary—even if it were possible to adjudicate such a thing precisely—than it is to recognize that for whatever combination of reasons Leopold, like Faulkner, came to embrace the literary as a way of exploring a style of ethical apprehension of the claims of the nonhuman on the human that surpassed his prior understandings and that he himself may not have grasped with full self-awareness. There was a certain relief and fitness in the retreat from polemical and monographic forms of writing to a more contemplative expression that would permit him to model as well as to decry how much remains locked away in environmental unconscious, even sometimes to take wry satisfaction in showing himself as only a few steps ahead of the layman: not knowing how muskrats think, or why Canada geese should favor waste corn grown on former prairies; realizing sheepishly that "no matter how intently one studies the hundred little dramas of the woods and meadows, one can never learn all of the salient facts about any one of them." In this sense, his editors did well to reverse the original order of the last two chapters so as to end not with insistence on scholarly expertise but with a manifesto on the "land ethic," which is characterized in evolutionary terms as "a product of social evolution," a project still in progress.[43]

Both Faulkner and Leopold, then, set in motion complex processes of ethical reconsideration whereby, in Faulkner, familiar hierarchies of gentry/subaltern and human/nonhuman were subjected to question in ways that intertwined them; and in Leopold the questioning of human priority became more sweeping and insistent, as he began to pursue the idea that Homo sapiens is but one among innumerable members of a biotic community that "includes the soil, waters, fauna, and flora, as well as people."[44]

For both writers, the scene of hunting became a favorite way of dramatizing the transition from traditional assumptions of human dominance to a newer kind of environmental-ethical awareness that might supersede it. When one considers that the common contemporary (sub)urbanite assumption of hunting as inherently evil was far less ingrained in the educated reading public a half-century ago, particularly among the male readers who almost certainly were these authors' primary contemplated audience, then their attempt to instill respect for the natural world via revisionist hunting stories (in both "The Old People" and "The Bear"), so as to make fulfillment come to the main character through epiphanic encounter with the big critter and tragedy when it is shot, begins to look more venturesome than at first it may seem.[45]

This kind of narrative does not come anywhere near approximating the more thoroughgoing ecocentrism one finds in, say, Felix Salten's novel *Bambi* (1924), the Disney film version of which was released almost simultaneously with *Go Down, Moses,* and which set off a storm of protest in sport-hunting circles.[46] Written in Weimar Germany in shocked recoil against the violence the Great War showed human beings were capable of, and adapted by Disney in a euphemized animated cartoon narrative released shortly after World War II began, *Bambi* is an overtly misanthropic dream of animal innocence, in which the nonhuman realm is both made a mirror of cherished middle-class values (family solidarity in particular) and imagined as a fragile sanctuary from human turpitude. So far as artistic propagation of an antihunting ethic is concerned, this is *the* twentieth-century breakthrough artistic work of environmental ethics *par excellence,* beside which Faulkner and Leopold seem temporizers. Even the comparatively watered-down and popularizing film version was as avant-garde ethically as it was aesthetically in the delicacy and sophistication (at ruinous expense) of its animation. And it was, of course, the film, more than the novel, that has made the Bambi story a lastingly influential part of western popular memory.

In taking the less romantic middle ground of trying to turn hunting rituals to more enlightened uses, Faulkner and Leopold recognized the human propensity for dominance as more complex and embedded than could be addressed by conjuring up a mirror opposite of animal innocence, which in fact was already a melodramatic cliché dating back to the nineteenth-century birth of the animal-protection movement and the modern animal story. For Leopold and Faulkner, human ruthlessness toward both nonhumans *and* other humans had to be addressed by raising the standard of what counts as civilized; one possible means was sublimating hunterly behavior into worthier expression.

Leopold put it this way at the end of *Game Management:*

> Twenty centuries of "progress" have brought the average citizen a vote, a national anthem, a Ford, a bank account, and a high opinion of himself, but not the capacity to live in high density without befouling and denuding his environment, nor a conviction that such a capacity, rather than such density, is the true test of whether he is civilized.[47]

Faulkner would not have agreed with this wholly; he would have found it too narrow. Leopold was a professional forester for whom the ethics of environmental stewardship ultimately became *the* central commitment; for Faulkner, environmental exploitation was one among a range of interlinked forms of regional pathology, among which (to name only one other) racism would certainly have seemed more important. To some readers of this chapter it may even seem perverse that I have put such emphasis on environmental issues in my account of *Go Down, Moses*, which began and ended more as a race book than as an environment book. On the other hand, I would argue that neither race nor any other social issue should be held up as *the* master referent of this or any other Faulkner text in terms of which its environmental representation must be decoded—as if the latter didn't proffer its own set of claims. The history and finished state of *Go Down, Moses* show otherwise: show that although the claims of the natural world were seldom paramount for Faulkner, they could take on a life of their own and produce unexpected changes in an original design. Our study shows too that Faulkner wrote with considerable knowledge of southern environmental history and its economic, social, and racial ramifications—even if these get sometimes bent or overridden in the interest of the narrative. The sense of postbellum and early twentieth-century southern history as a history of environmental degradation was integral to Faulkner's declensionary vision of southern history generally.[48] It is no mere window dressing, then, that leads southern historians of environmentalist persuasion to honor him as a harbinger of southern environmentalism.[49]

Indeed, Faulkner's generalist perspective enabled him to deal more profoundly with some aspects of the interests he and Leopold shared in common than if he had come to writing from the standpoint of an environmental professional. Leopold was chiefly a rhetor in the vein of documentary exposition, Faulkner in the vein of the psychohistorical case study—a mode better suited to exploring split allegiances, self-deception, and ironic unintended consequences. Of all these Leopold too was aware; but nowhere in his work, or the literature of conservationism generally, is there such profound awareness as there is in *Go Down, Moses* of how those who genuinely value wilderness can become, without fully reasoning through the implications of their acts, coconspirators with those who value it only as cash crop—and how sometimes, as with Ike McCaslin, they can become such even when they are scrupulous casuists and self-examiners. Indeed, not only in his role as "great novelist," but also in his capacity as thinking person and environmental amateur, Faulkner was better positioned to bring to consciousness how individuals become divided against themselves, how environmental concern manifests itself typically as a part-time concern in competition with others working to undermine it, and how factical and fantastical visions of the natural world coexist in uneasy and ever-shifting interdependence.[50]

At the start of Part 5 of "The Bear," for example, the narrator chuckles at the flimsiness of the scheme cooked up by General Compson and Walter Ewell "to corporate themselves, the old group, into a club and lease the camp and the hunting privileges of the woods—an invention doubtless of the somewhat childish old General but actually worthy of Boon Hogganbeck himself." For, adds the text, "even the boy"—even Ike, the perpetual naïf—"recognized it for the subterfuge it was: to change the leopard's spots when they could not alter the leopard," the leopard in this case being de Spain's decision to sell the timber rights to a "Memphis lumber company," a decision the hunting *confrères* hope against hope that he may be persuaded to revoke.[51] Faulkner here constructs a complicated ethical dilemma around environmental doublethink: the experience of being caught between one's environmentalist propensities and the inertial drag of tribal or selfish values, partly because one's commitment to something is always muddled by other commitments, distractions, or sheer inanity. On one of its wavelengths, the passage seems a self-parodic reflection: Faulkner good-humoredly mocking the quixoticism of his own recent Okatoba Hunting Club scheme.[52] More obviously, at the level of the nominal narrative, Faulkner exposes the chuckleheadedness of his wilderness lovers: their inability to think straight about wilderness issues. De Spain shows this as clearly as Compson and Ewell: he wants the Memphis entrepreneurs' money but hates himself for selling out.

At the level of the plot's deeper ideological structure, the passage reproduces the schizoid dichotomy between the wilderness of Parts 1–3 and the southern history-in-microcosm of Part 4. It thereby ensures that the logic of the denouement will mirror the doublethink by setting up an ironic distinction between the spiritual teleology (Old Ben's death means the end of wilderness) and the propertarian teleology (Major de Spain's sale means the death of wilderness) without resolving the issue of whether the former is a mystification of the latter or whether the former produces the latter. That both teleologies are invoked at moments in the text yet also shown to be interdependent, and at the same time the question is left unresolved as to which has priority, ensured that "The Bear" and indeed *Go Down, Moses* as a whole would become an unusually rich meditation in environmental ethics.

The split focus of "The Bear" reflects and accentuates an important complication in property ethics for Faulkner that broadly applies to Leopold as well. In Faulkner's novella, as in *Go Down, Moses* generally, the suggestion is planted (not just by Ike but also by the narrative voice) that land ownership is legal but metaphysically absurd and morally wrong (to possess is already to be dispossessed), although, again, there is something quixotic and even comic in believing as Ike McCaslin wants to believe that you can extricate yourself from the system.[53] These complications are partially echoed in the *Sand County Almanac* essay that was Leopold's personal favorite, "Great Possessions," also his personal choice for the title of the book. The title refers to the author's 120-acre upcountry retreat, which "according to the County Clerk, is the extent of my worldly domain." As this way of remarking suggests, however, we are to think of this acreage as "possessions" in quotation marks. What makes the possessions great is the plethora of wild "tenants"—the birds especially for present purposes—that the author loves to observe but does not pretend to be able to control.[54] This is quite close in spirit to Faulkner's insistence that fetishization of legal title is the opposite of ownership in a deep sense. Both writers were acutely sensitive to the inherent defects of the institution of private property: its historic legitimation of land abuse and (Faulkner's concern to an even greater extent) its legitimation of the abuses of slavery.[55] Yet it is also clear that neither Faulkner nor Leopold was ready to abandon private property. During the 1930s and 1940s, as remarked earlier, Faulkner was zestfully reenacting a latter-day version of the role of the planter-aristocrat from Rowan Oak, his estate at the outskirts of Oxford, Mississippi. Leopold, for his part, pointedly emphasized the personal importance to him of legal possession of his acreage: "I now realize," he wrote in a "Foreword" to *Sand County* not published until long after the book itself, "that I had always wanted to own land, and to study and enrich its fauna and flora by my own effort."[56]

For both writers, then, periodic imagination of idealized states of transaction with landscape when the concept of ownership is transcended or not yet invented must be understood not as radical critique of property so much as part of an attempted redefinition of property as trust to be held in the public interest.[57] In "The Bear," the problem of ownership of the Big Bottom land is not that it is privately held but that Major de Spain allows it to be harvested. The implied environmental-ethical inference is quite close in spirit to Leopold's admonition (with an upcountry Wisconsin neighbor in mind) that "there is something wrong about erasing the last remnant of pine timber from a country. When a farmer owns a rarity he should feel some obligation as its custodian, and a community should feel some obligation to help him carry the economic cost of custodianship."[58] Much of Leopold's later writing is devoted to trying to define that "something": to dramatizing its value and cogency through statistics, narrative, and example, and to promoting measures that would provide arenas and incentives for something better than narrow economic self-interest, and that would nudge owners and the general public toward behavior more in the interest of biotic and human community and less narrowly utilitarian. Property was to be respected—indeed, it was a key basis if not the primary guarantor of enlightened husbandry—but wildlife, a term that Leopold often extended to include all nonhuman life, was to be treated as a public trust, and all the more so when endangered.

With respect to their investment in a revisionary ethics of hunting, Leopold and Faulkner were actually more divergent in emphasis than in their conceptions of property, although more complementary than opposed. Leopold's views of hunting evolved as part of a broader philosophy of wilderness recreation informed by the priorities of democratic access and enlightened use. These priorities sometimes conflicted, though he ultimately made them synchronize. On the one hand, Leopold opposed the European system of privately owned preserves that raised "wild" game for profit, for shooting and marketing, in favor of a system of affordable licensing and active management of game to maximize supply consistent with ecosystem maintenance. ("I demand that game and wild life be one of the normal products of every farm, and the enjoyment of it a part of the normal environment of every boy, whether he live next door to a public sanctuary or elsewhere.")[59] On the other hand, faced with declining game stocks and his own second thoughts about literal hunting, Leopold increasingly promoted a refined conception of "enjoyment." Low-tech forms of hunting, like "the bow-and-arrow movement and the revival of falconry," seemed preferable because more difficult; and by the time of *Sand County Almanac* the displacement of hunting by nature study is advocated as a mark of culture's evolution from the frontier stage. "To promote perception" was the great challenge, indeed "the only truly creative part of recreational engineering." Here and elsewhere, Leopold enjoys using Daniel Boone as his straw man:

> Compared with the competent ecologist of the present day, Boone saw only the surface of things. The incredible intricacies of the plant and animal community—the intrinsic beauty of the organism called America . . . were as invisible and incomprehensible to Daniel Boone as they are today to Mr. Babbitt.

The lesson could not be more obvious: "trophy-hunting is the prerogative of youth," fine for a culture still in the bud; but not in today's world, where "the disquieting thing . . . is the trophy-hunter who never grows up." Whereupon Leopold launches into a jeremiad against "the motorized ant who swarms the continents before learning to see his own back yard."[60]

Faulkner would have sympathized with Leopold's concern about wildlife endangerment and his testiness toward the modern gun-toting Babbitts or Snopeses of the woods and highways; and he might have chuckled at a parody of Boon(e) parallel to his own. But he was no more than marginally interested in programs of wildlife management or environmental education as such. His environmentalist interest, such as it was, certainly as writer and probably also as person, was in conceiving hunting (in whatever sense) and ecological endangerment at the level of the individual encounter. Accordingly, though Faulkner was less environmentally literate than Leopold, and less the public citizen-guardian of the wild, he managed to effect an activation of environmental unconscious that Leopold's teaching, lecturing, lobbying, and writing could not. Amid his timely and eloquent warnings about the endangerment of land, game, and plant life in our time, Leopold remains by comparison blandly generic. It was not in his line of thinking to try to dramatize *the* last hunt for *the* last bear involving *the* last guardian of wilderness wisdom. The closest Leopold comes to this is the elegiac reminiscence "Thinking like a Mountain," when he remembers looking into the eyes of the wolf he has just killed as a varmint but in light of later wisdom knows is no less crucial to the ecosystem than the deer he was trying to protect. Otherwise, his propensity is not to linger on unique moments or objects but to stress that heightened ecological consciousness among the public at large, directed almost anywhere, is the key to reversing species decline. "When enough men," he writes, realize that there is "drama in every bush," then we shall "need fear no indifference to the welfare of bushes, or birds, or soil, or trees. We shall then have no need of the word conservation, for we shall have the thing itself."[61]

In Faulkner's novella, by contrast, Old Ben becomes a much more fully realized, compelling, charismatic icon of endangerment, at once a unique figure, a symbol of the doomed Delta bottomland wilderness generally, and a latter-day avatar of human-animal liminality that pervades sacred legends about human encounters with bears in many cultures, both western and nonwestern.[62] Such focalization, Leopold might reply, is stronger as cosmology than as ecology, for which the unique, individual creature has got to count for less than the biotic community. From a Leopoldian perspective, the novella's implication that the bottomland is doomed as a consequence of the death of Old Ben is perverse: a reversal of the ecological cart and horse. In a proper narrative of ecological degradation, habitat destruction produces the death of the game, first the big predators and then the rest. Yet Faulkner might reply to this that not only does his novella's way of imagining the situation make symbolic sense, it is also true in its own way to how environmental history works. It makes better historical (cultural) sense to define the integrity of the bottomland in terms of the critters with the greatest charisma, and to see the land as losing value when they disappear.

As we have seen, Leopold too was prepared to acknowledge that the rarity of a wild thing enhanced its value and—in an essay on the 1947 dedication of a Wisconsin monument to the passenger pigeon—to welcome public concern for the extinction of species as an advance of human civilization: "To love what *was* is a new thing under the sun, unknown to most people and to all pigeons." But Leopold was not about to waste any breath retailing the story of Martha (the last pigeon, who died in a Cincinnati zoo); on the contrary, he was careful to keep sentiment under control by putting the story in the proper ecological frame:

"Had the funeral been ours, the pigeons would hardly have mourned us."[63] This qualification of lyric or elegy with astringent afterbite is a hallmark of Leopoldian style that seems to express, among other implications, a professional reluctance to attach undue importance to individual feeling, individual experience, or the lives of individual creatures.

Finally, the respective literary biases of Leopold and Faulkner complement one another: the emphasis on the type against the background of theory and the emphasis on the instance in the context of narrative. This complementarity shows, among other things, that accurate, eloquent nature writing is not all there is to ecodiscourse. In order to activate for many readers "the ecological conscience" Leopold sought to cultivate, something like Faulkner's fictive imagination is needed, even if Faulkner's dramatization of Delta natural/cultural history was colored and selective relative to the more accurate chronicle Leopold would have produced. In the next chapter we shall see further evidence of how particularized human encounters with animal others remains a powerful, albeit hardly fail-safe, way of scripting environmental imagination.

Chapter 6

Global Commons as Resource and as Icon: Imagining Oceans and Whales

> We were the generation that searched Mars for the most tenuous evidence of life but couldn't rouse enough moral outrage to stop the destruction of the grandest manifestations of life here on earth. We will be like the Romans whose works of art, architecture, and engineering we find awesome but whose gladiators and traffic in slaves are mystifying and loathsome to us.
>
> —Roger Payne, *Among Whales*

> Prohibition is easy to legislate (though not necessarily to enforce); but how do we legislate temperance?
>
> —Garrett Hardin, "The Tragedy of the Commons"

One knows that nationalism and nation-states are facing a crisis of legitimacy when the most influential theorist of the subject defines nations as collective fictions, and when this feat of interpretative deliquescence is itself almost at once criticized for ridigity, for insufficient sensitivity to the history of migration, diaspora, and the interplay of contesting population groups.[1] Although the challenges of transnational dialogue and threats to civil order are bound, notwithstanding, to keep nation-states in business for a long time to come if not forever, it is no less self-evidently crucial in today's world to envisage cultural dynamics operating across transnational expanses: for example, in terms of historic macrocivilizational blocks[2] or in terms of a Eurocentric, capitalist, and in the late twentieth century U.S.-dominated global order whose origins lie in the early colonial era and whose present influence is without precedent in world history. Predictably, we find sharp disagreements as to whether, for example, the promise of this order (stabilization, rule of law, propagation of democratic values) outweighs its threats (neocolonialism, cultural standardization, unprecedented

196

power for transnational corporations) and as to how much of a mono-lith it really is.[3]

Environmental concerns have rightly figured in these discussions, again in conflicting ways. There are at least six (semi-interlinked) mod-els—or families of models—of what the defining emphases of global en-vironmental culture are or should be: the risk society paradigm (which puts the globe under the sign of toxic endangerment); the environmen-tal justice paradigm (which affirms ubiquitous grassroots resistance of environmentally oppressed peoples); the Gaia paradigm (which begins from envisionment of the biosphere as a single homeostasis); the ecotheology paradigm (which images the material world as a spiritually unified holism); the ecofeminist antidominationist ethics-of-care para-digm (which begins from the long conjuncture between patriarchal ideology and the subjugation of a female-imaged earth); and the sus-tainability paradigm or "ecological modernization" paradigm as some skeptics call it (which offers the prospect of a reformed global environ-mental order wherein economic development would be so regulated as not further to deplete earth's resources or further degrade environ-mental quality).[4]

None of these models is monolithic. For example, one could debate at length the question of whether Gaia is more than a metaphor for an assemblage of interactive biochemical processes, or which groups prop-erly count as victims of environmental injustice. Likewise, the models are perennially subject to change and erosion. Take sustainability. Up to a point, its history is a striking success story. Within the last quarter of the twentieth century, it has become the environmentalist paradigm of preference, achieving a canonical standing in international policymak-ing circles, especially since the 1987 United Nations report *Our Common Future* promoted "sustainable development" as the optimal planetary goal. The appeal is understandable: Who can be *against* a path where "sustainability" is maintained without "development" being sacrificed? But with the ethical-political advantages of an environmental lingua franca has come a high-stakes dispute over connotations. "Ecological modernization," geographer David Harvey warns, "provides a discur-sive basis for a contested rapprochement between [reformist environ-mentalism] and dominant forms of political-economic power. But on the other [hand], it presumes a certain kind of rationality that lessens the force of more purely moral arguments [Harvey cites Love Canal activist Lois Gibbs here] and exposes much of the environmental movement to the dangers of political cooptation."[5] Energy economist Herman Daly recalls a case in point: the World Bank's refusal to accept his group's minority recommendation to define "sustainable development" as "development without growth beyond environmental carrying capacity," though the Bank was on record as endorsing the underlying concept and has proven itself more responsive to environmental concerns than most member states.[6] Even a vague stipulation of a "limit" or "carrying capacity" felt too threatening to the Bank's commitment to support economic growth. A more Machiavellian discursive manipulation, one all newspaper readers and television watchers encounter daily, is greenwash: advertisement campaigns by oil, chemical, and other multinational corporations to persuade the public that their technological miracles will not disrupt the environment.[7]

The mass circulation of images of clean, shining storage tanks set amidst rolling pastures or amber waves of grain makes one fear that global environmental culture, if there really is such a thing, may be grounded in nothing better than a shallow cosmopolitanism and an evisceration of cultural particularity. The recalcitrance, horse trading, niggling, and obfuscation surrounding accords having to do with atmosphere, oceans, and water rights further demonstrate how tenuous transnational environmental discourse is. Yet the vitiation by interest-group politicking of projects like the post-Rio "Earth Charter" for United Nations general assembly ratification hardly invalidates the unprecedentedness and the worth, in principle, of attempts to establish green principles and treaties on a global scale.[8] Modest as its results so far have been, the growth of the felt need for a planetary environmental policy that does not conceive earth's resources to be "created for man's exclusive benefit" amounts, as a leading historian of international environmental regulation puts it, almost to "a second Copernican revolution."[9] Despite porousness, vacillation, and backsliding, the ozone accords of the 1980s and 1990s were of milestone significance as an indication of willingness to consider compromise of economic self-interest in order "to anticipate and manage a world problem before it becomes an irreversible crisis."[10] The awareness of air pollution's power to affect places far remote has reinforced the intuitive sense of atmospheric health as a transborder concern as well as the attempts of particular actors to evade responsibility. But by far the more anciently recognized global commons is the sea, which covers nearly three-quarters of the earth's surface.

No aspect of recent environmental thought more strikingly illustrates the significance and the difficulty of the "second Copernican revolution" than late twentieth-century concern about degradation of the world's oceans. For one thing, oceans are the closest thing on earth to a landscape of global scope. They are also incomparably the largest commons; if there is to be a "tragedy of the commons,"[11] this will be the biggest; and the possibility that such a thing might happen has captured international attention more suddenly and dramatically than has the degradation of land or air, which has been worried about for the better part of two centuries. By the same token, and more to the point of our present study, few developments in the history of environmentalism better exemplify at once the cultural power of environmental imagination, the cultural limits that also inevitably constrain it, and (oppositely) its capacity—sometimes—to speak with striking pertinence across borders of culture and time.

Resymbolizing Ocean

Modern science tells us that ocean is literally where we came from. Millennia before that, however, it was a common symbol for primordial reality, as in "the waters" of the Genesis creation narratives, or a symbol for what lies beyond the known world. In the mythical epitome of the ancient world fashioned by the god Hephaistos on the shield of Achilles in the *Iliad*, "the Ocean River" formed the perimeter of "the uttermost rim."[12] Later, water in general and ocean in particular came to symbolize unbounded inner space. Freud referred to the "sensation of 'eternity'" as the "oceanic" feeling. "Meditation and water are wedded for ever," affirms Herman Melville's narrator Ishmael in *Moby-Dick* (1851).[13] "And of all the elements," adds Joseph Conrad, "this is the one to which men have always been prone to trust themselves, as if its immensity held a reward as vast as itself." Mindful though Conrad was of the greed and rapacity of maritime enterprise at its worst, he lets his imagination be suffused momentarily by wonder at ocean's lure.[14] So too with the most significant book of the sea in the nature writing tradition, Rachel Carson's *The Sea Around Us* (1950).

Carson is today much better known for *Silent Spring*'s indictment of the toxic effects of DDT and other chemical pesticides. But throughout her life she was far more interested in the sea. Her college and graduate concentration was marine biology, and her main subjects during her formative years as a writer were estuaries, seacoasts, and oceans. *The Sea Around Us* was the book that won her fame as a scientifically serious nature writer, such that she was assured of a wide hearing for *Silent Spring*.

Carson's fascination with the sea, both as writer and as person, was quickened by the traditional symbolic sense of it as a mysterious realm apart, resistant to human meddling. In *The Sea Around Us,* the one chapter on islands, which focuses on anthropogenic degradation of island biogeography, has a satiric bite the rest do not, as they ruminate in a generally soothing lyrical way about both biology and commerce, treating the sea as an inexhaustible intellectual, spiritual, and economic resource without registering awareness of the possible conflict between these uses. The book tranquilly begins and ends with images of eternal return: it begins by evoking "that great mother of life, the sea," and ends by affirming that "all at last return to the sea—to Oceanus, the ocean river, like the ever-flowing stream of time, the beginning and the end." As Carson later mused, "It was pleasant to believe . . . that most of Nature was forever beyond the tampering reach of man," "to suppose that the stream of life would flow on through time in whatever course that God had appointed it." By the time she died a dozen years later, however, she had begun to reverse herself, begun especially to worry about promiscuous use of oceans as hazardous waste dumps.[15]

Silent Spring was the project that changed Carson's mind, and it is notable that one of that book's most powerful dimensions is its water pollution theme: "it is not possible to add pesticides to water anywhere without threatening the purity of water everywhere."[16] Reviewers were struck by Carson's insistence on massive carnage of marine life from pesticide "invasion of streams, ponds, rivers, and bays" and by her report of the tiny amounts that could be lethal: one-half part per billion in the case of shrimp killed by endrin.[17]

Carson's horror at insidious water-borne toxification may have been intensified by her attachment to the traditional romantic image of ocean as ultimate sanctuary. In any case, thanks in part to her most famous book, indignation and betrayal are now the controlling motifs in contemporary works of ocean-focused nature writing (often likened to the Carson of *Silent Spring*): for example, Anne W. Simon's *Neptune's Revenge* (1984), Sylvia Earle's *Sea Change* (1995), and Carl Safina's *Song for the Blue Ocean* (1998), which foreground issues like dumping, coral reef degradation, depleted stocks, and ecological fallout from the Gulf War. All testify to how swiftly the dominant image of the sea shifted in nature writing during the late twentieth century from inexhaustibleness to fragility.[18] Few episodes in the history of modern environmentalist consciousness have been more dramatic than this late twentieth-century awakening to the awareness that three-quarters of the globe, hitherto thought virtually immune from human tampering, might be gravely endangered.

This attitudinal shift can be thought of as a great demythologization: as a lesson taught by the hard evidence of dwindling and contaminated supplies of certain seafoods worldwide, evidence made more authoritative by increasingly precise methods of tracking species populations, based in turn on increasingly sophisticated mathematical modeling and data-gathering methods. But just as plausibly the shift is a great remythologization, marked by the creation of icons of endangerment. A prime example is the revaluation of whales. "Beyond the image of the planet Earth itself," Lynton Caldwell declares, "the most poignant symbol of the world environment movement has been the whale." He may be right. Certainly he is right that in many regions today "the economic returns from whale watching are now substantially greater than the profits once gained by whaling."[19]

All large creatures have the potential to become environmental icons: pandas, elephants, lions, tigers, white rhinos, bald eagles, deer, whooping cranes, and, of course, bears like Theodore Roosevelt's grizzly cub (the original Teddy bear) and Faulkner's Old Ben. This may reflect an endemic bias of human perception. In the United States there is a correlation between size of creature and federal expenditure for protection, and a further correlation according to whether the creature is considered "a higher form of life."[20] That environmentalists realize and are quick to avail themselves of the public sentiment implied by these correlations is evident from their reliance on domestic metaphors[21] and appealing photographs of cute, sensitive-looking animal faces in green magazines.[22] Sociologist Alison Anderson found that face-on photographs of North Sea common seals helped rouse public indignation against a 1988 virus epidemic allegedly pollution-caused, even though the scientific evidence was inconclusive.[23] This is arresting fortuitous corroboration of the power of the central metaphor in Emmanuel Levinas's ethical philosophy for one's responsibility for another.

A face, as Levinas writes in characteristically rhapsodic prose,

> presses the neighbor up against me. Immediacy is the collapse of the representation into a face, into a "concrete abstraction" torn up from the world, from horizons and conditions, incrusted in the signification without a context of the-one-for-the-other, coming from the emptiness of space . . . Such an order throws a "seed of folly" into the universality of the ego. It is given to me who answer before the one for whom I am responsible.[24]

Levinas himself had no interest in extending his idea of ethical obligation to human-nonhuman relations. His interest was exclusively in the face as the trace of the human and as activator of one's responsibility for another. But much of what he suggests here applies also to the activation of the human sense of accountability for (certain) animals, including the passage's implication that the appeal of the face is all the more compelling for being abrupt and unexpected, pressing itself on the experiencer seemingly out of nowhere.

By the criteria of size and "higher" life form, if not of face, whales have especially great charismatic potential. Langdon Winner's antithesis of "the whale and the reactor" as a late twentieth-century update of Henry Adams's antithesis between the virgin and the dynamo makes perfect intuitive sense.[25] As the largest of mammals, size alone makes whales easy to envision as planetary microcosms:

> The whales turn and glisten, plunge
> and sound and rise again,
> Hanging over subtly darkening deeps
> Flowing like breathing planets
> in the sparkling whorls of
> living light—[26]

It is not bulk alone that whales have going for them as icon candidates, but the combination of their size, their intelligence (which more easily makes them seem our "kindred"), their fascinating alterity (as creatures of a radically different scale inhabiting a radically different medium: the "subtly darkening deeps"), their increasing scarcity, and (to most, although not all, of earth's inhabitants today) their "nonessential" use-value: although one can make a profit from harvesting them, they are apparently not indispensable to the manufacture of any known product essential to human welfare. Cetaceans, whales and dolphins both, are also sociable, even sportive; and they have individuality as well as intelligence, including powers of adaptation, mimicry of human sounds, and even the capacity to transmit "'collective wisdom' from one generation to the next."[27] Cetaceans have remarkably sophisticated and acute vocal and auditory capacities that allow some species to communicate acoustically thousands of miles away[28] by a process still not fully understood. One evolutionary ecologist has even suggested that "dolphin language may in some ways be similar to written Chinese characters, in which analog pictures are given digital functions."[29] Perhaps most intriguingly of all from an anthropocentric standpoint, cetaceans seem to enjoy socializing with humans under certain conditions: to play, to race and follow boats, to listen and respond to flute music, and so on. Such interspecies behavior has been reported at least as far back as the mid-nineteenth century, not counting such ancient legends as Arion and the dolphin.[30]

Whales anciently seemed to partake of ocean's mysterious, radical, ambiguous otherness: to symbolize divine power, whether benign or threatening. Today whales still seem uncannily other, but with the uncanniness increasingly seen to reside in the "fact" that despite dramatic differences in scale and anatomy and habitat they are so much like us.[31]

Like modern primatology, cetacean studies are one of those areas where assumptions of species distinctiveness, and particularly the superiority of human mental powers to those of nonhuman species, are being most vigorously challenged. If western culture's representative ancient whale figuration was the unnamed sea creature in the Book of Jonah, the representative contemporary image is something like Shamu, Sea World's captive killer whale, or the winsome "Little Calf" (a baby sperm whale) whose early life and adventures Victor B. Scheffer narrates in *The Year of the Whale,* which won the annual John Burroughs Medal for the best book of natural history writing in 1969. "Remote indeed they are," Scheffer writes of the yearling calf and his mother, "but not lonely, for never are they out of range of the submarine voices of their own kind."[32] As this typical blend of exoticism and intimacy shows, domesticity has been even more important than physiognomy in modern literary efforts to give whales and other nonhuman creatures "a face."

In the century-old animal story tradition, of which Felix Salten's *Bambi* and Rachel Carson's first book *Under the Sea Wind* are more distinguished examples, *The Year of the Whale* inverts standard assumptions about the relation between hunter and hunted in the interest of dramatizing the claims of animal rights and animal suffering on human attention. This revisionary ethical thrust of the reimagination of cetaceans has itself been strongly pressed by whale conservationists. As animal rights advocate Peter Singer put it in a statement that influenced the Australian government's decision to discontinue whaling and adopt protectionist measures, whaling is morally objectionable for its acts of violence against "member[s] of an intelligent, social species, where the emotional links between different members of the group, and the capacity to enjoy life, are only too evident."[33] Singer's premise that "higher-order" creatures have higher moral claims on humans than "lower-order" creatures has been challenged,[34] but there is no question about the readiness of whale protectionists to reinforce their claims by promoting the sentiment of closeness between humans and whales.

Important as imaging has been for advocates of whale conservation and of ocean conservation more generally, and prolific as recent artistic imaging of whales has been (in film, painting, and music as well as literature), no modern work of maritime animal imagination, notwithstanding the award of Burroughs Medals and the like, seems likely to achieve the standing Herman Melville's *Moby-Dick* has long enjoyed. At first thought, the situation seems ironic. For *Moby-Dick* rose to the status of literary classic less because of than despite its prolix and obsessive preoccupation with cetology, and even today Melvillians chronically fail to take this aspect of the book seriously, except when preparing documentary apparatus; and from a present-day protectionist standpoint the novel is in some ways, to say the least, quite politically incorrect. At first sight, *Moby-Dick* seems considerably closer to the Book of Jonah than to *The Year of the Whale*. Yet if one turns back to Melville with contemporary concerns about the oceanic commons and the fate of cetaceans in mind, the complications of these issues and those of *Moby-Dick* itself become mutually illuminated in unexpected ways. Certainly no more modern feat of "whale versus reactor" imagination comes close to matching this astonishingly prescient work of the early industrial era.

Moby-Dick and the Hierarchies of Nation, Culture, and Species

Moby-Dick was written in and about the moment when the world was coming under the regime of global capitalism. It is the first canonical work of Anglophone literature to anatomize an extractive industry of global scope—an industry, furthermore, where American entrepreneurs had become the leading edge. "By 1850 the supremacy of American whaling had been established beyond question," as the classic American industry history states.[35] Melville makes much of this boast. The seas through which the *Pequod* sails are dominated by Yankee and particularly by Nantucket whalemen. The French and the Dutch whalers are pathetic; the British house of Enderby, which pioneered the Pacific sperm whale fishery, is represented by jovial triflers; and the crews of the New England vessels reflect this dominance. The *Pequod*— much like other New England whaling ships of the time—is a global village of ethnicities in which "the native American liberally provides the brains [i.e., the officers], the rest of the world . . . the muscles" (p. 108). This was one arena, then, where American imperial reach more than matched the British. As Ishmael puts it with characteristic panache, "let the English overswarm all India, and hang out their blazing banner

from the sun; two thirds of this terraqueous globe are the Nantuck-
eter's" (pp. 62–63).

The multimythic collage with which Melville overlays Captain
Ahab's fantastic quest, on the decoding of which Melvillians have ex-
pended far more intellectual energy than they have on its cetology, is an
abstract counterpart of the global reach and multiethnic composition of
the whaling industry itself. No wonder it takes on a life of its own, and
not just for biographical reasons but for broader cultural reasons as
well: this was also the moment of the birth of comparative anthropology and religion in the West. In suggesting a link, Melville anticipated
what today's global culture theory has formulated more analytically:
that the cultural and political-economic dimensions of globalism were
interconnected. Exploration made possible by technological advantage
led both to trade in which superior technology produced western (and,
in this case, Yankee) dominance and to cultural exchange in which
western cultural condescension normally prevailed, although not always. The same American subculture that opened up trade with the Far
East in the eighteenth century and forced entry into Japan in the mid-
nineteenth produced the first American converts to Buddhism a half-
century later. On the one hand, the expansionist impulse epitomized by
Ahab's imperial will is partially echoed by Ishmael's more innocent-
seeming desire to fathom unknown lands, customs, ideas.[36] On the
other hand, contact with unfamiliar geographies and cultures produced
disorientation and sometimes also reorientation of values in anyone
with a grain of receptivity.[37] In *Moby-Dick,* it is historically apt both that
the upcountry greenhorn Ishmael's first contact with the whaling industry should induce culture shock (his initial encounter with Queequeg),
followed by deparochialization; and also that the novel should not
know quite what to do with their relationship in the long run. The state
of the Yankee culture within as well as against which Melville wrote
was such as to make it hard even for an independent thinker to imagine
such companionship except as a brief glimpse of an alternative world.
Yet the novelty and audacity of that glimpse should not be underesti-
mated. The same holds for the novel's ecological vision.

Both latter-day chroniclers of whaling and whale conservationists
have laid claim to *Moby-Dick* as authority and/or as witness.[38] On the
face of it, the first claim seems more plausible, since this is a book more

concerned with whale-chasing and whale chasers than with whale-watching, let alone whale-saving. Professional Melvillians are taught to suppose that to the extent this highly ornate, stylized, self-consciously metaliterary book has historical-material reference it must be to the management-labor dynamics of emerging industrial capitalism or to contemporary debates over slavery and expansionism; and that as for the whale-watching dimension of *Moby-Dick,* its engagement is with whales as symbols rather than with whaleness as such.[39]

Notwithstanding the weight of such opinion, Roger Payne rightly holds *Moby-Dick* to be a book calculated to unsettle one's assumptions about the borderlines between the human and the nonhuman, so as to ensure "that whales would reconstitute themselves . . . at the point of origin of all the meridians of the imagination, its very pole, and there tie themselves forever into human consciousness by a kind of zenith knot."[40] In effect Payne asserts that, yes, Melvillian whales *are* signifiers, but of the intertwinement of humans with whaleness and by implication with all other nonhuman creatures as well. There is much to support this view.

First, of course, is the fact that the human characters in the book are fixated on whales, particularly the White Whale, to the point that they anxiously subject it/them to a multitude of interpretative constructions, all of which prove insufficent or downright wrong. It is not the captain alone who is umbilically tied to the monster that snatches him off at the end. Ishmael, for all his playfulness, is no less tied, and so too is Ahab's first mate and rival Starbuck, who is far too commonsensical to attach special significance to Moby Dick as against other whales, but no less bound to his own task-oriented mentality that whales equal barrels of oil equal profit. The plot is contrived so that cetacean materiality triumphs over all attempts to construe or contain it.

Second, and more important, the species boundary is perpetually being blurred, and the reader pulled back and forth across it. Through dozens of playful personifications, whales are given brows, bonnets, "chaste-looking" mouths, infant flukes like palms of hands. And negatively: whales are without voice, face, sense of smell, without a "proper nose" (p. 291). Right whales are stoic, sperm whales platonian. Right whales graze through brit like "morning mowers" (p. 234). Young bull sperm whales carry on "like a mob of young colleagians" (p. 330). The "desecrat[ion]" of a whale's corpse after the kill is the parody of a proper funeral (p. 262). Whales have families, and females care for their young and for each other. We are asked to imagine how nonbinocular vision might feel, to imagine the felt texture of the whale's isinglass skin, to appreciate that tiny earholes do not necessarily mean poor hearing.

Whaling narratives of Melville's day stressed the daring, risks, dangers, and excitement of whaling far more than the suffering of the whales when driven, maimed, and killed, but they were also capable of transient empathy for "the royal game of the seas." A graphic passage in J. Ross Browne's *Etchings of a Whaling Cruise,* one of Melville's sources, dwells on the "intensity of agony" of the whale toward the end of a chase. Another source, Francis Olmsted's *Incidents of a Whaling Voyage,* pauses affectingly to behold another whale in extremis, "exhausted with pain and the loss of blood." Still another, Henry Cheever, confessed that "I am not one that can coolly observe the last agony of so mighty an organized creature as the whale." Eliza Williams, who loyally accompanied her shipmaster-husband on several voyages and carefully noted their successes and failures, "could not bear the sight" of whales "tumbling and rolling about in the water, dying" that she had just seen "playing about, so happy in their native element, all unconscious, it seemed, of danger."[41] In *Moby-Dick* as well, most of the sympathy is reserved for sailors working under hazardous conditions, and humanitarian side-glimpses at their quarries are sparing, but they are also more pronounced. The account of the *Pequod*'s first kill is traumatic, not triumphal. Ishmael beholds the whale "spasmodically dilating and contracting his spout-hole, with sharp, cracking, agonized respirations," emitting the next instant "gush after gush of clotted red gore" (p. 245). Starbuck chides Flask for wanting to puncture a sick whale's ulcerated sore, and when Flask does anyhow, Ishmael calls it a "cruel wound" and proceeds to describe in detail the creature's "most piteous" death throes (p. 301).

The "Grand Armada" chapter, however, is the most poignant example of this fellow-creaturely identification. Ishmael's boat is becalmed in the center of a vast school where the newborn calves are crowded. Whether from "a wondrous fearlessness and confidence, or else a still, becharmed panic," the whales seem suddenly tame, letting themselves be stroked and scratched (p. 325). (Modern whale biologists are less likely to be surprised by this sociability.) This idyllic moment is then broken up by a whale one of the other boats has maimed, slashing about himself "in the extraordinary agony of the wound" and wounding others in the process (p. 326). The nominal lesson Ishmael obtusely draws after escaping from the melee is "the more whales the less fish. Of all the drugged whales only one was captured" (p. 328). He seems to have forgotten completely his becharmed delight, now that he has refocused on the chase that was the crew's practical objective. After all, the interlude was happenstance. But it also sets up the next chapter, on cetacean domesticity, in a more comic-pastoral vein ("Schools and Schoolmasters"), which avoids the poignancy yet continues the theme of whales as fellow creatures.

At moments like these, the book prepares one to think that it is not fancifulness but good sense to look upon whales generally and Moby Dick particularly as more than a "dumb brute" acting from "blindest instinct," as Starbuck holds him to be (p. 144). Although we need not take the ascription of intentionality at face value when the narrator tells us that "retribution, swift vengeance, eternal malice were in his whole aspect" (p. 468) as Moby Dick swam toward the *Pequod*, it is by no means out of keeping with the intelligence with which Melville (and modern zoology) has shown whales can behave to suppose that he might have targeted the ship as "the source of all his persecutions" (p. 466). That this language formulates his supposed reaction as the duplicate of Ahab's revengeful fixation comports with the quasi-equivalences between human and animal that the book has been suggesting all along.

Melville's whale ethnography also casts a new light on the sense of taboo with which "the fiery hunt" (p. 170) is invested. It is not merely a question of whether the whale should or should not be read as a providential (or Satanic) agent, or whether Ahab is or is not a providential (or Satanic) avenger. The taboo is created more fundamentally by imparting the sense that a limit has been transgressed when one revengefully picks a fight with a nonhuman creature who is thought to be an intelligent agent (or principal) in its own right: so "organized" a creature as the sperm whale. In *Moby-Dick* the taboo is of course mainly associated with the title figure, who is distinguished from other sperm whales. But the distinction is less sharp than it seems. First, Moby Dick is placed within a cohort of "famous whales" to which whalemen have given proper names (p. 177); second, Ishmael provides testimony from whaling history to corroborate most of Moby Dick's later exceptional acts, including the sinking of the ship; third, the whole series of whales with which the *Pequod* has significant previous encounters are also, as we have seen, to some extent "humanized." So the difference between Moby Dick and other cetaceans is more of degree than of kind, and appearances to the contrary can largely be written off as figments of overheated Ahabian and Ishmaelian imagination.

All this is not to say that some concealed save-the-whales message can be surgically extracted from *Moby-Dick*. Such was hardly to be expected given the conditions of whaling before harpoon guns and large high-speed vessels. Melville was acutely aware that under the paleotechnic constraints of 1840s whaling, whales posed a greater threat to their human pursuers than their pursuers did to them. He might have thought differently had he seriously believed that sperm whales were an endangered species—a point of dispute in his day, as he well knew. Certainly Ishmael longs to believe "the whale immortal in his species, however perishable in his individuality" (p. 384). But the book raises the endangerment question only to dimiss it.[42]

By the same token, the novel's predominant vision of the vast, unpredictable oceanic expanse as "a heartless immensity" (p. 347) is much more like Tennyson's proto-Darwinian "nature red in tooth and claw" than like Wordsworth or Thoreau, despite interludes of "The Grand Armada" sort. Indeed, one motive for the humanizing lyricalness and drollery with which Ishmael by turns invests whales seems to be to cope with "a horror" by being "social with it," as he freakishly remarks in the first chapter, "since it is but well to be on friendly terms with all the inmates of the place one lodges in" (p. 16). Melville's ocean is an arena of sudden violence daunting even to old salts. Within this context, however, the book distinguishes pretty consistently between different kinds of totemic creatures. Melville's sharks embody the sea's violent, predatory, "cannibalistic" aspect; whales, even though we are told what they eat and we sometimes see them do it, are not cast as sinister predators. On the contrary, more often they are typed as prey to the whalers, who themselves get slyly caricatured as the sharkish, cannibalistic ones.

Even at first sight, there is something atavistic about the *Pequod,* just as there is something archaic about Ishmael's wish to embark from the declining port of Nantucket rather than from thriving New Bedford, as the fountainhead of the industry. ("Where else but from Nantucket did those aboriginal whalemen, the Red-Men, first sally out to give chase to the Leviathan?" [p. 17].) Fittingly, the ship is named for a tribe Ishmael (wrongly) insists is extinct. "A cannibal of a craft," he calls it, intending the term in the most literal sense: tricked out "in the chased bones of her enemies," with whale teeth for fastening pins, the tiller carved from a jawbone (p. 67).

The book seems to be playing a dubious and equivocal game here with the notion of cannibalistic barbarity. After all, hasn't it just been at pains to discredit civilizationalism by honoring Queequeg's moral superiority and idealizing Ishmael's unlikely friendship with him? To a modern reader the mood swings between dismantling savagery and reinstating it in blatantly stereotypical ways can be disconcerting. Later, matters get worse, as in "The Try-Works," when Ishmael descries "the Tartarean shapes of the pagan harpooners" stoking the furnace, regaling each other at break-time with "their unholy adventures, their tales of terror told in words of mirth; as their uncivilized laughter forked upwards out of them, like the flames from the furnace" (p. 353). But I take it that the main point of having shown Queequeg and the others in more companionable ways beforehand is to demonstrate that they aren't "naturally" by disposition "cannibals" at all but at worst greenhorns in the ways of western culture, as Ishmael is in the ways of whaling. It is the exigency of the whaling industry that (re)produces them as savages. As the passage concludes: "the rushing Pequod, freighted with savages, and laden with fire, and burning a corpse, and plunging into that blackness of darkness, seemed the material counterpart of her monomaniac commander's soul" (p. 354). It is not the "pagans" but the captain who gives the order to pierce "the heathen flesh" in order to baptize his harpoon in their blood (p. 404).[43]

Ahab's inverted sacramentalism, here and elsewhere, gives this voyage an infernal titanicism quite unlike standard whaling narrative. Yet Melville was by no means the only writer of his time to imagine whaling as a devilish existence that bestialized the worker. "Before I had half finished my share of the labor," writes Browne of the cutting-in and trying-out process, "I heartily wished myself in the meanest dog-kennel ashore"; and as for off-hours, "if ever there was a miniature representation of the Black Hole of Calcutta, it was the forecastle of the Styx."[44] Here too one hears the self-indulgent exaggeration of the respectably bred young man abruptly thrust down into the proletariat without the vaguest notion of what would face him. But there is also plenty of bona fide vernacular testimony from the nineteenth century as to the stresses and privations of multiyear whaling voyages under tyrannical captains.[45]

On the one hand, then, *Moby-Dick* suggests that whaling forces many of those involved in it into more bestial lives than they would lead shoreside (whether they hail from Nantucket like Ahab or from Kokovoko like Queequeg). On the other hand, whales emerge as less bestial than one might expect. This is not, of course, the professional seaman's typical view, which if only as a survival tactic must not stray too far from Starbuck's utilitarianism. It takes a thinking person like Ishmael who is also an outsider to fashion a mental space in which these matters can be held up for contemplation: how whaling reduces people, how whale-beholding sometimes ennobles whales and impels one to imagine people and whales as semi-interchangeable.

Ishmael, then, is both a lens through which humans and sea creatures become coordinated into an informal comparative ethnology and a link between the amateur cetology in which premodern whaling narratives regularly indulge at least in passing, and late twentieth-century popular books about whales in which biology and/or environmental ethics get commingled with personal narrative, as in Payne's *Among Whales* or Scheffer's *Year of the Whale*.

Melville's ethnological cross-referencing between persons and beasts provides a zestful-skeptical running commentary on the age's passion for comparative anatomy and the more theoretical pseudosciences built upon it, like phrenology and craniology. Samuel Otter, who has delved furthest into this aspect of *Moby-Dick*, demonstrates how the novel disrupts racist pseudoscience by such devices as the deliberately overdone classificationism of the "Cetology" chapter and comical hyperfocus on cranial and skeletal measurement, on Moby Dick's chromatics, and so on.[46] The satirical treatment of classification, and the zest with which human and nonhuman get commingled, also express a more sweeping

unsettlement of Enlightenment rationalism by way of a deliciously ir-
reverent relish for the pedantic minutiae and incongruities of the pre-
Darwinian scene of clashing taxonomic systems, which belabored the
question of whether cetaceans were fish or mammals long after it had
been "resolved" and set off fierce disputes over the classifications of
"monsters," both human and nonhuman, including category-defying
new species from Europe's colonies.[47]

Even more central to *Moby-Dick* than the unsettlement of theories
about racial intelligence and potential, however, is its interest in animal
intelligence, specifically of course cetacean. This issue gets introduced
by way of the mystique with which whales are invested, both by tradition (especially the biblical-exegetical association of Leviathan, popu-
larly thought to be incarnated in the form of a whale, as divine
instrument and/or adversary) and by Ishmael's compulsive foreshad-
owings. At this level whales, especially sperm whales and most especially Moby Dick, are mysticized as the quintessence of "the full
awfulness of the sea which aboriginally belongs to it" (p. 235). But the
book is also concerned to make this "awfulness" plausible, so as to
refute in advance those who—as Ishmael puts it in a famous but imper-
fectly understood assertion—might "scout at Moby Dick as a monstrous fable, or still worse and more detestable, a hideous and
intolerable allegory" (p. 177). Here Melville protests too much, as he
later granted in an equally famous remark to Sophia Hawthorne that
her response to the novel made him realize its "part-&-parcel allegori-
calness" as never before.[48] But the context of the original passage is no
less important: a chapter purporting to argue for "the reasonableness of
the whole story of the White Whale, more especially the catastrophe"
(p. 177). "Reasonableness" also protests too much, and knowingly so:
Ishmael is perfectly aware of intermixing documentary with tall tale-
telling, as in the pretended vehemence of his jesuitical argument that
the sixth-century "sea-monster" of the Propontis "must in all probability
have been a sperm whale" (p. 182). Yet amidst the rhetorical hijinks are
more measured observations: that "it is very often observed that, if the
sperm whale, once struck, is allowed time to rally, he then acts, not so
often with blind rage, as with wilful, deliberate designs of destruction to
his pursuers" (p. 181); that "the Sperm Whale is in some cases sufficiently powerful, knowing, and judiciously malicious, as with direct af-

terthought to stave in, utterly destroy, and sink a large ship; and what is more, the Sperm Whale *has* done it" (p. 178). The best contemporary accounts of whaling bore out these claims: that sperm whales were "ordinarily of a peaceful and sluggish disposition," but when roused they could act like uncannily intelligent adversaries.[49]

It is important to stress Melville's differential handling of the whale's alleged malice versus its intelligence while not, in the process, overstating the distinction. The novel hints that imputing malice may be as superstitious as traditional demonizing of sea monsters as Leviathan,[50] that such "malice" as whales display is reactive and not initiatory. At the denouement, the White Whale's first reaction to the *Pequod* is to swim away, not to attack—as Starbuck is quick to point out to Ahab. This is in keeping with the reputation of his historical prototype Mocha Dick, for whom "it was not customary . . . while unmolested, to betray a malicious disposition."[51] Indeed, the novel at times goes much farther than this by imputing sinisterness to the whalemen instead: not only depicting Ahab as mad but whaling generally as "a butchering sort of business" (p. 98), and the *Pequod*'s routine kills as being like the "burglaries" of the Crusaders on their way to their holy assaults on Jerusalem (p. 184). At the same time, *Moby-Dick* by no means negates the impression of whales as Leviathanic adversaries, much as one might wish the novel to have done if approaching it from a presentist save-the-whales perspective. On the contrary, the plot, like conventional whaling narratives of the day, builds toward a climax in which resourceful hunters confront resourceful monster. The mirror opposition of whalemen (especially Ahab) bestialized by the hunt versus whale (especially Moby Dick) maddened by being hunted is culturally avant-garde insofar as it implies a comparative pathology of early capitalist enterprise and of intelligent mammals under pressure of systematic harassment. But the novel remains traditional insofar as it reproduces the familiar narrative and cosmic melodrama of the traditional symbolic hunt.

Imagining Interspeciesism: The Lure of the Megafauna

In short, *Moby-Dick* is still at some remove from Aldo Leopold's prescription of nature study as a more enlightened substitute for literal hunting. Indeed, from Leopold's "Conservation Esthetic" and the other three extended thinkpiece chapters that conclude *A Sand County Al-*

manac one might almost think Leopold believed that promiscuous sport hunting had become a greater social problem than promiscuous harvesting for gain. Of course, Leopold knew full well the enormous problem commercial exploitation of nature continued to pose—meaning for him most especially the shortsighted farming practices that had deforested, monocropped, and desertified the midcontinent and still remained orthodox despite the horrendous example of the Dust Bowl years just passed.[52] But the era of worst land abuse—somewhat evasively from one standpoint but prudently from another—Leopold prefers to diagnose as a Paleolithic stage of existence that most of his readers will be inclined to bracket off as a cultural memory of bygone times rather than as a description of the way they live now.

As we saw in Chapter 5, recreational hunting was for Leopold a trace of that pioneer stage that he hoped to refashion into a bridge toward a more advanced state of ecological enlightenment such as Faulkner's Ike McCaslin also grasps for. *Moby-Dick* stands closer to the frontier mentality, aware of the fragility of humankind before the power of first nature and empathetic albeit not uncritical of the emotional need and the romantic excitement of the adversarial struggle against brute force that this produces. Though Leopold had no more desire to place a ban on hunting than Faulkner did, the thrust of *Sand County Almanac* is to try to cajole the reader much more firmly than Melville does into laying down his gun for the sake of the nobler path of nature study.

Elsewhere in Melville's day we find the prehistory of this. Emerson had challenged his reader to "name all the birds without a gun"—a swipe at the then-standard ornithological practice of killing birds in order to study them.[53] Even Audubon, who did so promiscuously, confessed to twinges of guilt. Indeed, by the mid-1800s, animal watching in the United States was already a more common activity for the book-reading segment of the U.S. public than was animal hunting, whether for sport or subsistence: hence in part the brisk literary trade in books of maritime narrative, which afforded another kind of vicarity. It was no coincidence that the turn of that century marked the start of live exotic animal exhibits on a large scale in Europe and the United States. These were initially hawked by local entrepreneurs as curiosa, like "the REAL WHALE" beached at Salem and briefly exhibited at Boston before it began to stink.[54] Soon afterward aristocratic collections of exotic beasts, zoological gardens, and menagerie entrepreneurship became common, the taste for them whetted not only by an interest in living wonders that monster folklore suggests is more or less perenially appealing to the human mind, but more immediately by the quickened pace of western penetration of the rest of the world.

Human and animal wonders were coexhibited and even commingled, most notoriously in the form of "missing links" or fake Barnumesque collages of mermaids and the like.[55] But if the purpose of such exhibits was to titillate Caucasians with the thought that dark-skinned people were little different from primates, the late twentieth-century trend has been more to emphasize the humanity of the beast. In no case has the turnaround been more striking than in the case of how we think about whales. "Since the mid-1970s, whales and dolphins have been caught up in a tide of popular spiritualism and cross-species identification," Susan G. Davis observes in her ethnography of San Diego's Sea World experience.[56] This especially holds for killer whales, which have been semidomesticated in Sea World's theme parks. Only a half-century ago, Robinson Jeffers could unselfconsciously count on the reflex association of "orca" with "killer" as the basis for an "inhumanist" meditation on the terrible beauty of two predatory orcas snuffing out a panicky sea lion:

> Here was death, and with terror, yet it
> looked clean and bright, it was beautiful.
> Why? Because there was nothing human involved, suffering nor
> causing; no lies, no smirk and no malice;
> All strict and decent; the will of man had nothing to do
> here. The earth is a star, its human element
> Is what darkens it.[57]

Within less than a quarter of a century, however, "the captive-orca era," as one enthusiast exclaims, had produced "almost overnight [a] change in public opinion. People today no longer fear and hate the species; they have fallen in love with them."[58]

Davis unfolds in fascinating detail the manipulations that have helped produce this result: the extreme care to which impresarios and trainers go to perfect "the old circus trick of humanizing the animal," how this is scripted in the show by such ground rules as "the whale must never be an object of ridicule" and "it is positively important that humans be the butts of jokes"⁵⁹—jokes that involve such "human"-like behavior on the whale's part as splashing, head-bobbing, spitting, belching, and so on. This leads her to a jaundiced appraisal of a gullible public hoodwinked by an ersatz experience of "authentic" nature perpetrated by corporatism masquerading as patron of biological research and educational outreach. The trained orcas begin to look like a slightly more exotic version of Anheuser-Busch's other animal logo, Clydesdale horses, and Sea World a high-tech version of Barnum's American Museum.

Presumably a version of this argument about theme parks could be made about commercially organized whale-watching. Whale biologist Roger Payne, however, tenders an opposite verdict about whale-watching, a version of which he might well apply to theme parks also. Payne argues that it is important for large numbers of tourists "to become awestruck by whales" because "in the long run it is they who will determine the fate of whales more than many of the scientists who get to spend their lives with them." Such being the case, a carefully scripted live encounter is better than none at all.⁶⁰ But perhaps these claims are complementary, not irreconcilable. It may be true, as Davis claims, that commercial enterprises like Sea World offer a packaged version of nature in the interest of enhancing the corporate image, and yet it may also be true that such packaged experiences of contact with "nature" can reinforce or activate environmentalist commitment. Otherwise, one might add, why should environmentalists bother to write for publication, which demands another type of corporate packaging unless you run your own press on your own funds.

Contemporary regulation of the whaling industry presents a similarly mixed picture. Payne comes down on both sides of the fence in his remarks about the International Whaling Commission (IWC), an assemblage of representatives from member states charged to implement the International Convention for the Regulation of Whaling ratified after World War II by the major whaling nations. His annual trips "to the IWC constitute the most dispiriting, irritating, and outrageously frustrating activity of my life," rigged as the proceedings seem to him in favor of industry and porous as the IWC's oversight has been. Yet he believes that the IWC, meaning especially the minority of vigilant articulate conservationists who serve together with industry advocates and meretricious politicians, has saved a number of species from utter extinction, and that international organizations like it "constitute the only way forward."[61]

It is this mixed picture that leads Lynton Caldwell to conclude that the key to generating an effective system of protection for the transnational marine commons is neither scientific nor institutional but cultural: commitment to a better environmental philosophy. "Unless related to a holistic concept of humans-in-biosphere along with a realistic assessment of a sustainable future for mankind, facts alleged to be scientific may as easily be used to support exploitative policies as to protect the integrity of the earth."[62] Caldwell commensensically argues that institutions of mediation must supply the *structure* of any workable solution, but that public environmental values will determine whether they work well or poorly. From this standpoint, empathy for nonhumans as fellow creatures, however sentimental and subject to image manipulation, would seem a better augury than otherwise, especially when the creatures have the charisma to represent an entire ecological domain: indeed, to embody, like the great whales, the ocean or the planet within themselves.

Though this microcosmic way of thinking may seem fanciful, there is even, at least sometimes, a scientific as well as aesthetic eco-logic to it. Florida conservation biologists, for example, have looked to the vicissitudes of the endangered Cape Sable seaside sparrow as a "barometer" of the ecosystemic health of the Everglades.[63] The Endangered Species Act has been a powerful instrument for protecting ecosystems, not only individual creatures. This is not to say that ordinary citizens, creative writers, or advocacy journalists think "krill" or "squid" when they think "whale." Very likely, lay judgments as to why species extinction is wrong are driven by a more simplistic combination of large critter bias, higher-form-of-life bias, and uneasiness about seeing nature thrown "out of balance." Yet there is also a rough-and-ready wisdom to the fear that the disappearance of creatures at the top of the food chain will be harmful to "the environment," even if it is misguided to think that directing protectionist efforts toward them alone will ensure environmental health, ensure even their own survival.

Indeed, the latter-day shift in sentiment toward whales and whaling has been so pronounced—notwithstanding pockets of resistance in Japan, Iceland, Norway, and other scattered peoples—as to threaten to make old-time whaling imagination seem as retrograde as minstrel-show renditions of *Uncle Tom's Cabin's* Topsy or the late-imperial child's classic *Little Black Sambo*. Jeffers's poem about murderous orcas now looks even more atavastic than it meant to be. Disney's decision, entirely logical for 1940, to make the people-swallowing shark of Carlo Collodi's children's classic *Pinocchio* into "Monstro the Whale" would be a less automatic choice today.[64] Likewise, narratives of contemporary whaling adventure and derring-do have virtually dried up;[65] nature writing about whales has taken on a more explicitly protectionist cast; and *The Year of the Whale* has led to other whale-protagonist narratives. Robert Siegel's popular novel in the first person about the life and adventures of Hralekana-kolua—an improbably altruistic, sensitive young cetacean's attempts to rescue fellow whales from human predators though it may cost him his own life—comes close to turning *Moby-Dick* on its head.[66]

In contemporary nature writing the shift in imagination of the non-human is nowhere better seen than in the work of Barry Lopez, one of the leading figures most committed to reexamining human-animal relations. One of Lopez's signature achievements has been his sympathetic, scientifically informed meditations on selected large mammals with concurrent emphasis on the images, myths, and fantasies humans have constructed about them. A dual commitment to make literary representation more scientifically informed and at the same time to recover and advocate what he takes to be a lost understanding between humans and nonhumans is central to his work. In his essay "Renegotiating the Contracts," Lopez argues that western culture has been diminished by speciesism, by decline in contact with and sense of wonder about animals, by failure to appreciate that animals have cultures of their own that might in some respects even provide role models for ours. Lopez's claim that traditionally "among hunting peoples in general in the northern hemisphere, these agreements derived from a sense of mutual obligation and courtesy" may be a somewhat wishful romanticization.[67] But that does not affect the core of what he has to say about how species boundaries need to be renegotiated in order to strengthen human-animal intercommunity.

This essay was written in the aftermath of Lopez's first major book, *Of Wolves and Men* (1978), which went several steps beyond Aldo Leopold's "Thinking like a Mountain" in combatting the settler-culture "varmint" stereotype that had driven wolves to the brink of extinction. Lopez seconds Leopold's ecological argument (a wolf population keeps mountain forests from being defoliated by those "good" critters, the deer) with a rich account of wolf behavior set within an even richer tapestry of narrative and reflection about wolves as objects of human imagination. The book seeks thereby to demonstrate the antiquity of human fascination with wolves, to renew that interest, and to rechannel it so as to strengthen cross-species awareness.

Much the same is true of the three large mammal chapters that form the first main section of Lopez's *Arctic Dreams* (1985): on the musk ox, the polar bear, and the narwhal. None of these creatures are burdened with the negative stereotypes attached to wolves, but all have been thoughtlessly hunted, exploited, or taken for granted in ways that these chapters seek to supplant by education and reenchantment. In each case the Arctic ecosystem, which the initial chapter has sketched and which later chapters are to deepen, is made to revolve around the concentrated portraits of the individual creatures; and each portrait is transfused with a sense of past and present transactions between creatures and humans, with continual emphasis on the wonder and mysteriousness of encountering them, both experientially and contemplatively.

Interspecies communication, or rather the lack of it, is more centrally the subject of Lopez's essay "A Presentation of Whales," about the 1979 stranding of forty-one sperm whales on the Oregon coast.[68] Lopez stresses the well-meaning but ignorant and hence unintentionally cruel efforts to help the whales survive or die more quickly, and the ineffectiveness of these efforts given how little is known about the phenomenon of whale-stranding and even about sperm whale biology. The focus shifts back and forth from the suffering, death, and cleanup of the whales to the ethics and behavior of various people charged with crisis management: scientists, park officials, the press, and so on. In these ways "A Presentation of Whales" instantiates the diagnosis in "Renegotiating the Contracts" that western culture suffers from a pathetically meager ability to think across species lines. To Lopez, the loss on both sides, particularly for nonhumans, is sad indeed.

Lopez moves with greater sophistication along the path that Sea World and Disney protocols follow formulistically: interspecies understanding is important, animals shall no longer be treated as victims or scapegoats. Unlike popular culture's orchestrations of animal-human encounters, however, Lopez studiously refrains from familiarizing them. On the contrary, for Lopez the mysteries of animal behavior ("We know more about the rings of Saturn than we know about the narwhal") and the intricate perplexities of human wonderment in response ("My eye was drawn to them before my conscious mind, let alone my voice, could catch up") express an earnest, baffled thinking person's respect.[69] This attentive respectfulness differs sharply from the just-like-me illusion propagated by popular cetacean productions like the three *Free Willy* films, boy-critter melodramas about an initially hostile but actually tender, smart, and sensitive orca that evil mercenary Sea World-type entrepreneurs capture (in a boat ironically named the *Pequod*) and almost destroy, until Willy's new friend Jesse frees him with the combined aid of Jesse's wise Native American mentor, a disaffected trainer, and Jesse's foster parents. Willy and Jesse are playmates and soulmates. *Free Willy II* and *III* show the adolescent Jesse returning to shore to resume contact and, of course, to get embroiled in dangers from which orca and boy at different times save each other. What is finally most interesting about Willy is that he is Jesse's friend, an amazingly responsive wild pet.[70]

I do not mean to deny standing to the *Free Willy* films on this account as environmentalist interventions, despite their banal plotting and undistinguished cinematography. They remain preservationist, animal-rights-friendly texts even though Willy is not "freed" either literally (because a domesticated—or mechanical!—orca is needed for the role)[71] nor thematically (because Willy is made to matter chiefly in terms of Jesse's feelings toward him). As such, the films reaffirm—if reaffirmation be needed given the long history of the plot device—that dramatized rapport between individual human and individual nonhuman can be a powerful resource for imagining environmental concern. But how, if at all, can this be done at minimum sacrifice to ecological literacy and without reducing the new ethical paradigm of species relativism to nothing more than a friendly amendment to the old Adamic myth that the primary end of the animal creation is to serve human needs?

Lopez's recourse, as we have seen, is an intertwined lyric meditation and narrative descriptivism that amounts to a kind of supersensitive whale watcher's aesthetic of distance: a means of expressing intellectual interest and emotional empathy while keeping his hands off, the observer's ego conscientiously peripheral to his account of the creature.

Moby-Dick, on the other hand, insofar as it begins to deal with the issue of interspeciesism, generally follows a *via negativa* of dramatizing the pathogenic side of human preoccupation with it. The Nantucketers' thirst for dominance threatens to turn them into global predators. The root of Ahab's madness is that he is utterly sure that a MESSAGE has been delivered him from the cosmos through the medium of the White Whale (be it "agent" or "principal" [p. 144]). Ishmael too, although he would prefer to keep his distance, is almost as obsessive in his own quest for understanding: a quest also left hanging in an intellectual sense. *Moby-Dick* thereby reproaches in advance the sentimental side of animal rapport aesthetics, saying, in effect, "Don't assume it is in the interest of animals that we should act out our emotions toward them," and "It's understandable that you should care about the cosmos, but don't expect the cosmos to care about you." When your boat goes down, "the great shroud of the sea [will roll] on as it rolled five thousand years ago" (p. 469).

Melville might have rethought his ending, and other aspects of his book as well, had he foreseen that modern whalers would obtain the wherewithal to exterminate the globe's entire population of big cetaceans. As it was, he had no way to predict even the near-term collapse of American whaling less than a decade later as the result of the fuel oil revolution and the U.S. Civil War, let alone the twentieth-century revival of the industry with the aid of high-tech weaponry, factory ships, whale-disorienting sonar, and the like. But he would likely have stood by his narrative of obsession with "the whale" defeated by its own obsessiveness, and he would probably have taken *both* the excesses of modern whaling *and* the excesses of modern cetaceophilia as supporting testimony.

Moby-Dick's imagination of excess and Lopez's modeling of restraint (especially in *Arctic Dreams*) share at least two major ethical-aesthetic commitments. First, an agnostic fascination with human desire to find in animals configurations of behavior that seem symbolically significant (for those especially interested in cosmological reading of nature's book) or behaviorally meaningful from the standpoint of evidencing animal cognition. Second, a commitment to beholding the individual creature not merely as sui generis or qua species but in the context of a global vision of some sort, the chief ingredients of which for Melville are imperial enterprise and comparative mythology, and for Lopez polar ecology and comparative ethnography. These commitments produce a cosmopolitan vision that helps keep the novel from succumbing to trivialization of animal-human rapport such that the iconic beast loses its standing as an ecosystemic, ecocultural synecdoche, dwindling into an isolated case, and the experience of rapport into little more than an exotic episode of private life. That the latter seems more often the case in popular turn-of-the-twenty-first-century imaging of cetaceans suggests that the globalization of environmental imagination of the oceanic still has a long way to go before it can match its high-water marks with any frequency. Indeed, *Moby-Dick,* "A Presentation of Whales," *Free Willy,* and the Sea World experience all in their discrepant ways testify that when the mentality that produces grosser forms of abuse of commons is suspended or repressed—the conception of whales as commodities that are fair game for all entrepreneurs, for example—what may take its place is often little better than sublimated propertarianism: this is *my* trophy, my playmate, my unique and unprecedented experience. It then becomes the challenge of literature, and the discourses of cultural expression more generally, to make that insight common property in ways that resist the seductions of appropriation. This is the challenge a writer like Lopez has assumed, and it will surely remain a challenge for environmental writers throughout the new century.

Chapter 7

The Misery of Beasts and Humans: Nonanthropocentric Ethics versus Environmental Justice

> Wild animals protected in the conservation area, or protected species, outside it, can often affect the people adversely in various ways. Thus wild boar protected by the Bhimashankar Sanctuary in Pune district every year destroy extensive areas of standing crops in tribal hamlets which adjoin the reserve . . . In twenty-five hamlets surveyed in 1987, about 96,000 kg of grain has been destroyed by wild animals . . . These enormous losses suffered by ecosystem people in the interior rarely attract the attention of wildlife lovers in the city.
>
> —Madhav Gadgil and Ramachandra Guha, *Ecology and Equity: The Use and Abuse of Nature in Contemporary India*

> Here was a lunging, battering, stinking helicopter; men aiming, shooting, and shouting while around them elephants not yet crippled or killed screamed and ran in circles, charging into the dust-filled bush only to charge out again. Drawn back and back by their imperative to help; with each emergence giving fresh bellows of grief, horror, fear, and disbelief— their eyes wide and white, and temporin streaming down their cheeks as with tender trunks they freshly explored heads and bodies, reaching into ears, mouths, eye sockets, vulvas, hovering over pools of blood, dung, and urine, and awaiting their own death, as dictated by the mercy of the culling protocol.
>
> —Katy Payne, *Silent Thunder: In the Presence of Elephants*

Chapters 5 and 6 have taken us somewhat afield, in both senses of the word, from the preoccupations of Chapters 3 and 4, which concentrated more on metropolitan scenes. The opposite tendencies of these pairs of chapters underscore the difficulty of representing in a single book the interdependence of the "anthropocentric" and "ecocentric" dimensions of environmental imagination, even when one's premise is that compartmentalization of "nature" and "culture," settlement and outback, is too schematic a basis for conceiving environmental psychology, values, and aesthetics. In the remaining chapters, accordingly, I want first to reflect more pointedly on the history of this ethical/aesthetic schism and on how literature of the last two centuries helps both to explain its persistence as a cultural legacy and to expose its inadequacy as a way of thinking; then, in Chapter 8, to identify a specific tradition of environmental imaging that may help get us past the polarization imposed by such ethical rubrics as anthropocentric and ecocentric or genre categories like nature writing and urban fiction.

Schisms

For those concerned about environmental ethics, no phase of modern western thought has been more consequential than the steady, albeit uneven, extension of moral and sometimes even legal standing to wider circles of human *and* nonhuman community. The roots of extensionist thinking are so tangled that it would take a whole book in itself to explicate them, but certainly two of the catalysts have been the evolution of democratic values and the rise of evolutionary biology. The following two passages illustrate this. The first is a famous footnote from the last chapter of Jeremy Bentham's *Introduction to the Principles of Morals and Legislation* (1780; 1789), the second a pronouncement from Darwin's *The Descent of Man* (1871), that indispensable successor and companion piece to *The Origin of Species*.

The day has been, I grieve to say in many places it is not yet past, in which the greater part of the species, under the denomination of slaves, have been treated by the law exactly upon the same footing as, in England for example, the inferior races of animals are still. The day *may* come, when the rest of the animal creation may acquire those rights which never could have been withholden from them but by the hand of tyranny. The French have already discovered that the blackness of the skin is no reason why a human being should be abandoned without redress to the caprice of a tormentor. It may one day come to be recognized that the number of the legs, the villosity of the skin, or the termination of the *os sacrum* are reasons equally insufficient for abandoning a sensitive being to the same fate . . . the question is not, Can they *reason?* nor, Can they *talk?* but, Can they *suffer?*[1]

As man advances in civilization, and small tribes are united into larger communities, the simplest reason would tell each individual that he ought to extend his social instincts and sympathies to all the members of the same nation, though personally unknown to him. This point being once reached, there is only an artificial barrier to prevent his sympathies extending to the men of all nations and races . . . Sympathy beyond the confines of man, that is humanity to the lower animals, seems to be one of the latest moral acquisitions. It is apparently unfelt by savages, except towards their pets . . . This virtue, one of the noblest with which man is endowed, seems to arise incidentally from our sympathies becoming more tender and more widely diffused, until they are extended to all sentient beings.[2]

Bentham's is a discourse of rights, Darwin's a discourse of sympathy, but they concur in affirming that the criterion of civilizational advance is extension of respect to further realms of being: first to classes and/or races other than ours, then to other species than ours. Both are bold strokes of ethical transformationist evangelism. Yet they also beg some large questions and thus unconsciously foreshadow some of the characteristic problems with which a more developed, critically self-conscious moral extensionism must wrestle.

For example: What qualifies an entity for moral consideration? Is it sentience, as in Darwin, which would seem at least implicitly to valorize higher-order animal intelligence? Or is it capacity to suffer, as in Bentham, which might extend the circle further? Or might it instead be "interest," as Lawrence Johnson and certain other environmental ethicists argue, in which case all life-forms (even microorganisms) might be said to count?[3]

Again: What exactly is being extended? Is it rights, as in Bentham? A kind of utopian parliament of all beings? Is it humanitarian compassion, as in Darwin?—which sounds more like settlement house and SPCA activism. Or is the consideration to be extended to be thought of as something else? Tolerance, empathy, respect, or some other affect?

Then too, to the extent that we think of moral extension in terms of categories of being, as Bentham does exclusively and Darwin also for the most part, what is implied on the one hand about obligation to individuals as against groups, and what on the other hand about the moral claims of such complex entities as communities and ecosystems?[4]

But perhaps the most intensely debated of all the issues surrounding moral extensionism has been the more general question of the relative claims of an anthropocentric or humankind-first ethics versus a nonanthropocentric or ecosystem-first ethics of whatever kind. What values to assign to the welfare of endangered people as against the welfare of endangered nonhumans and/or bioregions? Shrinking elephant herds versus famine-threatened villagers? Loggers versus spotted owls, rainforest biodiversity versus urban public health? These are familiar avatars of the general issue. In recent years a veritable cottage industry of adjudication discourse has sprung up among environmental ethicists,[5] doubtless reinforced by realization that to the general public "environmental and human concerns are perceived to be mutually exclusive and even contradictory."[6]

As indicated in Chapter 1, mediation of this perception gap is of special import for contemporary environmentalism, insofar as the mainstream western-based organizations that constitute the global environmental establishment stand accused by the environmental justice movement of undue preoccupation with endangered species to the neglect of endangered humans. If we step back momentarily from this scene and examine classic statements like Bentham's and Darwin's more closely, we may better understand the logic of that impasse: understand why it makes sense for the expansion of environmental-ethical imagination that they so clearly envisaged as a both/and (both human and nonhuman others) to have led to a widespread perception of an inevitable either/or trade-off.

Both passages anticipate the claims of both contemporary human-centered environmental justice and nonanthropocentric ethics.[7] Both writers disdain the tribalisms of both race and of species, even though they partially reinstate those tribalisms via their assumptions of modern western history as a story of progressive moral enlightenment and of themselves as standing on a higher civilizational platform, implying that only the most highly civilized people are capable of appreciating the democracy of sentience or the sympathy that ought to bind a person to all other beings. But the harder difficulty these passages present is that the moment one starts to appreciate their prescience as prophecies of either environmental justice or nonanthropocentric ethics their judgments immediately begin to seem suspect from the standpoint of the other position. Focus on the ethical breakthrough of Bentham's approval of what he takes to be French egalitarianism toward blacks or Darwin's sympathy across lines of race, and immediately the anthropocentrism of each passage (its priority ordering of first humans and *then* nonhumans) is underscored. On the other hand, if one focuses on the idea of cross-species fraternity, then immediately one's teeth are set on edge by what seems a kind of ecofascist lumping of non-Europeans with nonhumans, and by the implication that the *real* test of civilization is not so much overcoming racialism as overcoming speciesism—as if prejudice and inequality at the human level were to be surmounted with relative ease.

Darwin's *Descent of Man* is particularly replete with such problematic moments. Take for instance what he has to say about pets and about Fuegians. The inhabitants of Tierra del Fuego were Darwin's first close-up specimens of what seemed a truly Paleolithic people; he liked to use them as examples of the most brutish order of humanity. Conversely, he liked to emphasize the near-human capacities of certain higher-order animals. Yet both pets and Fuegians are subjected to a rabbit-and-duck oscillation. Pets can seem by turns uncannily human (dogs can manifest "shame," "magnaminity," and "something very like a conscience") and intractably beneath us.[8] Fuegians are made to seem in some contexts appallingly animalistic and in others proof positive that all the races of humankind belong to a common species sharply distinct from higher-order nonhumans.[9] This ductility is typical of a general penchant for tacking back and forth between opposite positions that helps explain why Darwinism has lent itself to such opposite cartoon reductions: both that it debases men into monkeys and that it legitimates social hierarchicalism in the name of science. Such is the predictable legacy of the conservative radical, whose questioning of standard borders triggers an anxiety within himself as well as within others as to how completely those borders should be transgressed.

Darwin's writing shows, then, how a liminal stage of moral extensionism can produce in the same thinker such instability and compartmentalization that, by turns, human and animal others can be reduced or aggrandized in relation to advanced humans: either likened to each other (whether honorifically or slightingly) or treated as irreconcilably different, according to whether the emphasis is on the evolutionary threads that link them or the gradients between them. Once one begins to rethink the scope of moral agency and worth in this way, at least two opposite outcomes can be expected. First, an expansion of the ethical sphere beyond the classic Kantian position, according to which "rational being" is what qualifies a person (paradigmatically male) as a moral agent and "all animals exist only as means, and not for their own sakes, in that they have no self-consciousness."[10] But, second, a babel of applications in which rational western man's different others, other races and other species, can be played off against each other according to the writer's mood or persuasion.

With these complex possibilities in mind, we now turn from intellectual history to literature. Concurrent and symbiotic with the advent of western moral extensionist thinking comes an intensified interest in writing and reading about the imagined life-worlds of both social others and other species. Some symptomatic instances are Romantic poetry of peasant life; narratives of the lives of escaped slaves; biography, sociology, and fiction of the underclass; the rise of ethnography; and the birth of the modern animal story.

Concerning such bodies of writing, the following points roughly hold. First, literary recuperations of the life-worlds of human and nonhuman others tend for the most part to proceed more autonomously from each other than the linkage of the two concerns in those passages from Bentham and Darwin would imply. At a quite early date, the imagined miseries of beasts and of humans generate their own specialized genres. So, for example, Upton Sinclair's exposé of the Chicago meatpacking industry in *The Jungle* becomes the so-called "Uncle Tom's Cabin of wage slavery," while Anna Sewall's *Black Beauty* becomes the so-called "Uncle Tom's Cabin of the horse." The point of triangulation is the same but the trajectories disparate, the later texts privileging sharply discrepant realms of concern. Second, following from such discrepancies, the specialized discourses of human and nonhuman others have tended to attract different commentators: those who study naturalist novels, for example, have not tended to overlap much with those who study nature writing. Third, nonetheless, albeit perhaps serendipitously, one finds arresting parallels between these different bodies of critical commentary, such as interest in the ease with which narratorial sympathy shades into condescension or need to control; interest in the question of the representativeness of the individual case, in the question of whether and how one dares speak on behalf of a disempowered other, and in the question of whether subalterns can speak. Fourth, one also often sees in each discourse the shadow persistence of the other one—but so scripted as to make it ethically suspect if not disreputable. A familiar example is the analogy of the bestial in naturalist fiction: people brutalized into animals by social oppression, as in Zola's *Germinal* or Richard Wright's *Native Son*,[11] or (less pejorative but not exactly honorific either) oppressed people needing to practice animal-like adaptation if they are to become fully human, as in the opening image of the turtle as a resilient survivor in Steinbeck's *Grapes of Wrath*. Conversely, traditional nature writing often concentrates on the beauty and excitement of the natural world to the downplay if not the exclusion of social justice concerns, as with John Muir's disinterest in and even contempt for the Native American cultures that preceded him in the Sierras.

From this division of literary and critical labor, a spectacle of dissonant if not irreconcilable realms of thought has ensued, in light of which contemporary debates about rival environmental ethics start to look like a self-fulfilling prophecy.

Two late twentieth-century fictions will illustrate the result: Mahasweta Devi's Bengali novella translated in 1995 by Gayatri Spivak as "Pterodactyl, Puran Sahay, and Pirtha," and Canadian writer Barbara Gowdy's 1998 novel *The White Bone*. "Pterodactyl" narrates the visit of an investigative journalist (Puran, the protagonist and center of consciousness) to a remote immiserated village (Pirtha) of "tribal" (i.e., indigenous) people. *The White Bone* attempts to reconstruct from the inside the culture of an endangered nonhuman tribe, a clan of African elephants.

"Pterodactyl" is one of the most trenchant and challenging fictions of environmental justice ever written. Its sometimes esoteric cultural particularism, of which more in a moment, may seem to make it an odd detour from the U.S.-focused texts I have mainly been discussing, but the author herself has insisted on its applicability to the plights of first peoples worldwide, including Native Americans.[12]

The fictional Pirtha is one of a group of small villages in a district that gets ample rain for a short period annually but remains arid most of the year: a cycle, the story hints, aggravated by exploitative deforestation that has accelerated erosion and evaporation, deteriorating soil quality and endangering agriculture. Puran arrives in the midst of a famine caused not by the drought itself but by pollution of local wells—a disaster ironically resulting from the well-intended attempt by his host and former schoolmate, the local Block Development Officer (BDO), to stamp out profiteering in fertilizers, insecticides, and other items intended for the tribals. "To teach me a lesson," the BDO bitterly reports, his graft-deprived underlings sprayed the village's bare fields during the dry season,[13] and when rain came the runoff poisoned the residents' wells and the roots of their principal food crop, causing widespread sickness and death.

As Puran tries to make contact with the villagers, he confronts what come to seem gratuitously, insanely complicated layers of mediation: a nameless Sub-Divisional Officer (SDO); his friend the BDO; the Sarpanch or head of the village council (a tribal ethnic but also a caste-Hindu, who fulfills certain paternalistic oversight responsibilities within a cluster of local communities); the one literate, educated Pirthan; and an NGO (nongovernmental organization) relief agent who works partly in concert with, partly in defiance of, the aforesaid tiers of governmentally approved and locally sanctioned authority. Most seem more well-meaning than not but are frustrated by mutual jealousies, entrenched corruption, and disinterest on the part of the higher authorities. The SDO and BDO entertain a faint hope that Puran will put Pirtha on the map. Meanwhile, the Pirthans themselves expect nothing; indeed, they are demoralized to the point of willing collective suicide. Seemingly they have convinced themselves that they have brought disaster on themselves by uncleanness. The villagers are a paradigmatic example of what Madhav Gadgil and Ramachandra Guha call "ecosystem people": traditionally lococentric communities whose subsistence economies make them dependent on imperiled local resources for survival.[14]

The sensitive Puran perceives all this, though he too is wounded and self-absorbed: in flight from domestic responsibilities to his mother and his motherless child, skittish about committing himself to a long-term woman friend who has forgone other marriage options for his sake. Nonetheless, he develops a unique rapport with the remarkable youth who has seen and drawn the "pterodactyl," a mythic figure symbolizing tribal identity (including its imminent extinction), whose rumored apparition has aroused the ripple of attention that has brought Puran here. He himself "sees" it, and visits secret places no other outsider has seen. Rain comes with his arrival, and he is credited with being a miracle worker. Yet he remains painfully aware of the gulf separating himself from the villagers—"There is no communication-point between us and the pterodactyl."[15] When he leaves, neither he nor anyone else seems to expect that much will change in Pirtha, whatever he writes about it.

As with all ecocatastrophe writing, the story's apocalypticism presumably aims to disconfirm itself, to communicate the misery of the tribals over against the insistence on the impossibility of communication. Certainly the suggestion is planted that circulation of powerful images, partial and distortive though they are, is the only way to reach the national conscience. What makes "Pterodactyl" an especially striking example of its kind is its unsparingly self-critical dissection of the motives, the intelligence, and the efficacy of any and all institutionalized reform efforts. Its diagnosis is all the more trenchant given that these ecosystem people in fact do have, in principle, a viable modus vivendi, at least so far as water supply is concerned: self-dug wells adequate for domestic needs and small-scale irrigation when water is carefully rationed during the long droughts. So this particular doomsday was unnecessary, although culturally inevitable: inevitable both because "omnivores" are systemically bent on disabling "ecosystem people" and because ecosystem people, being cultural traditionalists, may internalize plague and famine in self-disenabling ways.

Barbara Gowdy's The White Bone is a bold attempt to imagine how elephants think and feel, following the misadventures of several small families as they negotiate an increasingly drought-ridden landscape that bristles with human predators, in vain search of The Safe Place of collective memory, decimated by slaughter and deprivation as they go. As such, The White Bone is a more epistemologically pretentious text than "Pterodactyl," which scrupulously refrains from anything more authoritative than an outsider's view of tribal culture. But although the novel personifies elephants to a marked degree (by allowing them articulate speech, for example), transgressing bounds that cautiously empirical nature writers like Rachel Carson always stay within, no less rigorously does it undo or put pressure on its own anthropomorphism by pressing elements of disanalogy, so that empathetic sentiment is repeatedly evoked only to be jolted. Yes, elephants intercommunicate, but using conventions and means quite alien from those of humans, relying much more on smell, touch, and a kind of sixth sense or ESP. Yes, they have emotions, affections, and close-knit family life, but not structured according to western norms, rather in intricate, matriarchally ordered clans disciplined by strange deference rituals; their reliance on dung as individual insignia and means of communication, intimacy, tracking; their mental mapping of social space and place. (The book begins with an enigmatically dispersed and atomized chart of landmarks as elephants might perceive them.)

The result is a far less reader-friendly text than *Bambi* or *Babar* or *The Year of the Whale*. As with "Pterodactyl," facile empathy with the misery of the beast or the human as the case may be is frustrated, the result being that each text becomes, in part, a strenuous meditation on the challenge of making good on its respective extensionist project. Elephants are claimed in *The White Bone* to be more emotionally and mentally complicated beings than most readers will have supposed, but there is no simple affinity between "them" and "us." Empathy is laced with disgust. The infant trauma of Gowdy's protagonist upon the death of her mother (cobra-bitten as she went into labor) is weirdly displaced onto a repulsive description of the corpse exploding ("the pop of gas, the slosh of innards tumbling out"), sending "rock-sized chunks of gore" "down Mud's face and into her eyes" until she vomits, "and the smaller of two [vultures] who were trolling the intestines across the ground" "lapped up the pool and then began to pluck at Mud's trunk." Later, the trials of desert crossing for Mud's mate get rendered this way: "Flies buzz at his anus, in his ears, in front of his eyes, colossal ticks rummage through the cuts on his skin. To fend off thirst, he sucks on a stone."[16]

What in present context I especially want to stress about *The White Bone* vis-à-vis "Pterodactyl," however, is how each marginalizes the other type of misery. In Gowdy's elephant world, humans—"the hindleggers" as the elephants call them—are grotesque and scary killers. Gowdy is not a self-identified writer-activist like Devi; *The White Bone* is much more a fictive thought experiment than a narrative tract, taking up the challenge of fathoming animal minds thrown down by such skeptical treatments of animal consciousness as Thomas Nagel's "What Is It Like to Be a Bat?" with a combination of research and poetic license.[17] Yet fidelity to the simulation of elephant consciousness would appear to necessitate demonizing humans—at least contemporary humans (for elephant collective memory can recall a distant epoch of more peaceful coexistence). Humans for all practical purposes equal poachers equal villains, with no thought at all of extenuating circumstances that might have driven marginal African people into poaching. In this respect the book has the same tunnel-visioned ferocity as Dian Fossey's *Gorillas in the Mist,* even more so than biologist Katy Payne's field narrative, *Silent Thunder: In the Presence of Elephants,* which—as this chapter's second epigraph shows—commits itself no less passionately to a pro-elephant position, but elsewhere takes account of how this commitment puts her at odds with colleagues she respects, who are more keenly concerned than she about the welfare of southern African economies endangered by elephant proliferation and benefited by population control programs that allow for ivory harvesting while keeping the herds at a decent size, well below the danger line. In *The White Bone,* the misery of resident humans, the kind of problem Gadgil and Guha identify in this chapter's first epigraph, simply doesn't count.

"Pterodactyl" is not so divisive. At least it implies that the villagers' plight is linked to the plight of the nonhuman environment. The two domains are not in opposition. But on the whole it is a counterpart of *The White Bone,* marginalizing the suffering of the other kind of other, the nonhuman other. At the novella's close the scope does widen beyond the scene of human devastation into a lament for the natural environment also: "A continent! We destroyed it undiscovered, as we are destroying the primordial forest, water, living beings, the human" (p. 196). But this is no more than a brief glimpse. For the most part, the two texts adhere to specialized forms of ethical-aesthetic extensionism that exclude each other's concerns.

Not that one should blame them greatly on that account. It is hard enough to extend oneself across one moral frontier, let alone two. Such I take to be the point of E. M. Forster's amusing passage in *Passage to India* about the generation gap between "old Mr. Graysford and young Mr. Sorley, the devoted missionaries who lived out beyond the slaughterhouses, always travelled third on the railways, and never came up to the club." Both teach that "[i]n our Father's house are many mansions . . . [that] not one shall be turned away by the servants on that verandah, be he black or white," but they quarrel over whether "the divine hospitality" should cease there.

> Consider, with all reverence, the monkeys. May there not be a mansion for the monkeys also? Old Mr. Graysford said No, but young Mr. Sorley, who was advanced, said Yes; he saw no reason why monkeys should not have their collateral share of bliss, and he had sympathetic discussions about them with his Hindi friends. And the jackals? Jackals were indeed less to Mr. Sorley's mind, but he admitted that the mercy of God, being infinite, may well embrace all mammals. And the wasps? He became uneasy during the descent to wasps, and was apt to change the conversation. And oranges, cactuses, crystals and mud? and the bacteria inside Mr. Sorley? No, no, this is going too far. We must exclude someone from our gathering, or we shall be left with nothing.[18]

As this passage suggests, moral extensionism is hard work, and in no small measure because one must labor on two fronts, not just one. Forster's satire hinges on the embarrassments of western moral extensionism not only insofar as it struggles self-consciously with ingrained speciesism, but also insofar as it tends to embroil one in ethnocentric self-deception. The root cause of why neither Mr. Graysford *nor* Mr. Sorley can get very far past their habituated anthropocentrism is insufficient adaptation to the *human* other in the form of Hindu culture and practice, despite the pains they have taken to share the lot of their native flock, to their considerable inconvenience and mortification. The principled relativism of the good missionaries—both of them—only goes so far. The narrator treats them condescendingly not so much because they aren't more stretchable but because they fancy they're more stretchable than they are: Mr. Graysford having stopped farther short of full sympathy with his clients than he doubtless supposes, Mr. Sorley prizing his open-mindedness more than is warranted. The narrator, by contrast, makes no pretense of trying to reform or even fathom the Hindu life-world and with it the "real India," as the European characters in the novel like to put it. Indeed, in the novel's last sequence, even the Hindu sage Godbole's far more practiced and supple extensionism is itself made to fail as his God-like afflatus successfully enfolds westerner, then insect, but founders when he tries to "attempt the stone" to which the wasp clung: "logic and conscious effort had seduced."[19] When adepts fall short, how much more will the outlanders.

Mediations

Can one then hope to find in the modern literature works that neither end in a state of ironic detachment about the prospects of ethical extension nor, if they do press forward, commit themselves to a self-limiting embrace of environmental justice to the exclusion of ecological ethics, or vice-versa? Fortunately, the answer is yes, although the challenge is arduous and its history suggests that success is never to be taken for granted.

Melville's *Moby-Dick,* the last chapter should have suggested, is one such work, insofar as it links exploitation of men to wanton slaughter of whales; and insofar as it asks the reader to imagine, on the one hand, that a figure so grotesque at first sight to western eyes as Queequeg might be a Yankee man's bosom friend, while, on the other hand, to reconceive whales—monstrous though they seem—as strangely analogous to people. Nor was Melville the first creative writer to succeed in coordinating both extensionist trajectories. A number of Romanticist precursors anticipated him. As ecocritic Onno Oerlemans remarks, "it is impossible to read through even a sampling of the poetry of John Clare without being struck by how his concern for the rural poor (figured very often by the poet himself) parallels his concern for animal life. Both are 'classes' of beings whose welfare is ignored by the oppressive classes that own and increasingly occupy the land they live on."[20] Blake, Burns, and Coleridge provide earlier cases in point. Coleridge's "To a Young Ass" (1794), for example, dares at the cost of ex post facto parody by Byron and others to take seriously a subject that Laurence Sterne had treated farcically in *A Sentimental Journey* (1768), greeting the stereotypically comical creature as "poor little foal of an oppressed race!" and then stressing the link between human and animal oppression:

> Poor ass! thy master should have learnt to show
> Pity—best taught by fellowship of Woe!
> For much I fear me, that He lives, like thee,
> Half famished in a land of Luxury.[21]

Coleridge might easily, Oerlemans notes, have imagined animal plight as nothing more than "an allegory for the situation of the working masses in England"²² or, conversely, he might just as easily have made a mere metaphor out of oppressive mastership, instead of stressing the special bond between animal and worker as mutual victims of oppression "in a land of Luxury."

This poem hardly shows Coleridge at his best, but as ethical reflection it is avant-garde. By the same token, the comparative rarity of so explicit a move in his writing suggests the difficulty of the project, just as the reception history of *Moby-Dick*—the long obtuseness of its exegetes to the novel's critique of speciesism—does in another way. Significantly, the quoted passage occupies but a small fraction of the poem, which concentrates on empathy with the creature. For Coleridge's strong point as an extensionist was definitely on the side of imagining the mutuality of the human spirit and the biological world: a perspective that M. H. Abrams, in an important bicentennial essay in 1972, calls "Cosmic Ecology."²³

So it is in Coleridge's greatest poem, "The Rime of the Ancient Mariner," which turns on the consequences of wanton killing of a totem creature, and makes atonement hinge on the murderer's later manifestation of spontaneous caring for even the slimy things of creation.²⁴ The curse is lifted at the epiphanic moment when, unexpectedly, the mariner beholds the water snakes as beautiful—"They moved in tracks of shining white, / And when they reared, / the elfish light / Fell off in hoary flakes"—and "I blessed them unaware." This is an even more striking turn than the equivalent point near the end of Faulkner's "The Bear," when Ike McCaslin overcomes his instinctive revulsion from the serpent by remembering the Indian ritual address: "Chief, Grandfather." For nothing in the mariner's prior experience has really prepared him for this sudden expansion of piety. But although it would be churlish to complain overmuch given the remarkable poetic result, there is also something disturbingly asymmetrical about the poem's drama of fall and redemption, contrasted with the awareness of dual victimage in "To a Young Ass." "Rime" is silent about the possibility of shipboard oppression, except insofar as the protagonist's stigmatization by his shipmates counts as such. By contrast, one can easily imagine Melville transfusing such a narrative with the suggestion of how boredom and brutalization might have predisposed the mariner to random violence against taboo, and his shipmates to their equally violent mood swings toward him of denunciation, approval, and chastisement.

Yet given the comparative recency of environmentalism as a matter of widespread, intense, and abiding public concern, it is only to be expected that not until considerably later would literary works begin to frame self-consciously the *relationship* between the claims of environmental justice and of nonanthropocentric ethics; and that recent writing would do so most pointedly, since the ethical debate has become prominent only within the past several decades. An instructive example is the fiction of Chickasaw writer Linda Hogan. Her novel *Solar Storms* (1995), like much other contemporary Native American writing, trenchantly depicts settler culture aggression (Canadian, in this case) against indigenous peoples and against nonhumans. Seen through native eyes, these are two sides of the same pathology of resource extraction: big lumber and big hydropower, made callous by a combination of racist contempt for the region's indigenous inhabitants and utter disregard for massive environmental disruption caused by rerouting rivers, radically changing water level of lakes, and extermination of fish and mammals. Hogan's later novel *Power* (1998), however, meditates more explicitly on the competition between and the (in)adequacy of the competing institutionalized conceptions of environmental ethics that supposedly regulate both settler and native communities.

The plot of *Power* turns on the trial of a Native American woman for killing an endangered species, a Florida panther, seen through the eyes of a sixteen-year-old kinswoman and protégée. Ama Eaton is actually tried twice: first in a highly publicized courtroom affair, which ends in a mistrial for lack of evidence; then by a native tribunal, which convicts her and exiles her from the tribe. The clear implication is that neither set of procedures arrives at the truth. This dual breakdown is part of a critique of our two environmental-ethical positions that amounts to a deliberately uneasy combination of both/and and neither/nor. Both environmental justice and nonanthropocentric ethics are up to a point sustained but also revealed, as discourses, to be formulistic. Protection of endangered species is professed by all parties (and indeed seemingly felt by most) to be a good thing. Yet its legalization is shown to be a pretext for whites to get at uppity Indians and a stumbling block for the Native Americans themselves, whose reverence for the natural world is at least in principle much more grounded and who revere the panther as their tribal ancestor, but whose spiritual practice includes a place for slaying the animal under certain specific circumstances. On the environmental justice side, the Taiga are portrayed sympathetically as an embattled remnant people quintessentially victimized by racism, at the bottom of the opportunity ladder, stuck on a patch of reservation land degraded by toxic pollution and arbitrary variations in water level beyond their control. Yet justice in the sense of due process, either statutory or tribal, even when conscientiously administered (as for the most part in both cases it is shown to be here), perverts rather than protects because it cannot get at the complexities of the individual case as it unfolds itself in a time of cultural breakdown. Justice is unachievable because both mainstream and native cultures are entangled in their own protocols. Neither ethical paradigm and neither cultural group can fathom that the accused woman has killed the panther in an intentional variation from proper ritual practice as a sacrificial act to the end of preserving the tribe by the loss of herself.

The plot comes to a generically sentimental return-of-the-native close, as when the narrator Omishto, Ama's teenage protégée, permanently drops out of school and home community to follow native ways and become the leader of her people that her mentor might have been but never was. But the book's overall conceptual design is far more interesting than this ethno-essentialist denouement in its combination of notional assent to values of both environmental justice and nonanthropocentric ethics together with insistence that both persuasions, *as* systems, become encumbrances to understanding an ethos or enabling a practice that embodies either.

This critique is given a strongly ecofeminist turn by *Power*'s dramatization of women leaders among the Taiga across several generations; by the casting of males as the book's most exploitative and bigoted figures, particularly concerned to rein in female truancy; by the importance of Omishto's avoidance of her stepfather's predatory harassments as a contributory factor in motivating her to forsake conventional suburban family and school life in favor of Ama's cabin in the swamps and offbeat traditional ways; and above all by the importance attached to the roles of Ama and Omishto after her as environmental and cultural caregivers. These two women emerge as the centers of wisdom about what really ought to count as either environmental justice or nonanthropocentric ethics. We see this especially in Ama's self-appointed but misunderstood (by all but Omishto) role as steward of Taiga survival and the responsiveness to the natural world and to Ama that leads Omishto to wish to become her successor. A gynocentric ethics of care surpasses all versions of ethics as code. "Someone had to find a way to renew the world," as Omishto muses at one point, "and no one else would do it. Yes, it was against the law, but I saw with my eyes the boys driving through the place in their swamp buggies killing the land and the men wouldn't hold up so much as a finger to stop them, so maybe Ama took it all on herself to do."[25]

As philosopher Karen Warren points out, because ethics of care must proceed more from affect than from ratiocination personal narrative is an especially fitting vehicle for conveying ecofeminist commitment: narrative that dramatizes sensitivity to relationships "often lacking in traditional ethical discourse," that grows out of lived experience, that takes form from specific events, that suggests in the process of its unfolding "*what counts* as an appropriate conclusion to an ethical situation."[26] Warren refers here to a particular first-person narrative of rock climbing, but she could just as easily have been writing about such a witness-oriented narrative as *Power,* both the frame narrative of Omishto and the inner narrative of Ama Eaton.

A good deal of what Warren claims, furthermore, and *Power* bears this out as well, could be argued more categorically on behalf of the advantage of environmental imagination over environmental justice versus nonanthropocentric ethics dilemma at the situational level, in flesh-and-blood cases. By identifying a secret "knowledge" shared by the accused woman and unfathomed by others except for the narrator who shares it with us, the novel suggests the folly of supposing that the dispute is soluble through formal argument without reckoning in lived experience. One need not agree with the novel's implications that the native's best hope is to go native, or that the most faithful stewards of environmental justice and ecological ethics are women, in order to respond to the suggestion, which the genre of narrative is so well suited to drive home, that the claims of both ethical orientations can only be dealt with profoundly when both are felt as basic to personal and collective life-worlds. Argument can state, but narrative can actually drama-

tize how Ama and eventually Omishto as well experience both endangered panther and endangered community as integral to their own fate
and well-being. In this sense, Darwin and Bentham were unconscious
prophets of the power of fictive imagination to depict moral extensionism taking the form of wider and wider circles of identification and belonging.[27]

On the other hand, *Power,* also to its credit, does not privilege acts of
environmental imagination without fear and trembling, even though it
insists on a scenario where the issues are "resolved" (at least in quotation marks), in contrast to, say, Melville's persistent skepticism both
about epistemology *and* about the rightness and even the possibility of
decisive action on the basis of what one believes or supposes to be the
truth about human and biotic community. One of the novel's most
striking features is its framing of the accused woman's unfathomable
behavior as an act of antinomian chutzpah that even she herself does
not seem to understand completely. In this way *Power* shows it knows
better than its ending suggests: knows that the legacy of disjuncture between ethical paradigms must in the first instance be addressed by acts
that look puzzlingly idiosyncratic proceeding from motives that may
seem impenetrable. The force of environmental unconscious is thereby
also acknowledged in both its opposite aspects: as blocked understanding and as basis of insight and awakening.

Does this supply a conceptual template of practical value in adjudi-
cating real-life controversies? No, not if what you want is a blueprint: a
set of guidelines or procedures. But that is not something literature was
necessarily supposed to furnish in the first place. As Hemingway is said
to have remarked, "If you're looking for messages, try Western
Union"—and he too was a strongly code-oriented writer. What *Power*
does provide is quite enough to ask: a critique of environmental ethics
as code, at the very point needed to compensate for the tendency to pit
the two domains of ethical extensionism against each other. It critiques
environmental ethics as code by dramatizing ethics as practice—a practice that does not pretend the codes don't exist, don't have power, don't
carry a certain emotional and even moral authority; but a practice that
in the long run also underscores the importance of resisting false dichotomies and formulism. As a narrative attempting to dramatize the
impact of a narrative (the saga of Ama Eaton) on the life of the person

who retells it, trying as she does to understand it, *Power* also affirms the importance of model in the sense of image against model as prescription. The next chapter will examine one of the images most vigorously set forth of late as having the potential to model cultural as well as personal mediation of the dichotomy whose ironies Hogan provocatively unpacks.

Chapter 8

Watershed Aesthetics

> We must therefore leave aside the contemporary notion of nature, insofar as we still have such a one in general, where the discourse is of streams and waters.
>
> —Martin Heidegger, *Holderlins Hymnen "Germanien" und "Der Rhein"*[1]

> To watch water, to watch running water
> Is to know a secret, seeing the twisted rope
> Of runnels on the hillside . . .
> . . . Or it is not to know
> The secret, but to have it in your keeping
>
> —Howard Nemerov, "Runes"

> Water is often described around San Luis [Valley, Colorado] through the metaphor of the cardiovascular system. People around San Luis can often be heard saying, "Water is our lifeblood." . . . when the human heart is affected because the arteries are clogged, people get sick and die . . . Pollute, destroy, or disrupt the hydrological cycles of the watershed, and you endanger the balance and health of the entire ecosystem.
>
> —Devon G. Peña, "A Gold Mine, an Orchard, and an Eleventh Commandment"

Rivers are ancient cultural symbols, and rightly so. Without water, no life. Without ample supply, no sizable human settlements. Whole civilizations have been defined by the arterial rivers without which they could not have come into existence: the Mesopotamian regimes of the "Fertile Crescent" by the Tigris and the Euphrates, Egypt by the Nile. Indeed, throughout the world rivers have become cultural icons by dint of size, extent, beauty, imputed sacrality, and utility as transportation routes: the Amazon, the Rhine, the Ganges, the Mississippi. Rivers may be regional and local signifiers as well as national: the Connecticut for the conservative Congregationalist culture of premodern New England, the Colorado for the southwestern aridlands of the United States. When Joseph Conrad in *Heart of Darkness* had his narrator Marlow call up, from the spectacle of "monstrous" London darkening at sunset from the distance of the Thames estuary, the mordant recollection that "this also has been one of the dark places of the earth,"[2] he did not need to belabor the analogy between Roman conquerors disoriented by ancient British barbarity and contemporary European imperialists in Africa in order for the basic river-empire topos to be intelligible to British readers. As early as Elizabethan times, topographical writing had taken the rivers of England and most especially the Thames as synecdoches for national identity and power, an obvious and plausible "natural symbol."[3]

From River to Watershed

Traditionally the "naturalness" of rivers as such was often quite subordinated to their anthropocentric connotations of civilizational felicity. In Michael Drayton's lavish panorama of the rivers of Britain, *Poly-Olbion* (1622), the Thames is "the *Isles* emperiall Flood,"[4] and passing by London affords the occasion for a chronicle of all the British monarchs from William the Conqueror through Elizabeth. John Denham's *Cooper's Hill*, the first of the great Neoclassical prospect pieces, is no more constrained by physical landscape description. "Thames, the eldest & noblest Sonne / Of ould Oceanus," is not so much a literal waterway as the defining motif in a rich imperial tapestry of global scope:

> As a wise king first settles fruitefull peace
> In his own Realmes & with their rich increase
> Seeks warre abroade & then in triumph brings
> The Spoyles of Kingdomes, & the Crownes of Kings,
> So Thames, to London doth at first present
> Those tributes, which the neighbouring Countreys sent:
> But at his second visite, from the East
> Spices he brings & treasures from the West:
> Findes wealth where tis, & gives it where it wants,

Cities in deserts, woods in Citties plants:
So that to us no thing, no place is strange,
While his faire Bosome is the Worlds exchange.[5]

But at the same time there is a latent acknowledgment here of prosperity founded on natural advantage; and by the nineteenth century this becomes more pronounced, personalized, and incipiently ecocentric, as when Wordsworth imagines in *The Prelude* how the River Derwent "loved / To blend his murmurs with my nurse's song," sending "a voice / That flowed along my dreams."

That indeed seems to have been the poem's inception point. The *Two-Part Prelude* (1799) begins with it; and later, with the short "glad preamble" and the long despondent search-for-a-theme sequence prefixed to Book I (1805, 1850), the lines provide at once transition for and answer to one of the great rhetorical questions in world literature: "Was it for this . . . ? / For this, / didst thou, / O Derwent!"[6] As the memory of having been nursed (in all senses of that word) by the river unfolds, self-condemnation gives way to calm assurance, arising from the felt power of the strength derived from foundational moments of intercourse with nature.

Conrad's Thames inverts Wordsworth's Derwent by its implication that nature can deform or destroy culture as well as nurture it. But what is most striking about this departure from Wordsworthian premises is not any critique of natural influence as such—for at other moments Conrad revels like a Romantic poet in the sunset's sensuous effects—as the sophisticated awareness of the problems that ensue from first nature becoming reproduced by second nature. As Chinua Achebe and later postcolonial critics have shown, when it reaches Africa itself, *Heart of Darkness* falls into a stereotypical otherizing of natives that is all too complicit with the colonial order it criticizes.[7] But Conrad's exordial reference to the British heart of darkness was even more socially as well as sensuously insightful than the revisionist critique of Conrad's Eurocentrism suggests. This was no mere historical allusion to late antiquity. Early Victorian sanitarian images of city as jungle or wilderness had been canonized in late Victorian investigative journalism and social work, like Charles Booth's monumental exposé of urban poverty, *Dark-*

est England (1890). Furthermore, Conrad would have been well aware that the lower Thames had since Dickens's day been afflicted with severe pollution, decried by environmental reformers as a hazard to public health and as a national disgrace. At certain seasons the Thames was as mephitic to its denizens as the Congo was to Kurtz and Marlow.[8]

These two very different nineteenth-century authors, then, each offer glimpses of something like an ecocultural understanding of peoples defined by waterways. Wordsworth's late work presciently anticipates later bioregionalist thinking. "The Vale of Grasmere," observes Jonathan Bate, "is imagined as a visionary republic; as Wordsworth put it in his *Guide to the Lakes* [5th ed., 1835], it is a 'pure Commonwealth; the members of which existed in the midst of a powerful empire like an ideal society or an organized community, whose constitution had been imposed and regulated by the mountains which protected it.'"[9]

Given the long-standingness of this sensibility it comes as no surprise to see "watershed" become the most popular defining gestalt in contemporary bioregionalism, at least in the United States.[10] The logic is not simply aesthetic, not simply that waterways are eye-catching, picturesque landscape definers. Equally if not more fundamental and long-standing have been the economic function of rivers as supply lines (and later also as power sources) and the social settlement patterns following from that. This combination of factors provided the impetus for Paterson, New Jersey, to try to become a model factory town in the early nineteenth century, and in the fullness of time helped inspire William Carlos Williams to create his protobioregionalist epic *Paterson,* discussed in Chapter 3. In addition to these traditional factors, the watershed as a defining image of community has the additional advantages of being a quick and easy way of calling attention to the arbitrariness of official borders (country, state, county, town, private property lines), an equally obvious reminder of common dependence on shared natural resources, and an appeal to an imagined community defined by "natural" rather than governmental fiat that promises to feel larger than most peoples' habitats or locales, yet still of manageable size.[11] Given the natural tendency of watercourses to meander, the watershed image has perhaps a special pertinence as a vision corrective in the United States, the vast majority of whose trans-Appalachian land parcels were laid out according to the rectilinear Jeffersonian survey grid regardless of terrain: "the most extensive uninterrupted cadastral system in the world."[12]

There are some problems with watershed as a defining image, notwithstanding. One is semantic: "watershed" is an Americanism for what in England and Europe denotes the borders between drainage systems rather than the drainage system itself. The decidedly noncharismatic "drainage basin" would translate better culturally.[13] Second, watershed borders are contestable. To a layperson, the image seems solider than it is (also one of its attractions, of course). The Mississippi basin, an enormous area that, with its tributaries, extends across much of the landmass of the lower forty-eight United States, would seem to comprise far more than a single bioregion; but if one starts trying to isolate subsidiary portions as cultural units, where to stop? It is impossible to stipulate categorically an order of ramification above or below which a subordinate waterway should not qualify for watershed status in a cultural sense. Third, watersheds are by no means necessarily even "natural" units so far as defining range and dispersal of plant and animal species is concerned, as anyone who climbs New Hampshire's Mount Washington with an eye to the changing plant life will immediately notice. Nor do surface watercourses and groundwater patterns correlate exactly. In the semiarid Great Plains of the United States, for example, since the advent of deep-well drilling technology in the mid-twentieth century it has made much more sense to conceive of water conservation districts according to the contours of the huge but fast-shrinking Ogallala Aquifer than according to the region's rivercourses.[14]

Yet none of these considerations detracts much from the power of watershed as a luminous aesthetic-ethical-political-ecological image, provided one recognizes it as a less than empirically airtight category and sometimes in need of cultural translation to boot.

Environmental historians credit the late nineteenth-century explorer-geologist-author John Wesley Powell with being the first great American formulator of something like the modern watershed concept, on the basis of Powell's contention that the western territories should be divided, and their settlements organized, according to their "hydrographic basins." This Powell felt to be a proper response to western water scarcity.[15] Each hydrographic district was "to be a commonwealth within itself" with respect to determining watershed-specific policies, empowered to "make [its] own laws for the division of the waters, for the protection and the use of the forests, for the protection of the pasturage on the hills."[16]

Powell's views were thought too utopian to implement, but concurrently smaller-scale plans were put in practice, perhaps the most significant being New York's creation of the first national forest preserve, in the Adirondacks, to prevent degradation of the Hudson River watershed.[17] Powell's vision has been reinvented during the last third of the twentieth century. Among creative writers contributing to its revival, none has been more prominent than Gary Snyder. Snyder's "Coming into the Watershed" defines the idea in an inclusive and resonant way, sensibly resisting a textbook definition:

> From the tiniest rivulet at the crest of a ridge to the main trunk of a river approaching the lowlands, the river is all one place and all one land.
>
> The water cycle includes our springs and wells, our Sierra snowpack, our irrigation canals, our car wash, and the spring salmon run. It's the spring peeper in the pond and the acorn woodpecker chattering in a snag. The watershed is beyond the dichotomies of orderly/disorderly, for its forms are free, but somehow inevitable. The life that comes to flourish within it constitutes the first kind of community.[18]

Snyder's "first kind of community," as sketched here, envisages a sort of Leopoldian "biotic community" where humans and nonhumans peacefully coexist, stressing not spatial positions within a topographic design but simultaneous and interacting processes, with an emphasis on how each activity or life-form depends on the shared supply of water. This finesses problems of pseudoprecision and border disputes (e.g., where exactly does this bioregion start and that one end?).

Snyder also manages to interweave many if not all of the main strands of environmental-ethical thought: for example, the nonanthropocentric spirit of "deep" ecology's claim that humans and all other creatures belong to the earth, rather than vice versa; post–Judeo-Christian stewardship thinking, which starts from the premise of human duty to care for nature, as does ecofeminist ethics of care in its own way; and even the populist principle of basing environmental policy on equity among inhabitants to achieve an equitable result, a keystone of environmental justice theory. The ethical eclecticism arises from a practical understanding that watershed environmentalism is potentially attractive on a number of grounds, and its attraction is likely to be strong in proportion to the breadth of that appeal. Likewise, the U.S. Riverkeepers movement has developed into a network of chapters nationwide from an alliance of wilderness advocates, sportsmen, commercial fishermen, and community advocates concerned about water quality.[19] So too with Trout Unlimited, which has diversified from its original base as a sportsman's interest group.[20] The organization American Rivers stresses nature protection and restoration as its top priorities ("Rescuing Rivers from Dams" is a typical article in its bulletin), but also publishes hygienic and stewardship-oriented pieces like "Keep Animal Waste out of Our Water."[21] Snyder seems mindful of all these constituencies.

That imagination is key to making watershed consciousness a potent force is corroborated by the instances of bioregionalist advocacy just mentioned. It is easier, however, to appeal to watershed consciousness than it is to define what it means with any specificity. As another western American writer remarks, "If we knew a word for the dark spaces between pebbles on the river bottom, if we had a name for the nests of dried grass deposited by floods high in riverside trees, if there were a word apiece for the smell of pines in the sunshine and in the shadows, we would walk a different trail."[22] This confession of failure partially surmounts itself by the enticement of its invitation, but the insufficiency is undeniable and long-standing. Wordsworth was constrained as well as empowered by the traditions of Neoclassical locodescriptivism and the lyric of nature symbolism. So too was Conrad by the novelistic and travel-writing conventions on which the plot of *Heart of Darkness* rests: a compound of nature description, ethnography, and adventure narrative. So too with the young Henry Thoreau's attempt, in *A Week on the Concord and Merrimack Rivers* (1849), to coordinate different environmental genres (the primary narrative of the voyage, the excursus nature essay on native fish, cameos of the other natural history of the region) with a potpourri of other agendas. In other words, the impediments to emergence of environmental imagination from environmental unconscious begin with the very templates on which it relies for expression.

More telling than premodern examples is the case of such a veteran contemporary ecologically self-conscious writer as the late British Poet Laureate Ted Hughes, whom Derek Walcott—whose own poetry entitles him to judgment on such matters—credits with having "brought us, in the most exact sense, closer to nature, its complete workings, than any English poet we can think of":[23]

> All night a music
> Like a needle sewing body
> And soul together, and sewing soul
> And sky together and sky and earth
> Together and sewing the river to the sea.[24]

This from *River* (1983), an interwoven collection of solstice-to-solstice lyrics that has won praise not only on aesthetic grounds (including this particular poem, "In the Dark Violin of the Valley") but also as "an ecological primer about learning to perceive the animistic energies that the fisherman persona experiences in nature."[25] The next stanzas relocate the music as a "scalpel"-like "lancing" within "the dark skull of the valley" and its "dark belly." Then the valley emerges as a whole person, itself a "rapt" musician, "hunched over its river"-instrument, with the personification doubled by the metaphor of the "attentive" night

> Bowed over its valley, the river
> Crying a violin in a grave
> All the dead singing in the river
>
> The river throbbing, the river the aorta
>
> And the hills unconscious with listening.

What I want to stress especially here is how metaphor works both for and against this poem's representation of riverness. The violin's "dead singing" imaginatively conjoins the sound of the valley's "aorta" with familiar associations of river with time, mortality, and perhaps also environmental endangerment; and the interactions that constitute this sad music are sensitively rendered, as in the "needle sewing" metaphor's delicately fateful rendering of the ecological web of life. The "scalpel"-like action of the river-violin on the bedrock aptly desentimentalizes what might otherwise have felt like old-fashioned prettification of an impersonal process. Still, the prosopopoeia seems to spin out of control and to take on more of a life of its own than the volume designed it to have. The insistent imagery of artifactual instrument and music threatens to displace the valley with a romantic cliché (nature's violin), leaving an aftertaste of clever phantasmal imposition: the kind of effect parodied in Wallace Stevens's "Anecdote of the Jar." Moral: for the ecopoet, metaphor is both indispensable tool and occupational hazard.

It is not merely the storehouse of conventional genres, plots, and tropes that creates such self-limitations. Hughes is also up against a barrier of lay versus trained perception. For example: for purposes of this poem, quite typical of traditional nature poetry in this respect, "river" equals the main channel, whereas river systems within watersheds are dendritic, "a network of channels much like the veination of a leaf."[26] For nonpotamologists it is likely to take a special effort of attention and training to project oneself into the kind of Whitmanian-aerial view nature writer Ted Levin provides of his local stream: "I see Blood Brook's waters merge with the flow from a dozen other valleys to feed the East Branch of the Ompomanoosuc, then the Connecticut River, before coursing to sea. I see a great green sprawl, dendritic drainages from valley to valley to the horizon, a three-dimensional map."[27] And the cost of such informed vision, as here, can be a kind of canned, pedantic recitation—as if the perception had not been fully internalized as part of felt experience or at least as part of one's repertoire of expressive possibilities. Indeed, until quite recently it was by no means self-evident that even the most exhaustive of "watershed" books would necessarily have a great deal to say about the ecological dimension of its subject. A case in point is Paul Horgan's *Great River: The Rio Grande in North American History* (1954), a monumental work of popular history about the dispensations of settlement and conflict in the Rio Grande Valley but with the titular protagonist figuring as little more than a theater of human discovery and contestation.

So the literary imagination of watersheds remains very much a work in process, just as bioregionalism itself is. Yet we are also in the midst of a renaissance of environmentally conscious watershed writing, which includes, for example (in addition to works already cited), Bruce Berger, *There Was a River;* Robert H. Boyle, *The Hudson River: A Natural and Unnatural History;* William deBuys and Alex Harris, *River of Traps;* Percival Everett, *Watershed;* Blaine Harden, *A River Lost: The Life and Death of the Columbia;* Freeman House, *Totem Salmon;* Barry Lopez, *River Notes;* Norman Maclean, *A River Runs Through It;* Greg McNamee, *Gila: The Life and Death of an American River;* John McPhee, "The River" (in his *Conversations with the Archdruid*); Ellen Meloy, *Raven's Exile;* Gary Snyder, *The Practice of the Wild;* David Rains Wallace, *The Klamath Knot*—and doubtless many, many more, especially if one were to extend beyond prose works by U.S. authors focused on rivers and watersheds.[28] Let us now look more closely at this emergence process.

Modern Watershed Consciousness: Mary Austin to the Present

Though negotiation of rivers was crucial to the history of settlement throughout the Americas, not until the nineteenth century do writers, at least in the United States, start to take note of riverine environmental problems of human causation, and then only fleetingly. Two transitional examples in U.S. literature are Thoreau's *A Week,* where we find some recognition of the unintended negative consequences of dams (as impediments to the migration of fish, as causes of upstream flooding),[29] and Mark Twain's *Life on the Mississippi* (1883), which notes with uncomprehending wonder the great flood of 1882, not thinking to connect it to the heroic feats of channelization engineered since his years as a pilot. The first approach to anything like modern watershed consciousness by a major U.S. creative writer was probably Mary Austin's *The Ford* (1917), which centers on the competition for water and land resources among small farmers and entrepreneurs in a turn-of-the-century California valley.

Austin made her reputation, and continues to be known today, as a writer about the southwestern desert, particularly in her first and best-known book of regional sketches, *Land of Little Rain* (1903). But equally important to that book, and crucial to Austin's grasp of desert ecology, is its perception of the region's watercourses, both natural and human-made: their service as borders and instigators of trails, both for animals and humans; the stunning visual and botanical effects of the sparse rain-fall; the vicious fights among ranchers over water supply. One mem-oirist recalls how "in her sunset years" Austin "was wont to autograph her books with a Shoshone symbol composed of a large tilted *E* and an arrow above a circle containing wavy lines"—a hieroglyph meaning "in this direction three bowshots is a spring of sweet water; look for it." This same symbol Austin had earlier described, explained, and illus-trated in *Land of Little Rain* as proof of Native American water wisdom.[30] *Land of Little Rain* may have been the first work of creative writing to re-flect at length upon the doubleness of "water borders" as both natural and legal boundary definers.[31]

Toward the end of her life, Austin dreamed of a never-executed mul-tivolume epic on water in the West. Fearing it would be too big for one person, she tried to enlist fellow novelist Sinclair Lewis (of all people!) as coadjutor, with this as her prospectus:

A first book, which I might do almost alone, covering the period reaching its dramatic climax in the wresting of the first irrigation sys-tem from Indians by the Whites. A middle phase might deal with the struggle between the ranch lands and the towns. The third—and this is where your genius would be triumphant, would illustrate the turn-ing of the indivisible utility of the acequia madre "mother ditch" with the equally indivisible utility of Power.

With characteristic immodesty, Austin immediately went on to reas-sure Lewis that

I know everything that needs to be known: How the Indians learned irrigation and taught it to the Whites; how the cities "framed" the farmers and stole the river for the use of the realtors, all the bitter-ness and greed; how three lives and fortunes are sacrificed to every title to irrigated lands. I was appointed to the Seven States Confer-ence on the Colorado. I know all about the corruption both commer-cial and political that goes to that business. I lived through the

Owens River theft . . . I think I know what threatens in Boulder Dam.[32]

Austin here recalls two periods of frustrated activism: the federal apportionment of Colorado River water rights among the southwestern states in the 1920s, when she sympathized with Arizona's claim that it provided the lion's share of the water but was being shortchanged on the rights; and her campaign twenty years before, seconding the efforts of her then-husband, to prevent Los Angeles from siphoning off the waters of the Owens Valley for its municipal water supply—an early phase of a metropolis-hinterland dispute that continues to this day.[33]

Although the trilogy was never written, Austin's prospectus stands as a reminder that her life and career in the West had as much to do with water as with land. Indeed *The Ford* might have served as volume two. Set in the "Tierra Longa" valley, the plot focuses on an Anglo family of pioneer farmers who together with an assortment of other small landowners find their lives increasingly dominated by vaguely understood entrepreneurial forces. By locating these in San Francisco, Austin may allude to John Muir's losing battle to save Hetch Hetchy from becoming a conduit for San Francisco's water supply as well as to the Owens Valley controversy.[34] In any case, the point was to fashion a narrative of competition for coveted resources that would go several steps beyond *Land of Little Rain,* with its predominant local colorist emphasis on sleepy backwater remoteness and self-containment. Here the central subject is the colonization of an earlier wave of rural settlement culture.

In its alignment of major interest groups *The Ford* recalls Frank Norris's *The Octopus* (1901) (wheat farmers versus grain merchants), but Austin is less schematic and panoramic, her evocation of environmental texture and psychological complication more nuanced, and her definition of the central issues and controversies more complex and oblique. The novel starts as if it will be a childhood-to-maturity story, with the heart of the book the education of center of consciousness Kenneth Brent, a dense filter whose loyalty to family and place are more admirable than his judgment. At first the father-son bond seems central, the two sharing the traits of conscientiousness, nonassertiveness, tactical innocence, and—above all—a "common consciousness of the earth" that makes them more devoted to the land than to success, better agrarian stewards than businessmen.[35] But soon it becomes clear that Steven and Kenneth are sensitive losers, easily manipulated by the enigmatic entrepreneur T. Rickart, as they and other small fry in the valley get caught in the losing game of trying to anticipate his big plays in land, oil, and water right speculation. The narrative design is to unfold its plot from the foreshortened, inside-the-whale perspective of subalterns like these. The one match for the "Old Man" is Kenneth's older sister Anne, every bit as landwise as her father and brother but endowed as well with a keen business sense, which makes her a successful real estate agent as well as rancher. It also enables her to manipulate the manipulator in the interest of her look-ahead version of the valley community's agrarian way of life by initiating a marriage-alliance with Rickart's son and heir (conveniently pre-cast as Kenneth's and Anne's old childhood playmate). This entraps the senior Rickart (who, fortunately, had admired her talents all along) into relenting on what had looked like a conclusive move to crush Kenneth's community-based farmers' organization's plot to control the valley's riverwater for local agriculture.

Thus modernization-savvy watershed citizenship triumphs, at least between the covers of this novel, over both ineffective environmental sensitivity and environmentally insensitive entrepreneurialism. For Anne, as she tells her brother earlier on, "Land doesn't mean crops to me the way it does to you and father; it means people—people who want land and are fitted for the land, and the land wants—how it wants them! I'm going back to Palomitas [where they had once lived, at the start of the novel] partly on account of father, and partly because it is the biggest opportunity I see to bring land and people together."[36]

Anne and the book's other major female character of her generation, Virginia Burke, a complementary pair of "new women,"[37] are part of a strong feminist-revisionary thrust that has a momentum of its own within the book (and within Austin's life) independent of the environmental thematics.[38] What raises Anne above the labor agitator-performer Virginia is a greater steadiness and perspicacity in keeping with and connected with (the book suggests) her greater rapport with the physical environment. In this way *The Ford* affirms through Anne's success a pragmatically nuanced ecofeminist ethic of care-based land stewardship, even though it also makes clear that environmental rapport is not exclusively female nor manipulation of physical environment confined to males.[39] The novel's unfolding of the complexity of environmental development issues in the context of maintaining an allegiance to regional environmental integrity both emotionally deepseated and shrewdly practical makes it a breakthrough achievement.

Just as one would expect of any work of intellectual pioneering, a number of moves *The Ford* makes sketchily are taken further in more recent watershed writing. One of these is recognition of cultural diversity as an ideal and/or lived reality of bioregional experience. Austin focuses overwhelmingly on winners and losers among Euro-American settler groups. The most remarked-upon cultural divide is Irish-English. Of course, the author knew full well that turn-of-the-century California demography was more diverse than this, as we see from *Land of Little Rain*'s sympathetic sketches of Shoshone and Paiute figures and its rosy glimpse of a Mexican-American community at the end. Later in life, after she had relocated to Santa Fe, Austin came to believe that "the next epoch in English-speaking culture" would arise along the Rio Grande as the result of Spanish and Indian influences.[40] This was a striking premonition of the contemporary renaissances in Chicano/a and Native American literature and art. Even at the start of her literary career, Austin knew full well that the first chapter of western water history was, as she later told Lewis, "the wresting of the first irrigation system from Indians by the Whites"; and *The Ford* shows she also knew that the second phase of that chapter was the dispossession of Mexicans by Anglos.[41] The point gets conveyed by planting the Romero family at the edges of the text, with laconic indications of how they have been socially displaced and economically exploited despite securing a tenuous hold in the new order, owing to the father's unique knowledge of ancient land titles. But they remain peripheral, rather stereotyped figures. So too the region's Chinese, to a far greater extent. As for Native Americans, although Austin crusaded lifelong for recognition of the "Amerindian" as a living culture, indeed as a model for Anglo cultural expression,[42] in *The Ford* she can sound as oblivious of aboriginal antecedence as Willa Cather's fiction of the Nebraska frontier—as when Austin's narrator registers with no more than the barest possible hint of irony the Brent family's foreshortened vision of local history: "they marked the shining waste of the river, and heard as always the clear call of the empty land to be put to human use."[43] Whereas Austin's oeuvre lays the groundwork for a more thorough rendering of cultural collision and diversity in the bioregion, *The Ford* remains more tied than the author herself to old Euro-American habits of imagining presettlement land as there for the taking and settlement culture as more monoculturally Anglocentric than it was. From here it is only one step to thinking—as Austin does *not,* but certain latter-day bioregionalists (like Wendell Berry) do—of monoculturalism as a communal value.[44]

Contemporary watershed consciousness often, and increasingly, has a more distinctly multicultural cast. Gary Snyder envisions watershed as a kind of global village in miniature. "The Great Central Valley region [of California]," writes Snyder, "does not prefer English over Spanish or Japanese or Hmong. If it had any preferences at all, it might best like the languages it heard for thousands of years, such as Maidu or Miwok, simply because it's used to them. Mythically speaking, it will welcome whoever chooses to observe the etiquette, express the gratitude, grasp the tools, and learn the songs that it takes to live there."[45] In this perception watershed and bioregion more generally are potential mediators of cultural difference. By observing their "etiquette," a certain communitarianism can be achieved; an assemblage becomes a collective.

The satirical complement of this utopian envisionment is the image of environmental *in*justice: of unequal citizenship on the watershed among mutually suspicious, differentially enfranchised actors. In Percival Everett's novel *Watershed,* an African-American hydrologist-detective discovers evidence of systematic federal toxic pollution of the portion of waterways flowing through reservation land. Throughout, the laconic protagonist-narrator Robert Hawks intersperses bits and flashes of personal/cultural memory that correlate mistreatment of Indians with mistreatment of blacks, but avoiding simplistic polarizations of citizens and authorities (two FBI agents have been killed trying to crack the case, both nonwhite; Hawks himself is a "hired gun," a state employee), as well as simplistic conflation of nonwhites (Hawks and the Native Americans never overcome their initial wariness of each other, though they develop a certain rapport).[46] The stain of environmental racism and, at best, fitful communication on the multicultural watershed are what get stressed here. But as in Snyder it is the environmental factor that finally brings folks of opposite backgrounds together, to the extent that they can cope with being brought together.

A related way in which contemporary river and watershed literature has deepened its environmental representations beyond what one finds in *The Ford* is by historicizing more fully backward (and sometimes forward as well) from the present moment. The late nineteenth-century regionalism in which Austin's early work was grounded generally portrays its places as places time has passed by, places with memories and legends to be sure, but subsisting now in a relatively static, tableaux-like state relative to the modernized world of the reader.[47] This sense of almost suspended time is reinforced by a comparatively plotless descriptivism. Such is the world of Sarah Orne Jewett's *Country of the Pointed Firs,* of Celia Thaxter's *Among the Isles of Shoals,* and of Austin's *Land of Little Rain. The Ford,* by contrast, imagines a fast-changing landscape and a densely packed series of events. But the time horizon is constrained to the decade or so of the plot. Rarely does the text become panoramic; the horizon of perception stays close to the ground level of the characters' vision of things, in an ironic echo of their nearsightedness. Contemporary watershed writing is more apt to range freely through the epochs, sometimes reaching all the way back through pre-Columbian America to geologic time ("One hundred and fifty million years B. P., the area of what today is the Gila drainage . . . lay beneath a vast saline lake"),[48] then unfolding in a series of eras in each of which the qualities of the human cultures are appraised in relation to their conduct as environmental stewards and their (mis)treatment of each other around river-related issues.

Such works draw on various subgenres. One strategy, used by the book from which I have just quoted, is to subsume social to natural history narrative, making the river more the protagonist than in (say) Horgan's *Great River* and judging the human communities drawn to it according to how sensitively they have coexisted with it and with each other. An important transitional example, contemporary with Horgan, is Marjory Stoneman Douglas's *The Everglades: River of Grass,* which allows a long chronicle of human possession and dispossession to take over the book after what seems a mandatory but self-contained natural history cameo, but takes another turn as it enters the twentieth century and confronts the big-time canal and drainage boosterism that she sees as threatening the region's integrity.[49] Then comes a far more jaundiced assessment of hydraulic manipulation than one finds in Powell and Austin, who accept irrigation projects as a necessity of river management.

The Everglades is especially significant as a harbinger of the contemporary rediscovery of seemingly useless and ugly "swamp" as ecologically and aesthetically attractive "wetland." This has been one of the most dramatic transformations of popular environmental values in the late twentieth-century United States: perhaps the most dramatic expansion in modern times of the nineteenth-century revaluation of wilderness from adversarial space, valued only in proportion to its capacity to be transformed into economic asset.[50] The antiutilitarian, environmental-protectionist aspect of watershed revaluation has been viewed suspiciously by environmental justice advocates,[51] but in most versions of watershed revisionism (including Douglas's), watershed ethics takes as its goal the mutual welfare of the region's population with each other as well as with the natural world. Douglas herself shows special concern for the effect of reclamation projects on the Everglades' "ecosystem people," the Native Americans.[52] In this, *Everglades* anticipates Linda Hogan's *Power*, discussed in Chapter 7.

Another revisionist strategy for reimagining watershed history is place-based micronarrative of an individual community's practices. One such case is recent creative and critical work on "acequia culture" (small-scale, communally maintained irrigation systems) that Mexican-American communities developed in the southwest borderlands from Native American origins long before U.S. annexation and that a number of them still maintain. There is local idiosyncrasy but also family resemblance among the various bodies of "acequia tales": "There are stories about who gets the water and who doesn't. There are stories about goats, sheep, and cows drowning in the ditches. There are stories about that last miserable drought and even stories about *la llorona*."[53] In this way communities define their history *as* watershed history. These oral histories are continuously evolving bodies of tales, shaped by traditional narrative practices, an equivalent within Chicano/a tradition of Native American place-based stories and legends, with which indeed they sometimes intertwine.

Revaluation of the ecological dimension of settler culture's transactions with watersheds has also affected the kind of writing that traditionally would have taken the form of naturalist tales of outback adventure (with much descriptive and didactic expatiation), as in Darwin's *Voyage of the Beagle,* Alfred Russell Wallace's *The Malay Archipelago,* and Powell's *The Exploration of the Colorado River and Its Canyons.* Such books tend to follow the unfolding sequence of personal experiences, infusing descriptive and documentary elaboration as they go. When risk or danger looms, the drama of experience is even more likely than otherwise to take precedence over all else, even in explicitly environmentalist writing. The "Down the [Colorado] River" chapter of Edward Abbey's *Desert Solitaire,* for instance, is framed as an angry *in memoriam* to the now-flooded Glen Canyon, but it is cast in the form of an excursion narrative and lyric interlude in which river and canyon become as much theater as subject: an occasion for diffuse musing inspired by natural wonders or simply the writer's random thoughts.

> Is this [side canyon of the Escalante] at last the *locus Dei?* There are enough cathedrals and temples and altars here for a Hindu pantheon of divinities. Each time I look up one of the secretive little side canyons I half expect to see not only the cottonwood tree rising over its tiny spring—the leafy god, the desert's liquid eye—but also a rainbow-colored corona of blazing light, pure spirit, pure being, pure disembodied intelligence, *about to speak my name.*[54]

This passage wonderfully conveys the excitement of a magical place, making the thought of its loss all the more poignant, but with an intensity of self-preoccupation, a longing to make the landscape *"speak my name,"* not as far different as the author might wish to imagine from graffiti inscriptions left by crasser adventurers.

Ellen Meloy's *Raven's Exile: A Season on the Green River,* built around another set of rafting excursions that cover much the same fluvial ground, is hardly less self-referential, but more careful to balance evocation of personal response to sojourn in a loved wilderness with demystification of the illusion of wilderness:

When you float Desolation [Canyon], you think, This is how wild a river is. But if you live on the river long enough, if you love it with all the ferocity of a passionate, surrendering affair, with love's innocence and erotica and its dizzying inertia, you will begin to see otherwise. If you memorize a single cottonwood and watch this tree season after season, if you peer over the shoulders of people who are taking the finest of measurements, you may begin to know. The land immediately beyond the river—so harsh, vertical, dry, rugged—is, relatively speaking, wild, wild land. But the River itself, to borrow a poet's words, is a snake nailed to the earth.[55]

This kind of passage provides a timely amendment to the new historiography of wilderness demystification, which tends to want to leave one with no alternative between deconstruction of the false consciousness of wilderness romanticization and the Marxian "truth" of nature as "organic machine."[56] Meloy claims in effect that wilderness is not delegitimated for being a relative term, and that it is possible for a wilderness sensibility to persist and thrive amid the self-consciousness of its own illusoriness, of nature's transformation by river engineering. This she does by refusing to allow the experience to subsist only in a single moment. That brings out the contrast between the "relatively" stable land—doubtless more modified by ranching than Meloy allows, however—and the abruptly manipulated river. The sensation of "original relation to the universe," as Emerson grandly called it,[57] and the corrective discipline that comes through the process of systematic nature study get wrapped up in a single package here, as Meloy recognizes how observing the single tree "season after season" and noting the measurements (of river level) change the quality of "wilderness" experience—not discrediting it but putting it in quotation marks. Whereas Thoreau's *Walden* extracts from a similar preoccupation with reexperience of the same seasonal phenomena a lesson of the constancy of natural process (despite awareness of flux, despite knowing that a good part of Walden Woods has recently been chopped down, and so on), Meloy sees not only this but also the signs of unseen artificial manipulation.

In the passage at hand, she does not identify the cause. Elsewhere she does. One of her boldest moves against the grain of traditional river adventure narrative is a surrealistic trip to Las Vegas: "mandatory" for all river rats, she insists. "We cannot know the River until we know this place," whose existence utterly depends on southern Nevada's control of water from the Colorado and its tributaries. "Las Vegas is the twentieth century's ultimate perversion of the River and the site of a twenty-first-century water war."[58] Not just here but throughout the book Meloy correlates the inherent instability of natural cycles with the still more destabilizing effects of human intervention, forecasting greater instabilities to come. In this way contemporary watershed writers give a disorienting wobble to linear-descriptivist excursion narrative by interrupting it with history's story of unfulfillment via environmental degradation.

Meloy's insistence that a person can't understand the Colorado without contemplating the 4,032 toilets in Las Vegas's Excalibur Hotel and Casino points toward a further way in which contemporary watershed imagination has built on what writers like Mary Austin began. *The Ford* qualifies its community-based ideal of watershed self-sufficiency with open-eyed awareness that such communities cannot expect to be hermetic but, on the contrary, must be able to negotiate with and turn to advantage the agendas of the outer world that impinge on them. If Thoreau's exotic analogizing between the pond and an Alpine tarn, between his hut vista and the plains of Tartary, between the waters of Walden and the Ganges marks a premodern anticipation of the think-global, act-local mentality in U.S. environmental writing, Austin's dramatization of the play of contending economic and social forces in Tierra Longa marks something like the start of a more practical analysis. But like Thoreau, although for a different reason, Austin wants these forces to remain somewhat mysterious—never, for example, to disclose exactly what the Old Man knows or what his motives are. The obverse strategy, used by Meloy, is to deparochialize watershed consciousness more aggressively by disclosing what initially seems to lie beyond its horizons altogether but, on further inspection, is shown to be interconnected.

Ted Levin's *Blood Brook* (1992) does this in another way. Most of this book consists of cozy around-home sketches of Vermont flora, fauna, scenes, seasonality: tadpoles, turtles, pileated woodpeckers, and so forth. Then in the last main chapter comes a surprising leap hundreds of miles north to the site of Quebec's gargantuan hydropower projects, the control center of "The Electrical Watershed," as Levin calls it. The point is not so much that a good rhetorical opportunity to plug for protectionism of nature and natives can't be passed up ("Hydro-Quebec has already begun gutting eastern North America's last and largest wilderness," its vast reservoirs flooding "the cathedral of the Cree") but the scandal of Vermont's dependence on power purchased from Quebec.[59] This makes Vermont both consumer and funding agent. The electrical watershed is becoming, like it or not, *the* watershed. The chapter is haunted by the irony of Levin's home place having become complicit, unawares, in an ecological colonization of another that has led to its own colonization as well.

When Levin and Meloy conjure up the specters of ecological colonization by Hydro-Quebec and the Las Vegas entertainment industry, they show an accentuated version of the anxiety with which modern watershed imagination, and bioregionalism more broadly, has always had to contend: that regional self-sufficiency just isn't possible any more (if indeed it ever was), whether because the natural resources aren't adequate or because the culture of environmentalism is too weak to contend against capitalism and consumerism. Behind Meloy's plumbing statistic is the knowledge that "toilet flushing is by far the largest single use of water in a home," not just in hotels,[60] indeed that indoor plumbing is the greatest source of water waste in history,[61] with the possible exception of high-tech irrigation for agricultural purposes.[62] Indeed, modernization of water supply infrastructure has led to a vastly increased conception of "minimum" water needs, at least for industrialized countries.[63]

Such anxieties need not be seen as self-undermining for watershed imagination, however, but as potentially strengthening its foundations. Its promise may lie precisely in offering up a double image of inclusive yet finite place-based communities of humans and land that, in the offering, also frustrates the complacent inference that actual modern communities come remotely close to the self-sufficiency and autonomy that cosier versions of watershed image evoke. In keeping with the theory of place-connectedness discussed in Chapter 2, watershed writing calls in principle for respect for environmental health, equity, and self-restraint within particular bailiwicks, implying that cocoon-like fantasies of self-containment fail to grasp the complexity and extent of the imbrication of cultures and environments. For, in principle, "watershed" ought to refer not only to a small, relatively finite unit but to a series of zones connecting local communities with larger stretches of continent. Christopher McGrory Klyza names four from his own home vantage point a little west of Ted Levin's in north central Vermont: the "small watershed" of his own creek system on the western slope of the Green Mountains; "the major drainage basins" that individually flow into lakes Champlain and Memphremagog, the Connecticut and Hudson rivers; the "larger watershed" level that encompasses all of these; and the "ecoregional province level," in this case comprising both "the Laurentian Mixed Forest Province and the Adirondack-New England Province." Thinking "watershed" in these terms challenges parochialism not only of jurisdictional borders of whatever sort but also of "natural" borders that fail to take larger interdependencies into account, interdependencies that finally reach out to include the whole planet.[64]

At a time of increasing metropolitanization, imagining of landscape in terms of watershed has the further advantage of reminding one of the copresence of "built" and "natural" elements even in dense urbanized centers (many of which were founded along bays or rivers to begin with) and of the impossibility of cordoning off country from city, or vice versa. Everywhere is either upstream or downstream (or both) from somewhere else. From a watershed perspective it is impossible to forget that country is destined to flow into city by gravitational laws more inexorable than the historic urbanization process itself; city is destined to remain integral with the half-forgotten hinterland it thinks it has displaced. For these reasons, if for no other, watershed is a potent environmental(ist) icon, if not an all-sufficient one.

Not by coincidence in Toronto, in Chattanooga, in Manchester, England, have metropolitan restoration projects based themselves upon the prior configuration of that city's major river. Not by coincidence did Ian McHarg, one of the patriarchs of contemporary green urban design, attach special importance to watersheds as keys to urban identity, seeing urban watersheds as both ecological and aesthetic compositions. ("Historic Washington," for example, he described as "in essence, a neoclassical composition set in a half bowl, defined by two confluent rivers and an escarpment, with a backdrop of low hills.")[65] "If rivers, flood plains, marshes, steep slopes, and woodlands in the city were accorded protection to remain in their natural condition or were retrieved and returned to such a condition where possible," McHarg declared, "this single device, as an aspect of water quality, quantity, flood and drought control, would ensure for many cities an immeasurable improvement in the aspect of nature in the city, in addition to the specific benefits of a planned watershed."[66] However fanciful—or professionally self-interested— these statements may be, their emphasis on rivercourses as signatures of metropolitan character synchronizes with urban ecopoetics from Dickens to the present. Will they, will any act of environmental imagination, achieve the kind of hearing an environmentalist would wish? Make the whole watershed cry out, as Joyce makes Dublin's River Liffey: "Rise up, man of the hooths [Howth], you have slept so long!"[67] Time will tell. Meantime, far better to hope and venture than forgo the chance.

Notes

Introduction

1. Richard N. L. Andrews, *Managing the Environment, Managing Ourselves: A History of American Environmental Policy* (New Haven: Yale University Press, 1999), p. 370.

2. Ulrich Beck, "Politics in Risk Society," *Ecological Enlightenment: Essays on the Politics of the Risk Society,* trans. Mark A. Ritter (Atlantic Highlands, N.J.: Humanities Press, 1995), p. 14; Roger Payne, *Among Whales* (New York: Dell, 1995), p. 339.

3. W. H. Auden, "In Memory of W. B. Yeats," *Collected Poems,* ed. Edward Mendelson (London: Faber, 1991), p. 248; Percy Bysshe Shelley, "A Defence of Poetry," *Shelley's Poetry and Prose,* ed. Donald H. Reiman and Sharon B. Powers (New York: Norton, 1977), p. 508; Auden, "Squares and Oblongs," in Rudolf Arnheim et al., *Poets at Work: Essays Based on the Modern Poetry Collection at the Lockwood Memorial Library, University of Buffalo* (New York: Harcourt, Brace and Co., 1948), p. 177.

4. Cheryl Glotfelty's "Introduction" to the *Ecocriticism Reader,* ed. Glotfelty and Harold Fromm (Athens: University of Georgia Press, 1996), p. xviii, defines ecocriticism very inclusively as "the study of the relationship between literature and the physical environment." I have defined it more specifically as the "study of the relation between literature and environment conducted in a spirit of commitment to environmentalist praxis" (*The Environmental Imagination* [Cambridge: Harvard University Press, 1995], p. 430), but within the last half-decade literature and environment studies, as they might neutrally be called, have so burgeoned that my activist stipulation may no longer apply and Glotfelty's big-tent definition may be more satisfactory. See, for example, Robert Kern, "Ecocriticism: What Is It Good For?" *ISLE,* 7 (2000): 9–32. Ecocriticism is methodologically eclectic too: in this respect it more closely resembles (say) feminist or ethnic revisionism than (say) new historicism or colonial discourse studies, although it patently differs also from the former in that it does not have a specific "identitarian" locus within the human or social body. I comment further on the movement's achievements and limitations in "The Ecocritical Insurgency," a commentary piece for a special ecocriticism issue of *New Literary History,* 30 (Summer 1999): 699–712.

5. Robert Pogue Harrison, *Forests: The Shadows of Civilization* (Chicago: University of Chicago Press, 1992); Louise Westling, *The Green Breast of the New World* (Athens: University of Georgia Press, 1996).

6. Arthur Lovejoy and Raymond Williams have famously emphasized the multifarious uses of "nature," which Williams calls "perhaps the most complex word in the language." See Lovejoy, "'Nature' as Aesthetic Norm," *Essays in the History of Ideas* (Baltimore: Johns Hopkins University Press, 1948), pp. 69–77; Williams, *Keywords* (New York: Oxford University Press, 1984), p. 184. A fine up-to-date extended philosophical overview is Kate Soper, *What Is Nature?* (Cambridge: Blackwell, 1995); a recent historical account is Peter Coates, *Nature: Western Attitudes since Ancient Times* (Berkeley: University of California Press, 1998).

7. Bill McKibben, *The End of Nature* (New York: Random House, 1980); Karl Marx, *The German Ideology*, in *Selected Writings*, ed. David McLellan (Oxford: Oxford University Press, 1977), p. 175 ("the nature that preceded human history . . . no longer exists anywhere [except perhaps on a few Australian coral islands of recent origin]"). In *Capital*, Marx characterizes nature as becoming "one of the organs" of man's activity, "one that he annexes to his own bodily organs, adding stature to himself in spite of the Bible" (ibid., p. 456). Neil Smith, *Uneven Development: Nature, Capital and the Production of Space* (Oxford: Blackwell, 1984), pp. 45–54, provides a historical sketch of the evolution of ideas of second nature from antiquity to Marx and the rise of capitalism.

8. Richard White, *The Organic Machine: The Remaking of the Columbia River* (New York: Hill & Wang, 1995). Some nature theory revisionists make a further distinction between physical reproduction of first nature and computer simulation, identifying as a "third nature" the virtual representations wrought by the revolution in informational technology. See McKenzie Wark, "Third Nature," *Cultural Studies*, 8 (January 1994): 115–132.

9. With this problem in mind, Soper usefully distinguishes between nature "as a realist concept" (denoting "the structures, processes and causal powers that are constantly operative within the physical world") and nature "as a 'lay' or 'surface' concept" (denoting popular misperception of ordinary landscape features as "natural" rather than produced). *What Is Nature?*, pp. 155–156.

10. Frost, "The Middleness of the Road," *The Poetry of Robert Frost* (New York: Holt, 1969), p. 388.

11. Richard T. T. Forman and Lauren E. Alexander, "Roads and Their Ecological Effects," *Annual Review of Ecological Systems*, 29 (1998): 207–231, synthesizes recent findings about the disruptive effects of road networks on ecosystems, including bird and animal avoidance, and possible genetic as well as demographic consequences.

12. *The Collected Poems of Wallace Stevens* (New York: Knopf, 1961), p. 94; *The Collected Earlier Poems of William Carlos Williams* (New York: New Directions, 1966), pp. 280–281. Stevens could be, of course, imagining a ride in a train rather than a car.

13. Although the avenue of poplars along the roadway was doubtless an engineered result, Williams presumably could have claimed that the engineering project itself was constructed in reminiscence of primordial forest.

14. Smith, *Uneven Development*, p. 62.

15. Michael Pollan, *Second Nature: A Gardener's Education* (New York: Delta, 1991), offers amusing testimony, as in "Nature Abhors a Garden" (pp. 45–64), which also recognizes the nonpristine nature of the resurgent "wilderness" with which gardeners contend.

16. David R. Foster, *Thoreau's Country: Journey Through a Transformed Landscape* (Cambridge: Harvard University Press, 1999), pp. 9–14 and passim; Kathleen Norris, *Dakota: A Spiritual Geography* (Boston: Houghton, 1993), pp. 36–37; John Elder, *Reading the Mountains of Home* (Cambridge: Harvard University Press, 1998), pp. 80–81.

17. For example, William Chaloupka and R. McGreggor Cawley argue that the imminent disappearance of wilderness has made wilderness all the more important as heterotopic space. "The Great Wild Hope: Nature, Environmentalism, and the Open Secret," *In the Nature of Things*, ed. Chaloupka and Jane Bennett (Minneapolis: University of Minnesota Press, 1993), pp. 3–24. In "Green Disputes: Nature, Culture, American(ist) Theory," a paper delivered April 15, 2000, at the biennial European American Studies conference in Graz, Austria, to be published in *Amerikastudien,* I have argued for the importance on environmental-restorationist and ethical grounds of modernized peoples maintaining a nonessentialist dualistic conception of nonhuman nature as an "other" entitled to respect, notwithstanding the necessity of recognizing the actual inseparableness of the "natural" from the fabricated.

18. N. Katherine Hayles, *How We Became Posthuman: Virtual Bodies in Cybernetics, Literature, and Informatics* (Chicago: University of Chicago Press, 1999), thoughtfully treats "embodiment" both as a site and as a ground of limitation of informatics. Jared Diamond's *Guns, Germs, and Steel: The Fates of Human Societies* (New York: Norton, 1997) sets forth an environmental determinist theory of human history that studiously avoids essentializing race and culture ("All human societies contain inventive people. It's just that some environments provide more starting materials, and more favorable conditions for utilizing inventions" [p. 408]).

19. See, for example, Roger S. Ulrich, "Biophilia, Biophobia, and Natural Landscapes," *The Biophilia Hypothesis,* ed. Stephen R. Kellert and Edward O. Wilson (Washington, D.C.: Island Press, 1993), pp. 73–137; Peter H. Kahn, Jr., *The Human Relationship with Nature: Development and Culture* (Cambridge: MIT Press, 1999), pp. 13–15 and chapters 6–10 passim.

20. Mutual constructivism is not species-specific either, insofar as even quite rudimentary organisms have powers of apprehension and seek to modify their environments as they can in the interest of survival and comfort.

21. See especially *Environmental Imagination,* pp. 143–308.

22. In humanistic environmental theory, "ethics of care" models have been articulated most influentially by ecofeminist theologians (e.g., Sallie McFague, *Models of God: Theology for an Ecological, Nuclear Age* [Philadelphia: Fortress Press, 1987]) and philosophers (e.g., Karen Warren, ed., *Ecological Feminist Philosophies* [Bloomington: Indiana University Press, 1996], and Warren, ed., *Ecofeminism: Women, Culture, Nature* [Bloomington: Indiana University Press, 1997])—although "care" ethics can rest on

other bases as well (see, e.g., Max Oelschlaeger, *Caring for Creation: An Ecumenical Approach to the Environmental Crisis* [New Haven: Yale University Press, 1994]). Some recent studies question both the identitarian implications of ecofeminism's "motherhood environmentalism" (e.g., Catriona Sandilands, *The Good-Natured Feminist: Ecofeminism and the Quest for Democracy* [Minneapolis: University of Minnesota Press, 1999], pp. 3–27) and the empirical difference between contemporary men and women with respect to caring for nature (e.g., Paul Mohai, "Gender Differences in the Perception of Most Important Problems," *Race, Gender and Class,* 5 [1997]: 153–169; and Kahn, *The Human Relationship with Nature,* pp. 184–187). But neither critique alters the historic fact of ubiquitous male-female, culture-nature stereotyping (see Sherry B. Ortner, "Is Female to Male as Nature Is to Culture?" *Woman, Culture, Nature,* ed. Michelle Zimbalist Rosaldo and Louise Lamphere [Stanford: Stanford University Press, 1974], pp. 67–87), nor the history of ecofeminism's leadership in advancing the ethics-of-care idea, nor the promise of an ethics of care as environmental-ethical starting point if not an all-encompassing model. Insofar as such caring begins with a frank acknowledgment of the legacy of human (especially male) domination of nature and with a model of self conceived in the first instance as relational rather than autonomous, critically sophisticated ecofeminism has the advantage—at least in principle—over most versions of "deep ecology," although critically sophisticated versions of deep ecology have the advantage of emphasizing dimensions of human commonality that might not be adequately grasped through a lens of gender difference. For a thoughtful comparison of resemblances and disputes between the two positions, see Michael E. Zimmerman, "Ecofeminism and Deep Ecology," *Contesting Earth's Future: Radical Ecology and Postmodernity* (Berkeley: University of California Press, 1994), pp. 276–313.

23. Ramachandra Guha, "Radical American Environmentalism and Wilderness Preservation: A Third World Critique," *Environmental Ethics,* 11 (1989): 71–83; Juan Martinez-Alier and Ramachandra Guha, *Varieties of Environmentalism: Essays North and South* (London: Earthscan, 1997), chapter 1: "The Environmentalism of the Poor" (pp. 3–21). Not that it is always easy to distinguish the voices of the truly disadvantaged from those of the embattled middle class.

24. Robyn Eckersley, *Environmentalism and Political Theory: Toward an Ecocentric Approach* (Albany: State University of New York Press, 1992). Chapters 2–3 (pp. 33–71) provide a lucid discussion of the variety of orientations (chapter 2) and a rejoinder to "common criticisms and misunderstandings" of relatively ecocentric orientations as more extreme than they are (chapter 3). Even extreme arguments about the moral claims of ecosystems over duties to individual creatures rarely advocate political coercion. Cf. J. Baird Callicott's well-known "Animal Liberation: A Triangular Affair," *Environmental Ethics,* 2 (1980): 311–338, which disqualifies animal liberationism from counting as environmental ethics because it fails to meet that moral test. Michael E. Zimmerman, "Ecofascism: A Threat to American Environmentalism?" *The Ecological Community* (New York: Routledge, 1997), pp. 229–253, is a thoughtful analysis of the arguments that finds the charge largely groundless. As for Nazism itself, Anna Bramwell, *Blood and Soil: Richard Walther Darré and Hitler's "Green Party"* (Abbots-

brook: Kensal, 1985), finds that the link between National Socialism and green science and philosophy was historically contingent rather than inherent.

25. Leo Marx, "The Full Thoreau," *New York Review of Books*, 46, no. 12 (July 15, 1999): 44, using my *Environmental Imagination* understandably, if reductively, to instantiate the ecocentric persuasion. For my reply and his rejoinder, see ibid., 46, no. 19 (December 2, 1999): 63–64.

26. Jonathan Bate, *The Dream of the Earth* (Cambridge: Harvard University Press, 2000), p. 38.

27. David Hall's *Worlds of Wonder, Days of Judgment: Popular Religious Belief in Early New England* (New York: Knopf, 1989) is particularly astute on this point.

28. The term used by Madhav Gadgil and Ramachandra Guha, *Ecology and Equity: The Use and Abuse of Nature in Contemporary India* (London: Routledge, 1995), pp. 3 and passim, to denote traditional rural communities dependent on increasingly imperiled local economies.

29. Lance Newman, "The Politics of Ecocriticism," *Review*, 20 (1998): 71.

30. Two significant historical accounts make this point in very different—but complementary—ways. Robert Gottlieb's contentious *Forcing the Spring: The Transformation of the American Environmental Movement* (Washington, D.C.: Island Press, 1993) links the rift between the insurgent environmental justice movement and mainstream preservationism to a long history of disrelation and conflict of interest between wilderness protection and urban public reform. Samuel P. Hays's cautious, exhaustively annotated scholarly monograph, *Beauty, Health, and Permanence: Environmental Politics in the United States, 1955–1985* (Cambridge: Cambridge University Press, 1985), takes a consensualist approach of defining late twentieth-century environmentalism in terms of a new emphasis within mainstream public thinking on the importance of quality of life concerns, including both nature preservation and environmental health. Whereas for Gottleib, race, class, and gender differentials are strongly emphasized, for Hays the central conflict at issue today is between various strains of environmentalism and vested (mostly corporate) antienvironmentalism.

31. The two most wide-ranging explorations of the cultural/ideological history and literary results of the naturist-urbanist dynamic in the Anglophone world illustrate the need for transnational, indeed global, range in their combination of frequent convergence of emphases and relative disinterest in each other's domain in the course of stressing national distinctiveness: Leo Marx, *The Machine in the Garden: Technology and the Pastoral Ideal in America* (New York: Oxford University Press, 1964), and Raymond Williams, *The Country and the City* (New York: Oxford University Press, 1973). One suggestive point of fortuitous confluence is the echo between Marx's diagnosis of American pastoral as arising in the first instance from European dreams of the new world and Williams's final chapter, which extends the country-city dynamic from a domestic context in British cultural history to the relation between British imperium and its former colonies.

32. Katharine Lee Bates, *America the Beautiful and Other Poems* (New York: Crowell, 1911), p. 3.

33. According to Bates's late-life recollection, "How I Came to Write 'America the Beautiful,'" Women's Clubs News (May 1929), p. 11 (Bates papers, Wellesley College Library), "I wrote out the entire song on my return that evening to Colorado Springs."

34. Of course Bates's "alabaster city," like its Chicago prototype, drew on the imagery of Christian idealism: the holy city of Revelation in the Christian New Testament and Augustine's City of God. Bates had previously used the image of the white city or community as an idealized rendering of Wellesley itself in an 1886 commencement poem and, more pietistically, in her 1887 poem "The New Jerusalem," printed in the Independent (Bates poetry scrapbook 1876–1885, Wellesley College).

35. Katharine Lee Bates, "America," The Congregationalist 80, no. 27 (July 4, 1895): 17. Dorothea Burgess, Dream and Deed: The Story of Katharine Lee Bates (Norman: University of Oklahoma Press, 1952), pp. 101–102, and Frank Tucker, "A Song Inspired," Colorado Heritage (issue 3, 1989), 32–43, provide brief biographical accounts of the western journey.

36. Bates, America the Beautiful and Other Poems, pp. 4–5.

37. Vida Denton Scudder, On Journey (New York: Dutton, 1937), p. 110.

38. Latter-day Wellesley students have protested this line by calling out "sisterhood!" when the hymn is sung at college convocations. Yet denigration of sisterhood would have been the farthest thing from Bates's own mind, who had committed herself to a Boston marriage ("Wellesley marriage" as it was called locally) to economist colleague-social activist Catherine Coman, a relationship she memorialized in what may be the first lesbian sonnet sequence in U.S. literary history, Yellow Clover (New York: Dutton, 1922), pp. 71–111, which prompted a letter from Jane Addams congratulating Bates for giving voice to "a new type of friendship" among women. Burgess, Dream and Deed, p. 209.

39. William Cronon, Nature's Metropolis: Chicago and the Great West (New York: Norton, 1991), pp. 142–147.

40. In 1913 Pinchot solicited a letter from Addams to support his campaign to prevent return of National Forest land to the states (Pinchot to Addams, 10 January 1913, Swarthmore College), and Addams replied that "I should be very happy indeed to serve the cause of conservation in any way" (Addams to Pinchot, 13 January 1913, Pinchot papers, Library of Congress). But it is not clear that she ever wrote such a testimonial.

41. Christopher Alexander, Sara Ishikawa, Murray Silverstein et al., A Pattern Language: Towns, Buildings, Construction (New York: Oxford University Press, 1977), p. 305. These authors stipulate that when more than three minutes away, facility use drops off; see also Tony Hiss, The Experience of Place (New York: Random House, 1990), pp. 15–16. Addams and her colleagues here followed the general line of Anglo-American turn-of-the-century urban reform thinking. British ambassador Lord James Bryce, addressing the Washington Playground Association in 1908, declared that British planners aimed "to have within a quarter of a mile from every house some spot of at least half an acre where the children may play." "The City Child," Charities and the Commons, 19, no. 22 (March 7, 1908), p. 1662. U.S. playground activist Henry S. Curtis, in The

Play Movement and Its Significance (New York: Macmillan, 1917), cautioned that "the maximum range of playground effectiveness is not more than one half mile" (p. 302).

42. Helen Lefcowitz Horwitz, *Culture and the City: Cultural Philanthropy in Chicago from the 1880s to 1917* (Chicago: University of Chicago Press, 1976), p. 140; quotation from Charles Zueblin, *American Municipal Progress* (New York: Macmillan, 1916), pp. 273–274. Galen Cranz, *The Politics of Park Design: A History of Urban Parks in America* (Cambridge: MIT Press, 1982), pp. 61–99, provides a useful survey of the small-scale "reform park" movement in New York, Chicago, and San Francisco between 1900–1930, making clear the difference between the neopastoral concept of the large-scale "pleasure ground" and the concept of the small-scale (sometimes only single-lot-sized) regulated recreational space of the "reform park." Not that the difference was absolute: Charles Zueblin's photo-illustrated "Municipal Playgrounds in Chicago," *American Journal of Sociology*, 4 (September 1898): 145–158, begins, for example, with the assertion that "a 'return to nature' is as necessary a demand for the modern city as it was for the romanticists of the eighteenth century." John C. Farrell, *Beloved Lady: A History of Jane Addams' Ideas on Reform and Peace* (Baltimore: Johns Hopkins University Press, 1967), pp. 104–119, discusses Addams's interest in playgrounds in the context of her various involvements in recreation reform.

43. Stephen Fox, *The American Conservation Movement: John Muir and His Legacy* (Madison: University of Wisconsin Press, 1985), pp. 134–135.

44. The individual in question, California congressman William Kent, was a self-declared conservationist (Kent to Addams, 7 December 1912, Woodrow Wilson papers, Library of Congress), but he was apparently an initially reluctant donor of the Chicago lot, and he opposed Muir's campaign to protect Hetch Hetchy.

45. John Muir, *Our National Parks* (1901; rpt., Madison: University of Wisconsin Press, 1981), p. 1; *John of the Mountains: The Unpublished Journals of John Muir*, ed. Linnie Marsh Wolfe (1938; rpt., Madison: University of Wisconsin Press, 1979), pp. 352, 191.

46. Shannon Jackson, *Lines of Activity: Performance, Historiography, Hull-House Domesticity* (Ann Arbor: University of Michigan Press, 2000), p. 120.

47. Robert Gottlieb observes that the division between mainstream "conservationist" and radical "preservationist" traditions represented by Pinchot and Muir "has tended to obscure the crucial role of the government agencies and their resource strategies in the framing of conservationist politics" generally. *Forcing the Spring*, p. 24. My comparison of Addams and Muir is inspired by, although it partly dissents from, Gottleib's appraisals of Muir and of Addams's protégée Alice Hamilton as examples of wilderness and urban strains of U.S. environmentalism. I discuss Hamilton in Chapter 1.

48. Paul Boyer, *Urban Masses and Moral Order in America, 1820–1920* (Cambridge: Harvard University Press, 1978), chapters 11–19.

49. Muir, *My First Summer in the Sierra* (1911; rpt., New York: Penguin, 1987), p. 122; Jane Addams, *Twenty Years at Hull-House*, ed. James Hurt (1910; Urbana: University of Illinois Press, 1990), p. 76.

50. Muir, *First Summer*, pp. 78, 77.

51. Muir, *The Mountains of California* (1894; rpt., New York: Penguin, 1985), p. 59.

52. Addams, *Twenty Years at Hull-House*, pp. 164–165.

53. I borrow this term from Yi-fu Tuan, *Landscapes of Fear* (New York: Pantheon, 1979), for whom, interestingly, scenes of natural danger (p. 137) are mentioned only in passing during a chapter on "Violence and Fear in the Country," which emphasizes fear of human violence, banditry for example. Although Muir makes no direct mention of this, he could not have failed to realize that the imagery of "shadowy cañon" and "wildest stronghold" would likely provoke "wild West" fantasies in late nineteenth-century readers.

54. Noted by Michael Smith, *Pacific Visions: California Scientists and the Environment: 1850–1915* (New Haven: Yale University Press, 1985), p. 97, and developed at length by Steven Holmes, *The Young John Muir: An Environmental Biography* (Madison: University of Wisconsin Press, 1999).

55. Robert L. Thayer, Jr., *Gray World, Green Heart: Technology, Nature, and the Sustainable Landscape* (New York: Wiley, 1994), p. xiii.

56. Pierre Bourdieu, *An Invitation to Reflexive Sociology*, by Bourdieu and Loïc J. D. Wacquant (Chicago: University of Chicago Press, 1992), p. 127.

57. Benjamin Franklin, *Writings*, ed. J. A. O. Leo Lemay (New York: Library of America, 1987), pp. 1428–29.

58. Ironically, the principal way in which they were "banished" in a *legal* sense during the first century of nationhood was by defining nuisance law so as to make it harder for an individual to win damages against an enterprise operating in what was considered the public interest. See Joel Franklin Brenner, "Nuisance Law and Industrial Revolution," *Journal of Legal Studies*, 3 (1974): 403–433.

59. William Bartram, *Travels and Other Writings*, ed. Thomas P. Slaughter (New York: Library of America, 1996), pp. 91–92.

60. Wolfe, ed., *John of the Mountains*, p. 68.

61. Ortiz, "Spreading Wings on Wind," *Harper's Anthology of 20th Century Native American Poetry*, ed. Duane Niatum (San Francisco: HarperCollins, 1988), p. 141.

62. Leslie Silko, "Landscape, History, and the Pueblo Imagination," *Antaeus*, 87 (Autumn 1986): 85.

63. Donatella Mazzoleni, "The City and the Imaginary," trans. John Koumantarakis, *Space and Place: Theories of Identity and Location*, ed. Erica Carter, James Donald, and Judith Squires (London: Lawrence & Wishart, 1993), p. 287.

64. The following passages are, respectively, from Frank O'Hara, *Collected Poems*, ed. Donald Allen (Berkeley: University of California Press, 1995), p. 131; Gary Snyder, *No Nature: New and Selected Poems* (New York: Pantheon, 1992), p. 191; Marianne Moore, *Collected Poems* (London: Faber, 1951), p. 60; Langston Hughes, *Collected Poems*, ed. Arnold Rampersad and David Roessel (New York: Knopf, 1994), p. 429.

65. Thayer, *Gray World, Green Heart*, p. 65.

66. Fredric Jameson, *The Political Unconscious: Narrative as a Socially Symbolic Act* (Ithaca: Cornell University Press, 1981), p. 81.

67. For a partially related critique of Jameson, see Bill Brown, *The Material Unconscious: American Amusement, Stephen Crane, and the Economies of Play* (Cambridge: Harvard University Press, 1996), pp. 13–19, whose special interest, however, is how the history of material objects and material culture functions in acts of literary representation to disrupt the overly abstract and unidimensional cast of ideology theory.

68. Madhav Gadgil and Ramachandra Guha, *This Fissured Land: An Ecological History of India* (Delhi: Oxford University Press, 1992), p. 12.

69. I deliberately refrain from writing *"the* environmental unconscious" because what I am attempting to describe is not an isolatable or invariant mental faculty but a process of response, and its tenor and range differ among individuals and cultures. Obvious examples would be the degree and manner, across cultures, of conscious versus unconscious responsiveness to the significance of minute gradations of color and physical texture.

70. Jameson's adaptation of Althusserian Marxism has produced a somewhat distracting cross-fire from his critics as to whether he is more the prisoner of ideology than he would wish to admit or less the Marxist than he would wish to represent himself as being. See, for example, Jerry Aline Flieger, "The Prison-House of Ideology: Critic as Inmate," *Diacritics,* 12, no. 3 (Fall 1982): 47–56, and Robert Scholes, "Interpretation and Narrative: Kermode and Jameson," *Novel,* 17 (Spring 1984): 266–278. I too have normative views about politics, literature, and environmentalism, but I have tried to avoid making them drive this particular model.

71. On biophilia, see, for example, Kellert and Wilson, eds., *The Biophilia Hypothesis,* especially the two essays by the editors, pp. 31–69; and Kahn, *The Human Relationship with Nature,* pp. 9–43. On the ecological unconscious, see Theodore Roszak, *The Voice of the Earth* (New York: Simon and Schuster, 1992), pp. 301–305 passim (I quote from pp. 96, 304), and "The Greening of Psychology: Exploring the Ecological Unconscious," *Gestalt Journal* 18, no. 1 (Spring 1995): 9–46. Warwick Fox, *Toward a Transpersonal Ecology: Developing New Foundations for Environmentalism* (Boston: Shambhala, 1990), shows how deep ecology (whose core idea of human rapport with nature developed from a base in phenomenology transfused by environmental ethics) easily lends itself to ecopsychological application.

72. Mitchell Thomashow, *Ecological Identity: Becoming a Reflective Environmentalist* (Cambridge: MIT Press, 1995), p. 3; Yi-fu Tuan, *Topophilia: A Study of Environmental Perception, Attitudes, and Values* (1974; rpt., with new preface, New York: Columbia University Press, 1990), pp. 4, 93, and passim; Robert David Sack, *Homo Geographicus: A Framework for Action, Awareness, and Moral Concern* (Baltimore: Johns Hopkins University Press, 1997), pp. 24–25 and passim.

73. In particular, I would distinguish environmental (un)conscious(ness) from the question of affect, that is, from place affinity (to be discussed more fully in Chapter 2) or place aversion; and to allow for the likelihood, as Brown certainly presumes, as Tuan recognizes, and as others have argued, that affinity for artifice is as "natural" (i.e., built into preconscious orientation) to humans as affinity for nature if not more

so. On this point, see, for example, David Rothenberg, *Hand's End: Technology and the Limits of Nature* (Berkeley: University of California Press, 1993), and Bruce Mazlish, *The Fourth Discontinuity: The Co-Evolution of Humans and Machines* (New Haven: Yale University Press, 1993). The point is complicated, however, by the fact that nonhumans also have an affinity for *techne:* there is not as much difference between the worst of architects and the best of bees as Karl Marx supposed (*Capital*, in *Selected Writings*, ed. McLellan, p. 456).

74. As Soper remarks of theories about the relation between humans and nonhumans, "We develop or respond to the theories in the light of the feelings we feel (or fail to feel) toward nature, and thus far it may be said that specific ontological commitments do not govern, even though they can exercise a considerable influence, upon ecological responses." *What Is Nature?*, p. 176.

75. On this issue, see Barry Lopez, "Landscape and Narrative," *Crossing Open Ground* (1978; rpt., New York: Vintage, 1989), pp. 61–71; and my discussion of "nonfictional aesthetics," *Environmental Imagination*, pp. 91–103, which attempts further to develop the implications of Lopez's essay.

1. Toxic Discourse

1. Ralph Waldo Emerson, *Nature*, in *Collected Works of Ralph Waldo Emerson*, vol. 1, ed. Robert E. Spiller et al. (Cambridge: Harvard University Press, 1971), p. 8.

2. On ecocriticism's origins and first consolidation, a helpful introductory overview, critical anthology, and annotated bibliography are provided by *The Ecocriticism Reader*, ed. Cheryll Glotfelty and Harold Fromm (Athens: University of Georgia Press, 1996). See "The Ecocritical Insurgency," a commentary-conspectus for a special ecocriticism issue of *New Literary History*, 30 (Summer 1999): 699–712, for my own assessment.

3. See, for example, Joni Adamson Clarke, "Toward an Ecology of Justice," *Reading the Earth: New Directions in the Study of Literature and the Environment*, ed. Michael P. Branch, Rochelle Johnson, Daniel Patterson, and Scott Slovic (Moscow, Idaho: University of Idaho Press, 1998), pp. 9–17; Michael Bennett and David Teauge, eds., *The Nature of Cities: Ecocriticism and Urban Environments* (Tucson: University of Arizona Press, 1999); *Green Culture: Environmental Rhetoric in Contemporary America*, ed. Carl G. Herndl and Stuart C. Brown (Madison: University of Wisconsin Press, 1996), particularly M. Jimmie Killingsworth and Jacqueline S. Palmer, "Millennial Ecology: The Apocalyptic Narrative from *Silent Spring* to Global Warming," pp. 21–45; Steven B. Katz and Carolyn R. Miller, "The Low-Level Radioactive Waste Siting Controversy in North Carolina," pp. 111–140; and Craig Waddell, "Saving the Great Lakes," pp. 141–165. The choice of environmental degradation as the theme for the 1999 ASLE (Association for the Study of Literature and Environment) convention is an auspicious sign.

4. For example, Fredric Jameson: "Pollution, although it's horrifying and dangerous, is maybe simply a spin-off of this new relationship to nature" (i.e., "the industrialization of agriculture and the transformation of peasants or farmers into agricultural

workers"). "Interview" with Paik Nak-chung, *Global/Local Cultural Production and the Transnational Imaginary*, ed. Rob Wilson and Wimal Dissanayake (Durham: Duke University Press, 1996), pp. 352–353. The reductive "simply" reflects the belief "that ecological politics tends to be bourgeois politics" (p. 353)—questionable in light of recent events, as I argue below. Two extended ecopolitical critiques from this basic perspective are Andrew Ross, *Strange Weather* (London: Verso, 1988), and *The Chicago Gangster Theory of Life* (London: Verso, 1994).

5. See, for example, Verena Andermatt Conley, *Ecopolitics: The Environment in Poststructuralist Thought* (London: Routledge, 1997); Jhan Hochman, *Green Cultural Studies: Nature in Film, Novel, and Theory* (Moscow, Idaho: University of Idaho Press, 1998); and the special issue of *Cultural Studies*, 8, no. 1 (January 1994), devoted to environmental issues, particularly the introduction by guest editors Jody Berland and Jennifer Daryl Slack, "On Environmental Matters," pp. 1–4, and Slack and Laurie Anne Whitt, "Communities, Environments and Cultural Studies," pp. 5–31.

6. N. Katherine Hayles, "Constrained Constructivism: Locating Scientific Inquiry in the Theater of Representation," *Realism and Representation: Essays on the Problem of Realism in Relation to Science, Literature and Culture*, ed. George Levine (Madison: University of Wisconsin Press, 1993), pp. 27–43; "Searching for Common Ground," *Reinventing Nature? Responses to Postmodern Deconstruction*, ed. Michael Soulé and Gary Lease (Washington, D.C.: Island Press, 1995), pp. 47–63; and "Simulated Nature and Natural Simulations: Rethinking the Relation Between the Beholder and the World," *Uncommon Ground: Toward Reinventing Nature*, ed. William Cronon (New York: Norton, 1995), pp. 409–425. Hayles seeks to coordinate scientific realism and social constructionism. For Hayles constrained constructivism "implies relativism" but "also indicates an active construction of a reality *that is meaningful to us* through the dynamic interplay between us and the world" (p. 42). See also Slack and Whitt's attempt to define "a non-anthropocentric account of solidarity" by contextualizing community as local "material" environment (using "material" in the fullest possible sense). "Communities, Environments and Cultural Studies," p. 19.

7. J. Donald Hughes, "Industrial Technology and Environmental Damage," in *Pan's Travail: Environmental Problems of the Ancient Greeks and Romans* (Baltimore: Johns Hopkins University Press, 1994), pp. 112–129.

8. Ulrich Beck, *Risk Society: Towards a New Modernity*, trans. Mark A. Ritter (1986; London: Sage, 1992), pp. 51, 49, and 19–84 passim; cf. also Beck's collection of essays, *Ecological Enlightenment: Essays on the Politics of the Risk Society*, trans. Mark A. Ritter (1991; Atlantic Highlands, N.J.: Humanities Press, 1995), and "World Risk Society as Cosmopolitan Society?" *Theory, Culture and Society*, 13, no. 4 (1996): 1–32. Likewise, Kai Erikson, "A New Species of Trouble," *Communities at Risk: Collective Responses to Technological Hazards*, ed. Stephen Robert Couch and J. Stephen Kroll-Smith (New York: Peter Lang, 1991), argues that latter-day "toxic emergencies really *are* different" from all precursor threats in the kind of "dread" they induce, since "they have no [distinct] frame" (temporally or spatially), they are invisible, there is no secure sanctuary, and

they surpass the capacity of science to specify physical, let alone emotional, risk (pp. 17–20). The difference in ideological valence between these two accounts is notable: Erikson's is a more or less politically neutral sociological overview, while Beck's is explicitly anti-industry, diagnosing toxic threat/fear as "the embodiment of the errors of a whole epoch of industrialism," "a kind of collective return of the repressed." "World Risk Society," p. 24.

9. Love Canal was a lower-middle-class subdivision of Niagara Falls, New York, built on a former waste dump created by the Hooker Chemical Company, a subsidiary of Occidental Petroleum. Advocates for residents claimed that they had experienced abnormal rates of birth defects and environmentally induced illness. The most detailed among numerous case studies, which places special emphasis on the discrepancy among different interest groups' accounts, is Allan Mazur, *A Hazardous Inquiry: The "Rashomon" Effect at Love Canal* (Cambridge: Harvard University Press, 1998), pp. 19–118.

10. The significance of this for the history and historiography of U.S. environmentalism is assessed succinctly by Martin V. Melosi, "Equity, Eco-racism, and Environmental History," *Environmental History Review*, 19, no. 3 (Fall 1995): 1–16, and in more detail by Robert Gottlieb, *Forcing the Spring: The Transformation of the American Environmental Movement* (Washington, D.C.: Island Press, 1993), chapters 5–8 and Conclusion. Gottlieb provides an overview of grassroots antitoxics activism, stressing the demographic diversification of this movement relative to mainstream environmentalism. Dorceta Taylor, "Can the Environmental Movement Attract and Maintain the Support of Minorities?" in *Race and the Incidence of Environmental Hazards*, ed. Bunyan Bryant and Paul Mohai (Boulder: Westview Press, 1992), pp. 28–54, argues in more specific terms that U.S. minorities are far more interested in environmental issues than has been supposed, but that their energy is being directed not toward environmental protection but toward fighting environmental degradation and discrimination. Not that the contrast between "mainstream" and "minority" or "disempowered" attitudes is clear-cut: environmental psychologist Peter H. Kahn, Jr., found little difference in attitudes toward nature between poor people in a black Houston neighborhood and groups studied elsewhere. *The Human Relationship with Nature: Development and Culture* (Cambridge: MIT Press, 1999), chapters 6–11. Samuel Hays, *Beauty, Health, and Permanence: Environmental Politics in the United States, 1955–1985* (Cambridge: Cambridge University Press, 1987), pp. 266–272 and passim, diagnoses "equity in [environmental] amenities" like forests and seashores and "equity in pollution contol" as a widely shared concern for environmental quality of life issues that cuts across lines of social division even as actual inequities define and exacerbate those divisions. In global studies, as in U.S. studies, one finds contention between a "postmaterialist"-consensual thesis that environmental concern is increasing worldwide in proportion to standard of living (see Ronald Inglehart, *Culture Shift in Advanced Industrial Society* [Princeton: Princeton University Press, 1990], and "Public Support for Environmental Protection: Objective Problems and Subjective Values in 43 Societies," *Political Science and Politics*, 28 [1995]: 57–71) and insistence that the environmentalism of the have-nots is sharply

different from (and more urgent than) that of the haves (see Steven R. Brechin and Willett Kempton, "Global Environmentalism: A Challenge to the Postmaterialism Thesis?" *Social Science Quarterly*, 75 [June 1994]: 245–269, and Juan Martinez-Alier, "'Environmental Justice' (Local and Global)," *The Cultures of Globalization*, ed. Fredric Jameson and Masao Miyoshi [Durham: Duke University Press, 1998], pp. 312–326). Where one comes down seems driven partly by ideology, partly by methodology: the sociocultural differences may loom greater if one focuses on patterns of organizational affiliation and activism than if one focuses on notional value preferences.

11. Mark Dowie, *Losing Ground: American Environmentalism at the Close of the Twentieth Century* (Cambridge: MIT Press, 1995), p. 141. Charles Lee, director of research for the Commission for Racial Justice for the United Church of Christ, whose 1987 report put "environmental racism" on the public agenda, states the case succinctly in "Toxic Waste and Race in the United States," in *Race and the Incidence of Environmental Hazards*, ed. Bryant and Mohai, pp. 10–27. The environmental racism diagnosis has not gone entirely unchallenged: in a Boston area study, Eric J. Krieg found that it held for the city but not the Route 128 suburbs, where the dependency of a community's tax base on industry was the best predictor of toxification. "The Two Faces of Toxic Waste: Trends in the Spread of Environmental Hazards," *Sociological Forum*, 13 (November 1998): 3–20. The article grants, however, that most U.S. studies have been quite consistent.

12. Richard Regan, "Environmental Equity: Risk and Race," *The Egg: An Eco-Justice Quarterly*, 13, no. 2 (Spring 1993): 7.

13. Andrew Szasz, *Ecopopulism: Toxic Waste and the Movement for Environmental Justice* (Minneapolis: University of Minnesota Press, 1994), p. 97. Although the quoted statements are broadly applicable, *Ecopopulism* sometimes fails to distinguish between suburban ecopopulist activism by middle-class whites and the activism of communities of poor whites and/or people of color, where the levels of initial domestic tranquility and naive civic trust were by no means so high. Of the latter especially it could not be claimed that before their environmental awakening "they pretty much believed in a textbook image of government: they trusted that officials do their jobs honestly and well" (ibid.). Andrew Hurley, *Environmental Inequalities: Class, Race, and Industrial Pollution in Gary, Indiana, 1945–1980* (Chapel Hill: University of North Carolina Press, 1995), is a splendid case study that differentiates more sensitively between the underlying political orientations and specific environmentalist priorities of Gary's middle-class whites, working-class whites, and African Americans.

14. Quoted in *Race, Poverty and the Environment*, 2, nos. 3–4 (Fall 1991/Winter 1992): 32. Mark I. Wallace, "Environmental Justice, Neopreservationism, and Sustainable Spirituality," *The Ecological Community*, ed. Roger S. Gottlieb (New York: Routledge, 1997), pp. 292–310, is a thoughtful attempt to imagine how environmental justice activism might be fortified by preservationist concerns.

15. By no means should this be taken as implying that environmental justice (EJ) advocates *don't* care for the earth. If EJ rhetoric sometimes sounds that way, the chief reason may be suspicion of the motives of protectionists and/or systemic bias of pro-

tectionist organizations. As African-American environmentalist Carl Anthony says, "People of color often view alarmist threats about the collapse of the ecosystem as the latest strategem by the elite to maintain control of political and economic discourse." Interview with Theodore Roszak, *Ecopsychology: Restoring the Earth, Healing the Mind* (San Francisco: Sierra Club, 1995), p. 265. An obvious example is third world resistance to species and wilderness protection in the name of biodiversity (pragmatically justified to governments of the "North" for the possible medical benefits of unknown species, from which transnational pharmaceutical firms stand to profit most). The EJ position on earthcare seems rather to be that "there will be little nature without justice and little justice without nature," as Indian environmentalist Smithu Kothari puts it. "Social Movements, Ecology, and Justice," *Earthly Goods: Environmental Change and Social Justice*, ed. Fen Osler Hampson and Judith Reppy (Ithaca: Cornell University Press, 1996), p. 161.

16. Szasz, *Ecopopulism*, p. 145. Lee Clarke, "Political Ecology of Protest Groups," in *Communities at Risk*, ed. Crouch and Kroll-Smith, observes that "national media coverage is necessary, if not sufficient, before grass roots associations can gain enough power to become real forces as protest associations" (pp. 103–104)—a view that seems almost universally accepted. "Thoreau and Gandhi," chuckles Beck, "would have beamed with delight to see Greenpeace using the methods of the media age to stage world-wide civil resistance." "World Risk Society as Cosmopolitan Society?" p. 23. Mazur, *A Hazardous Inquiry*, emphasizes the importance of intensive media coverage for canonizing Love Canal as the quintessential "exemplar of the toxic waste dump" ("just as Three Mile Island became the paradigmatic nuclear accident"), though in fact Love Canal "was not the worst chemical dump known to the press at that time" (p. 127).

17. See, for example, Roberto A. Sánchez, "Health and Environmental Risks of the Maquiladora in Mexicali," *Natural Resources Journal*, 30 (Winter 1990): 163–186, and Mutombo Mpanya, "The Dumping of Toxic Waste in African Countries: A Case of Poverty and Racism," in *Race and the Incidence of Environmental Hazards*, ed. Bryant and Mohai, pp. 204–214.

18. Henri Lefebvre, *The Production of Space*, trans. Donald Nicholson-Smith (1974; Oxford: Blackwell, 1991), p. 282.

19. In "Multinational Corporations and the Global Environment," for example, Nazli Choucri finds no corporate paragons of environmentalist self-restraint but also no countries that could be (yet) called extreme "pollution havens" either, and identifies a series of checks on exploitative behavior that seem to be starting to take effect, such as a worldwide movement toward restrictive environmental legislation and "increased acceptance of the 'polluter pays principle' . . . in international forums." *Global Accord: Environmental Challenges and International Responses*, ed. Choucri (Cambridge: MIT Press, 1993), pp. 205–253 (quotations, pp. 211, 249).

20. Willett Kempton, James S. Bolster, and Jennifer A. Hartley, *Environmental Values in American Culture* (Cambridge: MIT Press, 1995), p. 259. The percentages of each

group responding positively ranged from 77 to 97 percent. It is less clear how well environmental concern stacks up against other public priorities. A 1996 Wall Street Journal/NBC News survey of 2,000 U.S. citizens found, for example, that "Protecting the Environment" ranked 13th of 14 on the citizens' "highest priority" list (at 26 percent), against the top vote-getters of "Improving Public Education" and "Reducing Crime" (both 57 percent), although 81 percent of respondents rated the "environmental movement" as having had a "positive impact" on "today's values," versus only 13 percent dissent. *Wall Street Journal*, December 13, 1996, pp. R1, R4.

21. See, for example, Ramachandra Guha, "Radical American Environmentalism and Wilderness Preservation: A Third World Critique," *Environmental Ethics*, 11 (1989): 71–83, and Guha and Juan Martinez-Alier, *Varieties of Environmentalism* (London: Earthscan, 1997). The latter also suggests, however, at least to my mind, that a polarized differentiation between nature protectionist and social justice, ecocentric and anthropocentric, environmentalism makes more sense when contrasting the traditional thrust of big environmental nongovernmental organizations like the Wilderness Society and the World Wildlife Federation with populist environmentalism than it does as a diagnosis of the complexity of the environmentalist scene in nonwestern countries. For example, the strength of Gandhist antimodernism as an ingredient of mainstream environmental thought and the phenomenon of such land-based peasant activism as the Chipko movement render the anthropocentric-ecocentric distinction simplistic for characterizing Indian environmentalism(s), except to signal rejection of an ethic of concern *only* for nature preservation rather than people. (See *Varieties of Environmentalism*, chapter 8 ("Mahatma Gandhi and the Environmental Movement"), and Smitu Kothari and Pramod Parajuli, "No Nature Without Social Justice," *Global Ecology*, ed. Wolfgang Sachs (London: Zed, 1993), pp. 225–241.

22. Philip Fisher, "The Aesthetics of Fear," *Raritan*, 18 (Summer 1998): 72.

23. Cyrus Edson, "The Microbe as a Social Leveller," *North American Review*, 161 (October 1895): 422, 425.

24. Nancy Tomes, *The Gospel of Germs: Men, Women, and the Microbe in American Life* (Cambridge: Harvard University Press, 1998).

25. Alan M. Kraut, *Silent Travelers: Germs, Genes, and the "Immigrant Menace"* (New York: Basic Books, 1994).

26. Benjamin A. Goldman, "What Is the Future of Environmental Justice?" *Antipode*, 28 (1996): 128, advances this possibility in the course of arguing that "the struggle for environmental and economic justice will need to become profoundly more mainstream in order to succeed" (p. 125).

27. Rachel Carson, *Silent Spring* (Boston: Houghton, 1962), pp. 1, 3. The milestone status of this book and the controversy provoked by it in stimulating contemporary environmentalism and antitoxics agitation particularly are widely accepted (see, e.g., Gottlieb, *Forcing the Spring*, pp. 81ff, and Robert C. Paehlke, *Environmentalism and the Future of Progressive Politics* [New Haven: Yale University Press, 1989], p. 21), even though the actual success of Carson's campaign against chemical pesticides is debat-

able (see Martin J. Walker, "The Unquiet Voice of *Silent Spring:* The Legacy of Rachel Carson," *The Ecologist,* 29 [August/September 1999]: 322–325), and as noted below, toxic anxiety was invoked rather than invented by Carson.

28. Szasz, *Ecopopulism,* pp. 43, 44.

29. Lois Marie Gibbs, *Love Canal: My Story,* as told to Murray Levine (Albany: SUNY Press, 1982), pp. 9, 40.

30. See Michael R. Edelstein, *Contaminated Communities: The Social and Psychological Impacts of Residential Toxic Exposure* (Boulder: Westview Press, 1988), pp. 11–13, 57–60, 72.

31. Nathaniel Hawthorne, *Mosses from an Old Manse,* in *The Centenary Edition of the Works of Nathaniel Hawthorne,* ed. William Charvat et al. (Columbus: Ohio State University Press, 1974), pp. 91–128, 186–206.

32. Catherine Beecher, *Harper's New Monthly Magazine,* 33 (1866): 762–772. For the historical context, see Gavin Townsend, "Airborne Toxins and the American House, 1865–1895," *Winterthur Portfolio,* 24, no. 1 (Spring 1989): 29–42; John Duffy, *The Sanatarians: A History of American Public Health* (Urbana: University of Illinois Press, 1990), pp. 93–134; Tomes, *The Gospel of Germs,* particularly chapter 2.

33. Leo Marx, *The Machine in the Garden: Technology and the Pastoral Ideal in American Culture* (New York: Oxford University Press, 1964).

34. The cultural logic of the "rude awakening" topos in toxic discourse seems even more inevitable as one considers the range of other genres in which it figures: (certain forms of) autobiography, bildungsroman, and slave narrative, just to name three.

35. For suburbs, see, for example, Peter Rowe, *Making a Middle Landscape* (Cambridge: MIT Press, 1991); for cities, James L. Machor, *Pastoral Cities: Urban Ideals and the Symbolic Landscape of America* (Madison: University of Wisconsin Press, 1987). Robert Fishman, *Urban Utopias in the Twentieth Century* (New York: Basic Books, 1977), and Witold Rybczynski, *City Life: Urban Expectations in a New World* (New York: Scribner, 1995), testify to the transnational force and durability of urban pastoral as a model for energizing urban design.

36. Mary Douglas, *Risk Acceptability According to the Social Sciences* (New York: Russell Sage Foundation, 1985), p. 29.

37. Edelstein, *Contaminated Communities,* p. 55.

38. Kaye Kiker, "The Nation's Dumping Ground," *The Egg,* 10, no. 2 (Summer 1990): 17.

39. Although pastoral aesthetics itself was for much of western history more anthropocentric than ecocentric, since the early modern era, as I have argued in *Environmental Imagination* (Cambridge: Harvard University Press, 1995), pp. 31–82, it has developed the capacity to turn in the latter direction. The same may conceivably prove true of toxic discourse also. As Vera Norwood points out, running throughout Carson's work is a feminist-ecocentric implication that "human beings encounter the world most often as trespassers, alienated from both the organic home and the economic household." "The Nature of Knowing: Rachel Carson and the American Environment," *Signs,* 12 (Summer 1987): 742.

40. Carson, *Silent Spring*, p. 15.

41. Lily Lee, "Energy and Air Pollution Are Social Issues," *Race, Poverty and the Environment*, 22, no. 2 (Summer 1991): 1, 18; Celene Krauss, "Blue-Collar Women and Toxic-Waste Protests: The Process of Politicization," *Toxic Struggles: The Theory and Practice of Environmental Justice*, ed. Richard Hofrichter (Philadelphia: New Society, 1993), p. 109; Robert W. Collin and William Harris, Sr., "Race and Waste in Two Virginia Communities," *Confronting Environmental Racism: Voices from the Grassroots*, ed. Robert D. Bullard (Boston: South End, 1993), p. 100.

42. "Disasters," of which ecocatastrophe is one form, is one of the fifty genres identified in *Science Fiction A to Z: A Dictionary of the Great S. F. Themes*, ed. Isaac Asimov, Martin H. Greenberg, Charles G. Waugh (Boston: Houghton, 1982). Cynthia Deitering, in "The Postnatural Novel: Toxic Consciousness in Fiction of the 1980s," *Ecocriticism Reader*, pp. 196–203, a short analysis of selected toxic dystopian fiction, makes clear that sci-fi and representational realism are interpenetrating categories.

43. Quoted in Spencer R. Weart, *Nuclear Fear: A History of Images* (Cambridge: Harvard University Press, 1988), p. 215. Weart treats ecocatastrophical fear as an offshoot of nuclear fear. I am also indebted to Thomas Schaub's analysis of Carson as a self-conscious intervener in Cold War debates by turning right-wing tropes back on themselves. "Rachel Carson and the Cold War," American Studies Association Convention, November 3, 1996, Washington, D.C.

44. Carson, *Silent Spring*, p. 16. Cf. Ralph H. Lutts, "Chemical Fallout: Rachel Carson's *Silent Spring*, Radioactive Fallout, and the Environmental Movement," *Environmental Review*, 9 (1985): 210–225.

45. For example, Riley E. Dunlap and Kent D. Van Liere, "The 'New Environmental Paradigm': A Proposed Measuring Instrument and Preliminary Results," *Journal of Environmental Education*, 9 (1978): 10–19; John McCormick, *Reclaiming Paradise: The Global Environmental Movement* (Bloomington: Indiana University Press, 1989), p. 196.

46. The 1972 Club of Rome report prepared by Donella H. Meadows et al., *The Limits to Growth* (New York: Universe Books, 1972), may be said to have recanonized the theme of scarcity as a central premise of contemporary environmentalism. William Ophuls, *Ecology and the Politics of Scarcity* (San Francisco: Freeman, 1977), is one exemplary result, influential in its own right. In *Beyond the Limits* (Post Mills, Vt.: Chelsea Green, 1992), Meadows and associates have qualified yet reaffirmed their previous position. In diagnosing depletion anxiety as a rhetorical formation, I would not go so far as Ross, in *The Chicago Gangster Theory of Life* and subsequent conference papers, who debunks scarcity as an artifact of multinational corporatist manipulation. Although oligopolies *do* create maldistribution of wealth and of poverty, the causes of depletion anxiety are more complicated and the anxiety itself hardly without foundation.

47. Reproduced in David L. Lendt, *Ding: The Life of Jay Norwood Darling* (Ames, Iowa: Iowa State University Press, 1989), unpaginated illustrations between pp. 54–55: 1938 and 1947.

48. Richard Grove, *Green Imperialism: Colonial Expansion, Tropical Island Edens and the Origins of Environmentalism, 1600–1860* (Cambridge: Cambridge University Press, 1995),

especially chapters 1, 5, and 6. Still remoter antecedents lie in both Christian apocalyptics (particularly the Book of Revelation) and classical (particularly the close of Lucretius, *De Rerum Naturae*).

49. Hurley, *Environmental Inequalities*, p. 140.

50. Beck, *Risk Society*, p. 36.

51. Hurley, *Environmental Inequalities*, p. 112.

52. Muir, in the *Outlook* (November 2, 1907), quoted by Stephen Fox, *The American Conservation Movement: John Muir and His Legacy* (Madison: University of Wisconsin Press, 1985), p. 141, which then provides a concise summary of issues, players, and events. For a more extended discussion, itself influential in making this episode a canonical chapter in U.S. environmental historiography, see Roderick Nash, *Wilderness and the American Mind*, 3rd ed. (New Haven: Yale University Press, 1982), pp. 161–181.

53. Gottleib, *Forcing the Spring*, p. 65, is exceptional.

54. Victor Lewis, "Rachel Carson Remembered," *Race, Poverty and the Environment*, 2, no. 1 (Spring 1991): 5. The feminist implications of Carson's critique are developed especially in H. Patricia Hynes, *The Recurring Silent Spring* (New York: Pergamon, 1989), a study limited by its special interest in the issue of reproductive rights, yet incisive and significant in placing Carson's life and legacy in the context of women's achievement in science and victimage by patriarchally controlled technology.

55. Carson, *Silent Spring*, pp. 297, 178.

56. Lewis, "Rachel Carson Remembered," pp. 14, 5.

57. Elizabeth Martin, "Organizing for a Change," *Race, Poverty and the Environment*, 2, no. 1 (Spring 1991): 4.

58. Robert D. Bullard, *Dumping in Dixie: Race, Class, and Environmental Quality* (Boulder: Westview Press, 1994), pp. 45, 46.

59. Ibid., p. 65; Bullard, "Anatomy of Environmental Racism," *Toxic Struggles*, ed. Hofrichter, p. 30, elaborating on an article from the *San Francisco Examiner* describing Zip Code 99058 as "the 'dirtiest' in the state."

60. John A. Agnew, *Place and Politics: The Geographical Mediation of State and Society* (Boston: Allen & Unwin, 1987), p. 36. Not that there is *no* material referent to "place" at all: more on this and related matters in Chapter 2.

61. Carson, *Silent Spring*, pp. 174–175.

62. Lynn Lawson, *Staying Well in a Toxic World* (Chicago: Noble Press, 1993), pp. 82, 151.

63. Marla Cone, "Leaving a Generation Gasping for Breath," *Los Angeles Times*, October 27, 1996, p. A28.

64. Eric Homberger, *Scenes from the Life of a City: Corruption and Conscience in Old New York* (New Haven: Yale University Press, 1994), pp. 30, 13, quoting T. De Witt Talmadge, *The Masque Torn Off*. Christophe Den Tandt's chapter on "Naturalist Gothic" in *The Urban Sublime in American Literary Naturalism* (Urbana: University of Illinois Press, 1998), pp. 123–150, analyzes the conventions of the "descent into hell" (p. 125) in

turn-of-the-twentieth-century urban writing and its Darwinist assumptions about social victimage and struggle.

65. Melville, "The Paradise of Bachelors and the Tartarus of Maids," *Piazza Tales and Other Prose Pieces, 1839–1860*, ed. Harrison Hayford et al. (Evanston: Northwestern University Press and Newberry Library, 1987), p. 324; Rebecca Harding Davis, "Life in the Iron-Mills," *Norton Anthology of American Literature*, 5th ed., vol. 1, ed. Nina Baym et al. (New York: Norton, 1998), p. 2535.

66. Down even to today, as in a six-part 1996 *New York Times* series on the plight of housing for the urban poor. Deborah Sontag, "For Poorest, Life 'Trapped in a Cage,'" *New York Times*, October 6, 1996, p. 45, cites Riis as a precedent and benchmark.

67. Alice Hamilton, *Exploring the Dangerous Trades*, ed. Barbara Sicherman (1943; rpt., Boston: Northeastern University Press, 1985), p. 145.

68. Muriel Rukeyser, *U.S. 1* (New York: Covici, Friede, 1938), pp. 9–72.

69. The fullest biographical study of Carson's career is Linda Lear, *Rachel Carson: Witness for Nature* (New York: Holt, 1997). Also helpful on her later years and *Silent Spring* is her publisher's memoir, Paul Brooks's *The House of Life: Rachel Carson at Work* (Boston: Houghton, 1972). For a chronicle of the controversy that the book provoked in the 1960s, see Frank Graham, Jr., *Since Silent Spring* (Boston: Houghton, 1970). Carson would have taken no pleasure in the fact that a significant reason why her indictment now seems "universal" is that human casualties from toxification by pesticides are now more a global (third world) problem than an American (first world) problem. Marquita K. Hill, *Understanding Environmental Pollution* (Cambridge: Cambridge University Press, 1997), p. 230.

70. Karl Kroeber, *Ecological Literary Criticism* (New York: Columbia University Press, 1994), p. 32. On the other hand, toxic discourse fits Kroeber's characterization of "ecological literary criticism" as "sympathetic to the romantic premise that the imaginativeness essential to poetry is the primary human capability enabling us to interact in a responsible manner with our environment" (p. 21)—provided that one broadens out from poetry to include other forms of imaging and grants that imaging may be one, rather than *the* primary human capability that promotes reconnection with environment.

71. Derek Jarman, *Modern Nature: The Journals of Derek Jarman* (London: Century, 1991). Built around the anticipation of his imminent death from AIDS, Jarman's journals offer more poignant epiphanies in their scenes of human/(modern) nature encounter than does much traditional nature writing, partly because Jarman's expectations of what that encounter with physical nature ought to mean are less grandiose to begin with.

72. Alexander Wilson, *The Culture of Nature: North American Landscape from Disney to the "Exxon Valdez"* (Cambridge: Blackwell, 1992), pp. 203ff. See Introduction, pp. 5–6 and notes, for my reservations.

73. Victor Davis Hanson, *The Land Was Everything: Letters from an American Farmer* (New York: Scribner, 1999), accomplishes something of the same for the tradition of

the agrarian essay (from Jefferson through Wendell Berry), as does Jane Smiley's *A Thousand Acres* (New York: Knopf, 1991) for the tradition of the agrarian novel (e.g., Willa Cather's *O Pioneers!*).

74. Williams's *Refuge: An Unnatural History of Family and Place* (New York: Vintage, 1991) is actually one of a number of recent works by various writers and artists about law-abiding, God-fearing Mormon villages in southern Utah ravaged by what looks to have been a long history of faulty planning, botched execution, public relations duplicity, bureaucratic intimidation, and government cover-up. See also John G. Fuller, *The Day We Bombed Utah* (New York: New American Library, 1984); Philip L. Fradkin, *Fallout: An American Nuclear Tragedy* (Tucson: University of Arizona Press, 1989); and Carole Gallagher, *American Ground Zero: The Secret Nuclear War* (Cambridge: MIT Press, 1993). These books, all cited by Williams herself, are journalistic works (photojournalism in Gallagher's case) strongly judgmental toward the Atomic Energy Commission (AEC). For the other side, see Barton C. Hacker, *Elements of Controversy: The Atomic Energy Commission and Radiation Safety in Nuclear Weapons Testing 1947–1974* (Berkeley: University of California Press, 1994), a work commissioned by a Department of Energy (Nevada Operations) "prime contractor" (Reynolds Electrical and Engineering Company). Note that although Hacker absolves officials of conscious wrongdoing, he also concludes that the AEC's "carefully crafted press releases" "sometimes erred" and "rarely if ever revealed all" (p. 278).

75. Although ecoradical-anarchist Abbey was no euphemizer, he passes over the legacy of toxification in his evocations of desert wilderness, as SueEllen Campbell points out in "Magpie," *Writing the Environment: Ecocriticism and Literature,* ed. Richard Kerridge and Neil Sammels (London: Zed, 1998), pp. 13–26.

76. Edelstein, *Contaminated Communities,* p. 57. In "The Spirit of Rachel Carson," *Audubon,* 94, no. 4 (July–August 1992): 104–107, Williams pays homage to Carson's example of "passionate resistance" to toxification and to *Silent Spring*'s prophetic standing as "sacred text" (p. 107).

77. Henry D. Thoreau, *Walden,* ed. J. Lyndon Shanley (Princeton: Princeton University Press, 1971), p. 3.

78. Martha Nussbaum, *Poetic Justice: The Literary Imagination and Public Life* (Boston: Beacon Press, 1995), pp. 83, 115. The legal case of reference here is *Bowers v. Hardwick,* in which the U.S. Supreme Court in 1986 upheld a Georgia antisodomy law against the claim of privacy rights.

79. Szasz, *Ecopopulism,* p. 46. Some of the attendant social, scientific, and legal problems are explored from a skeptical perspective in *Phantom Risk: Scientific Inference and the Law,* ed. Kenneth R. Foster, David E. Bernstein, and Peter W. Huber (Cambridge: MIT Press, 1993).

80. David Bates, *Environmental Health Risks and Public Policy* (Seattle: University of Washington Press, 1994), p. 90.

81. Chauncy Starr, "Risk Management, Assessment, and Acceptability," *Risk Analysis,* 5, no. 2 (1985): 99 (italics in the original). Such considerations move risk assessment critic Joe Thornton, in *Pandora's Poison: Chlorine, Health, and a New Environmental Strat-*

egy (Cambridge: MIT Press, 2000), to contend that is procedures are so constrained by the myopia of testing discrete substances and so biased toward countenancing use when possible as opposed to preventing harm as to call for a radically different, democratically controlled regime that would whenever possible limit production to chemicals previously shown to be safe.

82. Gibbs, *Love Canal*, p. 170, corroborated by Mazur, *A Hazardous Inquiry*, which tends to emphasize homeowner overreaction (particularly residents beyond the "first" or central ring) and the flaws in the "scientific" studies that purported to establish the likelihood of environmentally induced medical problems. Mazur does not deny the possibility of the latter, but he confines himself to the available epidemiological evidence.

83. Phil Brown and Edwin J. Mikkelsen, *No Safe Place: Toxic Waste, Leukemia, and Community Action* (Berkeley: University of California Press, 1990), p. 30. Jonathan Harr's *A Civil Action* (New York: Vintage, 1995), a narrative reconstruction of the Woburn case, emphasizes the plaintiff's counsel's imminent fear of bankruptcy, judicial strictness, and tenuousness of the evidence as the reasons for the prosecution's acceptance of the out-of-court settlement rather than the confusion of the jury or the ordering of the new trial, which in Harr's account was nothing more than a public gesture orchestrated at the judge's request as part of the settlement arrangement. Whatever may have been the exact chain of events, Harr, like Brown and Mikkelsen, makes amply clear throughout his book the formidable technical and practical difficulties of gathering and interpreting the relevant evidence.

84. Williams, *Refuge*, p. 286.

85. Gibbs, *Love Canal*, p. 69.

86. Szasz, *Ecopopulism*, pp. 148, 149.

87. Paul Slovic, "Trust, Emotion, Sex, Politics, and Science: Surveying the Risk-Assessment Battlefield," *Environment, Ethics, and Behavior: The Psychology of Environmental Valuation and Degradation*, ed. Max Bazerman et al. (San Francisco: New Lexington Press, 1997), p. 307; Chauncy Starr, "Risk Management, Assessment, and Acceptability," p. 98. For further discussion of the significance of perceived as opposed to "real" risk, see Raphael G. Kasper, "Perceptions of Risk and Their Effects on Decision Making," and Paul Slovic, Baruch Fischhoff, and Sarah Lichtenstein, "Facts and Fears: Understanding Perceived Risk," both in *Societal Risk Assessment: How Safe Is Safe Enough?*, ed. Richard C. Schwing and Walter A. Alberts, Jr. (New York: Plenum, 1980), pp. 71–80, 181–214.

88. Charles Perrow, *Normal Accidents: Living with High-Risk Technologies* (New York: Basic, 1984), p. 4. After a lengthy critique of the assumptions and practices of the discipline of risk assessment, Perrow concludes that "a technology that raises even unreasonable fears is to be avoided because unreasonable fears are nevertheless real fears. A technology that produces confusion, deception, uncertainty, and incomprehensible events (as the [Three Mile Island crisis] did) is to be avoided . . . A worker's death is not the only measure of dread; the absence of death is not the only criterion of social benefit" (p. 323).

89. Niklas Luhmann, *Ecological Communication*, trans. John Bednarz, Jr. (Chicago: University of Chicago Press, 1989), p. 11. Interestingly, in his persona as systems theorist, Luhmann himself seems to regard this prospect with complete equanimity.

90. John Kavadny, "Varieties of Risk Representation," *Journal of Social Philosophy*, 28 (Winter 1997): 123–143, provides a thoughtful appraisal of risk epistemology, distinguishing "risk analysis" from "risk perception" and "risk interpretation": "the three paradigms take us from a direct . . . account of what risk is to an indirect account . . . of the social construction of risk, via an increasing emphasis on the processes of risk discourse" (p. 137). In Kavadny's terms, acts of creative and rhetorical imagination (as well as critical reflection) expose by focusing on the dimensions of perception and interpretation the "epistemic pluralism" (p. 138) that the normalizing discipline of risk analysis seeks to contain, even though its practitioners are themselves more aware than the general public of the climate of (scientific) uncertainty in which they operate.

91. Jane Addams, *Twenty Years at Hull-House, with Autobiographical Notes*, ed. James Hurt (1910; Urbana: University of Illinois Press, 1990), p. 43.

92. Don DeLillo, *White Noise* (New York: Penguin, 1985), pp. 117, 114.

93. John Kavadny, "Information out of Place," *Oxymoron: Annual Thematic Anthology of the Arts and Sciences*, ed. Edward Binkowski (New York: Oxymoron Media, 1997), p. 100: a shrewd, thoughtful reading more respectful of the novel than my own. Other environmentally oriented readings of *White Noise* that ascribe to it greater self-consistency than I do are Richard Kerridge, "Small Rooms and the Ecosystem: Environmentalism and DeLillo's *White Noise*," *Writing the Environment*, ed. Kerridge and Neil Sammels, pp. 182–195; and Dana Phillips, "Don DeLillo's Postmodern Pastoral," *Reading the Earth*, ed. Branch, Johnson, Patterson, and Slovic, pp. 235–246.

94. Whether it be confirmation of DeLillo's peripheralization of toxic discourse or simply of precontemporary literary-critical inattention, none of the contributors to *New Essays on "White Noise,"* ed. Frank Lentricchia (Cambridge: Cambridge University Press, 1991), interest themselves much in the text's environmental discourse.

95. Sontag, *Illness as Metaphor and AIDS and Its Metaphors* (New York: Doubleday, 1990). Ironically, one of Sontag's targets is the assumption of environmental causation of illness (pp. 71 and passim), which she opposes both questionably as bad science and more cogently as a possible slippery slope toward the depersonalization of the sufferer into a symptom of cultural pathology (e.g., this or that despised social group as a "cancer" on society). Pressing in this direction, however, keeps her analysis from anticipating what is problematic about the opposite move to which protagonist-centered novels are generically susceptible: privileging individual suffering to the elision of contextual ground.

96. The strongest version of this argument is set forth in George Lakoff and Mark Johnson, *Metaphors We Live By* (Chicago: University of Chicago Press, 1980). Naomi Quinn argues more cautiously that "metaphors, far from constituting understanding, are ordinarily selected to fit a preexisting and culturally shared model," though "they may well help the reasoner to follow out entailments of the preexisting cultural

model." "The Cultural Basis of Metaphor," *Beyond Metaphor: The Theory of Tropes in Anthropology*, ed. James W. Fernandez (Stanford: Stanford University Press, 1991), p. 60.

97. Stevens, "The Man on the Dump" in *Collected Poems* (New York: Knopf, 1961), pp. 201–203; Pynchon, *The Crying of Lot 49* (Philadelphia: Lippincott, 1966).

98. DeLillo, *Underworld* (New York: Scribner, 1997), pp. 286–287.

99. A. R. Ammons, *Garbage: A Poem* (New York: Norton, 1993), pp. 18, 35, 108, 75. On Ammons's responsiveness to environmental issues, see Jon Gertner, "A Walk with A. R. Ammons," *Audubon* (September-October 1996), pp. 74–82.

100. For an ecocritical reading of this poem that emphasizes the comedic trope of recycling more strongly than I have done, see Leonard M. Scigaj, "'The World Was the Beginning of the World': Agency and Homology in A. R. Ammons's *Garbage*," *Reading the Earth*, ed. Branch, Johnson, Patterson, and Slovic, pp. 247–258, and *Sustainable Poetry: Four American Ecopoets* (Lexington: University Press of Kentucky, 1999), pp. 109–116.

101. For example, Waddell, who, in "Saving the Great Lakes," reports one of the commissioners of the International Joint Commission on water quality telling him that "to see the people directly, in front of you, that were directly affected, there was an *emotional* impact . . . that had a *tremendous impact on me*" (p. 154). Folk eloquence in the context of organization and argument must be credited with carrying power even in defeat, as when citizen opposition fended off a proposed Alberta-Pacific pulp mill at two levels of appeal before reversal by provincial government manipulation. Mary Richardson, Joan Sherman, and Michael Gismondi, *Winning Back the Words: Confronting Experts in an Environmental Public Hearing* (Toronto: Garamond Press, 1993).

102. John T. Omohundro, "From Oil Slick to Greasepaint: Theatre's Role in Community's Response to Pollution Events," *Communities at Risk*, ed. Couch and Kroll-Smith, pp. 165–166.

103. Ammons, *Garbage*, pp. 24, 29.

2. The Place of Place

1. George Lakoff and Mark Johnson, *Philosophy in the Flesh: The Embodied Mind and Its Challenge to Western Thought* (New York: Basic, 1999), p. 566, summing up their synthesis of phenomenological philosophy and cognitive psychology.

2. Donna J. Haraway's "Cyborg Manifesto," in *Simians, Cyborgs, and Women: The Reinvention of Nature* (New York: Routledge, 1991), pp. 148–181, is a template for "Science, Technology, and Socialist-Feminism in the Late Twentieth Century" built on the premise of "three crucial boundary breakdowns" (p. 151)—human/animal, organism/machine, and physical/nonphysical—which seem to offer prospect for reconstruction of a "postmodern collective and personal self" liberated from dominationist essentializing regimes, especially of gender. N. Katherine Hayles, *How We Became Posthuman: Virtual Bodies in Cybernetics, Literature, and Informatics* (Chicago: University of Chicago Press, 1999), especially chapter 2 (pp. 25–49), provides a persuasive friendly

amendment to Haraway by arguing for "embodiment" (as material world, as physical body, as embodying narrative) as a necessary and desirable even if not precisely speci-fiable limit to the dematerializing impetus of different forms of postmodern theory and technology that undercut traditional conceptions of identity and presence.

3. Hayles, *How We Became Posthuman*, p. 35.

4. That Powers's fiction is no mere fiction is evidenced by Sandra Steingraber's con-current *Living Downstream: An Ecologist Looks at Cancer and the Environment* (Reading, Mass.: Addison-Wesley, 1997), a work at once scientific, ethnographic, and autobio-graphical with special reference to the high incidence of cancer in the small Illinois community of the author's girlhood, and her own battle with a form of cancer she sus-pects she contracted there. *Gain* and *Living Downstream* share with Terry Tempest Williams's *Refuge* the ecofeminist approach of emphasizing the female body as a pri-mary site, indicator, and victim of environmental toxification.

5. At the novel's end the town's economy is gutted when the company spins off the division to Monsanto, which ironically moves the plant to a *maquiladora*. Richard Powers, *Gain* (New York: Farrar, Straus, 1998), p. 354. Both the irony of this outcome and the never-had-a-chance quixoticism of the resistance effort seem telegraphed throughout the novel by the deliberately formulistic-symmetrical handling of the two plot strands.

6. Edward S. Casey, *The Fate of Place: A Philosophical History* (Berkeley: University of California Press, 1997), despite reading contemporary poststructuralism too wishfully (chapter 12), argues convincingly that theories of embodied, platially contexted know-ing have rebounded from their discreditation by Enlightenment rationalism.

7. Anthony Giddens, *The Consequences of Modernity* (Stanford: Stanford University Press, 1990), pp. 18–19. The most influential theoretical account of this transformation is Henri Lefebvre's *The Production of Space*, trans. Donald Nicholson-Smith (1974; Ox-ford: Blackwell, 1984), which provides a deeply disaffected grand narrative of human history as a process of "absolute space" increasingly desacralized by reappropriation as abstract space, culminating in industrial capitalism's intensified production of "a space in which reproducibility, repetition, and the reproduction of social relationships are deliberately given precedence over works, over natural reproduction, over nature it-self and over natural time" (p. 120).

8. William N. Parker, *Europe, America, and the Wider World*, vol. 2 (Cambridge: Cam-bridge University Press, 1991), p. 88.

9. Edward Soja, *Postmodern Geographies: The Reassertion of Space in Critical Social The-ory* (London: Verso, 1989), p. 246.

10. Dolores Hayden, *The Power of Place: Urban Landscapes as Public History* (Cam-bridge: MIT Press, 1995), pp. 103–104.

11. Mike Davis, *Ecology of Fear: Los Angeles and the Imagination of Disaster* (New York: Metropolitan Books, 1998), pp. 387–391.

12. Timothy Oakes, "Place and the Paradox of Modernity," *Annals of the Association of American Geographers*, 87 (1997): 509.

13. Linda Hogan, *Dwellings* (New York: Norton, 1995), p. 94.

14. Peter J. Taylor neatly exposes the messiness by pointing to the blurry borders between two apparent opposites: the "nation-state" and the "home-household" (both "enabling place and dis-enabling space," he argues). *Modernities: A Geohistorical Interpretation* (Minneapolis: University of Minnesota Press, 1999), pp. 100–108.

15. Hayden, *The Power of Place*, p. 15.

16. Erica Carter, James Donald, and Judith Squires, "Introduction," *Space and Place: Theories of Identity and Location*, ed. Carter, Donald, and Squires (London: Lawrence & Wishart, 1993), p. xii. Geographer Robert Sack introduces a further distinction between "secondary" and "primary" place: "secondary" denoting the physical distribution and interaction of entities in a designated place, "primary" for "when place, and not only the things in it, is a force" that influences human behavior. *Homo Geographicus: A Framework for Action, Awareness, and Moral Concern* (Baltimore: Johns Hopkins University Press, 1997), p. 32. "Place" in the sense I use it refers to Sack's "primary" place but his distinction is a helpful reminder that locality is a necessary but not sufficient condition for the creation of placeness.

17. Of course, "time" in the sense of epoch—"old times," "a man of his time," and so on—shows a similar elasticity.

18. Geographer Tim Cresswell observes: "while it is true that places are always socially constructed and that they are created in some image rather than in others, it is also true that every society and culture has places of some (socially constructed) kind. Any imagined or theorized future society will have places." In *Place/Out of Place: Geography, Ideology, and Transgression* (Minneapolis: University of Minnesota Press, 1996), p. 151.

19. John Agnew, *Place and Politics: The Geographical Mediation of State and Society* (Boston: Allen & Unwin, 1987), p. 28.

20. Cresswell, *In Place/Out of Place*, p. 157.

21. Anssi Paasi, "The Institutionalization of Regions: A Theoretical Framework for Understanding the Emergence of Regions and the Constitution of Regional Identity," *Fennia*, 164, no. 1 (1986): 131.

22. Tim Hall, "(Re)Placing the City: Cultural Relocation and the City as Centre," *Imagining Cities: Scripts, Signs, Memory*, ed. Sallie Westwood and John Williams (London: Routledge, 1997), p. 208.

23. Graham Woodgate and Michael Redclift, "From a 'Sociology of Nature' to Environmental Sociology: Beyond Social Construction," *Environmental Values*, 7 (February 1998): 3–24.

24. Henri Lefebvre's *The Production of Space* is the most seminal social constructionist statement. For a short critical analysis of the historical and conceptual rationale of the social constructionist formation, see John A. Agnew, "The Devaluation of Place in Social Science," *The Power of Place: Bringing Together Geographical and Social Imaginations*, ed. Agnew and James S. Duncan (Boston: Unwin Hyman, 1989), pp. 9–29. Edward S. Casey, "How to Get from Space to Place in a Fairly Short Stretch of Time,"

Senses of Place, ed. Steven Feld and Keith H. Basso (Santa Fe: School of American Research, 1996), pp. 13–51, is a thoughtful critique of social constructionism from a phenomenological perspective.

25. Edward S. Casey, *Getting Back into Place: Toward a Renewed Understanding of the Place-World* (Bloomington: Indiana University Press, 1993), p. 313.

26. Leslie Silko, *Ceremony* (New York: Viking, 1977), p. 35.

27. Thoreau, "Walking," *Excursions* (Boston: Ticknor and Fields, 1863), p. 169.

28. A. R. Ammons, "Corson's Inlet," *Collected Poems, 1951–1971* (New York: Norton, 1972), p. 151.

29. Keith H. Basso, *Wisdom Sits in Places: Landscape and Language among the Western Apache* (Albuquerque: University of New Mexico Press, 1996), p. 79. I print only Basso's translation of the exchange, not the accompanying Western Apache text.

30. Joyce, *Portrait* (1916; rpt., New York: Viking, 1956), p. 16.

31. Louise Chawla, "Childhood Place Attachments," *Place Attachment,* ed. Irwin Altman and Setha M. Low (New York: Plenum, 1992), p. 66.

32. Walt Whitman, "There Was a Child Went Forth," *Leaves of Grass: Comprehensive Readers Edition,* ed. Harold Blodgett and Sculley Bradley (New York: New York University Press, 1965), pp. 364, 366.

33. Yi-fu Tuan, *Topophilia: A Study of Environmental Perception, Attitudes, and Values* (1974; rpt., New York: Columbia University Press, 1990), p. 38.

34. Homi K. Bhabha, "DissemiNation: Time, Narrative and the Margins of the Modern Nation," *The Location of Culture* (London: Routledge, 1994), pp. 139–170.

35. Cf. Saskia Sassen, *The Global City: New York, London, Tokyo* (Princeton: Princeton University Press, 1991). Not that such claims as that "top-level control and management of the [financial] industry [have] become concentrated in a few leading financial centers" (p. 5) are hallucinations. (Powers's *Gain* provides a fictional rendition of this centralizing process.) Nor is "globalism" the only mode of nodal concentration eroding (local) place-centeredness, as so-called "central place studies" have made clear. Brian J. L. Berry, "Cities as Systems Within Systems of Cities," *Papers and Proceedings of the Regional Science Association,* 33 (1964): 147–163, is a classic statement.

36. Vandana Shiva, *Monocultures of the Mind: Perspectives on Biodiversity and Biotechnology* (London: Zed, 1993), p. 9.

37. See, for example, Roger Rouse's critique of received migration theory in "Mexican Migration and the Social Space of Postmodernism," *Diaspora,* 1 (1991): 9–12.

38. Sack, *Homo Geographicus,* p. 9.

39. Ibid., p. 158. John C. Ryan and Alan Thein Durning, *Stuff: The Secret Lives of Everyday Things* (Seattle: Northwest Environment Watch, 1997), is a readable down-to-earth guide to these interdependencies. As the authors suggest, there is scandal as well as fascination to this domestic-material drawdown of global resources. It is the mark of dependence of the bourgeois private sphere on the "omnivores," as Gadgil and Guha call neocolonial exploiters, who "draw resources from vast areas, . . . and process them to provide many different services." Madhav Gadgil and Ramachandra Guha, *Ecology*

and Equity: The Use and Abuse of Nature in Contemporary India (London: Routledge, 1995), p. 141.

40. Seymour Martin Lipset, American Exceptionalism: A Double-Edged Sword (New York: Norton, 1996), p. 17.

41. Casey, The Fate of Place, p. 337. In other words, place is less like a (discrete) entity than like a (transient) process of event.

42. Allan Pred, "Place as Historically Contingent Process: Structuration and the Time-Geography of Becoming Places," Annals of the Association of American Geographers, 74 (1984): 279.

43. Kent Ryden, Mapping the Invisible Landscape (Iowa City: University of Iowa Press, 1993), p. 40.

44. Geoff Park, Ngā Urora: The Groves of Life (Wellington: Victoria University Press, 1995), p. 207.

45. Doreen Massey, Space, Place, and Gender (Minneapolis: University of Minnesota Press, 1994), p. 121.

46. See, for example, William Jordan III, Michael E. Gilpin, and John D. Aber, eds., Restoration Ecology: A Synthetic Approach to Ecological Research (Cambridge: Cambridge University Press, 1987), and A. Dwight Baldwin, Jr., Judith DeLuce, and Carl Pletsch, eds., Beyond Preservation: Restoring and Inventing Landscapes (Minneapolis: University of Minnesota Press, 1994).

47. Barbara Adam, Timescapes of Modernity: The Environment and Invisible Hazards (London: Routledge, 1998), pp. 56 and 163–209. Geoff Park's Ngā Urora, a meditative travel narrative with running commentary on New Zealand's ecological degradation since colonization, accomplishes this in a more literary way for an entire country.

48. Aldo Leopold, Round River: From the Journals of Aldo Leopold, ed. Luna B. Leopold (1953; rpt., Minocqua, Wis.: NorthWord Press, 1991), p. 237.

49. Alfred Lord Tennyson, "Ulysses," Tennyson: A Selected Edition, ed. Christopher Ricks (Berkeley: University of California Press, 1989), p. 142; George Gordon, Lord Byron, Childe Harold's Pilgrimage III.lxxii, Byron's Poetry, ed. Frank D. McConnell (New York: Norton, 1978), p. 66.

50. Edith Cobb, The Ecology of Imagination in Childhood (New York: Columbia University Press, 1959); Gary Paul Nabhan and Stephen Trimble, The Geography of Childhood (Boston: Beacon Press, 1994).

51. Walden (1854), ed. J. Lyndon Shanley (Princeton: Princeton University Press, 1971), p. 156.

52. William Wordsworth, The Prelude (1850), 12.208, The Prelude: 1799, 1805, 1850, ed. Jonathan Wordsworth, M. H. Abrams, and Stephen Gill (New York: Norton, 1979), p. 429.

53. Susan Slyomovics, "The Memory of Place: Rebuilding the Pre-1948 Palestinian Village," Diaspora, 3 (1994): 157–168.

54. Hana Wirth-Nesher, City Codes: Reading the Modern Urban Novel (Cambridge: Cambridge University Press, 1996), pp. 29–47.

55. The novel's critics differ on whether the text should be read as fundamentally sympathetic or critical toward Gandhian revolution: for example, Jha Rama, *Gandhian Thought: Indo-Anglian Novelists* (Delhi: Chanakya Publications, 1983), pp. 88–111, takes the affirmative; Canadai Seshachari, "The Gandhian Dimension: Revolution and Tragedy in *Kanthapura*," *South Asian Review*, 5 (1981): 82–87, takes the negative. Much less contestable are the structural parallels between the fictive storyteller's exilic recreation of her village and the novelist's diasporic recreation of this microcosm of Indian peasant society, as well as between the eclectic traditional/revolutionary culture of anticolonial resistance and the syncretism of the text's Indian English and hybridized genre (novel/legend). (See Frederick Buell's discussion of the novel in *National Culture and the New Global System* (Baltimore: Johns Hopkins University Press, 1994), pp. 74–83.

56. Anthony D. Smith, *The Ethnic Origins of Nations* (Oxford: Blackwell, 1986), p. 183.

57. Quoted in Glenn Bowman, "Tales of the Lost Land: Palestinian Identity and the Formation of Nationalist Consciousness," *Space and Place: Theories of Identity and Location*, ed. Carter, Donald, and Squires, p. 88.

58. Slyomovics, "The Memory of Place," p. 162, on the function of luminous detail in Ghassan Kanafani's novel *'A'id ilā Hayfa (Return to Haifa)*.

59. The answer to the value question clearly seems "yes and no," although the negative has lately been given much greater emphasis. Clearly it *is* worrisome that "a global, information-processing society and the prevalence of media-transmitted images" might be pushing us "closer to becoming continual tourists and collectors of internal landscapes" (Robert B. Riley, "Attachment to the Ordinary Landscape," *Place Attachment*, ed. Altman and Low, p. 30), even if one discounts the paranoia of extreme statements like Jean Baudrillard's *The Gulf War Did Not Take Place*, trans. Paul Patton (1991; Bloomington: Indiana University Press, 1995), which insists that "coverage" of the war "is no more than a cover: its purpose is to produce consensus by flat encephalogram" (p. 68). My middle-of-the-road appraisal is that since high-tech imaging is obviously here to stay (as Baudrillard insists) and may be used in place-constructive as well as place-erasing ways, it behooves us to understand its place-constructive as well as its place-hallucinating possibilities.

60. Smith, *The Ethnic Origins of Nations*, p. 28.

61. Alexander Wilson, *The Culture of Nature: North American Landscape from Disney to the "Exxon Valdez"* (Cambridge: Blackwell, 1992), p. 12.

62. Thomas A. Birkland, *After Disaster: Agenda Setting, Public Policy, and Focusing Events* (Washington, D.C.: Georgetown University Press, 1997), p. 99.

63. Stephen Graham, "The End of Geography or the Explosion of Place? Conceptualizing Space, Place and Information Technology," *Progress in Human Geography*, 22 (June 1998): 171.

64. David M. Smith, "How Far Should We Care? On the Spatial Scope of Beneficence," *Progress in Human Geography*, 22 (1998): 21.

65. Andrew Ross's amusing ethnography, *The Celebration Chronicles* (New York: Ballantine, 1999), p. 18, quotes Celebration advertising pitches catering to these fantasies: for example, "Remember that place? perhaps from your childhood. Or maybe just

from stories. It held a magic all its own. The special magic of an American small town."

66. Frank Waters's popularized *Book of the Hopi* (New York: Viking, 1963), p. 35, translates *Túwanasavi* as "Center of the Universe," though "Center of the World" or "Earth Center" may be more indicative. See Armin Geertz, "A Reed Pierced the Sky: Hopi Cosmography on Third Mesa, Arizona," *Numen*, 31 (December 1984): 224; Ekkehart Malotki, *Hopitutuwutski/Hopi Tales* (n.p.: Museum of Northern Arizona Press, 1978), p. 159.

67. Ramson Lomatewama, *Drifting Through Ancestor Dreams* (Flagstaff, Ariz.: Northland, 1994), pp. 24–25.

68. Paul Bowles, *Without Stopping* (New York: Putnam's, 1972), p. 125.

69. John Haines, "The Writer as Alaskan: Beginnings and Reflections," *Living Off the Country: Essays on Poetry and Place* (Ann Arbor: University of Michigan Press, 1981), p. 5.

70. Berry, "Poetry and Place," *Standing by Words* (San Francisco: North Point, 1983), p. 103.

71. Basso, *Wisdom Sits in Places*, p. 59.

72. David Abram, *The Spell of the Sensuous: Perception and Language in a More-Than-Human World* (New York: Pantheon, 1996), p. 182.

73. Vine Deloria, Jr., *God Is Red: A Native View of Religion*, rev. ed. (Golden, Colo.: North American Press, 1992), pp. 267–282 and passim.

74. Wallace Stegner, "Thoughts in a Dry Land," *Where the Bluebird Sings to the Lemonade Springs: Living and Writing in the West* (New York: Penguin, 1992), p. 55.

75. To this Berry might reply, with some justice, that it caricatures his position by failing to take into account the broader perspectives of his critique of transnational corporatism; his strong interest in very different place-based cultures, such as the old-order Amish; and his translocal religiocentrism.

76. For a concisely elegant presentation of this idea from a Marxist perspective, see Doreen Massey, "A Global Sense of Place," *Space, Place, and Gender*, pp. 146–156.

77. Freeman House, *Totem Salmon: Life Lessons from Another Species* (Beacon Press, 1999), p. 159.

78. Particularly instructive here are Wideman's careful attempts to accommodate without oversimplification interviewers' desires that he situate himself as an African-American writer. See, for example, Wilfred D. Samuels, "Going Home: A Conversation with John Edgar Wideman" (1983), and James W. Coleman's interview of 1988, rpt. in *Conversations with Wideman*, ed. Bonnie TuSmith (Jackson: University Press of Mississippi, 1989), pp. 14–31, 62–80.

79. Wideman, "Preface" to *The Homewood Books* (Pittsburgh: University of Pittsburgh Press, 1992), pp. viii–ix. All subsequent quotations from the Homewood trilogy are taken from this edition and are indicated in parentheses.

80. Samuels, "Going Home," *Conversations*, pp. 15, 16.

81. Quotation from Melvin D. Williams, *On the Street Where I Lived* (New York: Holt, 1983), p. 4, who calls the place an "urban desert" (pp. 8, 45). This study of a district within Homewood by a Pittsburgh-born African-American anthropologist eight

years Wideman's senior, full of empathy and outrage for the neighborhood's plight, provides valuable documentary background, as does the revised edition, *The Human Dilemma* (New York: Harcourt, 1992). Speaking of Pittsburgh history of the period with reference to Homewood, Roy Lubove, *Twentieth-Century Pittsburgh: Government, Business, and Environmental Change*, vol. 2 (1969; rpt., Pittsburgh: University of Pittsburgh Press, 1995), notes that "Pittsburgh in 1960 ranked worst among the 14 largest cities in the percentage of nonwhite-occupied housing units that were classified as deteriorating or dilapidated" (p. 160). Laurence Glasco, "Double Burden: The Black Experience in Pittsburgh," *African Americans in Pennsylvania*, ed. Joe William Trotter, Jr., and Eric Ledell Smith (University Park, Pa.: Pennsylvania Historical and Museum Commission and the Pennsylvania State University Press, 1997), pp. 411–430, documents the steadily diminishing work prospects of Pittsburgh's black working-class population during the twentieth century, together with the improving prospects of the black middle class, including "a minor [sic] flowering of cultural life" exemplified by Wideman, playwright August Wilson, and others (p. 430).

82. Franklin Toker, *Pittsburgh: An Urban Portrait* (University Park, Pa.: Penn State University Press, 1986), p. 219.

83. Wideman told one interviewer that he worked from a trigenerational notion of a "pioneer" generation (John French's) who "prevailed"; a lost second generation (Carl's and his own father's) "who were wiped out because they didn't have the pioneers' struggle to survive"; and his own cohort, for whom "the future is open." Kay Bonetti, "An Interview with John Edgar Wideman" (1986), *Conversations*, pp. 56–57. The trilogy itself is not quite so consistent.

84. Toker, *Pittsburgh*, pp. 217–218. Wideman (through Tommy) realizes this: hiding out on Bruston Hill he knows that "he could see it all [the whole city] from where he stood" even though haze covers all (p. 204).

85. The memory of briefly and vainly harboring the real-life Robby on the run (see pp. 160–161 and *Brothers and Keepers* [New York: Vintage, 1984], pp. 8–19), which seems to lie in back of the Bess-Tommy bond that forms in *Hiding Place*, is one of two autobiographical episodes that Wideman has acknowledged as important provocation for the trilogy—the other being the experience of his grandmother's funeral in 1973, where family "stories I'd been hearing all my life without understanding" (p. x) began to seem luminous (cf. pp. 70–71, 155–156). Wideman connects the two in the idea of Tommy's incarceration as the unjust comeuppance for the "crime" of the ancestress-runaway, Sybela Owens (pp. 157, 161).

86. Williams, *On the Street Where I Lived*, pp. 14, 44. Most of the members of John's family in the Homewood trilogy, however, correspond to Williams's (excessively pejorative) category of "spurious" black: low economic status, identifying with "mainstream" values, who "detest the noise, the dirt, and the decay around them, but they do not possess the resources to leave" (p. 7). Notwithstanding that they share much in common (including a keen sense of irony), Wideman would presumably consider Williams's analysis too categorical and judgmental in its stratifications; Williams

would presumably consider Wideman's analysis too sympathetic to exemplars of middle-class values (e.g., in the treatment of mother Lizabeth and grandmother Freeda).
87. Williams, *On the Street Where I Lived*, p. 42.

3. *Flâneur*'s Progress

1. For analytical overviews of bioregionalism, see Kirkpatrick Sale, *Dwellers in the Land: The Bioregional Vision* (San Francisco: Sierra Club, 1985); and particularly *Bioregionalism*, ed. Michael Vincent McGinnis (London: Routledge, 1999), within which collection Doug Aberly, "Interpreting Bioregionalism: A Story from Many Voices," pp. 13–42, provides a fine starting point. A particularly thoughtful book-length expression of bioregional vision by a creative writer is Gary Snyder, *The Practice of the Wild* (San Francisco: North Point Press, 1990). Bioregionalism might be defined succinctly as an ethos and set of life practices directed toward achieving an ecologically sustainable coevolutionary symbiosis of human and nonhuman communities within a territory of limited magnitude whose borders may not be precisely specifiable but are conceived in terms of "natural" rather than jurisdictional units, often in terms of a watershed or constellation of watersheds. Bioregionalism seeks to make human community more self-consciously ecocentric than it has been in modern times but in such a way as to incorporate, not disallow, anthropocentric concerns.
2. The most widely circulated definition has been Peter Berg and Ray Dasmann's "learning to live-in-place in an area that has been disrupted and injured through past exploitation." "Reinhabiting California," *The Ecologist*, 7 (1977): 399. Another influential statement has been Gary Snyder, "Reinhabitation" (1977), rpt. in *A Place in Space: Ethics, Aesthetics, and Watersheds* (Washington: Counterpoint, 1995), pp. 183–191.
3. Wendell Berry, *Clearing* (New York: Harcourt, 1977), p. 5; John Elder, *Reading the Mountains of Home* (Cambridge: Harvard University Press, 1998), pp. 25–26; Gary Snyder, *The Practice of the Wild*, pp. 39–47.
4. Peter Berg, Beryl Magilavy, and Seth Zuckerman, *A Green City Program for the San Francisco Bay Area and Beyond* (San Francisco: Planet Drum Foundation, 1990), pp. 10, 17.
5. Peter Hall, *Cities of Tomorrow: An Intellectual History of Urban Planning and Design in the Twentieth Century* (Oxford: Blackwell, 1988), pp. 86–173, is a useful short account.
6. Sale, *Dwellers in the Land*, pp. 44–45.
7. This phase begins with Ian L. McHarg, *Design with Nature* (Garden City, N.Y.: Natural History Press, 1969), which contains an introduction by Mumford. Other significant statements from the United States, United Kingdom, and Canada include Anne Whiston Spirn, *The Granite Garden: Urban Nature and Human Design* (New York: Basic, 1984); David Nicholson-Lord, *The Greening of the Cities* (London: Routledge, 1987); Rutherford H. Platt, Rowan A. Rowntree, and Pamela C. Muick, eds., *The Ecological City: Preserving and Restoring Urban Biodiversity* (Amherst: University of Massa-

298 ▲ NOTES TO PAGES 86–89

chusetts Press, 1994); and Michael Hough, *Cities and Natural Process* (New York: Routledge, 1995).

8. Richard Lehan, *The City in Literature: An Intellectual and Cultural History* (Berkeley: University of California Press, 1998), p. 292.

9. Michael Vincent McGinnis, "Boundary Creatures and Bounded Spaces," *Bioregionalism*, ed. McGinnis, p. 75.

10. Frank Norris, *The Pit: A Story of Chicago* (New York: Collier, 1903), p. 243; cf. William Cronon, *Nature's Metropolis* (New York: Norton, 1991), especially chapter 3, "Pricing the Future: Grain."

11. Robert Frost, "A Brook in the City," *The Poetry of Robert Frost* (New York: Holt, 1969), p. 231.

12. Anne Whiston Spirn, *The Language of Landscape* (New Haven: Yale University Press, 1998), p. 268.

13. Hough, *Cities and Natural Process*, pp. 6, 9.

14. John Gay, *Trivia* III.101–110, *Poetry and Prose*, vol. 1, ed. Vinton A. Dearing (Oxford: Clarendon Press, 1974), p. 163.

15. John H. Johnston, *The Poet and the City: A Study in Urban Perspectives* (Athens: University of Georgia Press, 1984), p. 75.

16. Louis Wirth's classic summation near the end of his "Urbanism as a Way of Life," *American Journal of Sociology*, 44 (July 1938): 23.

17. In Priscilla Parkhurst Ferguson's useful definition: *flânerie* is "a social state that offers the inestimable, and paradoxical, privilege of moving about the street without losing one's individuality." *Paris as Revolution: Writing the Nineteenth-Century City* (Berkeley: University of California Press, 1994), p. 80. As Elizabeth Wilson writes in "The Invisible *Flâneur*," *Postmodern Cities and Spaces*, ed. Sophie Watson and Katherine Gibson (Oxford: Blackwell, 1995), the *flâneur*, "as a man who takes visual possession of the city," "has emerged in postmodern feminist discourse as the embodiment of the 'male gaze'" (p. 65). Yet, as we shall see, the *flâneur*-figure may modulate into one who is possessed by, as well as possessing, and although the figure is traditionally male, it need not inevitably be so. (See Virginia Woolf's Mrs. Dalloway, discussed later in this chapter, and, in Chapter 4, Theodore Dreiser's Carrie and, in part, the poetry of Gwendolyn Brooks.)

18. Contra Walter Benjamin's insistence that "the *flâneur* is the creation of Paris" (*Selected Writings*, vol. 2, ed. Michael W. Jennings et al. [Cambridge: Harvard University Press, 1999], p. 263), Dana Brand, *The Spectator and the City in Nineteenth-Century American Literature* (Cambridge: Cambridge University Press, 1991), persuasively argues for the antecedence of the English *flâneur* tradition and its influence on U.S. literature relative to French. As Brand sees it, the essayists "Addison and Steele create the flaneur, as Benjamin found him" (p. 33), with Gay a peripheral contributor. Gary Roberts traces the literature of British urban strolling back to the seventeenth century. "London Here and Now: Walking, Streets, and Urban Environments in English Poetry from Donne to Gay," *The Nature of Cities: Ecocriticism and Urban Environments*, ed.

Michael Bennett and David W. Teague (Tucson: University of Arizona Press, 1999), pp. 33–54.

19. See especially Georg Simmel, "The Metropolis and Mental Life" (1903), in *On Individuality and Social Forms*, ed. Donald N. Levine (Chicago: University of Chicago Press, 1971), pp. 324–339, and Walter Benjamin, *Charles Baudelaire: A Lyric Poet in the Era of High Capitalism*, trans. Harry Zohn (1973; rpt., London: Verso, 1983).

20. As Roger Gilbert makes clear in his *Walks in the World: Representation and Experience in Modern American Poetry* (Princeton: Princeton University Press, 1991). See also Jeffrey C. Robinson, *The Walk: Notes on a Romantic Image* (Norman: University of Oklahoma Press, 1989).

21. Blake, "London," *The Poetry and Prose of William Blake*, ed. David V. Erdman (Garden City: Doubleday, 1965), p. 27; Wordsworth, *The Prelude* (1850), 7.626, 644–646, in *The Prelude: 1799, 1805, 1850*, ed. Jonathan Wordsworth, M. H. Abrams, and Stephen Gill (New York: Norton, 1979), pp. 259, 261. As Jonathan Raban (among others) points out, Wordsworth's quintessential image of disoriented bafflement betokens a "greenhorn" mentality (*Soft City* [London: Hamish Hamilton, 1974], pp. 40–41), to be contrasted with the depth of the speaker's emotions confronting rural poor like the leech gatherer of "Resolution and Independence" or "The Cumberland Beggar," poems that catch hold of a single scene and meditate on it deeply. Book 7 of *The Prelude* by contrast "render[s] the confusion of his own hyperactive brain."

22. Thomas DeQuincey, "The Nation of London," *Autobiographic Sketches*, in *Collected Writings*, vol. 1, ed. David Masson (Edinburgh: Adam and Charles Black, 1889–1890), p. 181.

23. William B. Thesing, *The London Muse: Victorian Poetic Responses to the City* (Athens: University of Georgia Press, 1982), pp. 4–11.

24. William Blake, *Jerusalem: The Emanation of the Giant Albion*, ed. Morton D. Paley (Princeton: Princeton University Press, 1991), p. 179, Plate 31 (45). William Wordsworth, "Composed upon Westminster Bridge, September 3, 1902," *William Wordsworth: The Poems*, vol. 1, ed. John O. Hayden (New Haven: Yale University Press, 1981), p. 575.

25. See, for example, S. Xu and M. Madden, "Urban Ecosystems: A Holistic Approach to Urban Analysis," *Environment and Planning B*, 16 (1989): 187–200; and Abel Wolman, "The Metabolism of Cities," *Scientific American*, 213, no. 3 (September 1965): 178–190.

26. For example, Rodney R. White's survey, *Urban Environmental Management: Environmental Change and Urban Design* (Chichester: Wiley, 1994), cautions that although "the organic analogy of metabolism allows the planner and the citizen to think in system-wide terms over time," it "does not imply any commitment to organic analogues about the way in which a city might grow and then decline." Yet soon afterwards he begs exception for "a further analogy": that "urban systems sometimes produce a pathological condition, in that the built form and/or the inhabitants' experience decline, which may be fatal" (pp. 47, 67). See Elizabeth Grosz, "Bodies-Cities," in her

Essays on the Politics of Bodies (New York: Routledge, 1995), pp. 103–110, for an astute critique of the usual terms of the metaphor.

27. Walt Whitman, *Leaves of Grass: Comprehensive Reader's Edition*, ed. Harold W. Blodgett and Sculley Bradley (New York: New York University Press, 1965), p. 253, ll. 165–184; Dickens, *Dombey and Son*, chapter 16: "What the Waves Were Always Saying." Although Whitman developed strong reservations about what he took to be the unevenness and incoherence of *Dombey* as a whole, he enthusiastically reviewed volume 1 as "a sort of novel in itself—for it is the artistically complete life of one of Dickens' best drawn and most consistently sustained characters" (Paul) (*The Gathering of the Forces*, vol. 2, ed. Cleveland Rodgers and John Black [New York: Putnam, 1920], p. 296). All subsequent quotations from Whitman's poems are from the edition cited above and are indicated parenthetically in the text, first by page and then by line(s).

28. It was also of course symptomatic of a shared Romanticist susceptibility to sentimental renderings of youthful prescience and a shared Victorian idealization of motherhood.

29. Lyn H. Lofland, *A World of Strangers* (New York: Basic, 1973), pp. 158–168.

30. Jane Jacobs, *The Death and Life of Great American Cities* (New York: Vintage, 1961), pp. 82, 35, 56; emphasis hers. William Chapman Sharpe, *Unreal Cities: Urban Figuration in Wordsworth, Baudelaire, Whitman, Eliot, and Williams* (Baltimore: Johns Hopkins University Press, 1990), pp. 74–76, points out, correctly, that Whitman is more intent on dramatizing interpersonal connectedness as key to urban experience than that other great urban poet-*flâneur* of his day, Baudelaire.

31. Edward K. Spann, *The New Metropolis: New York City, 1840–1857* (New York: Columbia University Press, 1981), p. 137. Edwin G. Burrows and Mike Wallace, *Gotham: A History of New York City to 1898* (New York: Oxford University Press, 1999), pp. 649–863, provides a readable, up-to-date narrative of the city's extreme contrasts during these years.

32. *I Sit and Look Out: Editorials from the Brooklyn Daily Times by Walt Whitman*, ed. Emory Holloway and Vernolian Schwarz (New York: Columbia University Press, 1932), pp. 101–103; Whitman, *Collected Writings: The Journalism*, vol. 1, ed. Herbert Bergman et al. (New York: Peter Lang, 1998), pp. 172, 291, 302, 308, 320, 330, 334, 411, 446, 448, 454; Thomas L. Brasher, *Whitman as Editor of the Brooklyn Daily Eagle* (Detroit: Wayne State University Press, 1970), pp. 181–182.

33. *I Sit and Look Out*, p. 144.

34. Thomas Jefferson Whitman's daughter later gave Washington University a $72,764 endowment to set up a "Thomas Jefferson Whitman Engineering Library Fund." *Dear Brother Walt: The Letters of Thomas Jefferson Whitman*, ed. Dennis Berthold and Kenneth M. Price (Kent, Ohio: Kent State University Press, 1984), p. xxxv.

35. In Algernon Charles Swinburne's *William Blake: A Critical Essay* (1868; rpt., New York: Benjamin Blom, 1967), pp. 300–303. Ironically, Whitman disliked Blake's "wilful & uncontrolled" style. *Notebooks and Unpublished Fragments*, vol. 4, ed. Edward F. Grier (New York: New York University Press, 1984), pp. 1502–03. Whitman ironically never seems to have discussed Blake with his friend and would-be spouse Anne Gilchrist,

completer of the milestone biography by her late husband that precipitated the Blake revival. In the long run Blake's only influence on Whitman would seem to have been Whitman's borrowing the design of his tomb from Blake's engraving of "Death's Door" for Robert Blair's poem *The Grave* (reproduced for Horace Scudder's "William Blake, Painter and Poet," *Scribner's Monthly*, 20 [1880]: 225).

36. M. H. Abrams, "Structure and Style in the Greater Romantic Lyric," *From Sensibility to Romanticism*, ed. Frederick W. Hilles and Harold Bloom (New York: Oxford University Press, 1965), pp. 527–560, is the classic account of the genre.

37. Thoughtful previous discussions of "Brooklyn Ferry" as urban discourse, from all of which I have benefited even when in disagreement, include Wynn Thomas, *The Lunar Light of Whitman's Poetry* (Cambridge: Harvard University Press, 1987), pp. 92–116; Malcolm Andrews, "Walt Whitman and the American City," *The American City: Literary and Cultural Perspectives*, ed. Graham Clarke (London: Vision Press, 1988), pp. 179–197; William Sharpe, *Unreal Cities*, pp. 92–101; Sidney H. Bremmer, *Urban Intersections: Meetings of Life and Literature in United States Cities* (Urbana: University of Illinois Press, 1992), pp. 32–35; Dana Brand, *The Spectator and the City*, pp. 170–178; and Philip Fisher, *Still the New World: American Literature in a Culture of Creative Destruction* (Cambridge: Harvard University Press, 1999), pp. 65–70.

38. Henry Evelyn Pierrepont, *Historical Sketch of the Fulton Ferry, and Its Associated Ferries* (Brooklyn: Eagle Job and Book Department for the Union Ferry Company of Brooklyn, 1879), p. 74 (which reports 70,000 per day for the year 1854, two years before the poem was published).

39. *The Gathering of the Forces*, vol. 2, pp. 159–166; *I Sit and Look Out*, pp. 138–140; Brasher, *Whitman as Editor*, pp. 47–53.

40. Edward Winslow Martin, *The Secrets of the Great City* (Philadelphia: Jones, 1868), pp. 121–122.

41. Pierrepont, *Historical Sketch*, pp. 75–76, reports that in November 1856, less than two months after publication of "Brooklyn Ferry," the ferry directors, in order to expedite boarding and cut down on cheating, discontinued the practice of selling tickets to bona fide commuters at a half-cent cheaper than the two-cent pay-as-you-went rate, and discontinued free passes to "clergymen, reporters and others"—for which they were roasted as fat-cat predators by the city press. Although Whitman might not have anticipated that this would happen, he must have witnessed instances of crowding and cheating, and he would have known that the business had been operating at a loss for some time.

42. For an opposite interpretation, see James L. Machor, *Pastoral Cities: Urban Ideals and the Symbolic Landscape of America* (Madison: University of Wisconsin Press, 1987), pp. 179 and passim, which contends that Whitman should be considered an individual visionary rather than an urban reformer.

43. Raban, *Soft City*, p. 4.

44. Gay revisionist studies have rightly stressed the homoerotic overtones of these advances to the reader. It is even conceivable that such might have been the poem's most powerful biographical impetus. However that may be, what seems to me espe-

cially remarkable about "Brooklyn Ferry" is the amplitude of socioenvironmental vision that resulted from the inception point, whatever that may have been.

45. Walter Benjamin, "Some Motifs in Baudelaire," in *Charles Baudelaire*, p. 151 (quoting Simmel's "The Metropolis and Mental Life"); Nicholson-Lord, *The Greening of the Cities*, pp. 193, 192.

46. Paul Boyer, *Urban Masses and Moral Order in America, 1820–1920* (Cambridge: Harvard University Press, 1978), chapter 4.

47. Fisher, *Still the New World*, pp. 68–69.

48. Thomas, *Lunar Light of Whitman's Poetry*, p. 114. Thomas infers that lyric meditation would "appear to have ousted the objective world and appropriated its factuality" (p. 115). By contrast, Andrews, in "Walt Whitman and the American City," sees the foundry chimneys as a deliberately provocative act of reappropriating what had in Dickens and other British writers become a cliché of the baleful effects of industrialization (pp. 183ff). My diagnosis draws on both discussions but takes a position somewhat different from either.

49. Roger Gilbert, *Walks in the World*, pp. 45–48, begins his thoughtful comparison of Thoreau and Whitman with an observation along these lines.

50. On Olmsted's career, see especially Laura Wood Roper, *FLO: A Biography of Frederick Law Olmsted* (Baltimore: Johns Hopkins University Press, 1973), and Witold Rybczynski, *A Clearing in the Distance: Frederick Law Olmsted and America in the Nineteenth Century* (New York: Scribner, 1999). In drawing parallels between Olmsted and Whitman, I do not mean to imply close temperamental affinity. For one thing, Olmsted had a rigid, even military, disposition, giving precise directions, for example, to subordinates as to how they were to salute their superiors ("by raising a hand to the front of the cap, without bending the neck or body") and admonishing that superiors who neglected to return the salute should "be reported in a special report to the Superintendent." Olmsted, "Rules and Conditions of Service of the Central Park Keepers," *The Papers of Frederick Law Olmsted*, vol. 3, ed. Charles E. Beveridge and David Schuyler (Baltimore: Johns Hopkins University Press, 1983), p. 220.

51. Frederick Law Olmsted, "Public Parks and the Enlargement of Towns," *Civilizing American Cities: A Selection of Frederick Law Olmsted's Writings on City Landscapes*, ed. S. B. Sutton (Cambridge: MIT Press, 1971), pp. 94, 96.

52. For Whitman, see Number III (October 28, 1849) of "Letters from a Travelling Bachelor," rpt. in Joseph Jay Rubin, *The Historic Whitman* (University Park: Penn State University Press, 1973), pp. 318–323, and the poem "Give Me the Splendid Silent Sun" (1865). For Olmsted, a representative statement is "Observations on the Progress of Improvements in Street Plans, with Special Reference to the Parkway Proposed to be Laid Out in Brooklyn" (1868), *Civilizing American Cities*, pp. 23–42.

53. Whitman, *Journalism*, vol. 1, pp. 414, 424, 431, 433; "Brooklyn Parks," (April 17, 1858 editorial), *I Sit and Look Out*, pp. 140–141.

54. See Whitman, *Journalism*, vol. 1, pp. 169–172, 470. Whitman did not, so far as I know, comment on Olmsted's plan, but the attitude expressed by his journalism during the 1840s and 1850s seems more compatable with the rejected designs for Central Park, most of which stressed the "associational and educational purposes" of the park

by making the Croton Reservoir "the centerpiece of the park and . . . placing a promenade along its high retaining walls." David Schuyler, *The New Urban Landscape: The Redefinition of City Form in Nineteenth-Century America* (Baltimore: Johns Hopkins University Press, 1986), p. 84.

55. See, for example, Nelson Manfred Blake, *Water for the Cities: A History of the Urban Water Supply Problem in the United States* (Syracuse: Syracuse University Press, 1956), and Stanley K. Schultz and Clay McShane, "To Engineer the Metropolis: Sewers, Sanitation, and City Planning in Late Nineteenth-Century America," *Journal of American History*, 65 (1978): 389–411.

56. Brand, *The Spectator and the City*, p. 185.

57. James Joyce, *Ulysses* (1922), ed. Hans Walter Gabler et al. (London: Bodley Head, 1986), p. 133.

58. Michel de Certeau, *The Practice of Everyday Life*, trans. Stephen Rendall (Berkeley: University of California Press, 1984), pp. 93, 98.

59. One could argue that Bloom is *both* ordinary *and* subversive. Vincent Cheng discusses the symptomatic example of his oscillation between orientalizing stereotypes and exceptional (subversive?) capacity for projecting himself into the subject position of racial others, for example, imagining how cannibals might digest missionaries. *Joyce, Race, and Empire* (Cambridge: Cambridge University Press, 1995), pp. 175–184.

60. Thomas Moore, "The Meeting of the Waters," *Poetical Works of Thomas Moore*, ed. A. D. Godley (London: Oxford University Press, 1929), p. 185.

61. Simmel, *On Individuality and Social Forms*, pp. 325, 327–328, 330–331, 337–338.

62. Ibid., p. 324.

63. "A Painful Case," *Dubliners* (1919; New York: Modern Library, 1954), p. 134.

64. Quoted in Frank Delaney, *James Joyce's Odyssey: A Guide to the Dublin of "Ulysses"* (New York: Holt, 1981), p. 10. Michael Long concisely summarizes Joyce's evolution from conventional modernist urban nausea to urban affirmation in "Eliot, Pound, Joyce: Unreal City?" *Unreal City: Urban Experience in Modern European Literature and Art*, ed. Edward Timms and David Kelley (Manchester: Manchester University Press, 1985), pp. 144–157.

65. Joyce, *Ulysses*, p. 545.

66. For example, Sharpe, *Unreal Cities*, and Burton Pike, *The Image of the City in Modern Literature* (Princeton: Princeton University Press, 1981).

67. Simmel, *On Individuality and Social Forms*, p. 335.

68. Bloom illustrates what Tony Hiss calls "simultaneous perception"—a "sixth sense" that allows one to attend to multiple stimuli simultaneously, anticipate others' movements in public spaces, and relax the borders between one's personal body/space and that of others. *The Experience of Place* (New York: Random, 1990), pp. 19–21 and passim.

69. Hana Wirth-Nesher, *City Codes: Reading the Modern Urban Novel* (Cambridge: Cambridge University Press, 1996), p. 164.

70. Michael Seidel, *Epic Geography: James Joyce's "Ulysses"* (Princeton: Princeton University Press, 1976), emphasizes the tour-de-forcical minuteness with which the narrative geography of the *Odyssey* is encoded in the landscape of *Ulysses* as its plot unfolds.

71. Virginia Woolf, *Mrs. Dalloway* (New York: Harcourt, 1925), p. 12.

72. Henri Lefebvre, "Perspective or Prospective?" *Right to the City* (1968), rpt. in *Writings on Cities*, trans. and ed. Eleonore Kofman and Elizabeth Lebas (Cambridge: Blackwell, 1996), pp. 172–173.

73. Susan M. Squier, *Virginia Woolf and London: The Sexual Politics of the City* (Chapel Hill: University of North Carolina Press, 1985), sees Clarissa's "empathetic union with her surroundings" (p. 98) as a way of overcoming class barriers; Rachel Bowlby, treating other among Woolf's London writings in "Walking, Women and Writing: Virginia Woolf as *flâneuse*," *New Feminist Discourses*, ed. Isobel Armstrong (London: Routledge, 1992), pp. 26–47, places primary emphasis on female appropriation of the traditionally "masculine identity" (p. 29) of the *flâneur*.

74. This claim admittedly runs afoul of two strong, mutually discrepant readings of *Mrs. Dalloway* that stress agency—the feminist reading of Clarissa as "*flâneuse*" and a reading of the novel as a classist text: "Clarissa inhabits a city that, by virtue of her social class, can be experienced as a small town and can be appropriated for the sake of her aesthetic sensibility and spiritual needs." Wirth-Nesher, *City Codes*, p. 188.

75. For this and other insights into Woolf's ecocultural phenomenology, see Louise Westling, "Virginia Woolf and the Flesh of the World," *New Literary History*, 30 (Autumn 1999): 855–876, and Carol H. Cantrell, "'The Locus of Compossibility': Virginia Woolf, Modernism, and Place," *ISLE*, 52 (1998): 25–40.

76. Woolf, *Mrs. Dalloway*, pp. 122–123.

77. James Donald, in a thoughtfully evenhanded reading of the novel, diagnoses Smith's "hysteria" and Mrs. Dalloway's "neurasthenia" as urban disorders, arising from the sense of "boundaries between self and environment, like those between past and present, or male and female, becom[ing] uncertain and unreliable." "This, Here, Now: Imagining the Modern City," *Imagining Cities: Scripts, Signs, Memory*, ed. Sallie Westwood and John Williams (London: Routledge, 1997), pp. 193–194.

78. William Carlos Williams, *I Wanted to Write a Poem*, ed. Edith Heal (Boston: Beacon, 1958), p. 8. Stephen Tapscott, *American Beauty: William Carlos Williams and the Modernist Whitman* (New York: Columbia University Press, 1984), traces Williams's reserve to his friend Ezra Pound's youthful condescension toward Whitman (pp. 21–28), as well as to other modernist appraisals. See also Williams's important "An Essay on 'Leaves of Grass,'" *"Leaves of Grass" 100 Years After*, ed. Milton Hindus (Stanford: Stanford University Press, 1955), pp. 22–31.

79. Williams resided in suburban Rutherford, but he thought of Paterson, where he worked, as "my city."

80. *The Collected Earlier Poems of William Carlos Williams* (New York: New Directions, 1966), pp. 3, 459, 204, 389, 393, 300, 309–310.

81. Michael Hough, *Cities and Natural Process*, pp. 6, 8.

82. Williams, *Collected Earlier Poems*, pp. 96–97.

83. Nicholson-Lord, *The Greening of the Cities*, p. 90, which cites Richard Mabey as the originator of the phrase.

84. Subsequent quotations are from Williams, *Paterson*, rev. ed., ed. Christopher MacGowan (New York: New Directions, 1992). I concentrate on Books I–IV; Book V and the

fragmentary notes for Book VI were a belated revisitation, albeit important as testimony to the inherent endlessness of Williams's project. MacGowan's notes, as well as Benjamin Sankey, *A Companion to William Carlos Williams's "Paterson"* (Berkeley: University of California Press, 1971), and Joel Conarroe, *William Carlos Williams' "Paterson": Language and Landscape* (Philadelphia: University of Pennsylvania Press, 1970), provide introductory commentaries. On *Paterson* as an attempt to textualize the city, see also William Sharpe, "'That Complex Atom': The City and Form in William Carlos Williams's *Paterson*," *Poesis*, 6, no. 1 (1985): 65–93. Briefly as to structure: Book I establishes the literal/historical/archetypal landscape, establishes Paterson as "the giant in whose apertures we cohabit," linking city to persona and persona to citizenry ("Who are these people . . . among whom I see myself in the regularly ordered plateglass of his thoughts" [p. 9]) as well as to a range of historical figures. Books II and III loosely (re)process Paterson's physical, social, and historical landscapes from the standpoint of a stroll in the park (II) and a visit to the library (III), the latter's three sections each built around episodes of (respectively) tornado, fire, and flood that ravaged Paterson. Book IV focuses on a series of disintegrative forces: the lure of cosmopolitan metropolis personified by a wealthy lesbian New Yorker attempting to seduce a salty young working-class woman from Paterson; radiation and capitalism seen as comparable forms of cancer; and the degradation and demise of the Passaic River as it flows from city into the sea.

85. Williams to Harvey Breit, 1942, quoted in Paul Mariani, *William Carlos Williams: A New World Naked* (New York: McGraw-Hill, 1981), p. 459.

86. Tapscott, *American Beauty*, p. 17; Barry Ahearn, *William Carlos Williams and Alterity: The Early Poetry* (Cambridge: Cambridge University Press, 1994), p. 160. For the Pound-Williams connection, see Michael André Bernstein, *The Tale of the Tribe: Ezra Pound and the Modern Verse Epic* (Princeton: Princeton University Press, 1980), pp. 191–224. Note that these scholars vary greatly in the emphasis they put on Williams's perceptual limitations.

87. Walter Scott Peterson, *An Approach to "Paterson"* (New Haven: Yale University Press, 1967), p. 165, cautions that we can't be positive that Paterson/Williams was the bitten one, but I follow Sankey, *Companion*, p. 153, on the evidence of the earlier encounter between P and Chichi (p. 27).

88. Richard Sennett, *The Conscience of the Eye: The Design and Social Life of Cities* (New York: Norton, 1990), p. 129; and *The Uses of Disorder: Personal Identity and City Life* (New York: Knopf, 1970), pp. 141, 149, 160.

89. Berry, "A Homage to Dr. Williams," *A Continuous Harmony* (San Diego: Harcourt, 1972), pp. 56, 57. When Williams himself speaks about the theory of place, he can sound quite like Berry, as when insisting that "far from being bound by" place, "only through it do we realize freedom . . . if we only make ourselves sufficiently aware of it" we shall "join with others in other places." Williams, "A Fatal Blunder," *Quarterly Review of Literature*, 2 (1944): 126. On Berry's interest in Williams, see Andrew J. Angyal, *Wendell Berry* (New York: Twayne, 1995), pp. 12, 40, and 52–53.

90. Gary Snyder, *The Practice of the Wild*, p. 27.

91. Dan Flores, "Place: Thinking about Bioregional History," *Bioregionalism*, ed. McGinnis, p. 44.

92. Tapscott, *American Beauty*, pp. 185–189, assembles the evidence of the Whitmanian allusion, including a draft of the section in which it is made explicit. The whole near-death-followed-by-emergence sequence seems to engage both Whitman and T. S. Eliot in ways too complex to discuss fully here: for example, the pull of the erotics of death for Whitman while saving him from himself, and the substance but not the tone of Eliot's insight at the end of *The Waste Land* that impotent modernity is left with "fragments" to "shore" against its ruins.

93. Randall Jarrell, "Introduction," *Selected Poems by William Carlos Williams* (New York: New Directions, 1955), pp. xi–xii.

94. Nicholson-Lord, *The Greening of the Cities*, p. 94.

95. Robert L. Dorman, *Revolt of the Provinces: The Regionalist Movement in America, 1920–1945* (Chapel Hill: University of North Carolina Press, 1993), p. 318.

96. George Zabriskie, "The Geography of *Paterson*," *Perspective*, 6 (1953): 211. It is instructive to compare Paterson with novelist John Updike's more conventional realist chronicle approach in *In the Beauty of the Lilies* (New York: Knopf, 1996), whose initial sections follow the declining fortunes of a particular white middle-class family during the first three decades of the twentieth century. *Lilies* provides a more detailed account of the city's economic and demographic change, including loss of self-sufficiency, but its family-and-individual-character focus subordinates "place" to "individuals" notwithstanding its descriptive richness.

97. Cf. Sankey, *Companion*, pp. 42, 171–172, who points out that Phyllis is both P's would-be lover and counterpart. There may be an anti-Eliot sideswipe here too: Joel Conarroe calls Corydon "a blood sister" of the lonely neurotic woman in Book II of *The Waste Land* (*William Carlos Williams' "Paterson,"* p. 23), which also builds on stylized contrast between genteel and working-class women.

98. Benton MacKaye, *The New Exploration: A Philosophy of Regional Planning* (1928; rpt., Urbana: University of Illinois Press, 1962), p. 151; Lewis Mumford, "In Defense of the City," in *Metropolitan Politics: A Reader*, ed. Michael N. Danielson (Boston: Little, Brown, 1966), p. 22.

99. John C. Thirwall, "William Carlos Williams' *Paterson:* The Search for the Redeeming Language—A Personal Epic in Five Parts," *New Directions*, 17 (1961): 276–277.

100. See, for example, these essays on the rehabilitation of Chattanooga, Tennessee: Steve Lerner, "Brave New City?" *The Amicus Journal* (Spring 1995): 22–28; Ted Bernard and Jora Young, *The Ecology of Hope: Communities Collaborate for Sustainability* (Gabriola Island, B.C.: New Society Publishers, 1997), pp. 60–71.

101. Quoted in Sankey, *Companion*, p. 180.

102. William R. Klink, "William Carlos Williams' *Paterson:* Literature and Urban History," *Urban Affairs Quarterly*, 23 (December 1987): 179 and passim.

103. As William Sharpe writes of Book V, the originally unplanned resumption of *Paterson*, "the poet finally conceives of the poem as a process grounded not in failed myth but in recurrent beginnings." "'That Complex Atom': The City and Form in William Carlos Williams's *Paterson*," p. 85.

104. *The Collected Poems of Frank O'Hara*, ed. Donald Allen (Berkeley: University of California Press, 1995), pp. 476–477.

105. Joy Harjo, "Anchorage," *She Had Some Horses* (New York: Thunder's Mouth Press, 1983), pp. 14–15.

106. In a 1989 retrospect, geologist and former Anchorage assemblywoman Lidia Selkregg was quoted as saying caustically of present-day officials and developers: "They want to think they are more powerful than God. Nature is nature." Paul Jenkins, "Has Alaska Learned from Its Quake?" *Los Angeles Times*, March 26, 1989, Metro pt. 2, p. 1.

107. Gary Snyder, *Mountains and Rivers Without End* (Washington, D.C.: Counterpoint, 1996), pp. 62–63.

108. See, for example, Hough, *Cities and Natural Process*, pp. 39–96; Spirn, *The Language of Landscape*, pp. 185–188, 213–214, 267–272, and passim (on restoration of Mill Creek area).

109. John Edgar Wideman, *Philadelphia Fire* (New York: Vintage, 1990), pp. 44–45.

110. Barry Cullingworth, *Planning in the USA: Policies, Issues, and Processes* (New York: Routledge, 1997), p. 233.

111. Wideman, *Philadelphia Fire*, p. 82.

112. Sheri Hoem, "John Edgar Wideman: Connecting Truths" (1984 interview), rpt. in *Conversations with John Edgar Wideman*, ed. Bonnie TuSmith (Jackson: University Press of Mississippi, 1998), p. 35.

4. Discourses of Determinism

1. See, for example, Jared Diamond, *Guns, Germs, and Steel: The Fates of Human Societies* (New York: Norton, 1997), which argues passionately for an environmental-determinist view of history (linking the rise and fall of civilizations to such ecological advantages as the availability of domesticable grains and animals) as an antidote to racism and civilizationalist complacency. See also Alfred W. Crosby, *Ecological Imperialism: The Biological Expansion of Europe, 900–1900* (Cambridge: Cambridge University Press, 1986), and, for a quirky but intriguing defense of climate determinism by an intellectual from the "South," Jayantanuka Bandyopahyaya, *Climate and World Order: An Inquiry into the Natural Cause of Underdevelopment* (Atlantic Highlands, N.J.: Humanities Press, 1983).

2. For example, Edwin Chadwick's landmark *Report on the Sanitary Condition of the Labouring Population of Great Britain*, ed. M. W. Flinn (1842; Edinburgh: Edinburgh University Press, 1965), claimed on the basis of extensive statistical compilations and eyewitness accounts that disease could be attributed to "atmospheric impurities produced by decomposing animal and vegetable substances, by damp and filth, and close and overcrowded dwellings," and "that where those circumstances are removed" disease would abate to the vanishing point (p. 422). Mary Poovey, *Making a Social Body: British Cultural Formation, 1830–1864* (Chicago: University of Chicago Press, 1995), pp. 36–37, 115–131, confirms the influence of Chadwick's statisticalism on British public policy, though I take a more positive view of his reformist zeal than she does. For statisticalism in nineteenth-century American literature's social representations, see Mark Seltzer, *Bodies and Machines* (London: Routledge, 1992), pp. 82–84, 93–118, and passim.

3. Herbert Spencer, *Principles of Sociology,* vol. 1, 3rd. ed. (New York: Appleton, 1895), pp. 437–450. On the ideas and influence of Spencer and his American popularizers, see Ronald E. Martin, *American Literature and the Universe of Force* (Durham: Duke University Press, 1981), pp. 32–95.

4. Robert M. Young, "Darwinism *Is* Social," *The Darwinian Heritage,* ed. David Kohn (Princeton: Princeton University Press, 1985), pp. 609–638.

5. George Levine, *Darwin among the Novelists: Patterns of Science in Victorian Fiction* (Chicago: University of Chicago Press, 1988), pp. 21–55.

6. For Victorian writing, in addition to Levine, *Darwin among the Novelists,* see especially Gillian Beer, *Darwin's Plots: Evolutionary Narrative in Darwin, George Eliot and Nineteenth-Century Fiction* (London: Routledge, 1983), and James Krasner, *The Entangled Eye: Visual Perception and the Representation of Nature in Post-Darwinian Narrative* (New York: Oxford University Press, 1992).

7. See, for example, Alexander Welsh, *The City of Dickens* (Oxford: Clarendon Press, 1971), chapter 2 and passim; and F. S. Schwarzbach, *Dickens and the City* (London: Athlone Press, 1979). Dickens's ex-cathedra commitment to urban writing began with his first career as parliamentary reporter and culminated with the periodical he edited, *Household Words* (1850–1859), which includes many reformist pieces he wrote or coedited (see *Charles Dickens' Uncollected Writings from "Household Words,"* 2 vols., ed. Harry Stone [Bloomington: Indiana University Press, 1968]).

8. Georg Simmel, "The Metropolis and Mental Life" (1903), in *On Individuality and Social Forms,* ed. Donald N. Levine (Chicago: University of Chicago Press, 1971), pp. 324–339. See also Robert E. Park's essay, influenced by Simmel, "The City: Suggestions for the Investigation of Human Behavior in the City Environment," *American Journal of Sociology,* 20 (1915): 608–609: "The small community often tolerates eccentricity. The city, on the contrary, rewards it."

9. Ralph Waldo Emerson, "Experience," in *Collected Works,* vol. 3, ed. Joseph Slater et al. (Cambridge: Harvard University Press, 1983), p. 31. The Emerson-Dickens analogy also shows Dickens's transitionalness, for it is often no more explicit in him than it is in Emerson that such temperamental hyperfocus is a distinctively urban trait; both writers draw on traditions of caricature that had been staples of satire since antiquity. Welsh, *The City of Dickens,* p. 9.

10. F. S. Schwarzbach, *"Bleak House:* The Social Pathology of Urban Life," *Literature and Medicine,* 9 (1990): 95, and his *Dickens and the City,* pp. 125–127. For Dickens's interest in sanitary reform, see also his speeches of 1850 and 1851 before the London Metropolitan Sanitary Commission, of which he was a member: *Speeches of Charles Dickens,* ed. K. J. Fielding (Atlantic Highlands, N.J.: Humanities Press, 1988), pp. 104–109, 127–132. Dickens here follows the current "miasmatic" theory of contagious disease as originating from dirt and effluvia.

11. Dickens, *Little Dorrit* (1857; New York: Oxford University Press, 1953), pp. 28–29, 30, 31. Subsequent page references are given in parentheses.

12. See D. A. Miller, *Narrative and Its Discontents: Problems of Closure in the Traditional Novel* (Princeton: Princeton University Press, 1981), pp. 42–43. As Douglass Hewitt

writes, the plot "is not merely implausible; it is surely deliberately perfunctory." *The Approach to Fiction* (London: Longman's, 1972), p. 89.

13. J. Hillis Miller, *Charles Dickens: The World of His Novels* (1958; rpt., Bloomington: Indiana University Press, 1973), p. 101.

14. Hewitt, *The Approach to Fiction*, pp. 113–121, forecloses too abruptly on the out-door-indoor contrast by claiming that such solace as Amy finds on the Iron Bridge is a mere fantasy arising from her association of this place with Clennam, at odds with the actual grimness of the scene—though admittedly it is rather pathetic that the bridge feels to Amy like a place of "natural" freedom.

15. Miller, *Charles Dickens*, p. 295.

16. George Levine, *Darwin among the Novelists*, in a comparison that emphasizes Darwin's interest in Dickens's novels as well as their affinities with Darwinism, rightly concludes that for all the affinities between them Dickens "always struggled back toward the possibilities of essentialist thought and morality" (p. 151). Levine sees *Little Dorrit* as more influenced by the model of thermodynamics (the threat of entropy, specifically) than by Darwinism (pp. 153–176).

17. Amy Dorrit is, of course, also based on an essentialized type—the Wordsworthian sinless child, like Stowe's little Eva or Dickens's own little Paul and little Nell. But what is especially distinctive about her is the accompanying diagnosis of infantile innocence as a pathology wrought by circumstance.

18. Philip Collins, "Dickens and the City," in *Visions of the Modern City*, ed. William Sharpe and Leonard Wallock (New York: Columbia University Press, 1983), p. 99.

19. Anthony Vidler, *The Architectural Uncanny: Essays in the Modern Unhomely* (Cambridge: MIT Press, 1992), pp. 11, 200.

20. Chadwick, *Report*, p. 94, quoting from a report on the towns of Durham, Barnard Castle, and Carlisle.

21. Charles F. Wingate, "The Unsanitary Homes of the Rich," *North American Review*, 137 (1883): 172–173; Nancy Tomes, *The Gospel of Germs: Men, Women, and the Microbe in American Life* (Cambridge: Harvard University Press, 1997), pp. 68–77.

22. Catherine Beecher, *Letters to the People on Health and Happiness* (New York: Harper, 1855), p. 92.

23. Henry David Thoreau, *Walden* (1854), ed. J. Lyndon Shanley (Princeton: Princeton University Press, 1971), p. 84. Before winter came, however, Thoreau filled in the chinks. Thoreau's concern for his health (including sexual) comes out especially in *Walden* in his anxiety about diet ("Higher Laws"), though this is sublimated into a discourse of moral purity. See Christopher Sellers, "Thoreau's Body: Towards an Embodied Environmental History," *Environmental History*, 4 (October 1999): 486–514.

24. Gaston Bachelard, *The Poetics of Space*, trans. Maria Jolas (1958; Boston: Beacon Press, 1964), p. 32.

25. To be sure, dream-like destabilization has its own social-mimetic function—underscoring the disorientation attendant on trying to process multitudinous, dispersed urban inputs: see Taylor Stoehr, *Dickens: The Dreamer's Stance* (Ithaca: Cornell University Press, 1965), pp. 88–90.

26. I follow Lee Clark Mitchell's test of literary determinism, "a conception of men and women living as if no longer responsible for whatever they happen to do" (*Determined Fictions: American Literary Naturalism* [New York: Columbia University Press, 1989], p. 31)—that is, not whether or not they are credited with forethought or exercising choice, but whether such forethought or choice as they may show seems overridden by circumstance.

27. Upton Sinclair, *The Jungle* (1906; rpt., New York: Harper's, 1946), pp. 27–29, 72; Jack London, review of *The Jungle*, in *Novels and Social Writings*, ed. Donald Pizer (New York: Library of America, 1982), p. 1145.

28. Zola, *Germinal* (1885), trans. L. W. Tancock (Baltimore: Penguin, 1954), p. 136.

29. Jacob Riis, *How the Other Half Lives: Studies among the Tenements of New York*, ed. David Laviatin (1890; Boston: Bedford, 1996), pp. 69, 70, 72, 79, 201, 235.

30. Wright's encapsulation in his retrospective, "How 'Bigger' Was Born": "an indescribable city, huge, roaring, dirty, noisy, raw, stark, brutal; a city of extremes; torrid summers and sub-zero winters, white people and black people, the English language and strange tongues, foreign born and native born, scabby poverty and gaudy luxury, high idealism and hard cynicism! . . . A city which has become the pivot of the Eastern, Western, Northern, and Southern poles of the nation. But a city whose black smoke clouds shut out the sunshine for seven months of the year; a city in which, on a fine balmy May morning, one can sniff the stench of the stockyards; a city where people have grown so used to gangs and murders and graft that they have honestly forgotten that government can have a pretense of decency!" Richard Wright, *Early Works*, ed. Arnold Rampersad (New York: Library of America, 1984), pp. 872–873.

31. *Native Son*, ibid., pp. 447, 449, 456, 453.

32. Wright, "Ethnographic Aspects" and "Bibliography," ed. Michel Fabre, *New Letters*, 39 (Fall 1972): 61–75.

33. For Wright's introduction, see St. Clair Drake and Horace R. Cayton, *Black Metropolis: A Study of Negro Life in a Northern City* (New York: Harcourt, 1945), pp. xvii–xxxiv. For analysis of Wright and Chicago sociology, see especially Carla Cappetti, "Sociology of an Existence: Richard Wright and the Chicago School," *MELUS*, 12, no. 2 (1985): 25–43, and her *Writing Chicago: Modernism, Ethnography and the Novel* (New York: Columbia University Press, 1993), pp. 182–210; Werner Sollors, "Modernization as Adultery: Richard Wright, Zora Neale Hurston, and American Culture of the 1930s and 1940s," *Hebrew University Studies in Literature and the Arts*, 18 (1990): 134–143, and his "Anthropological and Sociological Tendencies in American Literature of the 1930's and 1940's: Richard Wright, Zora Neale Hurston, and American Culture," *Looking Inward, Looking Outward: From the 1930s Through the 1940s*, ed. Steve Ickringill (Amsterdam: VU University Press, 1990), pp. 22–75.

34. Wright, *12 Million Black Voices*, in *The Richard Wright Reader*, ed. Ellen Wright and Michel Fabre (New York: Harper, 1973), p. 212; Wright, *Native Son*, pp. 606, 452, 451.

35. Brooks, "Kitchenette Building," *A Street in Bronzeville*, collected in *Blacks* (Chicago: Third World Press, 1986), p. 20. For Wright's reaction to this book, see

Michel Fabre, *Richard Wright: Books and Writers* (Jackson, Miss.: University Press of Mississippi, 1990), p. 18. "Bronzeville" was one of the nicknames of the South Side Chicago black community for their neighborhood. Drake and Cayton, *Black Metropolis*, pp. 383–385.

36. Wright, "Introduction," *Black Metropolis*, p. xx. As "men became atoms crowding great industrial cities," Wright observes, "clocks replaced the sun as a symbolic measurement of time" (p. xxii).

37. Sollors, "Modernization as Adultery," pp. 112–116, and "Anthropological and Sociological Tendencies," pp. 23–40.

38. *The Autobiography of Upton Sinclair* (New York: Harcourt, 1962), pp. 110–114, 127.

39. As Sinclair's montage suggests, environmental determinism could figure in the literature of country as well as city life, as with the grimmer rural tales of Sarah Orne Jewett and Mary Wilkins Freeman. More on that below.

40. Michel Fabre, however, claims that the film's producer Pierre Chenal "insisted that Wright play the lead" and that "he consented" more "out of a desire to express everything that he had put in the novel, and from curiosity about his ability to do so, than from any ambition to shine as an actor." *The Unfinished Quest of Richard Wright*, trans. Isabel Barzun (New York: William Morrow, 1973), p. 338.

41. Wright, "How 'Bigger' Was Born," *Early Works*, pp. 867, 874, 866. In *Native Son* Bigger's attorney Max uses similar language to characterize Bigger as a "test symbol" isolated by "the complex forces of society," "like a germ stained for examination under the microscope" that provides the key to "our whole sick social organism" (p. 804).

42. Seltzer, *Bodies and Machines*, pp. 109, 105 (emphasis his).

43. Louis Wirth, "A Bibliography of the Urban Community," in Robert E. Park, Ernest W. Burgess, and Roderick D. McKenzie, *The City* (1925; rpt., Chicago: University of Chicago Press, 1967), pp. 187–188. A significant link between Chicago socioecology and the green design tradition is the holistic personification of the city as organism, which is key to the thinking of such urban and regional planning theorists as Patrick Geddes, Ebenezer Howard, Benton MacKaye, and Lewis Mumford, who have influenced contemporary green design theory from Ian McHarg's *Design with Nature* (Garden City, N.Y.: Natural History Press, 1969) to the present.

44. The confusions and fallacies inherent in Chicago ecology's reliance on biological models were first critiqued by Milla Aïssa Alihan, *Social Ecology: A Critical Analysis* (New York: Columbia University Press, 1938). For more recent appraisals, see Brian J. L. Berry and John D. Kasarda, *Contemporary Urban Ecology* (New York: Macmillan, 1977), pp. 3–18, and Lester Kurtz, *Evaluating Chicago Sociology* (Chicago: University of Chicago Press, 1984), pp. 17–29. As Alihan points out, the key architects of socioecological theory were the three primary coauthors of *The City*, but she rightly includes Wirth as accepting and elaborating their models. Two exemplary works read with interest by Wright were Wirth's *The Ghetto* (Chicago: University of Chicago, 1928) and his "Urbanism as a Way of Life," *American Journal of Sociology*, 44 (1938): 1–24. Ironically, the Chicago sociologists showed little interest in the Chicago life scientists' important work on population ecology. Greg Mitman, *The State of Nature: Ecology,*

Community, and American Social Thought, 1900–1950 (Chicago: University of Chicago Press, 1992), pp. 91–92.

45. William Wordsworth, "Lines Composed a Few Miles above Tintern Abbey," in *William Wordsworth: The Poems*, vol. 1, ed. John O. Hayden (New Haven: Yale University Press, 1981), p. 361; Ralph Waldo Emerson, *Nature*, in *Collected Works*, vol. 1, ed. Robert E. Spiller et al. (Cambridge: Harvard University Press, 1971), p. 39.

46. As Jonathan Bate observes in his reading of *Frankenstein* as a commentary on Rousseau, this wonderment is doomed to be disappointed because "it is Enlightenment man who invents the natural man." Bate, *Song of the Earth* (Cambridge: Harvard University Press, 2000), p. 52.

47. The modern antecedents of this countryside-nation symbolism go back to medieval times, as Raymond Williams showed in *The Country and the City* (New York: Oxford University Press, 1973). For the ideology's nineteenth-century crystallization, see Elizabeth K. Helsinger, *Rural Scenes and National Representation: Britain, 1815–1850* (Princeton: Princeton University Press, 1997). For a thoughtful short critical discussion linking two instances rarely paired, see Jonathan Bate, "Culture and Environment: From Austen to Hardy," *New Literary History*, 30 (1999): 541–560, revised as chapter 1 of *Song of the Earth*. Martin J. Wiener, *English Culture and the Decline of the Industrial Spirit 1850–1980* (1981; rpt., New York: Penguin, 1992), pp. 27–80, is helpful, albeit schematic, in his diagnosis of the ideology of English ruralism specifically as a recoil against the Industrial Revolution, entailing an attempt to shift England's iconic center of gravity from industrialized "North" to rural "South." See also Alun Howkins, "The Discovery of Rural England," *Englishness: Politics and Culture 1880–1920*, ed. Robert Colls and Philip Dodd (London: Croom Helm, 1986), pp. 62–89.

48. See, for example, Perry Miller, "Nature and the National Ego," (1954), rpt. in Miller, *Errand into the Wilderness* (Cambridge: Harvard University Press, 1956), pp. 204–216; Leo Marx, *The Machine and the Garden: Technology and the Pastoral Ideal in America* (New York: Oxford University Press, 1964); Roderick Nash, *Wilderness and the American Mind*, 3rd ed. (New Haven: Yale University Press, 1982); Myra Jehlen, *American Incarnation: The Individual, the Nation, and the Continent* (Cambridge: Harvard University Press, 1986); and Glen A. Love, "*Et in Arcadia Ego*: Pastoral Theory Meets Ecocriticism," *Western American Literature*, 27 (1992): 197–207, for a cluster of significant assessments that range across the spectrum from affirmation of (some version of) nature and/or wilderness as enabling national symbol to deconstruction of nature discourse as protective cover for expansionist ideology.

49. John Rennie Short, *Imagined Country: Environment, Culture and Society* (London: Routledge, 1991), p. 35—in the course of a comparative study of landscapes held to be quintessential of Britain, Australia, and the United States.

50. George Crabbe, *The Village* (1784), II.2, *The Poetical Works of George Crabbe*, ed. A. J. Carlyle and R. M. Carlyle (London: Henry Froude for Oxford University Press, 1908), p. 38.

51. Ann Radcliffe, *The Mysteries of Udolpho*, ed. Bonamy Dobrée (1794; New York: Oxford University Press, 1966), pp. 224, 226–227.

52. George Perkins Marsh, *Man and Nature,* ed. David Lowenthal (1864; Cambridge: Harvard University Press, 1965), pp. 226, 188.

53. Ibid., p. 43. However, George Levine rightly notes that Darwinian "theory was easily assimilable to both an anthropocentric—indeed Eurocentric—view of nature and a teleology whose final cause was the fullest development of mankind." *Darwin among the Novelists,* p. 27.

54. John Burroughs, "The Divine Soil," *Leaf and Tendril* (Boston: Houghton, 1908), pp. 231, 233. Burroughs continued a reluctant materialist to the last, however (see "A Critical Glance into Darwin," *The Last Harvest* [Boston: Houghton, 1922], pp. 172–200). Unsurprisingly, Burroughs responded most positively to the residue of teleological thinking in Darwin, especially in *The Descent of Man* (see Edward J. Renehan, Jr., *John Burroughs: An American Naturalist* [Post Mills, Vt.: Chelsea Green, 1992], p. 154).

55. Burroughs, "The Natural Providence," *Accepting the Universe* (Boston: Houghton, 1920), pp. 104, 103.

56. Scott Slovic, "Epistemology and Politics in American Nature Writing: Embedded Rhetoric and Discrete Rhetoric," *Green Culture: Environmental Rhetoric in Contemporary America,* ed. Carl G. Herndl and Stuart C. Brown (Madison: University of Wisconsin Press, 1996), pp. 82–110, provides a subtle, thoughtful discussion of nature writing's rhetorical strategies of implicit ethical and political self-positioning.

57. Mary Austin, *Land of Little Rain* (1903), in *Stories from the Country of Lost Borders,* ed. Marjorie Pryse (New Brunswick: Rutgers University Press, 1987), p. 17.

58. Edwin Markham, "The Man with the Hoe" (1899), in *American Poetry: The Nineteenth Century,* vol. 2, ed. John Hollander (New York: Library of America, 1993), p. 496.

59. Thomas Hardy, "In a Wood" (1898), in *The Complete Poems of Thomas Hardy,* ed. James Gibbon (New York: Macmillan, 1976), pp. 64–65.

60. Thomas Hardy, *Tess of the d'Urbervilles* (1891), ed. Scott Elledge (New York: Norton, 1965), pp. 330, 133.

61. Ibid., p. 9.

62. Beer, *Darwin's Plots,* p. 240.

63. Theodore Dreiser, *A Selection of Uncollected Prose,* ed. Donald Pizer (Detroit: Wayne State University Press, 1977), pp. 89, 216–217, 247: statements from 1896, 1918–1919, and 1929, respectively. Haeckel promulgated a monistic "law of substance" that purported to rule out "the three central dogmas of Metaphysics—God, freedom, and immortality," "assigning mechanical causes to phenomena everywhere." *The Riddle of the Universe,* trans. Joseph McCabe (New York: Harper, 1900), p. 232.

64. Dreiser, "A Counsel to Perfection," *Hey Rub-a-Dub-Dub: A Book of the Mystery and Wonder and Terror of Life* (New York: Boni and Liveright, 1920), p. 119; *Uncollected Prose,* p. 288; and *A Book about Myself* (New York: Boni and Liveright, 1922), pp. 457–458. Interestingly, Dreiser attached his theory of human futility to a Tocquevillian theory of American institutions as conducing to mass identity: "they are not after individuals; they are after types or schools of individuals, all to be very much alike." "Life, Art, and America," *Hey Rub-a-Dub-Dub,* p. 260.

65. Encomium from 1955 interview, diagnosis from unpublished essay, "Personalism," quoted by Michel Fabre, *Richard Wright: Books and Writers*, pp. 40, 41. At the end of his life Wright declared that "I'd give all [the great novelists] for one book by Dreiser: he encompasses them all" (ibid., p. 42).

66. Dreiser, *Uncollected Prose*, pp. 110, 141, 229.

67. Martin, *American Literature and the Universe of Force*, pp. 216–220.

68. Dreiser, *Dawn* (New York: Liveright, 1931), pp. 158, 156; *A Book about Myself*, pp. 19, 393. The long passage quoted here, from *A Book about Myself*, exemplifies what Christophe Den Tandt calls Dreiser's "gesture of pseudo-totalization": pseudo, because the view it provides is a stylized melodramatization of unknowable forces. *The Urban Sublime in American Literary Naturalism* (Urbana: University of Illinois Press, 1998), pp. 33–40.

69. Dreiser, *A Hoosier Holiday*, ed. Douglas Brinkley (1916; rpt., Bloomington: Indiana University Press, 1997), pp. 178, 66–68; *The Color of a Great City* (New York: Boni and Liveright, 1923), pp. 199, 204.

70. Dreiser, *Sister Carrie* (1900), ed. James L. W. West III et al. (Philadelphia: University of Pennsylvania Press, 1981), pp. 119, 157.

71. David E. E. Stone, *Sister Carrie: Theodore Dreiser's Sociological Tragedy* (New York: Twayne, 1992), p. 80; cf. Richard Lehan, "*Sister Carrie:* The City, the Self, and the Modes of Narrative Discourse," *New Essays on "Sister Carrie,"* ed. Donald Pizer (Cambridge: Cambridge University Press, 1991), pp. 65–85, and Philip Fisher, *Hard Facts: Setting and Form in the American Novel* (New York: Oxford University Press, 1985), pp. 155–178.

72. Dreiser, *The Titan* (1914; rpt., New York: New American Library, 1965), pp. 155, 157.

73. In *The Genius* (1915; rpt., New York: Boni & Liveright, 1923), the artist-protagonist's first glimpse of the very same Chicago River scene—"dirty, gloomy, but crowded with boats and lined with great warehouses, grain elevators, coal pockets"—fires his imagination with the thought that "here was something that could be done brilliantly in black—a spot of red or green for ship and bridge lights" (p. 37).

74. *The Titan*, p. 157. The mellowness of tone is somewhat at odds with Cowperwood's mood of impatience at this moment but congruent with the novel's prevailing conception of him as aesthetically sensitive, sensual, observant.

75. Robinson Jeffers, "Their Beauty Has More Meaning," *Collected Poetry*, vol. 3, ed. Tim Hunt (Stanford: Stanford University Press, 1991), p. 119.

76. Quotation from Jeffers, "Sign-Post," *Collected Poetry*, vol. 2, p. 418. The question of Jeffers's theology is much discussed, with many arguing the case for his theism, the most cogent presentation being William Everson, "All Flesh Is Grass," *Robinson Jeffers: Dimensions of a Poet*, ed. Robert Brophy (New York: Fordham University Press, 1995), pp. 204–238. I would start by taking "Things are the God" quite literally, recognizing that this kind of expression intends that sheer materiality feel numinous. Patrick D. Murphy thoughtfully characterizes Jeffers as a proto-Gaian thinker who falls short

chiefly in not being able to find a place for humankind within the natural order. "Robinson Jeffers, Gary Snyder, and the Problem of Civilization," *Robinson Jeffers and a Galaxy of Writers*, ed. William B. Thesing (Columbia: University of South Carolina Press, 1995), pp. 95–99.

77. Jeffers, "Inscription for a Gravestone" and "Roan Stallion," *Collected Poetry*, vol. 2, p. 125; vol. 1, p. 189.

78. Robert Zaller, *The Cliffs of Solitude: A Reading of Robinson Jeffers* (Cambridge: Cambridge University Press, 1983), p. 197; Jeffers, "Rock and Hawk" and "The Low Sky," *Collected Poetry*, vol. 2, pp. 416, 111.

79. Jeffers, "Calm and Full the Ocean," *Collected Poetry*, vol. 3, p. 124.

80. Czeslaw Milosz, *Visions from San Francisco Bay*, trans. Richard Lourie (New York: Farrar, Straus, 1982), p. 92. Cf. Alan Soldofsky, "Nature and the Symbolic Order: The Dialogue Between Czeslaw Milosz and Robinson Jeffers," *Robinson Jeffers: Dimensions of a Poet*, ed. Brophy, pp. 177–203.

81. In his preface to *The Double-Axe and Other Poems* (New York: Random House, 1948), p. vii, Jeffers characterizes "inhumanism" as "a shifting of emphasis and significance from man to not-man; the rejection of human solipsism and recognition of the transhuman magnificence."

82. Jeffers, "The World's Wonders," *Collected Poetry*, vol. 3, p. 371.

83. Jeffers, "Boats in a Fog," *Collected Poetry*, vol. 1, p. 110.

84. Jeffers, "What Are Cities For?" and "The Place for No Story," *Collected Poetry*, vol. 2, pp. 418, 157.

85. Jane Addams, *Twenty Years at Hull-House*, ed. James Hurt (1910; rpt., Urbana: University of Illinois Press, 1990), p. 159.

86. Wendell Berry, "The Regional Motive," *A Continuous Harmony* (New York: Harcourt, 1972), p. 67. This is a gloss on his definition of healthy regionalism as *"Local life aware of itself."*

87. Berry, "Writer and Region," *What Are People For?* (San Francisco: North Point, 1990), p. 85.

88. On Chicago's South Side, see William Julius Wilson, *When Work Disappears* (New York: Vintage, 1996), pp. 51–86 and passim; for Berry country, see his *The Unsettling of America: Culture and Agriculture* (San Francisco: Sierra Club, 1977), especially chapters 1–6, 8.

89. Wendell Berry, "Stay Home," *Collected Poems, 1957–1982* (San Francisco: North Point, 1985), p. 199.

90. Dickinson as quoted by Thomas Wentworth Higginson to Mary Elizabeth Channing Higginson (1870), *The Letters of Emily Dickinson*, vol. 2, ed. Thomas H. Johnson and Theodora Ward (Cambridge: Harvard University Press, 1958), p. 474; Brooks as per 1967 interview with Paul M. Angle, incorporated in Brooks, *Report from Part One* (Detroit: Broadside Press, 1972), p. 136.

91. Hortense J. Spillers, "Gwendolyn the Terrible: Propositions on Eleven Poems," *Shakespeare's Sisters* (1979), rpt. in Maria K. Moorty and Gary Smith, eds., *A Life*

Distilled: Gwendolyn Brooks, Her Poetry and Fiction (Urbana: University of Illinois Press, 1987), p. 226.

92. 1969 interview with George Stavros, incorporated in *Report from Part One*, p. 161.

93. In Berry's essays and poems, that is. His fiction focuses much more on the web of family and community relations. And the poems and essays always presuppose community, even when they do not foreground it.

94. Berry, "In This World," *Collected Poems, 1957–1982*, p. 112.

95. See, for instance, "Beverly Hills, Chicago," "The Lovers of the Poor," and "To a Winter Squirrel," in Brooks's collected poems *Blacks* (Chicago: Third World Press, 1994), pp. 128, 349, 437. All quotations are from this edition.

96. Gwendolyn Brooks, "The Sundays of Satin-Legs Smith," *Blacks*, p. 45.

97. *Report from Part One*, p. 170, from 1971 interview with Ida Lewis. The tradition in African-American writing, however, goes back to Dunbar, whose works Brooks read as a child. She remembered her mother telling her *"You* are going to be the *lady* Paul Laurence Dunbar" (ibid., p. 56).

98. Dickinson, poem 675, *The Poems of Emily Dickinson*, vol. 2, ed. R. W. Franklin (Cambridge: Harvard University Press, 1998), p. 653; Langston Hughes, *Collected Poems*, ed. Arnold Rampersad and David Roessel (New York: Knopf, 1994), p. 42. "Troubled Woman" first appeared in *The Weary Blues*.

99. Brooks, *Report from Part One*, p. 71.

100. A partial exception to the family values emphasis in Brooks is her treatment, in ibid., of midlife separation from her husband as a turning point in her unfolding life pilgrimage; but she more than makes up for this through the postreconciliation tributes to husband and marriage in *Report from Part Two* (Chicago: Third World Press, 1996).

101. Berry, "Elegy," *Collected Poems, 1957–1982*, p. 234.

102. Berry, ibid., p. 96; Brooks, *Blacks*, p. 502.

103. The extent of that shift, however, has been somewhat exaggerated by Brooks's commentators. Kathryne V. Lindberg, "Whose Canon? Gwendolyn Brooks: Founder at the Center of the 'Margins,'" *Gendered Modernisms: American Women Poets and Their Readers*, ed. Margaret Dickie and Thomas Travisano (Philadelphia: University of Pennsylvania Press, 1996), rightly points out that her "1967 announcement of a different public role for herself as poet, along with her embrace of the evolving role of New Black, might have been impossible and surely would not have been very forceful if she had not threaded a consistent meditation on racial and artistic self-construction . . . through her work" (p. 289).

104. Addams, *Twenty Years at Hull-House*, p. 254.

105. *Blacks*, p. 404, quoted from John Bartlow Martin, "The Strangest Place in Chicago," *Harper's*, 201 (December 1950): 87, a lengthy ethnographic-historical report, illustrated by Ben Shahn, that portrays individual residents respectfully, noting positive signs of community (several women's clubs, child care center) as well as overcrowding and blight, though at bottom seeing Mecca inhabitants as "imprisoned here

by the scarcity of dwellings for Negroes," their apartments arrayed "like tiers of cells in a prison cellblock" (pp. 94, 87).

106. George E. Kent, *A Life of Gwendolyn Brooks* (Lexington: University Press of Kentucky, 1990), p. 42. Kenny J. Williams, "The World of Satin-Legs, Mrs. Sallie, and the Blackstone Rangers: The Restricted Chicago of Gwendolyn Brooks," *A Life Distilled,* ed. Moorty and Smith, p. 60, notes the building's history, as does Martin.

107. Brooks, "A Song in the Front Yard," *Blacks,* p. 28.

108. Quoted in Kent, *A Life of Gwendolyn Brooks,* pp. 125, 128–130, 155.

109. Kent, *A Life of Gwendolyn Brooks,* pp. 212–213; *Life,* November 19, 1951.

110. Brooks, "In the Mecca," *Blacks,* p. 407. Subsequent references to this text given in parentheses. The Mecca "faced the Van der Rohe-designed Illinois Institute of Technology," which had bought up the Mecca property as well. D. H. Mehlem, *Gwendolyn Brooks: Poetry and the Heroic Voice* (Lexington: University Press of Kentucky, 1987), p. 160.

111. *Report from Part One,* p. 69.

112. Gayl Jones, "Community and Voice: Gwendolyn Brooks's 'In the Mecca,'" *A Life Distilled,* ed. Moorty and Smith, p. 195.

113. Brooks, *Blacks,* p. 438.

114. Berry, *Home Economics* (San Francisco: North Point, 1987), pp. 185–186; *The Unsettling of America,* p. 4.

115. Berry, *Clearing* (New York: Harcourt, 1977), p. 5. Further quotations from this text are given in parentheses.

116. Toni Morrison argues, in "City Limits, Village Values: Concepts of the Neighborhood in Black Fiction," *Literature and the Urban Experience,* ed. Michael Jay and Ann Chalmers Watts (New Brunswick: Rutgers University Press, 1981), p. 43, that "the absence of the ancestor, who cannot thrive in the dungeon of the city" helps explain urban alienation in African-American writing. Morrison cites a number of narratives of returns to small countries and villages as counterexamples and collateral evidence. Brooks's poetry also stresses the problem of deficits of kinship, community, and local history, though it shows scant nostalgia for country roots. All this is not to suggest that Berry's ascription to his region of communitarianism and a meaningful sense of the deep past is uniform within rural writing; on the contrary, as noted above regarding Hardy, Markham, Wharton, O'Neill, and others, urban literature has no monopoly on such naturalist themes as environmentally stunted mental and social horizons and personal/family/social dysfunctionallity.

117. Kent, *A Life of Gwendolyn Brooks,* p. 226.

118. D. H. Mehlem, "Afterword" to Kent, *Life of Gwendolyn Brooks,* p. 263.

119. Berry, "The New Politics of Community," *The Ecologist,* 29 (March/April 1999): 229–231, the centerpiece of which is a seventeen-point manifesto.

120. Item two of Berry's "New Politics" manifesto is "Always include local nature—the land, the water, the air, the native creatures—within the membership of the community" (p. 230). This consideration has become more a part of African-American

urban self-consciousness in the 1990s, at both the levels of popular culture and the intelligentsia, than it was for Brooks: see, for example, bell hooks, "Touching the Earth," *Sisters of the Yam* (Boston: South End Press, 1993); Peter H. Kahn, Jr.'s case studies of inner-city Houston families, *The Human Relationship with Nature: Development and Culture* (Cambridge: MIT Press, 1999), pp. 95–127; and the rise of environmental justice movements in minority communities discussed in Chapter 1.

121. Jane Addams, "A Modern Lear," *The Social Thought of Jane Addams,* ed. Christopher Lasch (Indianapolis: Bobbs-Merrill, 1965), pp. 108, 109, 114, 112.

122. Combining both lines of implication and giving them a further biographical turn, Shannon Jackson astutely suggests that Addams's essay "made a telling rhetorical link between the lives of workers and the lives of white, middle-class daughters, suggesting that such kinds of cross-class and cross-gender identifications could occur . . . by virtue of a shared experience under paternalism." Shannon Jackson, *Lines of Activity: Performance, Historiography, Hull-House Domesticity* (Ann Arbor: University of Michigan Press, 2000), pp. 80–81.

123. Addams argues that the self-restraint of Pullman's strikers goes to show that the code of "morals he had taught his men [sobriety, thrift, self-discipline] did not fail them in their hour of confusion." "A Modern Lear," p. 116.

124. Ibid., p. 122.

125. Ibid., p. 116.

5. Modernization and the Claims of the Natural World

1. William Faulkner, *Light in August* (1932; New York: Vintage, 1985), pp. 4–5.

2. Nollie W. Hickman, "Mississippi Forests," *A History of Mississippi,* vol. 2, ed. Richard Aubrey McLemore (Hattiesburg: University and College Press of Mississippi, 1973), pp. 217, 224.

3. Thomas D. Clark, *The Greening of the South* (Lexington: University Press of Kentucky, 1984), p. 34.

4. Nollie Hickman, *Mississippi Harvest: Lumbering in the Longleaf Pine Belt, 1840–1915* (University, Miss.: University of Mississippi, 1962), pp. 250–251.

5. Joseph Blotner, *Faulkner: A Biography,* vol. 1 (New York: Random House, 1974), p. 662.

6. Ilse Lind, "Faulkner and Nature," *Faulkner Studies,* 1 (1980): 115.

7. Frederick L. Gwynn and Joseph Blotner, eds., *Faulkner in the University* (New York: Vintage, 1965), p. 199.

8. Faulkner, *The Marble Faun* and *A Green Bough* (New York: Random House, n.d.), pp. 28–29.

9. E. N. Lowe, "Notes on Forests and Forestry in Mississippi," *Proceedings of the Third Southern Forestry Congress* (New Orleans: John J. Weihing, 1921), p. 195.

10. Faulkner, "Raid," *The Unvanquished* (New York: Vintage, 1966), p. 109.

11. Faulkner, "Nympholepsy," *Uncollected Stories,* ed. Joseph Blotner (New York: Vintage, 1981), p. 334.

12. Malcolm Cowley, *The Faulkner-Cowley File: Letters and Memories, 1944–1962* (New York: Viking, 1966), p. 111. John M. Barry, *Rising Tide: The Great Mississippi Flood of 1927 and How It Changed America* (New York: Simon & Schuster, 1997), is a readable history.

13. Faulkner mistakenly thought the flood simply to be "inherent in the geography and the climate." Gwynn and Blotner, eds., *Faulkner in the University*, p. 176. Barry, *Rising Tide*, emphasizes how aggressive channelization and other forms of "reclamation," not to mention imprudent patterns of land settlement, had made the Mississippi more disaster-prone.

14. Faulkner to Robert K. Haas, 1 May 1941, in Blotner, *Faulkner*, vol. 2, p. 1072.

15. Ibid., vol. 2, p. 1080.

16. Cooper's frontiersman Natty Bumppo, the Leatherstocking, makes his debut as a septuagenarian in *The Pioneers* (1823), and only in the last of the five novels in which he appears (*The Deerslayer* [1842]) does Cooper portray him as a youth.

17. Hickman emphasizes that "logging with skidders brought complete destruction of young timber of unmarketable size . . . No trees or vegetation of any kind except coarse wire grass remained on the skidder-logged hill and ridges. For miles and miles the landscape presented a picture of bare open land that graphically illustrated the work of destruction wrought by the economic activities of man." *Mississippi Harvest*, pp. 165–166.

18. Frank E. Smith, *The Yazoo River* (New York: Rinehart, 1954), observes that the "Delta lumberjacks were largely Negroes," not only because they were a ready-to-hand labor pool but because "traditionally only black men could work in the swamplands amid the distractions of heat, mosquitoes, bugs and snakes." "Few camps," he adds, "were complete without crap games and moonshine whiskey under the supervision of the foreman" (p. 210).

19. Faulkner, *Go Down, Moses* (New York: Random House, 1942), p. 354.

20. Faulkner, ibid., p. 102. Daniel Hoffman, *Faulkner's Country Matters: Folklore and Fable in Yoknapatawpha* (Baton Rouge: Louisiana State University Press, 1989), p. 130, also notes the parallel.

21. Consider comments to University of Virginia students that the evanescence of wilderness "to me is a sad and tragic thing . . . , providing you have the sort of background which a country boy like me had." Gwynn and Blotner, eds., *Faulkner in the University*, p. 68. On Faulkner's idea of wilderness, and on his use of Ike McCaslin as an imperfect instrument for perceiving wilderness, I am also indebted to Daniel J. Philippon's unpublished paper, "Faulkner's 'The Bear' as Ecological Fable."

22. Faulkner, "Address to the Delta Council" (1952), *Essays, Speeches, and Public Letters*, ed. James B. Meriwether (New York: Random House, 1965), p. 130. For the cultural context, see James C. Cobb, *The Most Southern Place on Earth: The Mississippi Delta and the Roots of Regional Identity* (New York: Oxford University Press, 1992), p. 254.

23. David H. Evans, "Taking the Place of Nature: 'The Bear' and the Incarnation of America," *Faulkner and the Natural World*, ed. Donald M. Kartiganer and Ann J. Abadie (Jackson: University Press of Mississippi, 1999), pp. 179–197, provides an insightful analysis of the formal separation of wilderness and settlement in "The Bear" as a wishful hal-

lucination imposed by Ike, though I think the essay takes a good thing too far by denying ontological standing to Faulknerian "wilderness" except as ideological artifact.

24. Susan Snell, *Phil Stone of Oxford: A Vicarious Life* (Athens: University of Georgia Press, 1991), pp. 51, 220, 236.

25. Blotner, *Faulkner*, vol. 1, pp. 879, 885. Charles S. Aiken, "A Geographical Approach to William Faulkner's 'The Bear,'" *Geographical Review*, 71 (October 1981): 446–459, meticulously reconstructs (with maps) the close relationships between the geography of the novel's fictive world and Stone's camp, as well as the camp farther up the Tallahatchie, closer to Jefferson/Oxford, which Faulkner had known as a child from his father's hunts. Faulkner's late-life (1954) essay, "Mississippi," in *Essays, Speeches, and Public Lectures*, deliberately montages autobiography with fiction ("he had shared in the yearly ritual of Old Ben" [p. 37]).

26. See, for example, Clark, *The Greening of the South*, especially chapters 7–8; Albert E. Cowdrey, *This Land, This South: An Environmental History*, rev. ed. (Lexington: University Press of Kentucky, 1996), pp. 149–166.

27. See, for example, Sherry H. Olson, *The Depletion Myth: A History of Railroad Use of Timber* (Cambridge: Harvard University Press, 1971), and Douglas W. MacCleery, *American Forests: A History of Resiliency and Recovery* (Durham, N.C.: Forest History Society, 1994).

28. Hickman, "Mississippi Forests," pp. 226, 227–229.

29. Clark, *The Greening of the South*, p. 24.

30. Thomas R. Dunlap, "Sport Hunting and Conservation, 1880–1920," *Environmental Review*, 12 (1988): 51. Dunlap's essay is cast, in good part, in the form of a helpfully discriminating critique of the merits and exaggerations of the most extended study, John F. Reiger's more wishfully pro-sportsman *American Sportsmen and the Origins of Conservation* (New York: Winchester Press, 1975).

31. H. L. Opie, "The Sportsman's Interest in the National Forests," *Proceedings of the Eighth Southern Forestry Congress* (1926), p. 74.

32. Reiger, *American Sportsmen and the Origins of Conservation*, pp. 21 and passim, though see Dunlap, pp. 56–57, on the elasticity of Reiger's criteria for what counts as "environmentalist" and/or "hunter." This is not to suggest that all the credit for instilling an ethics of restraint in hunting should go to men. Far from it. American women writers, as might be expected, although less socially influential during premodernity tended to be more critical of sport hunting, and even when they engaged in it they tended to romanticize it less than did men (see Vera Norwood, *Made from This Earth: American Women and Nature* [Chapel Hill: University of North Carolina Press, 1993], pp. 157–160, 219–229, and passim).

33. Wiley C. Prewitt, Jr., "Return of the Big Woods: Hunting and Habitat in Yoknapatawpha," *Faulkner and the Natural World*, ed. Kartiganer and Abadie, pp. 198–221, provides a thoughtful analysis of Faulkner's fiction in the context of popular hunting narratives, practices, and attitudes in the Deep South of his day. Prewitt also argues, arrestingly if not altogether conclusively, by reference to Ike's propitiation of the rattlesnake in Part 5 of "The Bear," that Faulkner anticipates not (only) the death but also

the partial rebound of wild places in the Deep South that latter-day environmentalist efforts have begun to bring about. For some examples of popular hunting narratives with a conservationist agenda contemporary with Faulkner, see Weldon Stone's 1938 story, "That Big Buffalo Bass" (the youthful fisherman wins the narrative's admiration by releasing the Moby Dick of the Ozarks after catching him), in *The Field and Stream Reader* (Garden City, N.Y.: Doubleday, 1946), pp. 106–116; and Nash Buckingham, "The Comedy of Long Range Duck Shooting," in *Blood Lines: Tales of Shooting and Fishing* (New York: Derrydale Press, 1938), pp. 151–172, which contrasts old-time skill with the bad sportsmanship of greedy, protocol-insouciant hunters equipped with more modern high-powered weaponry: a faint anticipation of Norman Mailer's sardonic high-tech bear hunt in *Why Are We in Vietnam?*

34. Aldo Leopold, *A Sand County Almanac* (New York: Oxford University Press, 1949), p. 211. This "rights" stipulation is supplemented and to some extent qualified by a "community" stipulation: "A thing is right when it tends to preserve the integrity, stability, and beauty of the biotic community. It is wrong when it tends otherwise" (pp. 224–225).

35. Curt Meine, *Aldo Leopold: His Life and Work* (Madison: University of Wisconsin Press, 1988), p. 163. On this and several other points I am also indebted to Judith Bryant Wittenberg's comparative discussion of Faulkner and Leopold, "*Go Down, Moses* and the Discourse of Environmentalism," *New Essays on "Go Down, Moses,"* ed. Linda Wagner-Martin (Cambridge: Cambridge University Press, 1996), pp. 61–67, despite various divergences of focus and interpretation.

36. *Sand County Almanac*, p. 176.

37. Ibid., pp. 130–131. Sublimation—though *not* to the point of actually forgoing the literal hunt, which Leopold was not prepared to advocate either—was, of course, also inherent in older codes of sportsmanship, introduced to the United States from Britain in the 1830s (Dunlap, "Sport Hunting and Conservation," pp. 52–53), which stressed rituals of procedure and practices of restraint. Genealogically speaking, Leopold and Faulkner belong to a further stage or generation of sublimators.

38. Matt Cartmill, *A View to a Death in the Morning: Hunting and Nature Through History* (Cambridge: Harvard University Press, 1993), p. 242.

39. John M. MacKenzie, *The Empire of Nature: Hunting, Conservation and British Imperialism* (Manchester: Manchester University Press, 1988), characterizes imperial hunting, complete with such ancilla as public and private displays of trophies, game books, and paintings of hunting scenes, as a specifically nineteenth-century institution.

40. Leopold, *Sand County Almanac*, pp. 200–201. The original typescript of the book is in the Steenbock Archives, University of Wisconsin, together with previous drafts and editorial correspondence, and annotated by Leopold's editors.

41. Robert L. Dorman, *Revolt of the Provinces: The Regionalist Movement in America, 1920–1945* (Chapel Hill: University of North Carolina Press, 1993), p. 316.

42. Dennis Ribbens, "The Making of *A Sand County Almanac*," in *Companion to "A Sand County Almanac": Interpretive and Critical Essays,* ed. J. Baird Callicott (Madison: University of Wisconsin Press, 1987), pp. 91–109.

43. Leopold, *Sand County Almanac*, pp. 32–33, 225.

44. Leopold, "The Ecological Conscience," *The River of the Mother of God and Other Essays*, ed. Susan L. Flader and J. Baird Callicott (Madison: University of Wisconsin Press, 1991), p. 345.

45. Cf. Scott Slovic's perceptive discussion of implicit ethical revisionism in other cases of what looks like romanticized nature writing: "Epistemology and Politics in American Nature Writing: Embedded Rhetoric and Discrete Rhetoric," *Green Culture: Environmental Rhetoric in Contemporary America*, ed. Carl G. Herndl and Stuart C. Brown (Madison: University of Wisconsin Press, 1996), pp. 82–110.

46. Cartmill, *A View to a Death in the Morning*, pp. 161–188, is an excellent case study. Cartmill accepts the gun lobby's verdict that *Bambi* (the film) was probably the most influential work of antihunting propaganda ever made, although he rightly sees the film's design as more complex than that. See also Greg Mitman's discussion of *Bambi* in relation to Disney's entire career as a maker of nature films, *Reel Nature: America's Romance with Wildlife on Film* (Cambridge: Harvard University Press, 2000), pp. 109–131.

47. Leopold, *Game Management* (New York: Scribner's, 1933), p. 423.

48. This interconnection manifests itself with special force in Faulkner's 1954 essay, "Mississippi," *Essays, Speeches, and Public Letters*, pp. 11–43.

49. See, for example, Albert E. Cowdrey, *This Land, This South*, p. 199.

50. Again, this is by no means to say that Leopold lacked a sense of irony, of self-reflexivity, and of awareness of the mixed motives and changing agendas of human beings toward nature, including himself. See, for example, H. Lewis Ulman, "'Thinking like a Mountain': Persona, Ethos, and Judgment in American Nature Writing," *Green Culture: Environmental Rhetoric in Contemporary America*, ed. Herndl and Brown, pp. 46–81, and my discussion in *The Environmental Imagination* (Cambridge: Harvard University Press, 1995), pp. 171–174.

51. Faulkner, *Go Down, Moses*, pp. 315, 316.

52. Aiken, "A Geographical Approach to William Faulkner's 'The Bear,'" pp. 450–451.

53. In Faulkner's fictive account, the aboriginal offense (in both senses of the word) is the first real estate transaction, involving sale of land to whites by Sam Fathers's father, Ikkemotubbe (who, ominously, during a sojourn in New Orleans had accepted a Gallic name for himself that gets Anglicized as "Doom"). Faulkner telescopes more than a century of native-settler contact into this one symbolic moment on the verge of Indian removal west, but his fantasy is eerily congruent with historian Richard White's finding: "they were never conquered. Instead, through the market they were made dependent and dispossessed." White, *The Roots of Dependency: Subsistence, Environment, and Social Change among the Choctaws, Pawnees, and Navajos* (Lincoln: University of Nebraska Press, 1983), p. 146. White refers to the Choctaws, whereas Ikkemotubbe is nominally Chickasaw; but in practice Faulkner tended to mix and hybridize the two histories. Lewis M. Dabney, *The Indians of Yoknapatawpha: A Study in Literature and History* (Baton Rouge: Louisiana State University Press, 1974).

54. Leopold, *Sand County Almanac*, pp. 41–44.

55. Peter Nicolaisen, "'The Dark Land Talking the Voiceless Speech': Faulkner and 'Native Soil,'" *Mississippi Quarterly*, 45 (Summer 1992): 253–276, offers a thoughtful meditation on Faulkner's ambivalence toward property (to which he adds the topic of literary property, p. 263), and is valuable also for its strong distinctions between Faulkner's mystique of land and the romanticization of land in German National Socialism.

56. Leopold, "Foreword," *Companion to "Sand County Almanac,"* p. 287. His explanation in "The Ecological Conscience" was simply that "I bought it because I wanted a place to plant pines." *River of the Mother of God*, p. 343.

57. Floyd C. Watkins, "Habet: Faulkner and the Ownership of Property," *Faulkner: Fifty Years after "The Marble Faun,"* ed. George H. Wolfe (University: University of Alabama Press, 1976), pp. 123–137, thoughtfully discusses some of these points. As Watkins points out, although Faulkner seems to idealize primordium he is careful in *Go Down, Moses* to desentimentalize not just settlement culture but also the Chickasaw dispensation before it: it too was founded on greed, slavery, and land profit. See also Daniel Hoffman, *Faulkner's Country Matters*, p. 138.

58. Leopold, "The Ecological Conscience," *River of the Mother of God*, p. 343, soon after emphasizing that one of the reasons for buying his chosen place "was that it adjoined the only remaining stand of mature pines in the County."

59. See, for example, Leopold, *River of the Mother of God*, pp. 62–67 ("Wild Lifers vs. Game Farmers"), 156–163 ("Game Methods: The American Way"), and 164–168 ("Game and Wild Life Conservation"); quotation from p. 167.

60. Leopold, *Sand County Almanac*, pp. 181, 173, 174, 176.

61. Ibid., pp. 129–133; "The Farmer as a Conservationist," *River of the Mother of God*, p. 263.

62. Paul Shepard and Barry Sanders, *The Sacred Paw: The Bear in Nature, Myth, and Literature* (New York: Viking, 1985), pp. 171–175 (on Faulkner's "The Bear") and passim. The authors suggest, interestingly, that Boon Hogganbeck, the character who actually killed the bear, might have been based on a historic nineteenth-century bear-tamer, Carl Hagenbeck, one of whose bears was named Ben Franklin; but the most provocative part of their discussion is a pairing of the novella to *Beowulf* as a mythic representation of cultural transition with a bear-man as central figure.

63. Leopold, *Sand County Almanac*, pp. 112, 110. For a cultural history of the extinction years, see Jennifer Price, *Flight Maps: Adventures with Nature in Modern America* (New York: Basic, 1999), pp. 1–55.

6. Global Commons as Resource and as Icon

1. See Benedict Anderson, *Imagined Communities* (London: Verso, 1983), for the definition; for two such critiques, see Homi Bhabha, "DissemiNation," *Nation and Narration* (London: Routledge, 1990), especially pp. 291–297, 308–311, and Arjun Appaduri, "Disjuncture and Difference in the Global Economy," *Public Culture*, 2, no. 2 (Spring 1990): 1–24.

2. Samuel P. Huntington, *The Clash of Civilizations and the Remaking of World Order* (New York: Simon & Schuster, 1996).

3. Fredric Jameson, "Notes on Globalization as a Philosophical Issue," *The Cultures of Globalization,* ed. Jameson and Masao Miyoshi (Durham: Duke University Press, 1998), pp. 54–77, and Joseph Nye, *Bound to Lead: The Changing Nature of American Power* (New York: Basic, 1990), exemplify saturnine versus hopeful perspectives. That Jameson's field is cultural theory and Nye's international politics is doubtless relevant to the contrast. Samir Amin, *Eurocentrism,* trans. Russell Moore (New York: Monthly Press, 1989), sketches the rise of Eurocentrism against the background of pre-Renaissance "tributary" antecedents; Frederick Buell, *National Culture and the New Global System* (Baltimore: Johns Hopkins University Press, 1994), offers a valuable history and anatomy of global theories. Amin's analysis emphasizes Eurocentric order; Buell emphasizes ways that order has permitted and even produced local difference.

4. The most seminal discussions for paradigms one, three, four, and six, respectively, are Ulrich Beck, *Risk Society: Towards a New Modernity,* trans. Mark Ritter (1986; New York: Sage, 1992); James Lovelock, *Gaia: A New Look at Life on Earth* (1979; rpt. with new preface, New York: Oxford University Press, 1987); Thomas Berry, *The Dream of the Earth* (San Francisco: Sierra Club, 1988); and Maarten A. Hajer, *The Politics of Environmental Discourse: Ecological Modernization and Their Policy Process* (Oxford: Clarendon Press, 1995). On paradigm two, Juan Martinez-Alier is exemplary for scope of vision; see, for example, "The Environmentalism of the Poor," in *Varieties of Environmentalism: Essays North and South,* written jointly by Ramachandra Guha and Martinez-Alier (London: Earthscan, 1997), pp. 3–21. On paradigm five, two especially significant works are Carolyn Merchant's historical diagnosis, *The Death of Nature: Women, Ecology, and the Scientific Revolution* (San Francisco: Harper, 1980), and Val Plumwood's philosophical analysis, *Feminism and the Mastery of Nature* (London: Routledge, 1993).

5. David Harvey, *Justice, Nature and the Geography of Difference* (Oxford: Blackwell, 1997), p. 378.

6. Herman Daly, *Beyond Growth: The Economics of Sustainable Development* (Boston: Beacon Press, 1996), p. 9.

7. Kenny Bruno, "Monsanto's Failing PR Strategy," *The Ecologist,* 28 (September/October 1998): 287–293, is a typical exposé.

8. For information about and current draft of the Earth Charter, in process under the leadership of Steven Rockefeller of Middlebury College since 1997, see *www.earthcharter.org/draft///fnottxt//*.

9. Lynton Keith Caldwell, *International Environmental Policy: From the Twentieth to the Twenty-First Century* (Durham: Duke University Press, 1996), p. 3.

10. Karen Liftin, *Ozone Discourses* (New York: Columbia University Press, 1994), p. 115, quoting Mustafa Tolba, the executive director of the United Nations Environment Programme (UNEP), which formulated the accords. Richard Elliot Benedick, *Ozone Diplomacy: New Directions in Safeguarding the Planet* (Cambridge: Harvard University Press, 1991), which agrees with this judgment, stresses the importance of the impetus created by the 1997 U.S. Clean Air Act in establishing the standard of "reason-

able expectation" rather than indubitable scientific proof of environmental endangerment (pp. 23–24). No less significantly for present purposes, in the course of emphasizing also the historic nature of the collaboration between political, corporate, and scientific communities both analyses stress the importance of heightened public imagination and concern arising from the unexpected discovery of the ozone hole over the Antarctic. The timing, Liftin observes, "could not have been much better for it to have had a major political impact" (p. 101). Sharon Beder, "Corporate Hijacking of the Greenhouse Debate," *The Ecologist*, 29 (March/April 1999): 199–122, angrily denounces the subsequent backsliding.

11. Garrett Hardin, "The Tragedy of the Commons," *Science*, 162 (December 1968): 1243–48, is the seminal formulation of this idea: it is in the interest of individuals to abuse the common territories that the group's interest is to maintain. Bonnie J. McCay and James M. Acheson, "Human Ecology and the Commons," provide a concise appraisal of the influence of this thesis and the major criticisms to which it has been subjected (e.g., its reduction of alternative solutions to privatization of property rights versus imposition of external authority). See *The Question of the Commons: The Culture and Ecology of Communal Resources* (Tucson: University of Arizona Press, 1987), ed. McCay and Acheson, pp. 1–34, which also serves as an introduction to a series of case studies, several of which discuss specific regional or national schemes for managing marine resources. I do not enter minutely into these debates here; my discussion starts from the premise that Hardin's paradox must be taken seriously, but my emphasis is on "management" at the level of cultural discourse (e.g., revisionary hunting narrative, interspecies solidarity), which Hardin does not take up.

12. Homer, *Iliad* XVIII.604–605, trans. Richmond Lattimore (Chicago: University of Chicago Press, 1964), p. 391.

13. Sigmund Freud, *Civilization and Its Discontents* (1930), trans. and ed. James Strachey (New York: Norton, 1961), p. 11; Herman Melville, *Moby-Dick* (1851), ed. Harrison Hayford and Hershel Parker (New York: Norton, 1967), p. 13. All subsequent quotations from this edition will be indicated in parentheses, as will items quoted from its various appendices.

14. Conrad, *The Mirror of the Sea* (1901; Garden City, N.J.: Doubleday, 1925), p. 101.

15. Carson, *The Sea Around Us* (New York: Oxford University Press, 1950), pp. 3, 216; Carson to Dorothy Freeman, quoted in Linda Lear, *Rachel Carson: Witness for Nature* (New York: Holt, 1997), p. 310; Carson, "Preface to the Second Edition of *The Sea Around Us*" (1961), in *Lost Woods: The Discovered Writing of Rachel Carson*, ed. Linda Lear (Boston: Beacon, 1998), pp. 106–109.

16. Carson, *Silent Spring* (Cambridge: Houghton, 1962), p. 42.

17. Ibid., pp. 140, 150, both from the chapter entitled "Rivers of Death"; see, for example, Edward Hyams, "People and Pests," *New Statesman*, February 15, 1963, p. 244; Loren Eiseley, "Using a Plague to Fight a Plague," *Saturday Review*, September 29, 1962, p. 18.

18. Simon, for example, muses on the innocence of Carson's era (obviously thinking of *The Sea Around Us*) compared to what already seemed familiar to the 1980s: "symbolically, an all-wise, all-protective Neptune still guarded the health of ocean in the

minds of distinguished scientists and of ordinary people in the 1950s. Each of us had the security of knowing that ocean was there, intact, as it always had been and always would be." *Neptune's Revenge: The Ocean of Tomorrow* (New York: Franklin Watts, 1984), p. 9.

19. Caldwell, *International Environmental Policy*, pp. 228, 231.

20. Andrew Metrick and Martin L. Weitzman, "Patterns of Behavior in Endangered Species Protection," *Land Economics*, 71 (1996): 1–15.

21. For example, John Tuxill, "Death in the Family Tree," *World Watch*, 10, no. 5 (September/October 1997): 13–21, on primate endangerment; and Will Nixon, "The Species Only a Mother Could Love," *Amicus Journal*, 21, no. 2 (Summer 1999): 28–32, attempting to promote concern for the plight of freshwater mussels.

22. For example, Susan Crystal, "Rockets in Paradise," *Amicus Journal*, 20, no. 3 (Fall 1998): 33; Meghan Houlihan, "Will the Stellers Survive?" *Greenpeace Magazine*, 4, no. 1 (Spring 1999): 20.

23. Alison Anderson, *Media, Culture and the Environment* (New Brunswick: Rutgers University Press, 1997), pp. 137–169, especially pp. 149–150.

24. Emmanuel Levinas, *Otherwise Than Being or Beyond Essence*, trans. Alphonso Lingis (1974; Dordrecht: Kluwer, 1991), p. 91.

25. As Winner puts it in the title essay of *The Whale and the Reactor: A Search for Limits in an Age of High Technology* (Chicago: University of Chicago Press, 1986), "Here were two tangible symbols of the power of nature and of human artifice: one an enormous creature swimming gracefully in a timeless ecosystem, the other a gigantic piece of apparatus linked by sheer determination to the complicated mechanisms of the technological society" (p. 168).

26. Gary Snyder, "Mother Earth: Her Whales," *No Nature* (New York: Pantheon, 1992), p. 236.

27. John Lilly, "A Feeling of Weirdness," *Mind in the Waters*, ed. Joan McIntyre (San Francisco: Sierra Club Books, 1974), pp. 71–77 (on mimicry); Norman Myers, "Sharing the Earth with Whales," *The Last Extinction*, 2d ed., ed. Les Kaufman and Kenneth Mallory (Cambridge: MIT Press, 1993), p. 192 (on whale "culture"). Jim Nollman, *The Charged Border: Where Whales and Humans Meet* (New York: Holt, 1999), provides an interesting though often tendentious account of the experiences of a specialist in interspecies communication through music.

28. Roger Payne, *Among Whales* (New York: Dell, 1995), pp. 168–211.

29. Sterling Bunnell, "The Evolution of Cetacean Intelligence," *Mind in the Waters*, ed. McIntyre, p. 58.

30. See *Mind in the Waters*, p. 145, for an 1850 anecdote; ibid., pp. 170–185, for orcas' response to flute music (Paul Spond, "The Whale Show"); and Payne, *Among Whales*, pp. 235 and passim, on cetacean sociability more generally. Payne muses on the similarity between "the songs of whales and our own songs" (p. 166).

31. Patti H. Clayton strongly stresses this point (together with several others noted above) in her case study of the 1988 rescue, at a cost of more than one million dollars, of three gray whales trapped in Arctic ice: a venture to which even President Ronald Reagan, of antienvironmentalist fame, lent his support. *Connection on the Ice: Environ-*

mental Ethics in Theory and Practice (Philadelphia: Temple University Press, 1998), pp. 79–80, 141–142, and passim.

32. Victor B. Scheffer, *The Year of the Whale* (New York: Scribner's, 1969), p. 229.

33. Peter Singer, "The Ethics of Whaling," unpublished 1978 paper quoted in Sydney Frost, *The Whaling Question* (San Francisco: Friends of the Earth, 1979), pp. 183–184.

34. See, for example, Eugene C. Hargrove, ed., *The Animal Rights/Environmental Ethics Debate: The Environmental Perspective* (Albany: State University of New York Press, 1992).

35. Elmo Paul Hohman, *The American Whaleman: A Study of Life and Labor in the Whaling Industry* (New York: Longmans, 1928), p. 6.

36. Russell Reising and Peter J. Kvidera, in "Fast Fish and Raw Fish: *Moby-Dick*, Japan, and Melville's Thematics of Geography," *New England Quarterly*, 70 (1997): 285–305, make this point cogently in the course of demonstrating the links between contemporary U.S.-Japan policy, the novel's various Japan and east Pacific references, and Ishmael's prophecy that "if that double-bolted land, Japan, is ever to become hospitable, it is the whale-ship alone to whom the credit will be due; for already she is on the threshold" (p. 100). Reising and Kvidera's skeptical reading of Ishmael's thirst for the unknown and receptivity to new experience is in keeping with the skeptical diagnosis of naturalist travel narrative as part of the armature of imperial expansion advanced by, for example, Mary Louise Pratt (*Imperial Eyes: Travel Writing and Transculturation* [New York: Routledge, 1992], pp. 15–68), and Myra Jehlen ("Traveling in America," *Cambridge History of American Literature*, ed. Sacvan Bercovitch [Cambridge: Cambridge University Press, 1994], pp. 126–139).

37. Melville, for one, was considerably deprovincialized by his sojourn in the Marquesas and his other contacts with nonwesterners. For thoughtful discussions of how Melville partially saw past, partially within, the received cultural stereotypes of his day, see T. Walter Herbert, Jr., *Marquesan Encounters: Melville and the Meaning of Civilization* (Cambridge: Harvard University Press, 1980), and Leonard Cassuto, *The Inhuman Race: The Racial Grotesque in American Literature and Culture* (New York: Columbia University Press, 1997), pp. 168–203. Christopher Herbert, *Culture and Anomie: Ethnographic Imagination in the Nineteenth Century* (Chicago: University of Chicago Press, 1991), pp. 150–203, ingeniously argues that even Polynesian missionaries (whom Melville satirized) tended to become incipient cultural relativists in spite of themselves.

38. See, for example, Clifford W. Ashley, *The Yankee Whaler* (1926; rpt., New York: Dover, 1966), p. 106: "There could be no truer picture of whaling or finer story of the sea than Herman Melville's 'Moby Dick'"; and Roger Payne, *Among Whales*, p. 324: "Alongside the profundity of his observations the fact that so many of Melville's perceptions about whales were wrong is entirely irrelevant."

39. A conspicuous exception is Elizabeth Schultz, "Melville's Environmental Vision in *Moby-Dick*," *ISLE*, 7 (2000): 97–113. Building partly on Robert Zoellner's earlier reflections on Ishmael's discourse of kinship between whales and humans, in his *The Salt-Sea Mastodon: A Reading of "Moby-Dick"* (Berkeley: University of California Press, 1973), Schultz argues persuasively that *Moby-Dick* is energized by a concern for the

nonhuman creatures that, however, by no means romanticizes nature. Although I think Schultz overstates the novel's concern for species extermination (see note 42 below), as my own analysis will make clear, I fully concur with her finding that the novel's critique of whaling is linked to its theme of human-nonhuman kinship.

40. Payne, *Among Whales*, p. 325.

41. "Huntsmen of the Sea," *Harper's New Monthly Magazine*, 49 (1874): 654; J. Ross Browne, *Etchings of a Whaling Cruise* (New York: Harper, 1850), pp. 297–298; Francis Allyn Olmsted, *Incidents of a Whaling Voyage* (1841; rpt., Rutland, Vt.: Tuttle, 1969), p. 58; Henry T. Cheever, *The Whale and His Captors* (New York: Harper, 1850), p. 114; Eliza A. Williams, "Journal of a Whaling Voyage . . . Commencing September 7th, 1858," *One Whaling Family* (Boston: Houghton, 1964), p. 138.

42. Chapter 105 ("Does the Whale's Magnitude Diminish?—Will He Perish?") notes that "the more recondite Nantucketers" wonder whether the whale population is about to go the way of the bison (pp. 382–383). A decade later, George Perkins Marsh agreed that "the 'hugest of living creatures' . . . has now almost wholly disappeared from many favorite fishing grounds, and in others is greatly diminished in numbers." *Man and Nature*, ed. David Lowenthal (1864; Cambridge: Harvard University Press, 1965), p. 100. American whaling voyages in the 1840s and 1850s seem to have been much longer on average than in the decade following the War of 1812 (42 versus 29 months: Hohman, *The American Whaleman*, p. 84). But the novel's inference that the whale population had become warier and more evasive rather than depleted (pp. 383–384) is reaffirmed by the most authoritative historical study of the subject: Lance E. Davis, Robert E. Gallman, and Karin Gleiter, *In Pursuit of Leviathan: Technology, Institutions, Productivity, and Profits in American Whaling, 1816–1906* (Chicago: University of Chicago Press, 1997), pp. 131–149.

43. This is not to say that degradation of the worker was the whole story of whaling, either historically or in Melville's estimation. In particular, as the novel hints throughout, the New England whaling industry, despite its risks and privations, supplied during the antebellum period a more egalitarian space of entrepreneurship for nonwhites, albeit diminishingly, than other fields of endeavor. For a short treatment, see Jeffrey Bolster, *Black Jacks* (Cambridge: Harvard University Press, 1997). Even though Captain Bildad lied when he told Queequeg that his wage would be "more than ever was given a harpooner yet out of Nantucket" (p. 84), even though "racial attitudes" aboard whalers "closely approximated those found ashore" (Briton Cooper Busch, *"Whaling Will Never Do for Me": American Whalemen in the Nineteenth Century* [Lexington: University Press of Kentucky, 1994], p. 35), few other lines of employment would have remunerated an uneducated nonwhite so well. For this and much more on the (qualified) multiculturalization of Nantucket and New Bedford whaling in the 1840s and 1850s, I am indebted to Jia-rui Chong's splendid Harvard University honors thesis, "'Federated Along One Keel': Race, Ethnicity, and the Alternative Spaces of Whaling Ships, 1830–1860" (1999).

44. Browne, *Etchings of a Whaling Cruise*, pp. 135, 214. Melville's review of Browne (*Literary World*, March 6, 1847) comments approvingly on Browne's deromanticization of whaling (rpt. in *Moby-Dick*, pp. 532–535).

45. Busch, *"Whaling Will Never Do for Me,"* especially chapters 2 ("Crime and Punishment") and 6 ("Desertion").

46. Samuel Otter, *Melville's Anatomies* (Berkeley: University of California Press, 1999), pp. 132–155.

47. On these points, see especially Harriet Ritvo, *The Platypus and the Mermaid; and Other Figments of the Classifying Imagination* (Cambridge: Harvard University Press, 1997), pp. 48–49, which includes a brief review of cetacean controversies.

48. Melville to Sophia Hawthorne, 8 January 1852, in *Moby-Dick*, p. 568.

49. Olmsted, *Incidents of a Whaling Voyage*, p. 141.

50. For example, Ishmael's dismissal of "some book naturalists—Olafsen and Povelsen—declaring the Sperm Whale not only to be a consternation to every other creature in the sea, but also to be so incredibly ferocious as continually to be athirst for human blood" (p. 157).

51. J. N. Reynolds, "Mocha Dick," *Knickerbocker* (May 1839), rpt. in *Moby-Dick*, p. 575.

52. Curt Meine, *Aldo Leopold: His Life and Work* (Madison: University of Wisconsin Press, 1988), pp. 348–349, 358, 372, makes clear that Leopold was well informed about the Dust Bowl crisis (for an environmental history, see Donald Worster, *Dust Bowl: The Southern Plains in the 1930s* [New York: Oxford University Press, 1979]). Leopold mentions the Dust Bowl disaster in *Sand County Almanac,* (New York: Oxford University Press, 1949), p. 132, and he also alludes to it in the 1935 essay in which he may have used the term "land ethic" for the first time, "Land Pathology," commenting tartly on the myopia of "rural" education's preoccupation "with the transplantation of machinery and city culture to the rural community, latterly in the face of economic conditions so adverse as to evict the occupants of submarginal soils." *The River of the Mother of God and Other Essays,* ed. Susan L. Flader and J. Baird Callicott (Madison: University of Wisconsin Press, 1991), p. 214.

53. Ralph Waldo Emerson, "Forbearance," *Poems, Complete Works of Ralph Waldo Emerson,* vol. 9, ed. Edward Waldo Emerson (Boston: Houghton, 1903–1904), p. 83.

54. "By permission of the gentlemen the Board of Health," broadside, American Antiquarian Society (Boston: Columbian Museum [Benjamin True, 1808]).

55. Ritvo, *The Platypus and the Mermaid,* pp. 120–187, and Christoph Irmscher, *The Poetics of Natural History: From John Bartram to William James* (New Brunswick: Rutgers University Press, 1999), pp. 122–146.

56. Susan G. Davis, *Spectacular Nature: Corporate Culture and the Sea World Experience* (Berkeley: University of California Press, 1997), p. 9. Davis takes note of the connection between modern theme parks and older modes of public amusement, pp. 20–21, 32–35.

57. Robinson Jeffers, "Orca," *The Collected Poetry of Robinson Jeffers,* vol. 3, ed. Tim Hunt (Stanford: Stanford University Press, 1991), p. 206.

58. Erich Hoyt, *Orca: The Whale Called Killer* (Camden East, Ontario: Camden House, 1984), p. 19.

59. Davis, *Spectacular Nature,* p. 216.

60. Payne, *Among Whales,* p. 223.

61. Ibid., pp. 277, 296. Payne appends a final warning that "whalers cannot be trusted" and that moratoria and/or designation of large areas like the Antarctic as

sanctuaries are the only viable regulatory approaches (pp. 300–301). Elizabeth R. DeSombre, "Distorting Global Governance: Membership, Voting, and the IWC," presents a more scholarly and evenhanded analysis of the politicking on both sides of the protection issue (in Robert Freidheim, ed., *Towards a Sustainable Whaling Regime* [Seattle: University of Washington Press, 2000]), which concludes, somewhat like Payne, that the IWC is patently unsatisfactory but without it matters might likely be worse.

62. Caldwell, *International Environmental Policy*, p. 239.

63. James C. McKinley, Jr., "A Tiny Sparrow Is Cast as a Test of Will to Restore the Everglades," *New York Times*, June 5, 1999, sec. A, pp. 1, 19.

64. Collodi's "pesce-cane" (shark) is regularly translated into English in a too literal way as "dogfish," despite the sacrifice of the sinister symbolic connotations that "shark" bears in both languages. However, as Nicolas J. Perella notes in his translation of *The Adventures of Pinocchio* (Berkeley: University of California Press, 1986), Collodi's beast has "more of the whale than the shark about him" (p. 22). A precedent in Italian literature, possibly known to Collodi, was the whale in Ariosto's *Cinque Canti*. See Allan Gilbert, "The Sea-Monster in Ariosto's 'Cinque Canti' and in 'Pinocchio,'" *Italica*, 33 (December 1956): 260–263.

65. One symptom of an endangered genre: Scottish ship doctor R. B. Robertson's admission toward the end of his personal chronicle of Antarctic voyaging, *Of Whales and Men* (New York: Knopf, 1954), p. 251, that "there was a common feeling among both scientists and whalemen that, though whaling was great fun and certainly the most dramatic way of tapping the vast food reserves of the ocean, it was really a wasteful and unnecessarily laborious way of doing so." The taste for popular history of bygone whaling adventures and disaster continues unabated, however; see, for example, G. A. Mawer, *Ahab's Trade: The Saga of South Sea Whaling* (St. Leonard's, New South Wales: Allen & Unwin, 1999), and Nat Philbrick, *In the Heart of the Sea: The Tragedy of the Whaleship "Essex"* (New York: Viking, 2000).

66. Robert Siegel, *White Whale* (San Francisco: HarperCollins, 1991).

67. Barry Lopez, "Renegotiating the Contracts," *Parabola* (1983), rpt. in Thomas Lyon, ed., *This Incomperable Lande* (Boston: Houghton, 1989), p. 381. For a more skeptical analysis of Indian respect for animals and the natural environment generally, see Shepard Krech III, *The Ecological Indian: Myth and History* (New York: Norton, 1999).

68. Barry Lopez, *Crossing Open Ground* (New York: Vintage, 1988), pp. 117–146.

69. Barry Lopez, *Arctic Dreams: Imagination and Desire in a Northern Landscape* (New York: Scribner's, 1986), pp. 128, 127.

70. Apropos Levinas's theory of the face versus *Moby-Dick*'s insistence that the sperm whale has no face, it is striking that the camera work in the *Free Willy* films does its best to compensate with affecting shots of Willy's eyes and particularly his mouth: that is, Willy likes to grin and have his tongue stroked.

71. The subsequent "freeing" of Keiko, the whale that played Willy, to a floating sea pen in a remote Icelandic cove became headline news. Marc Ramirez and Christine Clarridge, "Keiko Goes Home," *Seattle Times*, September 10, 1998, p. A1.

7. The Misery of Beasts and Humans

1. Jeremy Bentham, *An Introduction to the Principles of Morals and Legislation* (1780, 1789; Oxford: Clarendon Press, 1907), p. 311n.

2. Charles Darwin, *The Descent of Man, and Selection in Relation to Sex*, vol. 1 (1871; rpt., Princeton: Princeton University Press, 1981), pp. 100–101.

3. Lawrence Johnson, *A Morally Deep World: An Essay on Moral Significance and Environmental Ethics* (Cambridge: Cambridge University Press, 1991), pp. 97–147. Bioethicist Mary Anne Warren, *Moral Status: Obligations to Persons and Other Living Things* (Oxford: Clarendon Press, 1997), offers a perspicuous overview of alternative positions (pp. 1–147), proposing a "multi-criterial analysis of moral status" as a path to resolution (pp. 148–177).

4. For example, in a provocative, much-cited critique of animal liberation advocacy, J. Baird Callicott, "Animal Liberation: A Triangular Affair," *Environmental Ethics*, 2 (1980): 311–338, claimed Leopold's land ethic as authority for the position that accountability is preeminently to the ecosystem, not to the creature. The most influential animal liberationist, Peter Singer, enlists Bentham's passage as authority for what Warren calls a "sentience-only" criterion of moral accountability that privileges (certain) creatures rather than the ecosystem. *Animal Liberation*, rev. ed. (1975; New York: Avon, 1990), pp. 7–9.

5. Two among many examples (the first with an ecocentric tilt, the second anthropocentric) are Holmes Rolston III, "Feeding People Versus Saving Nature?" *The Ecological Community*, ed. Roger S. Gottlieb (New York: Routledge, 1997), pp. 208–225, and Joseph Sterba, "From Anthropocentrism to Nonanthropocentrism," *Justice for Here and Now* (Cambridge: Cambridge University Press, 1998), pp. 125–150. Sterba is willing to concede that "actions that meet nonbasic or luxury needs of humans are prohibited when they aggress against the basic needs of animals and plants" (p. 129); Rolston insists on the right of the poor "to a more equitable distribution of the good of the Earth that we, the wealthy, think we absolutely own," but denies their right to free use of nature (p. 223).

6. Patti H. Clayton, *Connection on the Ice: Environmental Ethics in Theory and Practice* (Philadelphia: Temple University Press, 1998), p. 85: apropos publicity surrounding the expensive 1988 rescue of three gray whales trapped in Arctic ice.

7. Here and below I deliberately lump together the discrepant positions of animal liberation, respect-for-life arguments founded on claims for the moral worth of other nonhuman entities as well, and ecosystem-first ethics like Callicott's (note 4), for it seems to me that the most fundamental distinction between types of environmental-ethical positions is whether or not they decisively privilege the human interest above the nonhuman, however the moral worth of the other-than-human be defined.

8. Darwin, *The Descent of Man*, vol. 1, pp. 42, 78. For further discussion of "Darwin's Anthropomorphism," with special reference to his *The Expression of Emotions in Man and Animals* (1872), see Eileen Crist, *Images of Animals: Anthropomorphism and Animal Mind* (Philadelphia: Temple University Press, 1999), pp. 11–50.

9. "The Fuegians rank amongst the lowest barbarians" yet contact with them on the *Beagle* persuaded Darwin of "how similar their minds were to ours." *The Descent of Man,* vol. 1, pp. 34, 232.

10. Immanuel Kant, *Groundwork of the Metaphysics of Morals* (1785), in *Practical Philosophy,* trans. and ed. Mary J. McGregor (Cambridge: Cambridge University Press, 1996), p. 87; and *Lectures on Ethics* (ca. 1775–1784), trans. Peter Heath, ed. Heath and J. B. Schneewind (Cambridge: Cambridge University Press, 1997), p. 212. On the other hand, although Kant's ethics rests on a sharp distinction between "a kingdom of ends" where moral action is possible because freedom of choice is possible versus the "kingdom of nature" where action proceeds from instinct (*Groundwork,* p. 87), he emphasizes also that "rational being" and "human" are not coextensive (e.g., humans can behave like animals [*Lectures on Ethics,* p. 147 and passim]) and that "we have duties to animals" (to treat them with consideration), although not because of anything we owe to them but because of what we owe ourselves: "a person who already displays such cruelty to animals is also no less hardened towards men" (ibid., p. 212). See, however, Holyn Wilson, "Kant and Ecofeminism," *Ecofeminism: Women, Culture, Nature,* ed. Karen J. Warren (Bloomington: Indiana University Press, 1997), pp. 390–411, for a vigorous defense of Kant against charges of speciesism and sexism.

11. In *Beasts of the Modern Imagination: Darwin, Nietzsche, Kafka, Ernst, and Lawrence* (Baltimore: Johns Hopkins University Press, 1985), Margot Norris pursues this configuration within the high modernist canon.

12. Devi describes the novella as "an abstract of my entire tribal experience," not confining itself "to the customs of one tribe alone" but designed to "communicate the agony of the tribals, of marginalized people all over the world," including the United States: "Everywhere it is the same story." "The Author in Conversation," *Imaginary Maps,* ed. and trans. Gayatri Spivak (New York: Routledge, 1995), pp. xx–xxi, xi. In India, however, tribals constitute a much higher fraction of the national population than do aborigines in the United States and even Canada: about 7 percent as opposed to 1 percent and 4 percent, respectively, according to a 1993 report. Alan Thein Durning, "Supporting Indigenous Peoples," *State of the World 1993: A Worldwatch Institute Report on Progress Toward a Sustainable Society* (New York: Norton, 1993), p. 83.

13. Devi, "Pterodactyl," p. 122.

14. Madhav Gadgil and Ramachandra Guha, *Ecology and Equity: The Use and Abuse of Nature in Contemporary India* (London: Routledge, 1995), pp. 3 and passim, contrast "ecosystem people" with "omnivores" (affluent, metropolitan-based entrepreneurs and consumers), whose exploitation turns ecosystem people into the "ecological refugees" of tent cities and urban slums.

15. Devi, "Pterodactyl," p. 195. It is crucial that the title image is never precisely described nor even explicitly identified with the pterodactyl of paleontology. Rather, "pterodactyl" is a fallback term devised by the outsiders as a way of making the figure halfway intelligible.

16. Barbara Gowdy, *The White Bone* (New York: Holt, 1999), pp. 13–14, 202.

17. Thomas Nagel, "What Is It Like to Be a Bat?" *Philosophical Review*, 83 (October 1974): 435–450, which actually invokes the bat example as a stalking horse for the problem of other (human) minds, has been a provocation for phenomenologists and cognitive ethologists alike: for example, Donald Griffin, *Animal Minds* (Chicago: University of Chicago Press, 1992), pp. 236–260; Ralph R. Acampora, "Bodily Being and Animal World: Toward a Somatology of Cross-Species Community," *Animal Others: On Ethics, Ontology, and Animal Life*, ed. H. Peter Steeves (Albany: State University of New York Press, 1999), pp. 117–131; and Daniel C. Dennett, "Animal Consciousness: What Matters and Why," *Humans and Other Animals*, ed. Arien Mack (Columbus: Ohio State University Press, 1999), pp. 281–300. Gowdy lists her chief sources (which do *not* include Nagel but only elephant studies) in *White Bone* at pp. 329–330. Another sort of precedent for Gowdy is her previous fictional experiments in imagining radically different forms of human being; for example, her short story collection, *We So Seldom Look on Love* (Toronto: Somerville House, 1992), depicts the life-worlds of a blind girl whose vision is surgically restored, a two-headed man, and a young woman with duplicate genitals and legs.

18. E. M. Forster, *A Passage to India* (1924; rpt., New York: Harcourt, 1952), pp. 31–32.

19. Ibid., p. 280.

20. Onno Oerlemans, "Romanticism and the Materiality of Nature," manuscript, pp. 89–90. Oerlemans calls special attention to "The Marten," "The Fox," "The Badger," and "The Hedgehog." I am grateful to Professor Oerlemans for allowing me to quote from his ground breaking study here and below.

21. *Samuel Taylor Coleridge*, ed. H. J. Jackson (Oxford: Oxford University Press, 1985), p. 10.

22. Oerlemans, "Romanticism and the Materiality of Nature," p. 94.

23. M. H. Abrams, "Coleridge and the Romantic Vision of the World," *The Correspondent Breeze* (New York: Norton, 1984), pp. 216–224. Karl Kroeber, *Ecological Literary Criticism: Romantic Imaging and the Biology of Mind* (New York: Columbia University Press, 1994), in the course of a more explicitly ecocritical reading of Romantic nature representation, points out that in certain instances, like "The Nightingale," although not typically, Coleridge's sense of cosmic ecology seems to derive more immediately from "interactive dialogue between man and [physical] nature" than from spiritual intuition (p. 75).

24. Leonard Lutwack, *Birds in Literature* (Gainesville: University Press of Florida, 1994), pp. 177–181, usefully discusses the poem in the context of the genre of "killing the sacred bird."

25. Linda Hogan, *Power* (New York: Norton, 1998), p. 125.

26. Karen J. Warren, "The Power and the Promise of Ecological Feminism," *Ecological Feminist Philosophies*, ed. Warren (Bloomington: Indiana University Press, 1996), pp. 27–28.

27. It is important to add that what Stacy Alaimo says of nature representation in Linda Hogan's poetry is also true of *Power:* although Hogan's work "evokes profound

connections with nature, it [also] strives to affirm nature's differences, in part by refusing to engulf it within human projections." Alaimo, "'Skin Dreaming': The Bodily Transfigurations of Fielding Burke, Octavia Butler, and Linda Hogan," *Ecofeminist Literary Criticism: Theory, Interpretation, Pedagogy,* ed. Greta Gaard and Patrick D. Murphy (Urbana: University of Illinois Press, 1998), p. 130.

8. Watershed Aesthetics

1. "Wir müssen daher die heutige Vorstellung von Natur, sofern wit überhaupt noch eine solche haben, beiseite lassen, wenn da von Strom und Gewässer die Rede ist." Heidegger, *Holderlins Hymnen "Germanien" und "Der Rhein"* (1934–1935; Frankfurt am Main: Klostermann, 1980), p. 196.

2. Joseph Conrad, *Heart of Darkness,* 3rd ed., ed. Robert Kimbrough (1899; New York: Norton, 1988), p. 9.

3. Gaston Bachelard, *Water and Dreams: An Essay on the Imagination of Matter,* trans. Edith R. Farrell (1942; Dallas: Dallas Institute of Humanities and Culture, 1983), p. 133, declares that fresh water "offers itself as a natural symbol of purity" (p. 133). Water obviously has other common symbolic connotations as well: life, time, and flux, among others. My own understanding of the concept of "natural symbol" itself, as will soon become apparent, derives from but is not identical to that of Mary Douglas, *Natural Symbols: Explorations in Cosmology* (1970; rpt. with new introduction, London: Routledge, 1996), for whom the concept implies specifically a transformation of first by second nature: symbols so culturally embedded as to seem "natural." In my rendering first nature is transformed but not on that account left behind.

4. Michael Drayton, *The Poly-Olbion: A Chorographicall Description of Great Britain* 2.283 (Manchester: Spenser Society, 1889–1890).

5. John Denham, *Cooper's Hill,* version 1, ll. 165–166, 186–198, in Brendan O Hehir, *Expans'd Hieroglyphicks: A Critical Edition of Sir John Denham's Cooper's Hill* (Berkeley: University of California Press, 1969), pp. 84, 85–86. However, Wyman H. Herendeen, *From Landscape to Literature: The River and the Myth of Geography* (Pittsburgh: Duquesne University Press, 1986), identifies the English apogee of river-nation troping especially with the age and figure of Spenser (pp. 257–262) and finds in Denham's frustrated royalism of *Cooper's Hill* a privatistic swerve away from national image-building (pp. 331–332).

6. William Wordsworth, *The Prelude: 1799, 1805, 1850,* ed. Jonathan Wordsworth, M. H. Abrams, and Stephen Gill (New York: Norton, 1979), pp. 1, 42–43. Although Wordsworth made some significant revisions in this passage from edition to edition, the phrases I have quoted, and the rhetorical formula, remained unchanged.

7. Chinua Achebe, "An Image of Africa: Racism in Conrad's *Heart of Darkness,*" *Massachusetts Review,* 18 (1977): 782–794; revised for inclusion together with other postcolonially oriented essays (two concurring, one dissenting) in *Heart of Darkness,* ed. Kimbrough, pp. 251–262.

8. As early as the thirteenth century "are recorded instances of Crown and City endeavoring to restrict the use of the river as a sewer and rubbish dump"; but the sanitation crisis came in the 1800s, after the population of London passed the one million mark: cholera epidemics, disappearance of anadromous fish, stinking effluvia. As elsewhere, the first results of modernization of water-sewer infrastructure were greatly increased water consumption and conversion from inadequate private cesspools to public sewers that drained into the Thames and its tributaries. Not until the twentieth century were effective wastewater treatment systems implemented; the great sanitary innovation of the 1880s and 1890s was the commissioning of vessels to dump city sludge in the open ocean. John Doxat, *The Living Thames: The Restoration of a Great Tidal River* (London: Hutchinson Benham, 1977), p. 32 and pp. 31–37 passim. For the connection between Victorian discourses of Africa and of urban reform, see Deborah Epstein Nord, "The Social Explorer as Anthropologist: Victorian Travellers among the Urban Poor," *Visions of the Modern City*, ed. William Sharpe and Leonard Wallock (New York: Columbia University, 1983), pp. 118–130.

9. Jonathan Bate, *Romantic Ecology: Wordsworth and the Environmental Tradition* (London: Routledge, 1991), p. 21.

10. James J. Parsons, "On 'Bioregionalism' and 'Watershed Consciousness,'" *The Professional Geographer*, 37 (1985): 2; Christopher McGrory Klyza, "Bioregional Possibilities in Vermont," *Bioregionalism*, ed. Michael Vincent McGinnis (London: Routledge: 1999), p. 89. An early manifestation of watershed as a defining image/concept for contemporary bioregionalism is the feature on "Watershed Consciousness" in *CoEvolution Quarterly*, no. 12 (Winter 1976): 4–45.

11. The title concept of *Imagined Communities* was given currency by anthropologist Benedict Anderson's use of it as the core definition of "nations" in his book of that title (London: Verso, 1983); but the concept works equally well for bioregionalism. Ironically, it can be no less useful in accounting for resistance to bioregional thinking by the defenders of a juridictional grid, once the grid has become "naturalized" through custom, institutionalization, and so forth.

12. H. B. Johnson, *Order upon the Land: The U.S. Rectangular Land Survey and the Upper Mississippi Country*, quoted in Curt Meine, "Inherit the Grid," *Placing Nature*, ed. Joan Iverson Nassauer (Washington, D.C.: Island Press, 1997), p. 50, an essay that—without focusing on watersheds especially—resourcefully discusses both the grid-boundedness of lay perception and life-practice and suggests several ways of seeing "ecologically" through or past the grid.

13. E. C. Pielou, *Fresh Water* (Chicago: University of Chicago Press, 1998), p. 84.

14. John Opie, *Ogallala: Water for a Dry Land—A Historical Study in the Possibilities for American Sustainable Agriculture* (Lincoln: University of Nebraska Press, 1993). Aquifers do, however, feed surface flow.

15. See especially Donald Worster, *Rivers of Empire: Water, Aridity, and the Growth of the American West* (New York: Pantheon, 1985), pp. 138, 332, and passim.

16. John Wesley Powell, "Institutions for the Arid Lands," *Century*, 40 (May 1890): 114.

17. Philip G. Terrie, *Forever Wild: Environmental Aesthetics and the Adirondack Forest Preserve* (Philadelphia: Temple University Press, 1985), pp. 95–97 and passim, which thoughtfully appraises the mixture of utilitarian and aesthetic motives underlying the long history of the evolution of the Adirondack idea.

18. Gary Snyder, "Coming into the Watershed," *A Place in Space* (Washington, D.C.: Counterpoint, 1995), pp. 229–230.

19. John Cronin and Robert Kennedy, Jr., *The Riverkeepers: Two Activists Fight to Reclaim Our Environment as a Basic Human Right* (New York: Scribner's, 1997).

20. See Owen D. Owens's autobiographical/case study narrative of the campaign to protect West Valley Creek in southeastern Pennsylvania, *Living Waters: How to Save Your Local Stream* (New Brunswick: Rutgers University Press, 1993), which acknowledges the influence of English riverkeeper Frank Sawyer's *Keeper of the Stream* (London: Allan Unwin, 1985), p. 148, whereas Cronin and Kennedy treat the U.S. Riverkeepers movement as a native-grown affair.

21. *American Rivers*, 26 (Fall 1998): 5, 10–11.

22. Kathleen Dean Moore, *Riverwalking: Reflections on Moving Water* (New York: Harcourt, 1995), p. 64.

23. Derek Walcott, "Medusa Face," *Critical Essays on Ted Hughes*, ed. Leonard M. Scigaj (New York: G. K. Hall, 1992), p. 43.

24. Ted Hughes, *River* (London: Faber & Faber, 1983), p. 86.

25. Leonard Scigaj, *Ted Hughes* (Boston: G. K. Hall, 1991), p. 134. Terry Gifford argues that Hughes's passion for angling is more inconsistent with his supposed ecocentrism than Scigaj assumes; but he agrees that Hughes has attained "a complex vision of nature that has gone beyond that of other contemporary poets." *Green Voices: Understanding Contemporary Nature Poetry* (Manchester: Manchester University Press, 1995), p. 136.

26. Luna Leopold, *A View of the River* (Cambridge: Harvard University Press, 1994), p. 223.

27. Ted Levin, *Blood Brook: A Naturalist's Home Ground* (Post Mills, Vt.: Chelsea Green, 1992), p. 21.

28. The first book I have found in any language that uses the device of making a waterway its central protagonist far antedates these: Élisée Reclus's charming *Histoire d'un Ruisseau* (1869). But its stream is a generic compound of different specific waterways and cultural traditions of water symbolism, organized partly in terms of source to outflow, partly in terms of topic (e.g., floods, waterfall, boating, islands).

29. Thoreau's predominantly pastoral agenda caused him, however, to shy away from confronting the full array of early-industrial environmental issues arising from the burgeoning factory towns in the Merrimack Valley. See Theodore Steinberg, *Nature Incorporated: Industrialization and the Waters of New England* (Cambridge: Cambridge University Press, 1991), pp. 1–9.

30. Vernon Young, "Mary Austin and the Earth Performance," *Southwest Review*, 35 (1950): 163; Austin, *Land of Little Rain* (1903), in *Stories from the Country of Lost Borders*, ed. Marjorie Pryse (New Brunswick: Rutgers University Press, 1987), p. 39.

31. *Land of Little Rain*, pp. 113–130. Significantly, the book starts by calling the territory by one of its Indian names, "the Country of Lost Borders," but later includes two chapters on "Water Borders," one botanical and the other propertarian in emphasis.

32. Mary Austin to Sinclair Lewis, 28 February 1931, *Literary America 1903–1934: The Mary Austin Letters*, ed. T. M. Pearce (Westport: Greenwood, 1979), p. 142. Ironically, in an essay published the next year, "Regionalism in American Fiction," Austin emphasized Lewis's propensity for portraying American life in generic rather than region-specific terms. *Beyond Borders: The Selected Essays of Mary Austin*, ed. Reuben J. Ellis (Carbondale: University of Southern Illinois Press, 1996), pp. 132–133.

33. For the Austins' role in the Owens Valley controversy (which for Mary Austin involved a second round in the 1920s when Los Angeles put a further, seemingly fatal, drain on valley resources), see William L. Kahrl, *Water and Power: The Conflict over Los Angeles' Water Supply in the Owens Valley* (Berkeley: University of California Press, 1981), pp. 104–108 and passim, and Abraham Hoffman, *Vision or Villainy: Origins of the Owens Valley-Los Angeles Water Controversy* (College Station: Texas A & M Press, 1981), pp. 99–103 and passim. Austin's peripheral involvement on behalf of Arizona in Colorado water rights debates of the late 1920s is noted in Worster, *Rivers of Empire*, pp. 209–210, and more fully evident from unpublished correspondence and newspaper clippings in the Mary Austin papers, Huntington Library, Pasadena, California.

34. Hoffman, *Vision or Villany*, p. 175, overstates the case when he claims that *The Ford* "provided roman à clef characterizations" of the key players in the Owens Valley water war. Kahrl, *Water and Power*, who discusses it together with two lesser novels about the case (pp. 322–324), is closer to the mark in seeing *The Ford* as a strongly stylized synthesis of elements of both the Owens Valley and Hetch Hetchy controversies.

35. Mary Austin, *The Ford* (1917; rpt., Berkeley: University of California Press, 1997), p. 92.

36. *The Ford*, p. 199. The uneasily both/and character of this speech (wanting both land development *and* earth-friendliness) might seem to be open to the same charge of sleazy temporizing that has been leveled in the 1990s against the motto of "sustainable development" as a protective cover for transnational corporatism (see Maartin A. Hajer, *The Politics of Environmental Discourse: Ecological Modernization and the Policy Process* [Oxford: Oxford University Press, 1995]). But on this point if not on other points (e.g., what Anne really thinks of her husband-to-be, Frank Rickart) the novel makes clear that she is sincere as well as wily; and in the world of Austin's fiction, if not in the extratextual world of history, this vision is sustained as the most responsible workable model of environmental citizenship.

37. Esther Lanigan Stineman, *Mary Austin: Song of a Maverick* (New Haven: Yale University Press, 1989), p. 47.

38. For example, in Austin's *A Woman of Genius* (New York: Doubleday, 1912) the feminist imagination clearly predominates; in *Land of Little Rain* it is a subsidiary but shaping aspect of the environmental imagination; in her autobiography *Earth Horizon* (Boston: Houghton, 1932) the emphases sometimes coordinate, sometimes alternate.

39. What Vera Norwood says of *Land of Little Rain* basically holds for *The Ford*: its criticism of "the arrogant development of arid landscapes" is linked with the identification of one's "own nature with the natural round" felt by Austin and other women writers Norwood discusses. *Made from This Earth: American Women and Nature* (Chapel Hill: University of North Carolina Press, 1993), p. 51.

40. From an interview with Harry Salpeter, "Mary Austin, Pioneer," *New York World*, February 23, 1930, Austin papers, Huntington Library, Box 126.

41. See also *Land of Little Rain*, p. 123.

42. See especially Austin's remarkable neoprimitivist manifesto *The American Rhythm* (New York: Harcourt, 1923), which argues that poetics in the United States must take the form of an earth-responsive free-verse expression of which Native chantways provide a prototype and Whitmanian poetics are at best a crude approximation.

43. *The Ford*, p. 294. Nor did this assumption of Indian evanescence entirely disappear; as Leah Dilworth points out in an astute analysis of *The American Rhythm* and Austin's other honorific comments on American Indian culture, her calls for a "new modern American literature" sometimes begin "to sound like literary eugenics" in their emphasis on "how these Native American literary origins could become the *inherited* legacy of modern non-Indian American writers." *Imagining Indians in the Southwest: Persistent Visions of a Primitive Past* (Washington, D.C.: Smithsonian Institution Press, 1996), p. 187.

44. This is not to say that Berry disdains cultures other than his own or that he is uncritical of Appalachian Euroculture's bigotry (he has written a whole book about the shame of racism in the region). But his local loyalties and his praised Amish community seem strongly cultural-particularistic as well as place-specific.

45. Snyder, "Coming into the Watershed," p. 234. In a collection of essays that reprints Snyder's, Japanese-American bioregionalist Carole Koda extends Snyder's cultural inclusivism by calling for a "diversity beyond multiculturalism" that honors different traditions while subsuming identity politics through a shared devotion to the ecology of place. "Dancing in the Borderland: Finding Our Common Ground in North America," in Snyder, Koda, and Wendell Berry, *Three on Community* (Boise, Idaho: Limberlost, 1996), pp. 63–64.

46. Percival Everett, *Watershed* (Minneapolis: Graywolf, 1996), p. 152.

47. The late nineteenth-century regionalist perspective is by no means, however, historically "innocent." In particular, the degree to which it might be conceived as complicit in nationalist and/or imperialist ideologies has been a subject of intense discussion during the past decade. See Sandra Zagarell, "Troubling Regionalism: Rural Life and the Cosmopolitan Eye in Jewett's *Deephaven*," *American Literary History*, 10 (1998): 639–663, for a thoughtful recent state-of-the-field reflection.

48. Gregory McNamee, *Gila: The Life and Death of an American River* (New York: Orion, 1994), p. 9.

49. Marjory Stoneman Douglas, *The Everglades: River of Grass* (1947; rpt. with two afterwords, Sarasota, Fla.: Pineapple Press, 1997), especially chapters 12–18.

50. William Howarth, "Imagined Territory: The Writing of Wetlands," *New Literary History*, 30 (Summer 1999): 509–540, is a wide-ranging meditation on the history and

uses of wetlands as cultural symbol in relation to wetlands' perceived ecological importance. Howarth rightly points out that long before the Wetlands Act of 1973 certain individual nature writers (like John Bartram and Henry Thoreau) had been drawn to swamplands out of aesthetic attraction as well as from scientific interest. The attitudinal shift in U.S. culture more broadly from negatively regarded "swamp" to positively esteemed "wetland" is a late twentieth-century phenomenon, however.

51. For example, Earth Island Institute's Carl Anthony's definition of "wetland" as "a swamp that white people care about." Interview with Theodore Roszak, *Ecopsychology: Restoring the Earth, Healing the Mind*, ed. Roszak, Mary E. Gomes, Allen D. Kramer (San Francisco: Sierra Club, 1995), p. 275.

52. Douglas, *The Everglades*, pp. 297–299, 364–373, 376. Despite a certain amount of exoticization (though nowhere near the level of the sentimental-cartoonish sketches of nubile women and diapered warriors contributed by illustrator Robert Fink), Douglas's portrait of Indians is remarkable for its respectful recognition of their resourceful strategies of economic adaptation and political maneuvering. She is emphatically not a simple primitivist with respect either to nature or to aboriginal culture.

53. Joseph C. Gallegos, "Acequia Tales: Stories from a Chicano Centennial Farm," *Chicano Culture, Ecology, Politics*, ed. Devon G. Peña (Tucson: University of Arizona Press, 1998), p. 237. Gallegos explains that "this" *la llorona* (weeping woman) is one who supposedly drowned her children (pp. 247–248). (More obliquely, the figure may descend from the figure of Cortez's native interpreter and mistress, La Malinche.) José A. Rivera, *Acequia Culture: Water, Land, and Community in the Southwest* (Albuquerque: University of New Mexico Press, 1998), is a well-documented history of the institutional arrangements. It argues that Hispanic settler culture was influenced by a preexisting "water ethic" derived from community-based conservation laws and practices in medieval Spain (pp. 29–30). Stanley Crawford, *Mayordomo: Chronicle of an Acequia in Northern New Mexico* (Albuquerque: University of New Mexico Press, 1988), and William deBuys and Alex Harris, *River of Traps* (Albuquerque: University of New Mexico Press, 1990), provide entertaining autobiographical narratives of Anglos attempting to master the sometimes arcane environmental and social intricacies of acequia culture.

54. Edward Abbey, *Desert Solitaire* (1968; New York: Ballantine, 1981), p. 200.

55. Ellen Meloy, *Raven's Exile: A Season on the Green River* (New York: Holt, 1994), p. 65.

56. *The Organic Machine* is the title of Richard White's book on "The Remaking of the Columbia River" (its subtitle) into a working river through engineering and (at another level) simulation technology (New York: Hill & Wang, 1995), such that the river has long since become "not just water flowing through its original bed" but "a partial human creation"; ergo, "natural" and "cultural" can no longer be disentangled: "What is real is the mixture" (pp. 110, 111). The most influential position statement by a revisionist environmental historian about "wilderness," conventionally understood, as cultural hallucination is William Cronon, "The Trouble with Wilderness; or, Getting Back to the Wrong Nature," *Uncommon Ground: Toward Reinventing Nature*, ed. Cronon (New York: Norton, 1995), pp. 69–90.

57. Ralph Waldo Emerson, *Nature, in Collected Works of Ralph Waldo Emerson*, vol. 1, ed. Robert E. Spiller et al. (Cambridge: Harvard University Press, 1971), p. 7.

58. Meloy, *Raven's Exile*, p. 182. Abbey's *Desert Solitaire*, by contrast, does not mix outback and urban landscapes in this manner.

59. Levin, *Blood Brook*, pp. 185, 195.

60. James M. Symons, *Drinking Water* (College Station: Texas A & M Press, 1995), p. 54.

61. All histories of modern infrastructure comment on the enormous jump in per capita consumption with the shift from outdoor wells and privies to indoor plumbing: in nineteenth-century Boston, for example, by a factor of eight. Alice Outwater, *Water: A Natural History* (New York: Basic, 1996), p. 141. When supply systems are not maintained, the problem is aggravated; Sandra Postel claims, for example, that "more than half the urban water supply simply disappears in Cairo, Jakarta, Lagos, Lima, and Mexico City." *Last Oasis* (New York: Norton, 1997), p. 159.

62. According to U.S. environmental historian John Opie, agriculture in the western states "consumes over 80 percent of the nation's fresh water supplies, probably half of which is wasted" (*Ogallala*, p. 299). Postel, *Last Oasis,* chapters 3–5, and Robin Clarke, *Water: The International Crisis* (Cambridge: MIT Press, 1992), chapters 4 and 8, draw similar conclusions on a global scale, citing chronic inefficiencies of large dams and irrigation schemes (siltation, evaporation, salinization, declining productivity per acre) as well as overpumping of nonrenewable groundwater.

63. According to Jean-Pierre Goubert, *The Conquest of Water,* trans. Andrew Wilson (Princeton: Princeton University Press, 1989), in French cities between 1760 and 1900 "the overall estimation of 'needs' evolved . . . from a few litres to several hundred litres per inhabitant per day" (p. 52). Peter Rogers, *America's Water: Federal Roles and Responsibilities* (Cambridge: MIT Press, 1993), reports that U.S. per capita consumption declined between 1965 and 1990, though average domestic use nationwide remained well above 200 liters (pp. 35–36).

64. Klyza, "Bioregional Possibilities in Vermont," *Bioregionalism,* ed. McGinnis, pp. 92–94.

65. Ian L. McHarg, *Design with Nature* (Garden City, N.Y.: Natural History Press, 1969), p. 184.

66. McHarg, "The Place of Nature in the City of Man," *To Heal the Earth: Selected Writings of Ian L. McHarg,* ed. McHarg and Frederick R. Steiner (Washington, D.C.: Island Press, 1998), p. 35. McHarg's watershed conservationism draws on a twentieth-century tradition of regional planning that goes back to the mentor of his own mentor (Lewis Mumford); see Patrick Geddes, *Cities in Evolution,* rev. ed. (1915; London: Williams & Norgate, 1949), pp. 51–52, and Geddes, "The Valley Plan of Civilization," *Survey,* 54 (June 1, 1925): 288–290, 322–325.

67. James Joyce, *Finnegans Wake* (New York: Viking, 1939), p. 619. The book grandiosely mythicizes its landscape, of course, transfiguring Liffey into Anna Livia Plurabelle, Howth Castle and Environs into Humphrey Chimpden Earwicker. But so too has "watershed" become a bioregionalist mythos at a more material level.

Not only has this book, like all works of research, been a collaborative effort in ways the notes indicate, it greatly benefited from the assistance of many people and institutions over a period of years, although the responsibility for its shortcomings rests with me alone.

For encouragement, support, and frank criticism at various stages of this project I thank all who have read and commented on prospecti, draft portions, in some cases even the entire manuscript, and/or who have patiently listened to my repeated expatiations. These include Jonathan Bate, Nina Baym, Bill Brown, Frederick Buell, Jia-rui Chong, Wai Chee Dimock, Richard Foreman, Wayne Franklin, John Mitchell, Nicholas Parrillo, H. Daniel Peck, Daniel J. Philippon, Leah Plunkett, Kent Ryden, Donald Swearer, Laura Thiemann, Lindsay Waters, Donald Worster, and the anonymous second reader of this manuscript for Harvard University Press. They also include many of my colleagues in Harvard's Department of English, from whom I have sought assistance on more occasions than I can count, and who have consistently been a source of encouragement and wise counsel.

The 1997 National Endowment for the Humanities Institute at Vassar College in Environmental Imagination allowed me over a period of some weeks to rethink my plans for this book in light of discussion of issues raised by my previous studies of literature and environment. For that I thank especially the Institute's director H. Daniel Peck, as well as my coteachers William Howarth, Wayne Franklin, Hertha Wong, and Barry Lopez, and the twenty-five university and college faculty members of the Institute.

Other institutions have provided welcome opportunities to test out earlier versions of certain chapters or arguments in lecture and conference paper form: the Association for the Study of Literature and Environment, Boston University, the Bread Loaf School of English, the

University of California at Davis, the California Institute of Technology, the University of Chicago, the University of Connecticut, the Humanities Center of Cornell University, Denison University, the Faulkner Conference at the University of Mississippi, Harvard University's Humanities Center, Harvard's Graduate School of Design, the Harvard Seminar in Environmental Values, Hope College, Indiana State University, the Japan Association for the Study of Literature and Environment, the Japan Society for the Promotion of Science, the University of Kansas, Kenyon College, Middlebury College, Oregon State University, the University of Oregon, the University of Rhode Island, the University of Southern Maine, Swarthmore College, the University of Virginia School of Architecture, the University of Wales Swansea (host of the first U.K. Conference on Literature and Environment), Washington University, and the University of Washington. On and around those occasions I was grateful for suggestions and criticisms offered by many colleagues, in addition to those already named, and doubtless a number of others who—to my shame—I cannot immediately recall: M. H. Abrams, Sara Blair, Bonnie Costello, John Elder, Fritz Fleischmann, Jonathan Freedman, Greg Garrard, Kevin Gilmartin, Daniel Kevles, Michael Holt, Lewis Hyde, Yoko Ima-izumi, Myra Jehlen, Abram Kaplan, Donald Kartiganer, Elizabeth Klimasmith, Dominic LaCapra, David Levin, Glen Love, James McConkey, Thomas McHaney, John McWilliams, Leo Marx, Bruce Mazlish, Elizabeth Meyer, Satya Mohanty, Michael Oriard, Robert Pack, Jay Parini, Noel Polk, Vivian Pollak, David Robinson, Peter Rogers, William Rossi, Marjorie Sabin, Elizabeth Schultz, Gary Snyder, John Tallmadge, Alfred Tauber, Wynn Thomas, Priscilla Wald, Mark Wallace, Cindy Weinstein, Timothy Weiskel, Louise Westling, and Bryan Wolf.

A number of present and former graduate and undergraduate students with whom I have had the pleasure to work during the last half-dozen years have helped me think through this book's ideas while working with me as students, and/or teaching fellows, and/or research assistants, in the course of moving on to higher endeavors. In addition to those already named above, I would especially thank Adam Bradley, James Dawes, Susan Ferguson, Rebecca Gould, Scott Hess, Steven Holmes, Stephanie LeMenager, Nathaniel Lewis, Runal Mehta, Sianne Ngai, William Pannapacker, Tovis Page, Judith Richardson,

Polina Rikoun, Woden Teachout, and Markella Zanni. I also thank the graduate students in my Harvard seminar on Space, Place, and Literary Imagination and the undergraduate students and graduate teaching fellows in my course in American Literature and the American Environment.

For a variety of other forms of assistance, I am indebted to Richard Audet, Elizabeth DeSombre, William Handley, Eric Higgs, Shannon Jackson, John Kavadny, Kathryne Lyndberg, Brett Mizelle, Leonard Neufeldt, Onno Oerlemans, Kimberley Patton, Sam Bass Warner, and Martin Weitzmann.

Portions of earlier versions of Chapters 1, 2, and 5 were published, respectively, in *Critical Inquiry, Borderlines,* and *Faulkner and the Natural World,* ed. Donald Kartiganer and Ann Abadie. I thank the University of Chicago, the University of Wales, and the University Press of Mississippi for permission to reprint. In addition I thank *New Literary History,* edited by Ralph Rader and Herbert Tucker, for the invitation to write a review-commentary for its special 2000 "Ecocriticism" issue that helped crystallize some of my ideas; and I thank Heinz Ickstadt and Walter Hoelbling of the European Association of American Studies for the invitation to address the 2000 EAAS Conference in Graz, Austria.

To the Guggenheim Foundation, to Oberlin College, and to Harvard University, I am indebted for tangible support at key points in my research on environmental imagination. The staff of the Wellesley College Archives and the Huntington Library were most helpful in assisting my consultation of their Katharine Lee Bates and Mary Austin collections, respectively.

The dedication marks my greatest single debt. What I have laboriously studied, she lives.

Index

Note: Instances of proper names appearing in endnotes are generally indexed only when the subject of remark as well as citation.

Abbey, Edward: adventure narrative tradition, 260; contemporary watershed consciousness, 268; monasticism, 156; toxic discourse overlooked by, 46

Abram, David, 75–76

Abrams, M. H., 237, 301n36

Acequia culture. *See* Mexican-American environmental issues

Achebe, Chinua, 245

Adam, Barbara, 69

Adams, Henry 10, 202

Addams, Jane: Bates and, 10; Chicago exposition, 160–161; class in/and, 17, 156, 318n122; commitment to democratic reform process, 13–14, 167–169; on discourse as self-protective sanctuary, 50–51; domesticity themes, 17, 168; environmental imagination as cultural construct vs. experience, 16–17; Muir and, as Progressive-era environmental reformers/writers, 12–18; park/playground reform, 12–13, 272–273nn41–42; paternalism of, 168; Pinchot and, 12; place-sense, 14–18; proto-ecofeminism of, 318n22; sanitarianism and, 15–17, 27, 160–161, 167; Tolstoi and, 156; voluntary submission to limits, 14, 152; mentioned, 2, 9, 28, 43

    Works: "A Modern Lear," 167–169; *Twenty Years at Hull-House,* 14–18; quoted, 50, 156

Advertising. *See* Media

African-American culture/literature: "c.p. time," 59; environmental justice commitment vs. conservation/preservation, 275n15; environmental values relative to other populations, 39–40, 288n10, 317n120; environmental victimage and, 37, 39–40, 41–43, 92, 123, 323–330, 359–365, 411–412; *flânerie* tradition and, 125–128, 158–159, 162; great migration (South-North), 58; place/race relation and, 37, 41–42, 57–58, 78–83, 123, 157–167; supposed fitness for southern swampland labor, 319n18; urban reform/representation and, 73–83, 125–128, 138–142; watershed consciousness and, 257–258, 339n50; as whalemen, 328n43. *See also* Environmental justice; Place; Race; Urban(ism)

Agnew, John, 42, 60

Agrarianism: in Berry, 157–158, 160, 164–170, 257, 338n44; of Indian tribals, 230–232; satirized, 146–147; watershed imagination, 247–248, 252–257, 239, 339n53. *See also* Bioregionalism; Rural(ism)

"America the Beautiful." *See* Bates

American Rivers (organization), 249

Amin, Samir, 324n3

Ammons, Archibald: *flânerie* in, 89; place-sense in, 62–63; toxic discourse in *(Garbage),* 53, 54

Anderson, Alison, 202

Andrews, Malcolm, 302n48
Animal liberation, 7, 204, 331n7. *See also*
Extensionism
Animal story, 187–188, 204–205, 229,
232–233
Animals (and birds): big-creature bias in
human view of, 201–203; communities
of, 14, 208–209, 232–234; Endangered
Species Act, 8, 218, 238–239; extension
of moral and/or legal standing to,
194–195; face, power of, 202, 330n70;
game management, 185–186, 188, 192;
as icons of environmental endangerment, 190, 193–195, 201–205; images of
human bestialization, 139–140, 149,
212, 237–238; intelligence, 203, 213–214;
interspecies imagination, 193–195,
207–210, 216–223, 233–234, 234–248; as
moral mirrors, 187–188

Species: albatross, 237; ass, 236–237;
black bear, 176, 187, 190, 194, 323n62;
Canada goose, 186–187; Cape Sable
seaside sparrow, 218; cetaceans,
202–223; deer, 178, 184, 187–188, 194,
220; dog, 114–115, 116; dolphin, 203;
(African) elephant, 224, 232–234; grizzly bear, 210; muskrat, 186; narwhal,
220; (Florida) panther, 238–240; passenger pigeon, 194–195; polar bear,
220; (North Sea common) seal, 184;
wasp, 235–236; grey whale, 326n31;
killer/orca whale, 204, 216–217, 219,
220–221, 223; sperm whale, 204,
205–214, 220–223; (grey) wolf, 184, 194,
220

See also Extensionism; Metaphor;
Whales
Anthony, Carl, 280n15, 339n51
Anthropocentric environmentalism: environmental justice movement as, 6,
32–33, 38, 39–40, 278n10, 281n21; interdependence with ecocentric concerns, 7–9, 18, 33, 38, 45, 84–85, 193–195,
224–225, 236–242, 252–265, 278n10,
279n15, 281n21, 282n39; origins/conse-

quence of western anthropocentric/
ecocentric division in aesthetics/
ethics, 224–236; pragmatic attraction
relative to ecocentricism, 6–10, 32;
species protection, motive for,
201–204; toxic discourse and/as, 8–9,
32–45, 53–56. *See also* Ecocentric; Environmental ethics; Extensionism;
Race; Toxic discourse; Watershed
Apache, Western, place sense of, 63, 75.
See also Native American writing
Architecture: architectural restoration,
68–69, 87, 119–120, 125; "architectural
uncanny," 135, 162; contaminated domestic spaces, 36–37, 42, 49, 135–136; in
gothic fiction, 144; home-centric place
sense, 64, 65–66, 81; houses, 23, 36, 37,
60, 66, 81; as imposition on nature, 87,
122–128; infrastructure, 94–95, 101–102,
262; landscape, 85–86, 87, 100–102, 125;
malls/stores, 23, 42; and/as metaphor, 91, 127, 135–136; monuments,
103–104, 105; planned communities,
73, 167–168; prisons, 69, 133; schools,
35, 42–43; slums/tenements, 10, 15–16,
90–91, 138–141, 160–164; suburbs, 37,
41; theme parks, 57, 204, 216–217;
towns and villages, 37, 43–44, 64, 73,
143–144; urban design/planning,
85–87, 107, 110, 115, 119, 127, 264–265;
urban entrapment, 42–43, 80–83,
132–142, 160–164; urban panoramas,
23–24, 57–58, 80–81, 87–88, 90–91,
92–93, 95–97, 103–104, 106–108, 109–112,
114–115, 121–128, 132–134, 150–153,
158–159, 264–265. *See also Flâneur;*
Metaphor; Urban(ism)
Auden, Wystan Hugh, 1–2
Audubon, John James, 215
Austin, Mary: Anglo-Hispanic-Native relations, depictions of, 253–254, 256–257,
338n43; anti-anthropocentrism, 146;
ecofeminism in, 255–256, 338n39; historical consciousness in, 253–254, 258;
local colorism and, 252, 258; percep-

tion of watercourses as key to desert ecology, 253; proposed water epic, 253–254, 256; regional water rights activism, of 254; view of irrigation, 259; watershed imagination in, 252–257, 262; mentioned, 2, 29
  Works: The American Rhythm, 338n42; *Earth Horizon,* 337n38; *The Ford,* 252–257; *Land of Little Rain,* 89, 146, 253, 254, 256, 258; *A Woman of Genius,* 337n38

Baraka, Amiri, 117
Bartram, William: Franklin and, 20–21; hyperfocus on descriptive detail, 21–22
Basso, Keith, 63, 66, 75, 76
Bate, Jonathan 7, 246, 312n46
Bates, Katharine Lee: "America the Beautiful," composition and ideology, 9–12, 18, 27, 272n33; Chicago Exposition and, 10, 160; dual urban-rural reference of, 10–12; expansionism in, 11; religiocentric dimension of, 272n34; settlement house movement and, 11; "Year of the Vision" as companion piece, 11; *Yellow Clover* and lesbian affirmation, 272n38
Baudelaire, Charles, 89, 103, 300n30
Baudrillard, Jean, 57, 294n59
Beck, Ulrich 1, 30, 32, 280n16, 324n4
Beecher, Catherine, 36, 136
Beer, Gillian, 149
Benjamin, Walter, 89, 298n18
Bentham, Jeremy, compared with Darwin as moral extensionist, 225–229, 241
Bergson, Henri, 145
Berry, Thomas, 324n4
Berry, Wendell: agrarianism of, 157–158, 160, 164; communitarian commitment of, 157–158, 164–165, 257; decorum in, 159; elegiac dimension of, 159–160, 166; environmental restoration priority, 85, 165–167; family values in, 159, 164; patriarchalism/androcentrism of, 158, 160; place, valuation of, 75, 76, 77,

78, 115–116; poetic persona, 158; as reinhabitor, 85, 157–158, 165–167; voluntary acceptance of limits of regional/ethnic culture, 157–167; mentioned, 2, 28
  Other authors: Brooks and, 156–167; Frost and, 157; Jeffers and, 166; W. C. Williams and, 115–116
  Works: Clearing, 68, 160, 164–166; *A Continuous Harmony* (quoted), 115–116, 157; "Elegy" (quoted), 159–160; *Home Economics* (quoted), 164; "In this World" (quoted), 158; "The New Politics of Community," 165–166; "Poetry and Place" (quoted), 55, 75; "Stay Home," 157; "To a Siberian Woodman," 160; *The Unsettling of America* (quoted), 164; *What Are People For?* (quoted), 157
Bhabha, Homi, 65
Biophilia hypothesis, 25
Bioregionalism: defined, 297n1; Austin, watershed representation and, 252–258; Berry and, 84–85, 115–116, 257 and n44; environmental justice and, 249, 257–258; ethnocentricity vs. multicultural inclusiveness of, 256–258; reinhabitation as goal of, 84–87; Snyder and, 85, 124–125, 248–249, 257; urban manifestations of, 85–87, 110–112, 115–116, 117–120, 264–265; utopian work in progress, 116–117, 120; watershed consciousness and, 124–125, 244–265; in W. C. Williams, urban bioregionalism and, 110–112, 115–116, 117–120, 246. *See also* Place; Regionalism; Reinhabitation; Watershed
Blake, William: *Jerusalem* anticipating urban ecology, 90–91; "London," 90; Whitman and, 95, 300–301n35; W.C. Williams and, 115, 120; mentioned, 236, 281
Blotner, Joseph, 177
Body: "body-machine complex," 141; environmental determinism and,

Body (*continued*)
137–141, 146–147, 162; place sense and, 26, 55–56, 61, 71, 75–76, 158–159, 290n6; "posthuman" embodiment, 6, 55; toxic discourse/toxification and, 42–43, 45–47, 48–49, 53–56; urban metaphor and, 91, 109, 118–120, 127, 311n43; watershed-body metaphor, 243
Booth, Charles, 245
Bourdieu, Pierre, 19
Bowlby, Rachel, 304n73
Bowles, Paul, 74
Boyer, Paul, 14–15
Brand, Dana, 298n18
Brontë, Emily, 144
Brooks, Gwendolyn: architectural uncanny in, 161–162; and/on Chicago, 157–164; communitarian commitment of, 157, 161–166; decorum in, 159; family values in, 159–160, 165; *flânerie* tradition and, 158–159, 162, 298n17; gynocentrism, 158, 160–162; Pan-Africanism, 160; place sense, 158–165; politicization of later work, 161–165, 316n103; portrait poem tradition and, 158–159, 163; voluntary acceptance of limits of place/culture, 157–167; mentioned, 2, 28
    Other authors: Berry and, 156–167; Dickinson and, 157, 159; Dunbar and, 316n97; L. Hughes and, 159; Wright and, 140
    Works: Annie Allen, 161; "Horses Graze" (quoted), 129; "In the Mecca," 160–164; *Jump Bad,* 161; "Kitchenette Building," 140; *Maud Martha,* 161; *Report from Part One* (quoted), 159; *Report from Part Two,* 316n100; "Song in the Front Yard" (quoted), 161; "Sundays of Satin-Legs Smith," 158–159; "To Black Women," 160
Brown, Bill, 275nn67, 73
Brown, Charles Brockden, 43, 95
Browne, J. Ross, 208, 212

Brunner, John, 39
Buell, Frederick, 324n3
Bunyan, John, 36, 73
Burns, Robert, 236
Burroughs, John, 145–146, 204
Byron, George Gordon Lord, 69, 136

Caldwell, Lynton, 201, 218; quoted, 198
Capitalism. *See* Global environmental consciousness; Imperialism; Settler culture
Carson, Rachel: animal story and, 204; *The Sea Around Us* and traditional mythologization of ocean, 200, 325n18; mentioned, 2, 22, 47, 232
    Silent Spring: as awakening from previous marine romanticism, 200–201; Cold War and, 39; conventions of contemporary toxic discourse articulated in, 27, 35–45; domesticity emphasis/exemplification, 35, 42; eco-catastrophe tradition and, 36–39; environmental justice movement and, 40–42, 44–45; feminism of, 41, 282n39; influence of, 8, 36, 281n27, 285n69; middle class target audience of, 44–45; pastoralism in, 37–38; respect for scientific authority, 44
Cartmill, Matt, 322n46; quoted, 185
Casey, Edward, 55, 61, 67
Cather, Willa, 171, 256, 286n73
Chadwick, Edwin, 135, 307n2
Chatwin, Bruce, 66
Cheever, Henry, 208
Cheng, Vincent, 303n59
Chicago: Addams on, 12–18; Bates on, 10–12; Chicago, University of, sociology, 142; Columbian Exposition/White City, 10–11, 160–161; Dreiser on, 150–153; economic dominance of hinterland, 11, 86; North Side, 158; park/playground reform in early 20th century, 12–13; Pullman strike (Adams), 167–169; South Side/Black

Belt/Bronzeville, 138–142 (Wright), 157–167 (Brooks); stockyards (Sinclair), 136–137; transit history of, 152–153

Chickasaw. *See* Faulkner; Hogan; Native American writing

Child, Lydia: *Letters from New-York,* 94, 103

Choucri, Nazli, 280

City. *See* Urban(ism)

Clare, John, 236

Class, and environment(alism): environmental justice movements and, 6, 32–35, 257, 270n23, 278–280nn10–11,13,16, 281n26; (socio)environmental victimization of nonelites, 32–35, 37–38, 41–44, 80–83, 110–112, 118–120, 122–124, 129–132, 136–143, 146–149, 150–152, 157, 160–165, 167–169, 211–212, 229–232, 234, 236–242, 259, 263; *flânerie* and class privilege, 88–89, 99, 101, 107, 110–115, 121–122, 162; genteel environmentalist attitudes, 12–14, 44–45, 50–51, 167–169; hunting, views of, 182–185; intergroup environmental(ist) coalitions, 33–35, 39–40, 53–54; middle-class environmental victimage, 35–37, 42, 44–45, 49–50, 51–52, 55–56, 132–136, 279n13, 196n83; middle-class naïvete about stability of place, 19, 56, 64–65, 67–68; preservationism, class basis of, 32, 37; problems in correlating environmental attitudes by class, 270n23, 278n10, 279n13, 296n86; watershed ethics and, 248–249, 253, 257; western vs. nonwestern, 33–34, 279n15, 281n21. *See also* Community; Determinism; Environmental justice; *Flâneur;* Preservation; Race; Toxic discourse

Clayton, Patti, 326n31

Coleridge, Samuel Taylor: moral extensionism in "To a Young Ass," 236–237; "cosmic ecology," 237–238 ("Rime"), 333n23 ("Nightingale")

Collodi, Carlo: *Pinocchio,* 219

Commons: global, 196–199; oceanic, 199–201; "tragedy of," 199, 325n11. *See also* Global environmental consciousness: Ocean; Whales

Community, and environment(alism): biotic and other nonhuman, 14, 183, 187–188, 203–205, 207–209, 232–234; "disaster subcultures," 53–54; *flânerie* and, 92–93, 95, 97–100, 104, 106–109, 113–115, 162; place sense and sense of, 14–18, 57–58, 61–62, 63–64, 68–69, 70–75, 78–83, 157–167; toxic/other environmental victimage, resistance and sense of, 32–42, 47, 53–56, 122–124, 136–142, 157, 163–164, 230–232, 238–242, 279n13, 289n101; watershed consciousness and, 247–249, 243–259, 263–265. *See also* Bioregionalism; Environmental justice; Love Canal; Place; Reinhabitation; Toxic discourse; Watershed

Conrad, Joseph: identity refashioning, 70; lure of ocean in, 199–200

Heart of Darkness: genre traditions behind, 249; implication of London squalor, 245–246; and river-empire topos, 224

Conservation. *See* Preservation

Cooper, James Fenimore, 171, 174, 178, 442

Cooper, Susan Fenimore, 171

Country. *See* Rural(ism)

Crabbe, George, 143–144, 147

Crane, Hart, 117

Cresswell, Tim: quoted, 129

Cronon, William, 11, 86, 291n18

Cullingworth, Barry, 127

Daly, Herman, 198

Darling, J. Norwood, 39

Darwin, Charles: Bentham and, 225–229, 241; Burroughs and, 145–146; Dickens and, 309n16; evolutionary theory, 131,

Darwin, Charles (*continued*)
245, 210; Hardy and, 148–149; Marsh and, 145; moral extensionism in, 225–229, 241; natural theology in, 131, 313n53; putative deterministic materialism of, 131, 145–147; social Darwinism and, 131, 145; species theory and, 213, 228
    Works: Descent of Man, 225–229; *Origin of Species*, 145, 225; *Voyage of the Beagle*, 260
Davis, Mike, 57–58
Davis, Rebecca Harding: "Life in the Iron Mills," 43, 137
Davis, Susan G., 216–217
DeCerteau, Michel, 104
Deep ecology, 7, 25, 248, 270nn22–23, 275n71. *See also* Ecocentric
DeLillo, Don: *Underworld* and imagination of waste, 52; *White Noise*, risk society, and metaphorization of toxicity, 51–52
Denham, John: "Cooper's Hill," 126, 244–245
Den Tandt, Christophe, 284n64, 314n68
DeQuincey, Thomas, 50, 90
Determinism, (socio)environmental: attractions of, 130–131, 149–157; conflations of building-occupant-context imagined, 133, 135, 136–138; Darwinism/social Darwinism and, 131, 136–150; environmental ethics and, 170–171; gothic fiction and, 136, 144; literary, defined, 310n26; modern origins of, 129–131; natural dis/advantage of regional environment, 6 and n18; naturalist fiction and, 136–142, 149–153; philosophic materialism and, 149–150, 153–155; Progressive-era "positive environmentalism" and, 13–14; resistance to, 129–130, 133–134, 136, 155–156, 167–169; rise of statistics and, 131; rural representation and, 143–149, 155, 166; sanitarianism and, 131, 135–136; in (Chicago) sociology, 142; toxic dis-

course and, 129; urban ghettoes and, 136–142, 160–165; voluntarily self-imposed, in allegiance to bounded community, 14, 156–169. *See also* Class; Environmental justice
Devi, Masheweta: "Pterodactyl," 230, 232–234
Diamond, Jared, 269n18, 307n1
Dick, Philip, 39
Dickens, Charles: dweller-dwelling metaphor in, 135–136; environmental deterministic elements in, 131–137, 144; essentialization of character in, 131, 134, 136, 308n9; exurban scenes, 92, 143; gothic and, 135, 136, 144; prison experience and/in, 69, 132–134; sanitarianism/toxic discourse in, 132–136, 246; mentioned, 28, 44, 46, 95, 265
    Other authors: Darwin and, 309n16; Emerson and, 131–132; Stowe and, 309n17; Thoreau and, 136; Whitman and, 91–94, 300n27, 302n48; Wordsworth and, 309n17
    Works: Bleak House, 77, 132; *Dombey and Son*, 91–92, 144, 300n27, 309n17; *Great Expectations*, 136; *Hard Times*, 43, 47–48, 132; *Household Words*, 308n7; *Little Dorrit*, 132–137, 144; *Oliver Twist*, 94; *Our Mutual Friend*, 94; *Sketches by Boz*, 103
Dickinson, Emily, 157, 159
Dillard, Annie, 156
Disney, Walt: *Bambi* (film), 187–188; Celebration (Florida), 73, 294n65; Disneyworld, 57; *Pinocchio* (film), 219; mentioned, 220
Donald, James, 304n77
Dorman, Robert L., 186
Dos Passos, John, 55
Dostoyevsky, Fyodor, 142
Douglas, Marjory Stoneman, 258–259
Drayton, Thomas: *Poly-Olbion*, 244
Dreiser, Theodore: aesthetic impressionism in, 150–151, 152–153; on Chicago, 150–151, 152, 153; determin-

ism of, 149–153; urban ecology in, 152–153; mentioned, 2

Other authors: Haeckel and, 149; Jeffers and, 153–155; Sinclair and, 150; Spencer and, 149–150; Whitman and, 152; Wright and, 142, 150, 153

Works: American Tragedy, 152; *A Book about Myself* (quoted), 150–151; *The Color of a Great City* (quoted), 151; *Dawn* (quoted), 150, 151, 390n73; *The Genius,* 314n73; *A Hoosier Holiday* (quoted), 151; *Jennie Gerhardt,* 152, quoted 129; *Sister Carrie,* 152, 298n17; *The Titan,* 152–153

Dunbar, Paul Laurence, 316n97

Dunlap, Thomas, 320ns30,32

Eckersley, Robyn, 270n24

Ecocentric/ecocentrism: in *Bambi,* 187–188; diversity of positions encompassed by, 6, 269–270n24; 226–228, ethics of care and/as, 6, 269–270n22; as ideal vs. practicality, 6–7; interdependence with anthropocentric(ism), 7–9, 18, 33, 38, 45, 84–85, 183–195, 224–225, 236–242, 262–265 passim, 278n10, 279n15, 281n21, 282n39; in Jeffers, 153–155; in nature writing, 146; vs. nonanthropocentrism, 331n7; origins/consequence of anthropocentric/ecocentric antithesis, 224–226; Puritanism and/as, 7. *See also* Anthropocentric environmentalism; Ecofeminism; Extensionism; Reinhabitation

Ecocriticism: defined, 2–3, 267n4; general applicability, 3; multidimensionality of, 17–18; prior range and limits of, 6–7, 45; mentioned, 67

Ecofascism, 6–7, 130, 155, 228, 270n24, 323n55

Ecofeminism: in Addams, 318n22; Austin and, 255–256, 338n39; in body as site of toxification, 290n4; Carson and, 282n39, 284n54; deep ecology and, 270n22; ethics of care and, 6, 239–241,

255, 269–270n22; as global environmentalist paradigm, 197, 324n4; in Hogan's *Power,* 239–241; narrative's significance for, 239–242; toxified body and, 54, 290n4. *See also* Gender

Ecological conscience. *See* Leopold

Ecopopulism. *See* Environmental justice

"Ecosystem people." *See* Imperialism

Elder, John, 85

Eliot, Thomas Stearns: "Love Song of J. Alfred Prufrock," 127; *The Waste Land,* 99; mentioned 70, 115, 117, 159

Emerson, Ralph Waldo, 31, 131–132, 143, 145, 215, 261

Engels, Freidrich, 43, 103, 137

Environment: first usage of term, 2; implies both "natural" and "human-built" dimensions, 3; increasing anthropogenic remolding of, 3–5; limits of human dominance of, 5–6; mutual construction of culture and, 6, 16–17, 31, 45–46, 60–61, 280n15; as present-day public priority, 1, 8–9, 18, 32–35, 196–199, 263–265. *See also* Nature; Rural(ism); Urban(ism)

Environmental ethics. *See* Animal liberation; Anthropocentric environmentalism; Ecocentric; Ecofeminism; Environmental justice; Extensionism; Hunting; Imagination; *individual authors*

Environmental justice; antiracist dimension of, 32–33, 38, 41–42, 44–45, 230–232, 238–240, 257–259, 263; community orientation of, 35–40, 47, 53–54; as global environmentalist paradigm, 33–34, 197; in literature, 46–48, 230–232, 236–242, 253–259, 262–263; and mainstream environmentalism, 6–8, 33–35, 38–40, 258–259; as movement of the disempowered, 6, 8, 32–35, 38–42, 44–45, 53–56; pastoral and, 37–38; preservation/conservation and, 8, 32–33, 38, 40, 45–46; toxic anxiety and, 32–33, 35–38, 40–45, 47–50; in Whit-

Environmental justice (*continued*)
man's journalism, 94, 97. *See also*
Class; Love Canal; Race; Toxic discourse
Environmental restoration, 60, 69,
84–87, 120, 125; Berry and, 85, 165–167;
Leopold and, 191. *See also* Reinhabitation; Urban(ism)
Environmental unconscious: defined,
22–27; distinguished from semi-ana-
logues, 25–26; Faulkner, 177–183,
190–191; Hogan, 241; Leopold, 186;
place sense and, 28, 61–62; reflecting
foreshortened perception, 18–22;
virtues of imperception, 19, 21–22;
Whitman, 96–97; W. C. Williams,
114–115. *See also* Imagination
Eurocentrism, 65, 185–196. *See also*
Global environmental consciousness;
Imperialism; Settler culture
Everett, Percival: *Watershed*, 257–258
Everson, William, 314n76
Extensionism, moral: anthropocentric
vs. nonanthropocentric, 225–230; con-
temporary examples of polarity
(Gowdy vs. Devi), 230–234; difficulties
of overcoming (Forster), 234–236; lit-
erary mediations (Clare, Coleridge,
Melville, Hogan), 236–242. *See also*
Anthropocentric environmentalism;
Ecocentric

Fabre, Michel, 311n40
Faulkner, William: androcentrism, 172,
182–185; class consciousness/classism,
185, 187, 191; endangerment of wilderness and/or species concerns, 180–183,
190, 193–194, 201; environmental-ethical revisionism, 186–195; environmental history interests (deforestation,
agribusiness), 178–183; environmental
inquiry through fictive approach,
189–191, 193–195; environmental unconscious and, 177–183, 190–191; geography of works, 320n25; hunting

revisionism, 179–183, 187–195, 214–215;
limits of environmental
interests/knowledge, 176, 188–189,
193; literary marketplace pragmatism,
176, 179; Native American culture/his-
tory in works of, 237, 322n53, 323n57;
property, views of, 191–192; mentioned, 2, 28
    Other authors: Coleridge and, 237;
Leopold and, 171, 183–195; Melville
(*Moby-Dick*) and, 215; Thoreau and,
174; W.C. Williams and, 119
    Works: Absalom, Absalom! 144, 175;
"Address to the Delta Council," 180;
"The Bear Hunt," 177; *The Big Woods*,
176; *Flags in the Dust*, 171; *Light in August*, 172–174; "Lion," 177, 180; *The
Marble Faun*, 174; "Nympholepsy," 175;
"Old Man" *(If I Forget Thee, Jerusalem)*,
175–176; *The Unvanquished*, 175, 177
    Go Down, Moses: Bambi and,
187–188; "The Bear," 170, 176, 177,
178–183, 187, 190–194, 237; composition
of, 176–183; critique of property in,
191–192; cultural nostalgia in, 179–180,
189; "Delta Autumn," 177–180, 182;
"The Fire and the Hearth," 177, 179;
"Go Down, Moses," 177; Ike Mc-
Caslin's significance, 176–179, 185,
190–191, 215, 237; "The Old People,"
177–179, 187; "Pantaloon in Black," 177,
178, 182; as refraction of biographical
experiences, 180–181, 183, 190, 191; as
refraction of forest/conservationist
history, 176–183, 188–195; relation between issues of race and environment, 178–179, 187–189 passim; "Was,"
177; mentioned, 28, 175
Ferguson, Priscilla Parkhurst, 298n17
Film. *See* Media
Fisher, Philip, 34
Flâneur/Flânerie: definition, 298n17;
Brooks and, 158–159, 162, 298n17; Gay
and, 87–89; genderization of, 298n17;
Harjo and, 122–124; Joyce and,
103–107; literary origins of, 298n18;

O'Hara and, 121–122; Olmsted and, 100–102; rural, 89; urban (re)inhabitation and, 92–128 passim; Whitman and, 91–103; Wideman and, 125–128; W. C. Williams and, 113–115, 116; Woolf and, 107–109; mentioned, 8

Forster, E. M., 234–236

Fossey, Dian, 234

Foucault, Michel, 58

Franklin, Benjamin: Bartram and, 20–21; environmental perception/reform in, 19–22; mentioned, 3, 94, 126, 323n62

Free Willy, 221, 223

Freeman, Mary Wilkins, 147

Freud, Sigmund, 199

Frost, Robert: "A Brook in the City," 86–87, 125; "Design," 153; "Directive," 85; "Mending Wall," 147; "The Middleness of the Road," 3–4; "The Pasture," 157; mentioned, 70

Gadgil, Mahdav, 24–25, 231, 292n39; quoted, 224

Gaia paradigm, 197

Gaskell, Elizabeth, 137

Gay, John: Trivia, 87–90, 85, 98–99

Geddes, Patrick, 85, 127, 340n66

Gender, and environmental imagination: androcentrism/patriarchalism in W. Berry, 158, 160; androcentrism/partriarchalism in Faulkner and Leopold, 172, 182–185; city-hinterland binary in W. C. Williams, 118–119; class and, 118–119, 318n122; critique of hunting and, 182–185; elephant matriarchalism in Gowdy, 233; environmental ethics and, 238–240, 269n22; environmentalism, demography of, 32; flânerie tradition and, 298n17, 304nn73–74; gynocentrism in Brooks, 158, 160–162. See also Ecofeminism

Geography. See Environment; Place; Rural(ism); Urban(ism)

Gibbs, Lois, 36–37, 47, 49, 56, 198. See also Love Canal

Giddens, Anthony, 57

Ginsberg, Allen, 113, 117, 119

Global environmental consciousness/culture: capitalism and, 33–34, 52, 196–199, 280n19; country-city dynamic and, 65, 271n31; environmental(ist) paradigms of 197, 278n10; global scope of anthropogenic transformation of environment, 3, 30–31, 33–35, 38–39, 290n7; imperialism and, 199–200, 205–206, 244–245, 253–254; place sense affected by, 65–66, 71–73, 77–78, 160; scarcity anxiety and, 39; toxic anxiety/impact and, 30–31, 33–35, 38–39, 45–46, 52, 54, 69, 197–201 285n69; transnational accords and organizations, 196–199, 217–218, 249, 281n21, 289n101; watershed consciousness and, 244–245, 262–264, western and/vs. nonwestern environmentalism, 278n10, 281n21. See also Imperialism; Ocean; Settler culture

Glotfelty, Cheryll, 267n4

Gothic: architectural imagery, 135–136, 144; environmental determinism and, 135–136, 144; Melville on barbarity of whaling, 211–212; regionalism and, 174–175, toxic discourse and, 42–44, 135, 137, 144

Gottleib, Robert, 271n30, 278n10

Gowdy, Barbara: The White Bone, 230, 232–234; animal story tradition and, 233

Guha, Ramachandra, 24–25, 231, 281n21, 292n39, 324n4; quoted, 224

Haeckel, Ernst, 149

Haines, John, 74–76

Hajer, Maarten, 324n4

Hamilton, Alice 43–44

Haraway, Donna, 289n2

Hardin, Garrett, 325n11; quoted, 196

Hardy, Thomas: determinism in, 147–149; mentioned, 46, 317n116
    Works: "In a Wood," 147–148; *Tess of the D'Urbervilles,* 148–149; *Under the Greenwood Tree,* 148; *The Woodlanders,* 148
Harjo, Joy, 121, 122–125, 128
Harrison, Robert Pogue, 3
Harvey, David, 197–198
Hawthorne, Nathaniel, 36
Hawthorne, Sophia, 213
Hayden, Dolores, 57–58, 59
Hayles, N. Katherine, 31, 55, 269n18, 277n6, 289n2
Hays, Samuel, 271n30, 278n10
Hearn, Lafcadio, 70
Heidegger, Martin: quoted, 243
Hemingway, Ernest, 185, 241
Hewitt, Douglas, 309n14
Hiss, Tony, 303n68
Hogan, Linda: coordination of environmental justice and nonanthropocentric ethics, 238 *(Solar Storms),* 238–242 *(Power);* Douglas and, 259; ecofeminism of, 239–240; ethics as code or narrative, 240–242; Melville and, 241; nondualism, 59; mentioned, 2, 29
Hopkins, Gerard Manley, 175
Horgan, Paul, 251, 258
Hough, Michael, 87; quoted, 110
House, Freeman, 78, 252
Housman, A. E., 174
Howard, Ebenezer, 85
Hughes, Langston, 23–24, 26, 117, 159
Hughes, Ted, 250–251
Hunting: Audubon, 215; *Bambi,* 187–188; conservationism and revisionist narratives of, 182–194; contemporary (sub)urbanization and, 184–185; Emerson, 215; Faulkner, 173, 177–195; imperialism and, 185, 205–206; Jewett, 184; Leopold, 183–195; Melville's *Moby-Dick,* 205–215, 222–223; women writers on, 184, 320n32. *See also* Animals; Gender; Imperialism; Settler culture; Urban(ism); Whales

Hurley, Andrew, 279n13
Hurston, Zora Neale, 46, 140

Imagination, environmental: advantages of experientially oriented narrative for environmental(ist) inquiry, 186–189, 193–195, 240–242; ecofeminism and, 239–242; environmental unconscious and, 18–27; forms of engagement with world prompted by, 1–2; fusion of cultural construction and experiential receptivity, 16–19; images, place-creating and/or motivating power of, 1–2, 17–18, 31, 35–36, 71–75, 83, 120, 137, 182–184, 189–191, 193–195, 200–204, 216–217. *See also* Environmental unconscious; Metaphor; Place; Reinhabitation; Watershed
Imperialism; in children's literature, 219; commodity flow, 66; ecological colonization/degradation, 308; English riverine literature and, 244–246; environmental determinism and, 130–131; environmental representation and, 294n59; Eurocentrism, ecocolonization, and place theory, 65–66, 68, 130; hunting and, 185, 205–206; internal colonization of (white) place-based settlers, 164, 263; internal colonization of first peoples, 211, 230–232, 238–240, 253, 256–259, 263, 322n53; local colorist regionalism and, 338n47; moral extensionism impeded by, 228, 230–237; "omnivores" vs. "ecosystem people," 7, 224, 231, 259, 292n39; toxic exportation as, 33–34, 52, 290n5; whaling industry and, 205–206, 211–212. *See also* Devi; Global environmental consciousness; Melville; Settler culture
India: Devi's environmental justice fiction of tribals, 230–232, 234; diasporic construction of place-based commu-

nity in Rao, 71; Indian environmental movements, 281n21; mentioned, 25, 65, 224

Interspeciesism. *See* Animals; Ecocentric; Whales

Jackson, Shannon, 13, 318n22
Jackson, Wes, 84, 85
Jacobs, Jane, 93
James, Henry, 70
Jameson, Fredric, 24, 275nn67, 69, 276n4, 324n3
Jarman, Derek, 25
Jarrell, Randall, 117–118
Jeffers, Robinson: Berry and, 166; determinism in, 153–156; Dreiser and, 153–155; "inhumanism" of, 154–155; materialist cosmology / theology, 153–155; whale imaging ("Orca"), 216, 219
Jewett, Sarah Orne, 184, 258
Johnson, Lawrence, 226
Johnson, Samuel, 95
Jones, Gayl, 163
Jones, Leroi. *See* Baraka, Amiri
Joyce, James: deCerteau and, 104; *flâneur* tradition and, 103–107; Simmel and, 105; Whitman and, 106; W.C. Williams and, 109, 113, 115, 116, 120; Woolf and, 106–107, 113, 116, 119, 120; mentioned, 28
   Works: Dubliners, 105–106; *Finnegans Wake,* 109, 120, 365; *Portrait,* 64, 105; *Ulysses,* 103–107, 109, 115, 116

Kant, Immanuel, 229, 332n10
Kavadny, John, 288nn90,93; quoted, 51
Klyza, Christopher McGrory, 264
Kroeber, Karl, 285n70; quoted, 45
Kvidera, Peter, 327n36

Land ethic. *See* Leopold
Landscape. *See* Architecture; Nature
Least Heat Moon, William, 66

Lefebvre, Henri: spatial transformationist theory, 33–34, 57, 290n7; urban theory and Woolf's fiction, 107–108

Leopold, Aldo: androcentrism, 182–185; *Bambi* and, 187–188; "biotic community" and ethical critique of speciesism, 186–187, 192, 194–195; conservatism of, 188, 191, 192; critique of property, 171, 191–192; on Dust Bowl, 215; "ecological conscience," 186, 195; environmental unconscious in, 186–187; Faulkner and, 171, 183–195; as forestry professional, 185–186, 193–195; hunting experiences of, 183–184; hunting revisionism in, 183–185, 187–188, 192–193, 214–215; land ethic of, 183, 186–187, 329n52; literary vs. environmental-professional commitments, 186–187, 189, 193–194; literary marketplace pragmatism, 186; literary persona, 186–187, 322n50; Melville's *Moby-Dick* and, 214–215; persona, 425–426; mentioned, 2, 28; quoted, 170
   Works: Game Management, 185, 188; *Round River* (quoted), 69
   Sand County Almanac: composition of, 185–186; hunting revisionism in, 183–185; "Conservation Esthetic," 183, 192–193, 214; "Foreword," 191; "Good Oak," 68; "Great Possessions," 191; "Smoky Gold," 183, 186; "Thinking Like a Mountain," 184, 186, 193–194, 219

Levin, Ted: *Blood Brook,* 251, 262–264
Levinas, Emmanuel, and the face, 202, 330n70
Levine, George, 309n16, 313n53
Lewis, Sinclair, 253, 256
Lindberg, Kathryne, 316n103
Lipset, Seymour Martin, 66
Literature and environment studies. *See* Ecocriticism
Lomatewama, Ramson, 74
London: as global city 65; in Conrad, 245–246; in Denham, 244–245; in Dick-

London (*continued*)
ens, 131–136; in Eliot, 98; environmental problems, 132–136, 245–246; metaphorical representation of, 127; Thames, 132–134, 244–246; Woolf's fiction and, 107–109

London, Jack, 43, 44, 137, 146, 149

Lopez, Barry: interspecies imagination, 219–223; Melville and, 222–223; two-landscapes theory, 276n75; mentioned, 66
    Works: Arctic Dreams, 220–221, 223; "Landscape and Narrative," 276n75; *Of Wolves and Men*, 219–220; "A Presentation of Whales," 220, 223; "Renegotiating the Contracts," 219, 220; *River Notes*, 252

Los Angeles: contesting place theory, 57–58; metropolitan expansion/transformation, 57–58, 68; Snyder on, 124–125; toxification of, 42–43; watershed imagination/activism and, 124–125, 253–254

Love Canal, 32, 35–37, 48, 52, 198, 278n9, 280n16, 287n82. *See also* Gibbs; Toxic discourse

McHarg, Ian, 166, 264–265, 297n7

MacKaye, Benton, 85, 119, 166

McKibben, Bill, 3

McNamee, Greg, 252; quoted, 258

McPhee, John, 252

Machor, James, 301n42

Maclean, Norman, 252

Madhubuti, Haki (Don L. Lee), 161, 165

Mailer, Norman, 321n33

Markham, Edwin: "Man with a Hoe," 146–147, 317n116

Marsh, George Perkins, 39, 144–145, 171, 328n42

Martinez-Alier, Juan, 281n21, 324n4

Marvell, Andrew, 174

Masters, Edgar Lee: *Spoon River Anthology*, 44, 159

Marx, Karl, and Marxist theory: first vs. second nature distinction, 3, 5, 268n7, 276n73; mode of production concept, 24–25; production of space in capitalism, 33–34, 261. *See also* Global environmental consciousness; Imperialism; Modernization

Marx, Leo, 37, 271n31; quoted, 7

Massey, Doreen, 68

Mazzoleni, Donatella, 22

Mazur, Allan, 278n9, 280n16, 287n82

Media, mass, and environmental representation/environmentalism, 32–33, 202; advertising, 1, 72, 198, 217, 294n65; cartoons, 39; film, 49–50, 187–188, 219, 220–221, 223; journalism, 42–45, 138, 294n59; photography, 72, 139, 202; television, 32, 72, 73, 280n16, 294n59, 326n31

Meloy, Ellen: *Raven's Exile*, 252, 260–263

Melville, Herman, 2, 29, 37, 174
    Works: "Bartleby the Scrivener," 94; *Pierre*, 94; "Tartarus of Maids," 43, 137
    Moby-Dick: cetology, critical underestimation of, 205, 207, 327n39; Coleridge's "Rime of the Ancient Mariner" and, 237–238; critiques of dominance over human and nonhuman others interlinked in, 205–214, 236; cultural deparochialism reflected in, 206; epistemological skepticism relative to Hogan, 241; hunting revisionism vis-à-vis Faulkner, 215; interspecies links between whales and humans, 207–210, 211–214; Leopold's hunting critique and, 214–215; Lopez's animal representations and, 222–223; rise of New England/global capitalism dramatized by, 205–206; romance of ocean, 199; whaling, critique of, 208–209, 211–212; whaling, limits of critique, 210, 214–215

Merchant, Carolyn, 324n4

Metaphor: animals as ecosystemic/planetary synecdoches, 193–195, 201–203, 218, 238–239; body-city, 91, 109,

118–120, 126–127; domestic (for wild animals), 202, 204, 207–209; dweller dwelling, 135–136; ethics of, 51–53, 250–251; land-woman, 118–119, 172, 338n39; linking humans to nonhumans, 110, 138–139, 149, 194, 207–209, 230, 236, 238–239; property as, 171, 190–192; river/watershed as, 243–251, 263–265; toxicity/waste and, 51–53, 119–120; wilderness as urban metaphor, 12, 245–246. *See also* Animals; Environmental unconscious; Imagination; Watershed

Metropolis. *See* Urban(ism)

Mexican-American environmental issues: acequia culture, 253, 259; maquiladoras, 33, 290n5; migrant farmwork, 66, settler culture watershed writing on, 256–257

Miller, J. Hillis, 133

Mitchell, John, 68

Mitchell, Lee Clark, 310n26

Modernism: Dreiser and impressionist painting, 150–151, 153; urban theory and fictional, 103–109; Whitmanian (W. C. Williams), 109–120

Modernization: "ecological modernization," 197–198; Faulkner and southern forest history, 170–173, 177–183, 188–194; global reorganization of space, 33–34; Leopold, game management, and 188, 192–193; place sense and place theory, consequences for, 57–59, 65–78; semitransformation of first by second nature, 3–6; stimulus to environmental perception, 144–145, 170–171. *See also* Global environmental consciousness; Imperialism; Settler culture; Toxic discourse

Moore, Kathleen Dean: quoted, 259

Moore, Marianne, 23, 26, 153

Morrison, Toni, 317n116

Muir, John: Addams and, as environmental writers/reformers, 12–18; dis-

dain for Native American cultures, 230; domestic images in, 17; and Hetch Hetchy dam controversy, 12, 40, 254; moral passion of, 40; pastoralism of, 15–16, 27; as public health advocate, 13; sense of place in, 12–18; as wilderness/national parks advocate, 14–17, 40; mentioned, 9, 21

    Works: Mountains of California, 14–18; *My First Summer in the Sierra* (quoted), 14; *Our National Parks* (quoted), 13

Mumford, Lewis, 95, 118, 119, 166

Murphy, Patrick, 314n26

Mutual constructionism. *See* Environment

Nagel, Thomas, 233

Narrative, and environmental values, 1, 189–195, 240–242

Nation/nationalism: countryside as national identity symbol, 143; environmental imagination and the nation form, 8–12, 335n11; globalism and, 196–197

Native American writing/cultures: environmental justice and preservation, 238–242, exploitation/dispossession of NA peoples, 38, 238–242, 253–254, 256–258, 269, 322n53, 452n57; Indian "tribals" and (Devi), 230; nondualism of, 59; place attachment of, 21–22, 61–64, 73–74, 75–76, 78; spirituality and 1991 environmental racism manifesto, 33; watershed imagination and, 253–254, 256–258, 269; white locals as symbolic "redskins," 154

    Specific peoples: Apache, Western, 63, 75; Chickasaw, 59, 238, 322n53; Choctaw, 322n53, 323n57; Gwichen, 38; Hopi, 21, 73–74; Laguna, 61–62, 78; Navajo, 21, 152; Nisenan, 85; Paiute, 256; Shoshone, 253, 256; Taiga, 237–242, 259

    See also Austin; Faulkner; Hogan; Silko

358 · INDEX

Naturalism, fictional: ecocritical neglect of, 8, 229–230; ecology of place in, 46; environmental determinist tendencies of, 136, 143, 149–153; novelist as "scientist," 142, 311n41; mentioned, 11

Nature: body/technology hybridization (cyborg), 6, 55; elusiveness of term, 268n6; first/second distinction, 3–6, 25; limits of dominance and rationale for retaining nature/culture and country/city distinctions, 5–6; psychological preference for natural environments, 6; "third nature," 278n8. *See also* Environment; Rural(ism)

Nature writing: Darwinism and, 146–147; ecocriticism's traditional focus on, 8, 46; environmental justice and, 46–49, 54, 229–230, 256, 259, 262–263; ethical/political orientation of, 46–49, 68, 75, 84–85, 146, 153, 186–187, 193–194, 200–201, 204–205, 219–223; ocean representation in, 200–201, 204–205; place sense and, 66–68, 74–76, 84–85; toxic discourse and, 46–49, 54; urban fiction and, 3, 46, 229–230; watershed imagination in, 248–249, 252, 253, 256, 258–263; mentioned, 98. *See also* Austin; Burroughs; Carson; Levin; Lopez; Meloy; Thoreau; Williams, T. T.

Navajo. *See* Native American writing

Nemerov, Howard: quoted, 243

Neoclassical/Neoclassicism: country bumpkin figures in, 147; urban *flânerie* and, 87–89; watershed imagination and, 244–245, 264–265; mentioned, 27

Newman, Lance: quoted, 7

New York City: Central Park, 100–102; colonization of hinterland as seen by W. C. Williams, 117–120; Croton Reservoir, 101; Dreiser, 151; ferry history of, 95–100; *flânerie* in, 92–100 (Whitman), 121–122; as global city, 65; Hughes, 23–24, 159, 19th-century infrastructure problems of, 94–95, 95, 138;

O'Hara, 121–122; Olmsted, 100–102; Petry, 139; Riis, 238; slums/ghettoes of, 43, 138, 139; Whitman, 91–100; W. C. Williams, 109, 117–120

Nicholson-Lord, David: quoted, 99, 112

Nicolaisen, Peter, 323n55

Norris, Frank, 11, 86, 149, 254

Norris, Kathleen, 156

Nussbaum, Martha, 47

Nye, Joseph, 324n3

Ocean: as endangered global commons, 199–201; traditional symbolism of, 199–200; whales as icons of, 201–223. *See also* Carson; Melville; Whales

Oerlemans, Onno, 236–237

O'Hara, Frank 23, 26, 117, 121–122, 125, 128

Olmsted, Francis, 208

Olmsted, Frederick Law: Whitman, urban reform, and, 100–102; mentioned, 2, 12, 85, 90

Olson, Charles, 177

O'Neill, Eugene, 147, 317n116

Ortiz, Simon, 21

Otter, Samuel, 212

Park, Geoff, 68, 293n47

Parks and playgrounds: Chicago, 12–13; national parks movement, 12; New York City, 23, 24, 100–102; pastoral impulse behind, 101–102; Paterson, N.J., 113, 304n84; "pedigreed landscape" vs. "unofficial countryside" in cities, 110–112; urban park/playground movement, 12–13, 100–102. *See also* Anthropocentric environmentalism; Ecocentric; Preservation; Rural(ism); Urban(ism); Wilderness

Pastoral: anthropocentric vs. ecocentric facets of, 282n39; in Faulkner, 174; as romantic idealization of wilderness (in Muir), 15–16, 27; simple vs. complex, 37; toxic discourse ingredient, 37–39; urban park movement and,

101–102; *Walden* and traditional locus of, 70; W. C. Williams's satirical idyll in *Paterson*, 118–119. *See also* Rural(ism)

Payne, Katy, 234; quoted, 224

Payne, Roger: *Among Whales*, 207, 212, 217–218, 326n30, 327n38; quoted, 196

Peña, Devon: quoted, 243

Perrow, Charles, 50

Petry, Ann, 139

Philadelphia: environmental deterioration of, 125–128 (Wideman); Franklin and urban reform, 19; Mill Creek restoration, 87, 307n108; yellow fever epidemic of 1793, 43 (C. B. Brown)

Photography. *See* Media

Pinchot, Gifford, 12, 40, 185

Pittsburgh, Pa.: Dreiser on, 151; Wideman on Homewood district, 78–83

Place, place attachment: defined, 59–74; as "archipelago" of dispersed locales, 65–67; body and, 55–56, 61; childhood vs. adulthood as stages in construction of, 69–71; community/culture and construction/valuation of, 35–37, 39–42, 57–59, 60–62, 63–64, 70–77, 79–83, 157–167, 256–257; contestedness and/or instability of, 66–69, 79–80, 117–120, 160–167; cultural hybridization of, 66–67; discreditation of place (in recent social theory) and revival of, 56–59, displacement/diaspora/uprooting and, 69–74, 76–78; elusiveness of, 59–63; ethnocentricsm and/or maladaptiveness as hazard of place attachment, 76–77, 231–232, 256–257; imagined retrieval/redemption of unloved places, 16–17; 78–86, 109–120, 124–125, 157–167; local-global awareness of, as ideal, 75–78; memorial/diasporic reconstruction of, 70–73, 75–76, 78–83; modernization as threat and/or provocation to attachment, 56–59, 75–78; place-based resistance to toxicity and other environmental endangerment, 35–42, 55–56, 257–258; pri-

mary vs. secondary, 291n16; space vs., 57, 59, 78; "timescape," 69; topophilia and topophobia, 19; toxification and sense of, 35–37, 39–42, 69; translocal/global construction of, 66–67, 76–78; trauma and construction of, 69–70, 161, 163; virtual vs. actual, 71–74, 77. *See also* Space

Plumwood, Val, 324n4

Poe, Edgar Allan, 89, 95, 144

Pollution. *See* Public health; Toxic discourse

Poovey, Mary, 307n22

Pope, Alexander, 90, 95, 160

Posthumanism, 6, 289n2

Postmodernism: Berry's resistance to, 160; challenges to traditional place assumptions, 145 57–58, 65; critique of nation form, 196; prosthetic body/environment as claim of, 6, 55; spatial transformationist geography, 33–34, 57–58; mentioned, 27

Pound, Ezra, 113, 119, 304n78

Powell, John Wesley: early watershed planner, 247–248; irrigation advocate, 259; *Exploration of the Colorado*, 260

Powers, Richard: *Gain*, 55–56, 292n35

Pred, Alan, 67

Preservation: conservation vs., 12, 40; conservation/preservation and environmental justice, 8–9, 32–34, 38, 45–46, 207–212, 224–242, 248–249, 253–254; preservation/public health priorities' interdependence, 8–9, 13–14, 19–29; toxic discourse and, 32–34, 38, 45–46. *See also* Anthropocentric environmentalism; Ecocentric; Rural(ism); Urban(ism); Wilderness

Property: ethics of ownership/stewardship, 171, 190–192; as metaphor, 190–192

Public health environmentalism. *See* Sanitarianism; Urban(ism)

Puritanism, 71

Pynchon, Thomas, 52, 57

Quinn, Naomi, 288n96

Raban, Jonathan, 98, 99, 299n21
Race/ethnicity and environment(alism):
ecocriticism compared with ethnic revisionism, 267n4; environmental victimage of nonwhites, 32–33, 37–43
passim, 78–83, 122–124, 126–127, 138–
142, 158–164, 178–179, 211–212, 230–232,
238–240, 253, 256–260, 263, 322n53; in
Faulkner, as synchrononous vs. competing interests, 188–189; human vs.
nonhuman others, 211–212, 224–242; in-
terracial coalitions, 32–33, 39–40; multiethnic demography of 19th-century
whaling and in Melville, 205, 211–212;
nonwhite participation in environmental justice movements and preservation, 32–33, 39–40, 238–240, 257–258,
278–280nn10–16, 317n120; place sense/
attachment and race/ethnicity, 60–62,
63–65, 70–74, 76–83, 117–118, 122–128,
157–167, 230–232, 238–240, 257–258,
263; and environmental determinism,
130–131, 142; watershed ethics/citizen-
ship and, 248–249, 253–259, 263. See also
African-American culture; Community; Mexican-American environmental issues; Native American writing;
Settler culture
Radcliffe, Ann, 144
Rao, Raja, 71
Regionalism (U.S.): Austin and watershed consciousness/regional realist
traditions, 252–257; in Berry, 157–160,
164–167; in Faulkner, 171–195 passim;
and national consolidation, 58; J. W.
Powell's bioregionalism, 247–248;
Snyder's bioregionalism, 248–249,
257; W. C. Williams's bioregional
aesthetic, 117–120. See also Bioregionalism; Reinhabitation; Watershed
Reinhabitation: defined, 84–85; Berry
and, 85, 157–158, 165–167; failure, in
Wideman's fiction, 125–128; meditative engagement as dimension of, 100,
165–166; moral extensionist implication of, 170; reciprocities between person and place, 92–120 (Whitman,
Joyce, Woolf, Williams); traditionally
exurban sites of, 84–85; urban application of, 85–87, 92–125 passim; voluntarism of, 128–129, 168–169; watershed
imagination and, 255–256, 259,
262–265; Snyder and, 85, 116, 124–126;
W. C. Williams's Paterson and, 113–120
passim. See also Bioregionalism; Environmental restoration; Regionalism;
Watershed
Reising, Russell, 327n36
Reznikoff, Charles, 117
Riis, Jacob, 43, 138
Risk: risk analysis and its discontents,
48–50; risk as literary
provocation/theme, 45–56; "risk society," 32. See also Toxic discourse
Riverkeepers, 249
Rivers/streams: "archetypal" symbolism
of, 109, 243; images of environmental
health or endangerment, 86–87, 124–
126, 132–134, 246–249, 254–264, 305n84;
problems/limits in literary representation of, 249–252; symbols of re-
gional-national identity, 95–97, 109,
118, 243–249, 257–264, 305n84. See also
Bioregionalism; Reinhabitation;
Watershed
Robinson, Edwin Arlington, 159
Robinson, Marilynne: quoted, 30
Romanticism: environmental determinism and, 143–144; environmental
ethics and, 236–238; greater romantic
lyric, 95, 301n36; lyric contemplation
vs. satire in, 95; ruralism and, 90, 92,
100–101, 143–144; urban environmental
consciousness and, 90–103; watershed
imagination and, 245–246, 252; youthful prescience idealized by, 300n28;
mentioned, 29. See also Gothic; Victo-
rian(ism); Wordsworth

Roosevelt, Theodore, 185, 201
Ross, Andrew, 283n46, 294n65
Roszak, Theodore, 25
Rukeyser, Muriel, 44
Rural(ism): countryside as traditional symbol of national identity, 143; deterministic elements in representation of, 143–149; portrait poem and, 159; Romantic idealization of, 90, 91, 100–101, 143–144; rustic blockhead stereotype, 147; traditional salubrity of, 86, 100–101, 143; urban/rural interdependencies, 3–5, 7–9, 9–12 (Bates), 12–18 (Addams-Muir), 19–21 (Franklin-Bartram), 91–92 (Dickens-Whitman), 100 (Thoreau-Whitman), 104–105 (Joyce), 108 (Woolf), 117–120 (Williams), 122–124 (Harjo), 127–128 (Wideman), 141 (Sinclair), 149–156 (Dreiser-Jeffers), 157–167 (Berry-Brooks), 177–183 (Faulkner), 243–265 passim (watershed consciousness). See also Agrarianism; Bioregionalism; Urban(ism); Watershed
Ruskin, John, 137
Ryden, Kent, 67, 78

Sack, Robert, 25–26, 65–66, 291n16
Safe, 49–50
Salten, Felix: Bambi, 187–188, 204, 233
Sanitarianism: defined, 8; Addams and, 15–17, 27, 160–161, 167; Beecher and, 135; beginnings of urban-public health environmentalism marked by, 8, 13, 307n2; deterministic aspect of, 130–136 passim, 374n2; Dickens and, 132–136, 246; disease, theory of, 131; Franklin and, 19–20; Sinclair and, 136–137; Thoreau and, 136; Whitman and, 94, 97–98; Wright and, 139–140. See also Toxic discourse
Scheffer, Victor: Year of the Whale, 104, 105, 212, 219, 233
Schultz, Elizabeth, 327n39
Sea World, 204, 216–217, 223

Seltzer, Mark, 141
Sennett, Richard, 115
Settler culture (chiefly U.S.): "America the Beautiful" as artifact of, 9–12; environmental transformation wrought by, 4–6, 8, 68–69, 84–85, 116, 117–120, 170–195 passim, 252–265 passim; first peoples' dominance, 38, 230–232, 238–240, 253–254, 257–259, 263; internal variety of, 266; place awareness attenuated/foreshortened in, 3–4, 23, 67–68, 127–128, 258; reinhabitory imagination and, 84–87, 116, 117–120, 171–172, 190–192, 248–249, 257; watershed consciousness and, 244–245, 247–248, 254–265. See also Global environmental consciousness; Imperialism; Native American writing; Race; Reinhabitation
Sewall, Anna, 229
Sexuality, representation of: in Bates, 272n38; in landscape metaphor, 118–119 (Williams), 172 (Faulkner); in response to landscape (Dickens), 133–134; Thoreau, 309n23; in Whitman, 301n44
Shaw, George Bernard, 168
Shelley, Mary, 143
Shelley, Percy Bysshe, 2
Shiva, Vandana, 65
Siegel, Robert, 219
Silko, Leslie: on Anglo vs. Native American landscape representation, 21; Ceremony, 61–62, 75–76, 78
Simmel, Georg: "Metropolis and Mental Life," 89, 105–106, 131
Simon, Anne W., 201, 325n18
Sinclair, Upton, The Jungle: anticipates toxic discourse, 40, 43, 44, 136–137; determinism in, 136–138, 140–141, 147; Dreiser and, 150; Stowe's Uncle Tom's Cabin and, 137, 229; Wright and, 138, 140–141; Zola and, 137–138
Singer, Isaac Bashevis, 71
Singer, Peter, 204

Slovic, Paul, 49
Slovic, Scott, 322n45
Smith, Anthony, 72
Smith, David, 73
Smith, Neal, 5
Snyder, Gary: on bioregionalism, 297n1;
    flânerie and, 124–125; place sense in,
    66–67, 116, 248–249, 257; as reinhab-
    itor/on reinhabitation, 85, 116,
    124–126; watershed ethics/aesthetics
    of, 248–249, 257; mentioned, 121, 128
    Works: "Coming into the Water-
    shed," 248–249, 257; "Mother Earth:
    Her Whales," 203; "Night Song of the
    Los Angeles Basin," 124–125; *The Prac-
    tice of the Wild,* 252, 297n1;
    "Reinhabitation," 297n1; "The
    Trade," 23, 26
Sociology: informs Addams's prose, 17;
    naturalist narrative as, 139–142; of
    Pittsburgh, 80–83; of risk, 37, 49–50;
    Univ. of Chicago urban "ecology,"
    142, 152; urban social theory, 57–58,
    88–89, 103–109
Soja, Edward, 57–58
Sollors, Werner, 140
Sontag, Susan, 288n95
Soper, Kate, 268n9, 276n74
Space: globalization and, 33–34; illusori-
    ness of constructed urban, 122–123,
    127–128; and place, 57, 59, 78; produc-
    tion of, under capitalist moderniza-
    tion, 33–34, 55–58, 61, 65–66; urban
    spatial determinism, 131–142 passim;
    wilderness as heterotopic space, 5–6,
    184–185, 269n17. *See also* Determinism;
    Global environmental consciousness;
    Imperialism; Modernization; Place;
    Wilderness
Spencer, Herbert, 149–150
Spirn, Anne Whiston, 87
Spivak, Gayatri, 230
Stegner, Wallace, 77
Steinbeck, John, 230
Steingraber, Sandra, 290n4

Sterne, Laurence, 236
Stevens, Wallace 4–5, 52–53, 153, 251
Stowe, Harriet Beecher: *Uncle Tom's
    Cabin,* 137, 219, 229, 309n17
Sustainability paradigm, 197–198,
    261–265, 337n36. *See also* Agrarianism;
    Bioregionalism; Global environmen-
    tal consciousness; Watershed
Swift, Jonathan, 90, 95
Swinburne, Algernon Charles, 95
Szasz, Andrew, 279n13

Tapscott, Stephen, 304n78, 306n92
Taylor, Peter J., 291n14
Tennyson, Alfred, 69, 210
Thaxter, Celia, 258
Thayer, Robert, 19, 24
Theroux, Paul, 39
Thomas, Wynn, 302n48
Thomashaw, Mitchell, 25
Thomson, James, 87
Thoreau, Henry David: "complex" pas-
    toral and, 37; ecocentrism and/vs. an-
    thropocentrism in, 7, 47; Faulkner
    and, 174; *flânerie* and, 89; limits of en-
    vironmental perception in, 249–250,
    252, 261–262; place sense and, 66, 69,
    70; Whitmanian resistance to work
    ethic, 100; mentioned, 5, 22, 38, 60, 210
    Works: Journal, 89; "Walking"
    (quoted), 62; *A Week on the Concord
    and Merrimack Rivers,* 249–250, 251
    Walden: critique of hunting, 184;
    early childhood recollection in, 70;
    ethos of deliberate living, 100; house-
    person correlations, 136; human mate-
    rial needs acknowledged in, 7; limits
    of environmental perception in,
    261–262; pastoral *locus amoenus* and,
    70; post-return perspective of, 47; san-
    itarianism and, 136
Tolstoi, Leo, 156
Toxic discourse: defined, 30–31; anthro-
    pocentrism (vs. ecocentrism) of, 38,
    45–46; capitalism and, 31, 33–34, 38,

40–41, 43–45, 55–56, 135–136, 196–199; class/race/gender specificity vs. consensualism of, 32–40, 50–54; Cold War and, 30, 40–41, 286n74; conventions and genealogy of, 35–45; country-city binary challenged by, 43–47; determinism and, 33–34, 38, 129, 132–137 passim; discursive/metaphorical evasion and, 50–53; domestic/family concerns and, 35–38, 41–43, 46–47, 52, 55–56; ecofeminism in, 40–41, 46–47, 54–56; environmental justice movement and, 32–35, 28–45 passim; evidential basis of, 47–50; globalism/transnationalism and, 30–35, 38, 52–56, 69, 72–73, 197–199; gothic(ism) and, 43–44, 135–139; media construction of, 35–36, 72–73; nature writing and, 45–47; pastoral and, 35–38; place attachment and, 35–42, 55–56, 80–81; risk analysis and, 48–50; risk society concept and, 32; scientific authority and, 44–45, 48–50; suburbanization and, 35–38, 51–52, 55–56; timescape concept and, 69; urban entrapment and, 39–43 passim, 132–142 passim, 119–120; waste/waste disposal issues, 15–17, 33–38, 49–50, 52–54, 140; water/ocean pollution, 72–73, 200–201. *See also* Environmental justice; Gothic; Love Canal; Race; Sanitarianism

Transportation/technology: automobile culture-induced hallucinations, 3–5; riding as alienating experience, 3–5, 50, 90, 97–100; streets/roadways as impositions on landscape, 23–24, 121–127 passim; streets/roadways as place-definers (Wideman), 81–82, 103–105, 107–108, 121–123; tramlines, ecopoetics of, 105, 152–153, 158–159; transit as reinhabitation (Whitman), 95–103

Trout Unlimited, 249

Tuan, Yi-fu, 25, 64–65, 274n53

Turner, Frederick Jackson, 10

Twain, Mark, 174, 252

Updike, John, 306n96

Urban(ism): "accessible green," 12; Addams and, 12–18; body-city metaphor, 91, 109, 118, 120, 126–127; dependence of cities on natural systems, 8, 85–87, 100–103, 105, 109–120 passim, 122–125, 262–265; environmental determinism and, 131–142; fictions of ghetto representation, 136–142, 158–164; green urban planning traditions, 12, 85–87, 100–102, 110, 119–120, 125, 264–265, 311n43; idiosyncrasy of character and, 105, 131–132; individual isolation and, 88–90, 92–93, 95–103, 105, 113, 121–122; modernism and, 103–120 passim; reinhabitation and, 85–87, 92–125 passim; Romanticism and, 91–103; segmentation of urban experience, 88, 93; transpersonality/interpersonality and, 88–109 passim, 113–115, 117–118. *See also Flâneur;* Rural(ism); Toxic discourse

Victorian(ism): and (socio)environmental reform, 12; happy endings, 133; imperial hunting, 185; investigative journalism, 245–246; poetry of city, 95; sanitarianism, 131, 246; urban wilderness metaphor in, 12, 245–246. *See also* Dickens; Sanitarianism

Virgilian mode, 42–44

Wallace, David Rains, 252

Walcott, Derek, 70, 250

Warren, Karen, 240

Waste. *See* Toxic discourse

Watershed/watershed imagination: definition, 246–247; definitional complications, 247, 263, 264; Austin as literary pioneer of, 252–258; as defining bioregional conception/image, 246–249, 263–265; ethno-cultural diversity and environmental justice as

Watershed (*continued*)
concerns of, 247–249, 253–254, 256–258, 259, 263; green urbanism tradition and, 264–265; impediments to literary imagination of, 249–252; Mexican-American acequia culture, 259; modern revaluation of wetlands, 258–259; nature writing and, 252–253, 258–263; premodern literary anticipations of, 243–246; sustainability, 247–248, 261–265. *See also* Bioregionalism

Watkins, Floyd, 323n57

Westling, Louise, 3

Whales: charisma as environmental(ist) icons, 202–204; contemporary symbol of environmental (oceanic) endangerment, 201; exhibitions of, 215–217; intelligence of, 203, 477, 482; interspecies (human-whale) relations/links, actual and/or imagined, 203–205, 207–210, 212–214, 216–217, 220–223; in popular culture, 219, 204–205, 221, 223, protection of, 204, 217–218, 221; traditional ominous symbolism of, 213–214, 216, 219; whale watching, 201, 217, whaling, 201, 204, 205–214 (in *Moby-Dick*), 217–218, 222; whaling narratives (nonfictional), 208, 330n65. *See also* Animals; Extensionism; Lopez; Melville; Ocean

Wharton, Edith, 144, 317n116

Whistler, James McNeill, 151, 153

White, Richard, 3, 322n53

White, Rodney, 299n26

Whitman, Walt: body-city metaphor, 95–97, 127; ecopoetics of *flânerie* in, 91–103; journalism, 91, 94–95, 97–98; persona/transpersonality in 91–93, 97; rural roots, 64, 91–92, 143; sanitarianism and, 94, 97–98; sexuality, representation of, 301n44; transit/commutation and, 95–103; on urban parks, 101; mentioned, 2, 28, 90, 160, 251

Other authors: Baudelaire and, 300n30; Blake and, 95, 300n35; Dickens and, 91–94, 300n27, 302n48; Dreiser and, 152; Harjo and, 123; Joyce and, 106; O'Hara and, 122; Olmsted and, 100–103; Thoreau and, 100; W. C. Williams and, 109, 116–117, 118, 120; Woolf and, 107, 108; Wordsworth and, 92, 95

Works: "Crossing Brooklyn Ferry," 95–100, 103–104; "Give Me the Splendid Silent Sun," 122, 302n50; "Out of the Cradle," 92; "Song of Myself," 92, 93, 100, 116, 123; "Sparkles from the Wheel," 92–93; "There Was a Child Went Forth," 64, 65, 92

Wideman, John Edgar: body-city metaphor in 126–127; *flânerie* and, 125–128; nature vs. culture in, 127–128; place recuperation, 79–83; reinhabitation (failure of), 125–128; mentioned, 2, 28, 156

Works: *Brothers and Keepers*, 79, 81–82; *Fatheralong*, 79; Homewood trilogy (*Damballah, Hiding Place, Sent for You Yesterday*), 79–83, 156; *Philadelphia Fire*, 125–128; *Reuben*, 79

Wilderness: decline of, 3, 5, 8, 171, 176–183, 189–191; decline produces ideal of, as heterotopic space, 5–6, 184–185; as ideological artifact vs. factical location, 319n23; Muir and preservation, 12–18 passim, 40; recreation in and/vs. conservation of, 182–189; regional recoveries of, 5, 320n33; romantic reification of, 67–68, 260–261; wetland protection and, 259. *See also:* Nature; Preservation; Rural(ism); Settler culture

Wildlife. *See* Animals

Williams, Eliza, 208

Williams, Raymond, 268n6, 271n31

Williams, Terry Tempest: *Refuge* and toxic discourse, 46–47, 49–50, 54,

290n4; place-connectedness and, 72; mentioned, 2

Williams, William Carlos: aesthetics of breakdown/fragmentation/disorder, 112–113, 115, 119–120; bioregionalism/reinhabitation and, 110–112, 115–120, 246; class consciousness/conflict in, 112, 113, 114–115, 117–119; *flâneur* tradition and, 113–115, 116; imagism, 109–110; mutual construction of culture and environment, 4–5, 117–118; Native American allusions, 113, 114, 117, 118; Passaic River/falls in poetry of, 109, 117–118, 246; persona/transpersonality in, 113–115, 117; place destabilized by, 115–116, 117–120; suburban residence, 304n79; toxic discourse in, 119–120; mentioned, 2, 28

Other authors: Baraka and, 117; Berry and, 115–116; Blake and, 115, 120; Crane and, 117; Eliot and, 115, 117, 306n97; Faulkner and, 119; Ginsberg and, 113, 117, 119; L. Hughes and, 117; Joyce and, 109, 113, 115, 116, 119, 120; Mumford and, 118; O'Hara and, 117, 121; Pound and, 113, 119, 304n78; Updike and, 306n96; Whitman and, 109, 116–117, 118, 120; Woolf and, 113, 116, 120

Works: Autobiography, 117; "Avenue of Poplars," 4–5; *Paterson,* 109, 304n84; "View of a Lake," 110–112

Wilson, Alexander, 46, 72

Wilson, Elizabeth, 298n17

Winner, Langdon, 202

Wirth, Louis, 142; quoted, 88

Wirth-Nesher, Hana, 106, 304n74

Wittenberg, Judith Bryant, 321n35

Woolf, Virginia: ecofeminism of, 108; *flânerie* in *Mrs. Dalloway,* 106–109, 120,

298n17; Joyce and, 106–107, 113, 116, 120; Lefebvre and, 107–108; Whitman and, 107, 108; W. C. Williams and, 113, 116, 120; mentioned, 28

Wordsworth, William: anticipates watershed bioregionalism, 246; Neoclassical locodescriptivism and, 249; Romantic idealization of nature, 122, 143; rural determinism in, 143, 147; sinless child motif, 309n17; "spots of time" and place attachment, 69–70; urban imagination, 90, 91, 99; Whitman and, 92, 95

Works: "The Cumberland Beggar," 299n21; *Guide to the Lakes,* 245; "Michael," 143; *The Prelude,* 69–70, 90, 245, 299n21; "Resolution and Independence," 143, 299n21; "Tintern Abbey," 143; "Westminster Bridge" sonnet, 91, 127

Wright, Richard: Brooks and, 140; Dostoyevsky and, 142; Dreiser and, 142, 150, 153; environmental determinism in, 138–142; Hurston and, 140; Petry and, 139; sanitarian tradition and, 139–140; Sinclair and, 138, 140–141, 147; urban (Chicago) sociology and, 139, 141–142; mentioned, 28, 46, 161

Works: "How 'Bigger' Was Born," 310n30, 311n41; *Native Son,* 138–142, 230; *Native Son* (film), 141; *Twelve Million Black Voices,* 139–140

Yeats, William Butler, 2

Zola, Emile: "The Experimental Novel," 142; *Germinal,* 137–138, 230

Zukovsky, Louis, 117